W9-BEL-788

GERIATRICS *At Your* FINGERTIPS®

2012, 14th EDITION

GERIATRICS *At Your* FINGERTIPS®

2012, 14th EDITION

AUTHORS

David B. Reuben, MD

Keela A. Herr, PhD, RN

James T. Pacala, MD, MS

Bruce G. Pollock, MD, PhD

Jane F. Potter, MD

Todd P. Semla, MS, PharmD

Geriatrics At Your Fingertips® is published by the American Geriatrics Society as a service to health care providers involved in the care of older adults.

Although *Geriatrics At Your Fingertips*® is distributed by various companies in the health care field, it is independently prepared and published. All decisions regarding its content are solely the responsibility of the authors. Their decisions are not subject to any form of approval by other interests or organizations.

Some recommendations in this publication suggest the use of agents for purposes or in dosages other than those recommended in product labeling. Such recommendations are based on reports in peer-reviewed publications and are not based on or influenced by any material or advice from pharmaceutical or health care product manufacturers.

No responsibility is assumed by the authors or the American Geriatrics Society for any injury or damage to persons or property, as a matter of product liability, negligence, warranty, or otherwise, arising out of the use or application of any methods, products, instructions, or ideas contained herein. No guarantee, endorsement, or warranty of any kind, express or implied (including specifically no warrant of merchantability or of fitness for a particular purpose) is given by the Society in connection with any information contained herein. Independent verification of any diagnosis, treatment, or drug use or dosage should be obtained. No test or procedure should be performed unless, in the judgment of an independent, qualified physician, it is justified in the light of the risk involved.

Citation: Reuben DB, Herr KA, Pacala JT, *et al. Geriatrics At Your Fingertips: 2012, 14th Edition.* New York: The American Geriatrics Society; 2012.

Copyright © 2012 by the American Geriatrics Society.

All rights reserved. Except where authorized, no part of this publication may be reproduced, stored in a retrieval system, or transmitted in any form or by any means, electronic, mechanical, photocopying, recording, or otherwise without prior written permission of the American Geriatrics Society, 40 Fulton Street, 18th Floor, New York, NY 10038.

ISSN 1553-152X
ISBN 978-1-886775-57-2

TABLE OF CONTENTS

AUTHORS

David B. Reuben, MD
Director, Multicampus Program in Geriatric Medicine and Gerontology
Chief, Division of Geriatrics
Archstone Foundation Chair
Professor of Medicine
David Geffen School of Medicine at UCLA, Los Angeles, CA

Keela A. Herr, PhD, RN
Professor and Associate Dean for Faculty
Co-Director, Iowa John A. Hartford Center of Geriatric Nursing Excellence
College of Nursing
The University of Iowa, Iowa City, IA

James T. Pacala, MD, MS
Associate Professor and Associate Head
Distinguished University Teaching Professor
Department of Family Medicine and Community Health
University of Minnesota School of Medicine, Minneapolis, MN

Bruce G. Pollock, MD, PhD
VP Research
Centre for Addiction and Mental Health
Professor and Head, Division of Geriatric Psychiatry
Faculty of Medicine
University of Toronto, Toronto, Ontario, Canada

Jane F. Potter, MD
Chief, Division of Geriatrics and Gerontology
Director, Home Instead Center for Successful Aging
Harris Professor of Geriatric Medicine
University of Nebraska Medical Center, Omaha, NE

Todd P. Semla, MS, PharmD
Clinical Pharmacy Specialist
Department of Veterans Affairs
Pharmacy Benefits Management
Associate Professor
The Feinberg School of Medicine
Northwestern University, Chicago, IL

ABBREVIATIONS

AAA	abdominal aortic aneurysm
ABG	arterial blood gas
ABI	ankle-brachial index
ACC	American College of Cardiology
ACE	angiotensin-converting enzyme
ACEI	angiotensin-converting enzyme inhibitor
ACIP	Advisory Committee on Immunization Practices
ACOG	American College of Obstetrics and Gynecology
ACR	American College of Rheumatology
ACTH	adrenocorticotropic hormone
AD	Alzheimer's disease
ADA	American Diabetes Association
ADLs	activities of daily living
AFB	acid-fast bacillus
AGS	American Geriatrics Society
AHA	American Heart Association
AHRQ	Agency for Healthcare Research and Quality
AIDS	acquired immune deficiency syndrome
AIMS	Abnormal Involuntary Movement Scale
ALT	alanine aminotransferase
AMD	age-related macular degeneration
APAP	acetaminophen
ARB	angiotensin receptor blocker
AS	aortic stenosis
ASA	acetylsalicylic acid or aspirin
ASA class	American Society of Anesthesiologists grading scale for surgical patients
AST	aspartate aminotransferase
ATA	American Thyroid Association
ATS	American Thoracic Society
AUA	American Urological Association
BMD	bone mineral density
BMI	body mass index
BP	blood pressure
BPH	benign prostatic hyperplasia
bpm	beats per minute
BUN	blood urea nitrogen
C&S	culture and sensitivity
CABG	coronary artery bypass graft
CAD	coronary artery disease
CBC	complete blood cell count
cfu	colony-forming unit
$CHADS_2$	congestive heart failure, hypertension, age, diabetes, stroke
CHD	coronary heart disease
CI	confidence interval
CKD	chronic kidney disease
CMS	Centers for Medicare and Medicaid Services
CNS	central nervous system
COPD	chronic obstructive pulmonary disease

CPAP	continuous positive airway pressure
CPK	creatine phosphokinase
CPR	cardiopulmonary resuscitation
Cr	creatinine
CrCl	creatinine clearance
CT	computed tomography
CXR	chest x-ray
CYP	cytochrome P-450
D&C	dilation and curettage
D5W	dextrose 5% in water
DBP	diastolic blood pressure
D/C	discontinue
DHIC	detrusor hyperactivity with impaired contractility
DMARD	disease-modifying antirheumatoid drug
DSM-IV	*Diagnostic and Statistical Manual of Mental Disorders*, 4th ed. (Washington, DC: American Psychiatric Association; 1994)
DVT	deep-vein thrombosis
ECF	extracellular fluid
ECG	electrocardiogram, electrocardiography
EEG	electroencephalogram
EF	ejection fraction
eGFR	estimated glomerular filtration rate
EPS	extrapyramidal symptoms
ESR	erythrocyte sedimentation rate
FDA	Food and Drug Administration
FEV_1	forced expiratory volume in 1 sec
FI	fecal incontinence
FOBT	fecal occult blood test
FVC	forced vital capacity
GAD	generalized anxiety disorder
GDS	Geriatric Depression Scale
GERD	gastroesophageal reflux disease
GFR	glomerular filtration rate
GI	gastrointestinal
GnRH	gonadotropin-releasing hormone
GU	genitourinary
Hb	hemoglobin
HbA_{1c}	glycosylated hemoglobin
HCTZ	hydrochlorothiazide
HDL	high-density lipoprotein
HF	heart failure
HR	heart rate
HT	hormone therapy
HTN	hypertension
hx	history
IADLs	instrumental activities of daily living
IBS	irritable bowel syndrome
IBW	ideal body weight
ICD	implantable cardiac defibrillator
INH	isoniazid
INR	international normalized ratio

IOP	intraocular pressure
iPTH	intact parathyroid hormone
JNC 7	Seventh Joint National Committee on Prevention, Detection, Evaluation, and Treatment of High Blood Pressure
K^+	potassium ion
LBW	lean body weight
LDL	low-density lipoprotein
LFT	liver function test
LMWH	low-molecular-weight heparin
LVEF	left ventricular ejection fraction
LVH	left ventricular hypertrophy
MAOI	monoamine oxidase inhibitor
MCV	mean corpuscular volume
MDI	metered-dose inhaler
MDRD	Modification of Diet in Renal Disease
MI	myocardial infarction
MMA	methylmalonic acid
MMSE	Mini-Mental State Examination (Folstein's)
MoCA	Montreal Cognitive Assessment
MRA	magnetic resonance angiography
MRI	magnetic resonance imaging
MRSA	methicillin-resistant *Staphylococcus aureus*
MSE	mental status examination
NG	nasogastric
NNRTIs	non-nucleoside reverse transcriptase inhibitors
NSAIDs	nonsteroidal anti-inflammatory drugs
NPH	neutral protamine Hagedorn (insulin)
OCD	obsessive-compulsive disorder
OGTT	oral glucose tolerance test
OT	occupational therapy
PAD	peripheral arterial disease
PAH	pulmonary arterial hypertension
PCA	patient-controlled analgesia
PE	pulmonary embolism
PEF	peak expiratory flow
PNS	peripheral nervous system
POLST	Physician Orders for Life-Sustaining Treatment
POMA	Performance-Oriented Mobility Assessment
PONV	postoperative nausea and vomiting
PPD	purified protein derivative (of tuberculin)
PPI	proton-pump inhibitor
PSA	prostate-specific antigen
PT	prothrombin time *or* physical therapy
PTCA	percutaneous transluminal coronary angioplasty
PTH	parathyroid hormone
PTT	partial thromboplastin time
PUVA	psoralen plus ultraviolet light of A wavelength
QT_c	QT (cardiac output) corrected for heart rate
RA	rheumatoid arthritis
RBC	red blood cells *or* ranitidine bismuth citrate
RF	rheumatoid factor

RLS	restless legs syndrome
sats	saturations
SBP	systolic blood pressure
SD	standard deviation
SIADH	syndrome of inappropriate secretion of antidiuretic hormone
SNRIs	serotonin norepinephrine-reuptake inhibitors
SPEP	serum protein electrophoresis
SSRIs	selective serotonin-reuptake inhibitors
sTfR	soluble transferrin receptor
TCA	tricyclic antidepressant
TD	tardive dyskinesia
TDD	telephone device for the deaf
TG	triglycerides
TIA	transient ischemic attack
TIBC	total iron-binding capacity
TSG	thyroid-stimulating globulin
TSH	thyroid-stimulating hormone
TTP	thrombotic thrombocytopenic purpura
TUIP	transurethral incision of the prostate
TURP	transurethral resection of the prostate
U	unit(s)
UA	urinalysis
UFH	unfractionated heparin
UI	urinary incontinence
UTI	urinary tract infection
UV	ultraviolet
VF	ventricular fibrillation
VIN	vulvar intraepithelial neoplasia
VT	ventricular tachycardia
VTE	venous thromboembolism
WBC	white blood cell(s)
WHO	World Health Organization
wt	weight

Drug Prescribing and Elimination

Drugs are listed by generic names; trade names are in *italics*. An asterisk (*) indicates that the drug is available OTC. Check marks (✔) indicate drugs preferred for treating older adults. A triangle (▲) following the drug name indicates that the drug is available as a generic formulation. A triangle following a combination medication indicates that the combination is available as a generic, not the individual drugs. Note that even though individual drugs in a combination medication are available as generics, the combination may not be. Formulations in text are bracketed and expressed in milligrams (mg) unless otherwise specified. Abbreviations for dosing, formulations, and route of elimination are defined below.

ac	before meals	crm	cream
C	capsule, caplet	d	day(s)
ChT	chewable tablet	ER	extended release
conc	concentrate	F	fecal elimination
CR	controlled release	fl	fluid

g	gram(s)		wk	week(s)
gran	granules		XR	extended release
gtt	drop(s)		yr	year(s)
h	hour(s)			
hs	at bedtime			
IM	intramuscular(ly)			
inj	injectable(s)			
IT	intrathecal(ly)			
IV	intravenous(ly)			
K	renal elimination			
L	hepatic elimination			
lot	lotion			
max	maximum			
mcg	microgram(s)			
MDI	metered-dose inhaler			
min	minute(s)			
mo	month(s)			
npo	nothing by mouth			
NS	normal saline			
ODT	oral disintegrating tablet			
oint	ointment			
OTC	over-the-counter			
OU	both eyes			
pc	after meals			
pch	patch			
pk	pack, packet			
po	by mouth			
pr	per rectum			
prn	as needed			
pwd	powder			
qam	every morning			
qhs	each bedtime			
S	liquid (includes concentrate, elixir, solution, suspension, syrup, tincture)			
SC	subcutaneous(ly)			
sec	second(s)			
shp	shampoo			
sl	sublingual			
sol	solution			
Sp	suppository			
spr	spray(s)			
SR	sustained release			
sus	suspension			
syr	syrup			
T	tablet			
tab(s)	tablet(s)			
tbsp	tablespoon(s)			
tinc	tincture			
TR	timed release			
tsp	teaspoon(s)			

Providing high-quality health care for older adults requires special knowledge and skills. *Geriatrics At Your Fingertips® (GAYF)* is an annually updated, pocket-sized reference that provides quick, easy access to the specific information clinicians need to make decisions about the care of older adults. Since its initial publication in 1998, *GAYF's* up-to-date content and portable format quickly made it the American Geriatrics Society's (AGS) best-selling publication.

In response to the increased use of electronic media in clinical settings, the AGS has also developed *GAYF* for the Web and for mobile devices. Schools can acquire licenses to provide mobile device access for all their faculty and trainees. More information on these formats can be found at www.geriatricsatyourfingertips.org.

In this updated 14th edition, we have added new sections on the Medicare Annual Wellness Visit, interprofessional team care, transcatheter aortic valve replacement, new treatments for hearing loss, refeeding syndrome, perioperative management of antiplatelet drugs in patients with drug-eluting stents, and rapid eye movement sleep disorder. The text and tables contain newly recommended diagnostic tests and management strategies. Among the many updates included in this edition are new criteria for the diagnosis of rheumatoid arthritis, short-course colchicine for gout flares, and treatment of asthma in older adults. Medication tables were updated shortly before publication and include specific caveats and cautions to facilitate appropriate prescribing in older adults. Medications available as generic formulations are indicated, because these are often less expensive.

Given its portable size, *GAYF* does not explain in detail the rationale underlying the strategies presented. Many of these strategies have been derived from guidelines published by the Agency for Healthcare Research and Quality and various medical societies (see the National Guideline Clearinghouse at www.guidelines.gov). When no such guidelines exist, the strategies recommended represent the best opinions of the authors and reviewers, based on clinical experience and the most recent medical literature. References are provided sparingly, but many others are available from the organizations listed below, as well as from the current edition of the AGS *Geriatrics Review Syllabus*.

The authors welcome comments about *GAYF*, which should be addressed to the AGS at infoamger@americangeriatrics.org or 40 Fulton Street, 18th Floor, New York, NY 10038.

The authors are particularly grateful to the following organizations and individuals: the John A. Hartford Foundation, for generously supporting the initial development and distribution of *GAYF* and its PDA version; AGS staff, Nancy Lundebjerg, Carol Goodwin and Elvy Ickowicz, who have served a vital role in *GAYF's* development and its continued distribution and expansion; and the following experts who reviewed portions of this edition:

Daniel Blumberger, MD

Catherine E. DuBeau, MD

Perry Fine, MD

Gail Greendale, MD

Gerald C. Groggel, MD

Jason M. Johanning, MD

Jerry C. Johnson, MD

James Judge, MD

Joy Laramie, MSN, NP

Andrew Lee, MD

Eric J. Lenze, MD

Arash Naeim, MD, PhD

Larissa Rodriguez, MD

Thomas T. Yoshikawa, MD

Guidelines of the following organizations are the basis of parts of specific chapters:

Advisory Committee on Immunization Practices
Agency for Healthcare Research and Quality
Alzheimer's Association
American Academy of Neurology
American Academy of Orthopaedic Surgeons
American Association for Geriatric Psychiatry
American College of Cardiology
American College of Chest Physicians
American College of Gastroenterology
American College of Obstetrics and Gynecology
American College of Rheumatology
American Diabetes Association
American Geriatrics Society
American Heart Association
American Lung Association
American Pain Society
American Psychiatric Association
American Society of Anesthesiologists
American Thyroid Association
American Urological Association
The Endocrine Society
Ethnogeriatrics Committee, American Geriatrics Society
National Cholesterol Education Program
National Heart, Lung and Blood Institute
National Osteoporosis Foundation
U.S. Preventive Services Task Force
World Health Organization

Editorial Staff
Susan E. Aiello, DVM, ELS, Medical Editor
Joseph Douglas, Managing Editor
Pilar Wyman, Medical Indexer

Technical development and production of print and electronic versions:
Fry Communications, Inc.
Melissa Durborow, Group Manager
Rhonda Liddick, Composition Manager
Denise DeNicholas, Composition
Jason Hughes, Technical Services Manager
Julie Stevens, Project Manager

U.S. Biomedical Information Systems, Inc. (USBMIS, Inc.)
Eric Poirier, Chief Operations Officer

Table 1. Conversions		
Temperature	**Liquid**	**Weight**
$F = (1.8)C + 32$	1 fl oz = 30 mL	1 lb = 0.453 kg
$C = (F - 32) / (1.8)$	1 tsp = 5 mL	1 kg = 2.2 lb
	1 tbsp = 15 mL	1 oz = 30 g

Alveolar-Arterial Oxygen Gradient
$A - a = 148 - 1.2(Paco_2) - Pao_2$ [normal = $10-20$ mmHg, breathing room air at sea level]

Calculated Osmolality
$Osm = 2Na + glucose / 18 + BUN / 2.8$ [normal = 280–295]

Golden Rules of Arterial Blood Gases
• Pco_2 change of 10 corresponds to a pH change of 0.08.
• pH change of 0.15 corresponds to base excess change of 10 mEq/L.

Creatinine Clearance
See Appropriate Prescribing, p 14.
For renally eliminated drugs, dosage adjustments may be necessary if CrCl <60 mL/min.
Cockcroft-Gault formula:

$$\frac{IBW(140 - age)\ (0.85\ if\ female)}{(72)\ (stable\ serum\ creatinine)}$$

Many laboratories are reporting MDRD as an estimate of GFR (eGFR). This measure is used for staging chronic kidney disease. The MDRD has not been validated in adults >70 yr old. GFR should not be equated to CrCl. The use of the MDRD eGFR to adjust drug dosages overestimates renal function in many older adults. The use of Cockcroft-Gault is more accurate to adjust drug dosages. FDA package insert dosing recommendations are almost entirely based on the Cockcroft-Gault estimate of CrCl.

Erythrocyte Sedimentation Rate
Westergren: women = (age + 10) / 2
men = age / 2

Ideal Body Weight
• Men = 50 kg + (2.3 kg) (each inch of height >5 feet)
• Women = 45.5 kg + (2.3 kg) (each inch of height >5 feet)

Lean Body Weight

IBW + 0.4 (actual body weight − IBW)

Body Mass Index

$$\frac{\text{weight in kg}}{(\text{height in meters})^2} \quad or \quad \frac{\text{weight in lb}}{(\text{height in inches})^2} \times 704.5$$

Partial Pressure of Oxygen, Arterial (Pao_2) While Breathing Room Air

100 − (age/3) estimates decline

Table 2. Motor Function by Nerve Roots			
Level	**Motor Function**	**Level**	**Motor Function**
C4	Spontaneous breathing	L1–L2	Hip flexion
C5	Shoulder shrug	L3	Hip adduction
C6	Elbow flexion	L4	Hip abduction
C7	Elbow extension	L5	Great toe dorsiflexion
C8/T1	Finger flexion	S1–S2	Foot plantar flexion
T1–T12	Intercostal abdominal muscles	S2–S4	Rectal tone

Table 3. Lumbosacral Nerve Root Compression			
Root	**Motor**	**Sensory**	**Reflex**
L4	Quadriceps	Medial foot	Knee jerk
	Dorsiflexors	Dorsum of foot	Medial hamstring
L5	Great toe dorsiflexors	Dorsum of foot	Medial hamstring
S1	Plantar flexors	Lateral foot	Ankle jerk

Figure 1. Dermatomes

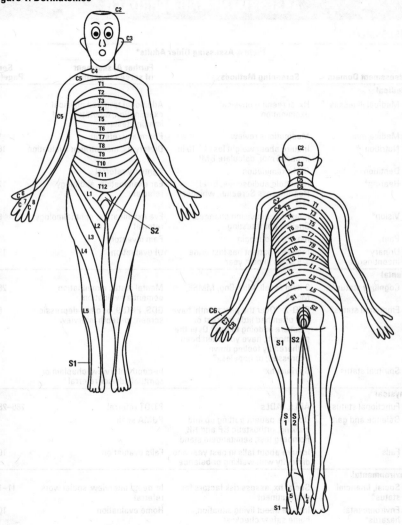

Source: Hamilton, RJ, ed. *The Tarascon Pocket Pharmacopoeia*, 2012 classic shirt-pocket edition. Jones and Bartlett Learning, 2012:134. Sudbury, MA. www.jblearning.com. Reprinted with permission.

ASSESSMENT

Table 4. Assessing Older Adults*

Assessment Domain	Screening Methods	Further Assessment (if screen is positive)	See Page(s)
Medical			
Medical illnesses[a,b]	Hx, screening physical examination	Additional targeted physical examination, laboratory and imaging tests	
Medications[a,b]	Medications review	Pharmacy referral	14
Nutrition[a,b]	Inquire about weight loss (>10 lb in past 6 mo), calculate BMI	Dietary hx, malnutrition evaluation	166
Dentition	Oral examination	Dentistry referral	
Hearing[a]	Handheld audioscope, Brief Hearing Loss Screener, whisper test	Ear examination, audiology referral	120
Vision[a]	Inquire about vision changes, Snellen chart testing	Eye examination, ophthalmology referral	92
Pain	Inquire about pain	Pain inventory	203
Urinary incontinence	Inquire if patient has lost urine >5 times in past year	UI evaluation	132
Mental			
Cognitive status[a,b]	3-item recall, Mini-Cog, MMSE, MoCA	Mental status examination, dementia evaluation	285
Emotional status[a]	PHQ-2: "Over the past month, have you often had little interest or pleasure in doing things? Over the past month, have you often been bothered by feeling down, depressed, or hopeless?"	GDS, PHQ-9, or other depression screen; in-depth interview	68
Spiritual status	Spiritual hx	In-depth interview, chaplain or spiritual advisor referral	
Physical			
Functional status[a]	ADLs, IADLs	PT/OT referral	286–287
Balance and gait[a]	Observe patient getting up and walking, orthostatic BP and HR, Romberg test, semitandem stand	POMA scale	
Falls	Inquire about falls in past year and difficulty with walking or balance	Falls evaluation	101
Environmental			
Social, financial status[a]	Social hx, assess risk factors for mistreatment	In-depth interview, social work referral	11–13
Environmental hazards[a]	Inquire about living situation, home safety checklist	Home evaluation	105

(cont.)

Table 4. **Assessing Older Adults* (cont.)**			
Assessment Domain	**Screening Methods**	**Further Assessment** (if screen is positive)	**See Page(s)**
Care Preferences			
Life-sustaining treatment[a,b]	Inquire about preferences; complete POLST form		9–11

*See also Assessment Instruments, p 285.

[a] Required elements of the Medicare Initial Annual Wellness Visit

[b] Required elements of Medicare Subsequent Annual Wellness Visits

Medicare Annual Wellness Visit (AWV)

- Can be performed by a physician, physician's assistant, nurse practitioner, or clinical nurse specialist, or a health professional (eg, health educator, dietitian) under the direct supervision of a physician.
- Initial and subsequent AWVs must include documentation of elements indicated in **Table 4**, plus the following items that are to be established at the initial AWV and updated at subsequent AWVs:
  - A family hx
  - A list of current providers caring for the patient
  - A written 5- to 10-yr schedule of screening activities based on USPSTF/CDC recommendations (see Prevention, p 229)
  - A list of risk factors and conditions for which primary, secondary, and tertiary preventive interventions are being applied

INTERPROFESSIONAL GERIATRIC TEAM CARE

- Most effective for care of frail older adults with multiple comorbidities
- Also appropriate for management of complex geriatric syndromes (eg, falls, confusion, dementia, depression, incontinence, weight loss, persistent pain, immobility)
- Common features of team care include:
  - Proactive assessment of multiple domains (see **Table 4**)
  - Care coordination, usually performed by an advanced practice nurse or social worker
  - Care planning performed by team members (see **Table 5**)

Table 5. **Interprofessional Team Members**[a]			
Profession	**Degree/Certification**	**Training**	**Team Role/Expertise**
Advance practice nurse	APRN	2–4 yr PB	Disease management, care coordination, primary care, skin and pain assessment
Nurse	RN/LPN (LVN)	4 yr B/1–2 yr B	Care coordination, skin and pain assessment, ADL/IADL screening

(cont.)

Table 5. Interprofessional Team Members[a] (cont.)

Profession	Degree/Certification	Training	Team Role/Expertise
Occupational therapist	OTR	2–4 yr PB	ADL/IADL assessment and improvement (including driving and home safety assessments)
Pharmacist	PharmD	4 yr PB ± 1–2 yr PG	Medication review, patient education, drug monitoring
Physical therapist	PT	2–3 yr PB	Mobility, strength, upper extremity assessment and improvement
Physician	MD, DO	4 yr PB + 3 or more yr PG	Diagnosis and management of medical problems, primary care
Social worker	MSW, DSW	2–4 yr PB	Complete psychosocial assessment and improvement, individual and family counseling

Note: B = baccalaureate (post-high school), PB = post-baccalaureate, PG = post-graduate (ie, residency training)

[a] This is not an exhaustive list. Other common team members include audiologists, dentists, dietitians, physician's assistants, speech therapists, and spiritual care professionals.

SITES OF CARE FOR OLDER ADULTS

Table 6. Sites of Care[a]

Site	Patient Needs and Services	Principal Funding Source
Home	ADL or IADL assistance	PP for caregiving services
	Skilled nursing and/or rehabilitation services when patient can only occasionally leave the home at great effort	Medicare Part A for most nonphysician professional services (eg, nursing, OT, PT); PP for caregiving services
Senior citizen housing	Housing	PP[b]
Assisted living, residential care, board-and-care facilities	IADL assistance, primarily with meals, housekeeping, and medication management	PP, Medicaid for some facilities
Hospital		
Acute care	Acute hospital care	Medicare Part A
Chronic care	Chronic skilled care (eg, chronic ventilator)	Medicare Part A, PP, Medicaid
Inpatient rehabilitation	Intensive multidisciplinary team rehabilitation	Medicare Part A[c]

(cont.)

Table 6. Sites of Care (cont.)[a]

Site	Patient Needs and Services	Principal Funding Source
Skilled nursing facility		
Transitional care unit	Skilled nursing care and/or intensive multidisciplinary team rehabilitation	Medicare Part A[c]
Short stay/ Rehabilitation	Skilled nursing care and/or straight-forward rehabilitation	Medicare Part A[c]
Long-term care	ADL assistance and/or skilled nursing care	PP, Medicaid
Continuing care retirement communities	Variety of living arrangements ranging from independent to skilled	PP
Hospice (home or facility-based)	Palliative/comfort care for life expectancy <6 mo	Medicare Part A

Note: PP = private pay (may include long-term care insurance)

[a] For useful information about sites of care for patients and families, see www.payingforseniorcare.com.

[b] May be subsidized for older adults spending over one-third of income for rent. Some facilities may have access to a social worker or caregiving services for hire.

[c] Medicare Part A pays for 20 days after a hospital stay of ≥3 days, patient or co-insurance pays $144.50/d (in 2012) for days 21–100 with Part A covering the rest; patient or co-insurance pays 100% after day 100.

HOSPITAL CARE

Common Problems to Monitor

- Delirium (see p 59)
- Intra- and postoperative coronary events: postoperative ECG to check
- Malnutrition (see p 166)
- Pain (see p 203)
- Polypharmacy: review medications daily
- Pulmonary complications: minimized by incentive spirometry, coughing, early ambulation after surgery
- Rehabilitation: encourage early mobility
- Skin breakdown (see p 258)

Discharge Planning

- Ideally, all team members should participate in discharge planning, beginning early in the hospitalization.
- For a safe and effective transfer from the hospital to the nursing home, the following should be completed by the time the patient arrives at the nursing home:
  - Interfacility transfer form (the medication administration record is inadequate) that includes a discharge medication list noting new and discontinued medications, discontinuation dates for short-term medications, and any dosage changes in all medications
  - Discharge summary (performed by physician) that includes the patient's baseline functional status, "red flags" for rare but potentially serious complications of conditions or treatments, orders including medications, important tests for which results are pending, and needed next steps
  - Verbal physician-to-physician sign-out

- Tools are available (see www.caretransitions.org) for patients and caregivers to assert care preferences, clarify discharge instructions, resolve medication discrepancies, and facilitate communication across care sites after discharge.
- Site of care after discharge should be warranted by patient's needs (see **Table 6**).

SCHEDULED NURSING-HOME VISIT CHECKLIST
1. Evaluate patient for interval functional change
2. Check vital signs, weight, laboratory tests, consultant reports since last visit
3. Review medications (correlate to active diagnoses)
4. Sign orders
5. Address nursing staff concerns
6. Write a SOAP note (subjective data, objective data, assessment, plan)
7. Revise problem list as needed
8. Update advance directives at least yearly
9. Update resident; update family member(s) as needed

LIFE EXPECTANCY AND MEDICAL DECISION MAKING
- Many medical decisions are predicated on estimated life expectancy of the patient. **Table 7** shows life expectancy by age and sex.
- Life expectancy is associated with a number of factors in addition to age and sex, including health behaviors, presence of disease, nutritional status, race/ethnicity, and educational and financial status.
- Conditions commonly leading to death are frailty, cancer, organ failure (heart, lung, kidney, liver), and advanced dementia.
- Active life expectancy reflects the remaining years of disability-free existence. At age 65, active life expectancy is about 90% of total life expectancy; this percentage decreases with further aging.
- Estimated life expectancy can aid individualized medical decision making, particularly when considering preventive tests. A clinician can judge the patient's health status as being above (75th percentile), at (50th percentile), or below average (25th percentile) for age and sex, and then roughly determine life expectancy using **Table 7**. Then, the period of time needed for the treatment to result in a positive clinical outcome is estimated and compared with the life expectancy of the patient.
  - If estimated life expectancy is longer than the time needed to achieve a positive outcome, the treatment is encouraged.
  - If estimated life expectancy is shorter than the time needed to achieve a positive outcome, the treatment is discouraged.
  - If estimated life expectancy is about the same as the time needed to achieve a positive outcome, the potential risks and benefits of the treatment should be discussed neutrally with the patient.

For example, the benefit of many cancer screening tests is not realized for ~5 yr after detection of asymptomatic malignancies. If a patient's life expectancy is 4 yr based only on age and sex, and the patient has poor overall health status compared with age-matched peers, cancer screening would be discouraged because the likelihood of benefit from having the test is low.

Table 7. **Life Expectancy (yr) by Age (United States)***						
	25th percentile		**50th percentile**		**75th percentile**	
Age	**Men**	**Women**	**Men**	**Women**	**Men**	**Women**
65	10	13	17	20	23	26
70	7	10	13	16	19	21
75	6	7	10	12	15	17
80	4	5	8	9	11	13
85	2	3	6	7	8	10
90	1	2	4	5	6	7

*Figures indicate the number of years in which a percentage of the corresponding age and sex cohort will die. For example, in a cohort of 65-yr-old men, 25% will be dead in 10 yr (by age 75), 50% will be dead in 17 yr, and 75% will be dead in 23 yr.
Source: Data from Arias E, Rostron BL, Tejada-Vera B. United States Life Tables, 2005. National Vital Statistics Reports, vol 59, no 10, Mar 3, 2010.

INFORMED DECISION MAKING AND PATIENT PREFERENCES FOR LIFE-SUSTAINING CARE
Physicians have no ethical obligation to offer care that is judged to be futile.
Three elements are needed for a patient's choices to be legally and ethically valid:
- A capable decision maker: Capacity is for the decision being made; patient may be capable of making some but not all decisions. If a person is sufficiently impaired, a surrogate decision maker must be involved. (See also **Figure 2**.)
- Patient's voluntary participation in the decision-making process.

Figure 2. Informed Decision Making

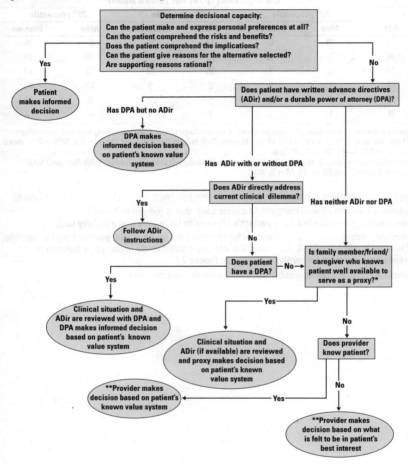

* Most states have laws specifying who should serve as proxy when no ADir or DPA exists. For most of these states, the specified hierarchy of decision makers is (in order): legal guardian, spouse or domestic partner, adult children, parents, adult siblings, closest living relative, close friend.

** Or court-appointed decision maker; laws vary by state.

- Sufficient information: Patient must be sufficiently informed; items to disclose in informed consent include:
  - Diagnosis
  - Nature, risks, costs, and benefits of possible interventions
  - Alternative treatments; relative benefits, risks, and costs
  - Likely results of no treatment
  - Likelihood of success
  - Advice or recommendation of the clinician

Ideally, patient preferences for life-sustaining care should be established before the patient is critically ill.

- Preferences should be established for use of the following interventions and the conditions under which they would be used: cardiopulmonary resuscitation, hospitalization, intravenous hydration, antibiotics, artificially administered nutrition, other life-extending medical treatment, and palliative/comfort care (see Palliative Care, p 216).
- Patients should be encouraged to complete a living will and/or to establish a durable power of attorney for health-care decision making.
- Use of a POLST (Physician Orders for Life-Sustaining Treatment) form can be very useful in formalizing patient preferences (see www.polst.org).

MISTREATMENT OF OLDER ADULTS

Risk Factors for Inadequate or Abusive Caregiving

- Cognitive impairment in patient, caregiver, or both
- Dependency (financial, psychological, etc) of caregiver on elderly patient, or vice versa
- Family conflict
- Family history of abusive behavior, alcohol or drug problems, mental illness, or mental retardation
- Financial stress
- Isolation of patient or caregiver, or both
- Depression or malnutrition in the patient
- Living arrangements inadequate for needs of the patient
- Stressful events in the family, such as death of a loved one or loss of employment

Table 8. Determining Suspicion and Clinical Signs of Possible Mistreatment of Older Adults

Abandonment

Question to Ask Patient: Is there anyone you can call to come and take care of you?
Clinical Signs:

- Evidence that patient is left alone unsafely
- Evidence of sudden withdrawal of care by caregiver
- Statements by patient about abandonment

Physical Abuse

Question to Ask Patient: Has anyone at home ever hit you or hurt you?
Clinical Signs:

- Anxiety, nervousness, especially toward caregiver
- Bruising, in various healing stages, especially bilateral or on inner arms or thighs
- Fractures, especially in various healing stages
- Lacerations
- Repeated emergency department visits
- Repeated falls
- Signs of sexual abuse
- Statements by patient about physical abuse

Exploitation

Question to Ask Patient: Has anyone taken your things?
Clinical Signs:

- Evidence of misuse of patient's assets
- Inability of patient to account for money and property or to pay for essential care
- Reports of demands for money or goods in exchange for caregiving or services
- Unexplained loss of Social Security or pension checks
- Statements by patient about exploitation

Neglect

Question to Ask Patient: Are you receiving enough care at home?
Clinical Signs:

- Contractures
- Dehydration
- Depression
- Diarrhea
- Fecal impaction
- Malnutrition
- Inappropriate use of medications
- Poor hygiene
- Pressure ulcers
- Repeated falls
- Repeated hospital admissions
- Urine burns
- Failure to respond to warning of obvious disease
- Statements by patient about neglect

Psychological Abuse

Questions to Ask Patient: Has anyone ever scolded or threatened you? Has anyone made fun of you?
Clinical Signs:

- Observed impatience, irritability, or demeaning behavior toward patient by caregiver
- Anxiety, fearfulness, ambivalence, or anger shown by patient about caregiver
- Statements by patient about psychological abuse

Assessment and Management
- Interview patient and caregiver separately.
- Ask patient some general screening questions, such as, "Are there any problems with family or household members that you would like to tell me about?" Follow up a positive response with more direct questions such as those suggested in **Table 8**.
- On physical examination, look for any unusual marks, signs of injury, or conditions listed in **Table 8**.
- If mistreatment is suspected, report case to Adult Protective Services (most states have mandatory reporting laws).
- If patient is in immediate danger of harm, create and implement plan to remove patient from danger (hospital admission, court protective order, placement in safe environment, etc).

CROSS-CULTURAL GERIATRICS
Clinicians should remember that:
- Individuals within every ethnic group can differ widely.
- Familiarity with a patient's background is useful only if his or her preferences are linked to the cultural heritage.
- Ethnic groups differ widely in
  - approach to decision making (eg, involvement of family and friends)
  - disclosure of medical information (eg, cancer diagnosis)
  - end-of-life care (eg, advance directives and resuscitation preferences)

In caring for older adults of any ethnicity:
- Use the patient's preferred terminology for his or her cultural identity in conversation and in health records.
- Determine whether interpretation services are needed; if possible, use professional interpreter rather than family member. When interpreters are not available, online translation services (eg, www.babelfish.com or http://translate.google.com) can be useful.
- Recognize that the patient may not conceive of illness in Western terms.
- Determine whether the patient is a refugee or survivor of violence or genocide.
- Explore early on the patient's preferences for disclosure of serious clinical findings, and reconfirm at intervals.
- Ask if the patient prefers to involve or defer to others in the decision-making process.
- Follow the patient's preferences regarding gender roles.

For further information, see *Doorway Thoughts: Cross Cultural Health Care for Older Adults Series* (www.americangeriatrics.org/publications/shop_publications/).

APPROPRIATE PRESCRIBING, DRUG INTERACTIONS, AND ADVERSE EVENTS

HOW TO PRESCRIBE APPROPRIATELY

- **Obtain a complete medication history.** Ask about previous treatments and responses as well as about other prescribers. Ask about allergies, OTC drugs, nutritional supplements, alternative medications, alcohol, tobacco, caffeine, and recreational drugs.
- **Use e-prescribing to reduce risk of transcription and medication errors, check insurance coverage, and receive CMS bonus payment (1% in 2012 and 0.5% in 2013) and avoid 1% penalty in 2012 and 1.5% in 2013.**
- **Avoid prescribing before a diagnosis is made.** Consider nondrug therapy.
- **Review medications regularly and before prescribing a new medication.** D/C medications that have not had the intended response, are no longer needed, or do not have a corresponding diagnosis.
- **Know the actions, adverse events, and toxicity profiles of prescribed medications.** Consider how new prescriptions might interact or complement current medications.
- **Consider the following for new medications:** Is the dosing regimen practical? Is the new medication the least expensive alternative if efficacy and safety are comparable to others in the drug class?
- **Start long-term medications at a low dose and titrate dose on the basis of tolerability and response.** Use drug concentration monitoring when available.
- **Attempt to reach a therapeutic dose before switching to or adding another medication.** Use combinations cautiously: titrate each medication to a therapeutic dose before switching to a combination product.
- **Educate patient and/or caregiver about each medication.** Include the regimen, therapeutic goal, cost, and potential adverse events or drug interactions. Provide written instructions.
- **Avoid using one medication to treat the adverse events caused by another.**
- **Attempt to use one medication to treat two or more conditions.**
- **Communicate with other prescribers.** Don't assume patients do—they assume you do!
- **Avoid using drugs from the same class or with similar actions** (eg, alprazolam and zolpidem).

WAYS TO REDUCE MEDICATION ERRORS

- Be knowledgeable about the medication's dose, adverse events, interactions, and monitoring.
- Write legibly to avoid misreading of the drug name (eg, *Lamictal* vs *Lamisil*).
- Write out the directions, strength, route, quantity, and number of refills.
- Always precede a decimal expression of <1 with a zero (0); never use a zero after a decimal.
- Write out directions, avoid using abbreviations, especially easily confused ones (qd and qid).
- Assess patient's or caregiver's ability to correctly and safely administer each medication.
- Avoid confusion: Brand name products can contain different ingredients depending on their indication, eg, *Mylanta Classic*, maximum and regular strength liquid contains aluminum

and magnesium hydroxide plus simethicone, while *Mylanta Gas Maximum Strength* contains only simethicone; *Lotrimin Ultra* crm contains butenafine, while *Lotrimin AF* and *Gyne-lotrimin* crm contain clotrimazole, and *Lotrimin AF* aerosol topical contains miconazole.

- Do not use ambiguous directions, eg, as directed (ud) or as needed (prn).
- Include the medication's purpose in the directions (eg, for high blood pressure).
- Write dosages for thyroid replacement therapy in mcg, not mg.
- Always re-read what you've written.
- For more information, see www.fda.gov/Drugs/DrugSafety/MedicationErrors/default.htm or www.ismp.org/tools/abbreviations/

CRITERIA FOR MEDICATIONS OF CHOICE FOR OLDER ADULTS

- Established efficacy
- Compatible safety and adverse-event profile
- Low risk of drug or nutrient interactions
- Half-life <24 h with no active metabolites
- Elimination does not change with age, or there are known dosage adjustments for renal or hepatic function
- Convenient dosing—once or twice daily
- Strength and dosage forms match recommended dosages for older adults
- Affordable for the patient
- See also Medicare Part D Prescription Drug Plan, www.medicare.gov/navigation/medicare-basics/medicare-benefits/part-d.aspx or call Medicare at 1-800-633-4227.

DE-PRESCRIBING: WHEN AND HOW TO DISCONTINUE MEDICATIONS

- Recognize opportunities to stop a medication:
  ○ Care transitions
  ○ Annual/semiannual medication review
  ○ Review existing medications before starting a new medication
  ○ Presentation or identification of a new problem or complaint
- Discontinue medication if:
  ○ Harms outweigh benefits
  ○ Minimal or no effectiveness
  ○ No indication
  ○ Not being taken, and adherence is not critical
- Plan, communicate, and coordinate:
  ○ Include patient, caregiver, and other healthcare providers
  ○ What to expect/intent
  ○ Instructions, eg, how to taper (if indicated)
- Monitor and follow-up:
  ○ Withdrawal reactions
  ○ Exacerbation of underlying conditions

Source: Adapted from Bain KT, Holmes HM, Beers MH, et al. *JAGS* 2008;56:1946–1952.

CMS GUIDANCE ON UNNECESSARY DRUGS IN THE NURSING HOME

See the complete guidance at www.cms.hhs.gov/transmittals/downloads/R22SOMA.pdf or Appendix PP of the CMS State Operations Manual.

PHARMACOLOGIC THERAPY AND AGE-ASSOCIATED CHANGES

Table 9. **Age-associated Changes in Pharmacokinetics and Pharmacodynamics**

Parameter	Age Effect	Disease, Factor Effect	Prescribing Implications
Absorption	Rate and extent are usually unaffected	Achlorhydria, concurrent medications, tube feedings	Drug-drug and drug-food interactions are more likely to alter absorption
Distribution	Increase in fat:water ratio; decreased plasma protein, particularly albumin	HF, ascites, and other conditions increase body water	Fat-soluble drugs have a larger volume of distribution; highly protein-bound drugs have a greater (active) free concentration
Metabolism	Decreases in liver mass and liver blood flow decrease drug clearance; may be age-related changes in CYP2C19, while CYP3A4 and -2D6 are not affected	Smoking, genotype, concurrent drug therapy, alcohol and caffeine intake may have more effect than aging	Lower dosages may be therapeutic
Elimination	Primarily renal; age-related decrease in GFR	Kidney impairment with acute and chronic diseases; decreased muscle mass results in less Cr production	Serum Cr not a reliable measure of kidney function; best to estimate CrCl using formula (see p 1)
Pharmaco-dynamics	Less predictable and often altered drug response at usual or lower concentrations	Drug-drug and drug-disease interactions may alter responses	Prolonged pain relief with opioids at lower dosages; increased sedation and postural instability to benzodiazepines; altered sensitivity to β-blockers

COMPLICATING FACTORS

Drug-Food or -Nutrient Interactions

Physical Interactions: Mg^{++}, Ca^{++}, Fe^{++}, Al^{++}, or zinc can lower oral absorption of levothyroxine and some quinolone antibiotics. Tube feedings decrease absorption of oral phenytoin and levothyroxine.

Decreased Drug Effect: Warfarin and vitamin K-containing foods (eg, green leafy vegetables, broccoli, brussels sprouts, greens, cabbage).

Decreased Oral Intake or Appetite: Medications can alter the taste of food (dysgeusia) or decrease saliva production (xerostomia), making mastication and swallowing difficult. Medications associated with dysgeusia include captopril and clarithromycin. Medications that can cause xerostomia include antihistamines, antidepressants, antipsychotics, clonidine, and diuretics.

Drug-Drug Interactions

A drug's effect can be increased or decreased by another drug because of impaired absorption (eg, sucralfate and ciprofloxacin), displacement from protein-binding sites (eg, warfarin and sulfonamides), inhibition or induction of metabolic enzymes (see **Table 10**), or because two or more drugs have a similar pharmacologic effect (eg, potassium-sparing diuretics, potassium supplements, and ACEIs).

Enzyme Inhibitors and Inducers: **Table 10** is a list of common drug-drug interactions via this mechanism.

Table 10. Selected CYP Isozyme Substrates, Inducers, and Inhibitors			
Isozyme	**Substrates[a]**	**Inducers[b]**	**Inhibitors[c]**
CYP1A2			
	Amitriptyline APAP Clozapine Clomipramine Cyclobenzaprine Duloxetine Estradiol Fluroxamine Haloperidol Imipramine Mexiletine	Naproxen Olanzapine Ondansetron Riluzole Theophylline Triamterene Verapamil Warfarin-R[d]	Cigarette smoke Modafinil Omeprazole Phenobarbital	Amiodarone Cimetidine Fluoroquinolones Fluvoxamine Ticlopidine
CYP2C9			
	Celecoxib Diclofenac Fluoxetine Fluvastatin Glimepiride Glipizide Glyburide Ibuprofen Irbesartan Losartan	Meloxicam Naproxen Phenytoin Piroxicam Rosiglitazone Sulfamethoxazole Tamoxifen Tolbutamide Torsemide Warfarin-S	Rifampin Secobarbital	Amiodarone Fenofibrate Fluconazole Fluvastatin Fluvoxamine Isoniazid Sertraline
CYP2C8			
	Amodiaquine Paclitaxel Repaglinide Torsemide			Gemfibrozil Montelukast

(cont.)

Table 10. Selected CYP Isozyme Substrates, Inducers, and Inhibitors (cont.)

Isozyme	Substrates[a]		Inducers[b]	Inhibitors[c]
CYP2B6				
	Bupropion		Phenobarbital	Thiotepa
	Cyclophosphamide		Phenytoin	Ticlopidine
	Efavirenz		Rifampin	
	Methadone			
CYP2C19				
	Amitriptyline	Omeprazole	Carbamazepine	Fluoxetine
	Citalopram	Pantoprazole	Norethindrone	Fluvoxamine
	Clomipramine	Phenobarbital	Prednisone	Ketoconazole
	Clopidogrel	Phenytoin	Rifampin	Lansoprazole
	Cyclophosphamide	Progesterone		Omeprazole
	Diazepam	Rabeprazole		Pantroprazole
	Escitalopram	Warfarin-R[d]		Rabeprazole
	Lansoprazole			Ticlopidine
CYP2D6				
	Amitriptyline	Metoprolol	Dexamethasone	Amiodarone
	Aripiprazole	Mexiletine	Rifampin	Bupropion
	Carvedilol	Nortriptyline		Chlorpheniramine
	Codeine[d]	Ondansetron		Cimetidine
	Clomipramine	Paroxetine		Clomipramine
	Desipramine	Perphenazine		Darifenacin
	Dextromethorphan	Propafenone		Diltiazem
	Donepezil	Risperidone		Doxepin
	Duloxetine	Tamoxifen		Duloxetine
	Flecainide	Thioridazine		Fluoxetine
	Fluoxetine	Timolol		Haloperidol
	Haloperidol	Tramadol[e]		Methadone
	Imipramine	Venlafaxine		Paroxetine
				Perphenazine
				Quinidine
				Ritonavir
				Sertraline
				Valproic acid

(cont.)

Table 10. Selected CYP Isozyme Substrates, Inducers, and Inhibitors (cont.)

Isozyme	Substrates[a]		Inducers[b]	Inhibitors[c]
CYP3A4,5,7				
	Alprazolam	Methadone	Carbamazepine	Amiodarone
	Amiodarone	Midazolam	Glucocorticoids	Cimetidine
	Amlodipine	Nefazodone	Oxcarbazepine	Clarithromycin
	Aripiprazole	Nifedipine	Phenobarbital	Diltiazem
	Astemizole	Nisoldipine	Phenytoin	Erythromycin
	Atorvastatin	Nitrendipine	Pioglitazone	Fluconazole
	Boceprevir	Omeprazole	Rifabutin	Fluoxetine
	Buspirone	Pioglitazone	Rifampin	Fluvoxamine
	Carbamazepine	Quetiapine	St. John's wort	Grapefruit juice
	Chlorpheniramine	Quinidine	Troglitazone	Indinavir
	Cisapride	Quinine		Itraconazole
	Clarithromycin	Risperidone		Ketoconazole
	Clozapine	Ritonavir		Mibefradil
	Codeine	Saquinavir		Nefazodone
	Cyclosporine	Sildenafil		Nelfinavir
	Darifenacin	Simvastatin		Norfloxacin
	Dextromethorphan	Solifenacin		Norfloxacin
	Diazepam	Tacrolimus		Ritonavir
	Diltiazem	Tadalafil		Star fruit
	Donepezil	Tamoxifen		Telithromycin
	Eplerenone	Telaprevir		Verapamil
	Erythromycin	Telithromycin		Voriconazole
	Estradiol	Trazodone		
	Felodipine	Triazolam		
	Finasteride	Vardenafil		
	Fluoxetine	Venlafaxine		
	Gleevec	Verapamil		
	Haloperidol	Vilazodone		
	Imatinib	Vincristine		
	Indinavir	Warfarin		
	Itraconazole	Zaleplon		
	Ketoconazole	Ziprasidone		
	Lovastatin	Zolpidem		

[a] Substrate: a drug metabolized by the isozyme.

[b] Inducer: a drug that increases the capacity of the isozyme to metabolize the substrate and potentially decreases the therapeutic effect of the substrate.

[c] Inhibitor: a drug that prevents the isozyme from metabolizing the substrate and increases the risk of toxicity of the substrate.

[d] R-isomer

[e] Analgesic effect decreased because of inhibition of substrate metabolism to its active metabolite by an inhibitor.

Note: The list of medications is not comprehensive but represents medications often prescribed for older adults or medications involved in very serious drug interactions (eg, cyclosporine). Some interactions in vivo or in vitro have been documented, whereas others are theoretical. For more information, consult a drug-drug interaction text or Internet resource, eg, http://medicine.iupui.edu/flockhart/.

Drug-induced Changes in Cardiac Conduction

• Intrinsic changes associated with aging in cardiac pacemaker cells and conduction system

• Altered pharmacokinetics

• Increased sensitivity to drug-induced conduction disorders, eg, bradycardia and tachyarrhythmias

• QT_c prolongation exacerbated by drug interactions and medications (see **Table 11**)

Table 11. Medications That May Prolong the QT$_c$ Interval Alone or in Combination with Other Medications That Affect the QT$_c$ Interval or as a Result of Pharmacokinetic Changes*

Analgesics	**Anti-infectives** *(cont'd)*	**Antiretrovirals** *(cont'd)*
Buprenorphine	Ketoconazole	Ritonavir
Methadone	Moxifloxacin	Saquinavir
Oxycodone	Telithromycin	Tipranavir
Antidepressants	Voriconazole	**Cardiovascular**
Amitriptyline	**Antimigraines**	Amiodarone
Citalopram	Sumatriptan	Disopyramide
Desipramine	Zolmitriptan	Dofetilide
Doxepin	**Antipsychotics**	Ibutilide
Imipramine	Clozapine	Procainamide
Nortriptyline	Fluphenazine	Quinidine
Sertraline	Haloperidol	Sotalol
Trazodone	Loxapine	**Chemotherapy**
Venlafaxine	Molindone	Degarelix
Antiemetics	Olanzapine	Dosatinib
Dolasetron	Perphenazine	Nilotinib
Droperidol	Pimozide	**Gastrointestinal**
Granisetron	Quetiapine	Cisapride
Ondansetron	Risperidone	**Urinary**
Palonosetron	Thioridazine	Alfuzosin
Anti-infectives	Ziprasidone	Solfenacin
Ciprofloxacin	**Antiretrovirals**	Tolterodine
Clarithromycin	Atazanavir	Vardenafil
Erythromycin	Darunavir	**Other**
Gatifloxacin	Fosamprenavir	Tetrabenazine
Itraconazole	Indinavir	

*Level of risk depends on dosage, baseline QT$_c$ (mild risk if <450 millisec), other patient characteristics, and comorbidity.

COMMONLY USED HERBAL AND ALTERNATIVE MEDICATIONS

Note: Herbal and dietary supplements are not subject to the same regulatory process by the FDA as prescription and OTC medications. Product and lot-to-lot variations can occur in composition and concentration of active ingredient(s), or be tainted with heavy metals or prescription medications (eg, sildenafil). Consumers are advised to purchase products by reputable manufacturers who follow good manufacturing procedures.

Chondroitin

Common Uses: Osteoarthritis

Adverse Events: Nausea, dyspepsia, changes in intraocular pressure

Comments: Knee pain did not respond better to chondroitin alone or in combination with glucosamine compared with placebo in >1500 patients with osteoarthritis. If patients choose a trial of chondroitin in combination, it should be with glucosamine sulfate.

Coenzyme Q$_{10}$

Common Uses: Cardiovascular diseases (angina, HF, HTN), musculoskeletal disorders, periodontal diseases, diabetes, obesity, AD; may lessen toxic effects of doxorubicin and daunorubicin

Adverse Events: Abdominal discomfort, headache, nausea, vomiting

Comments: May increase risk of bleeding; use with caution in patients with hepatic impairment, may decrease response to warfarin; may further decrease BP if taking antihypertensives or other medications that decrease BP; ubiquinol is a reduced form of coenzyme Q$_{10}$

Echinacea

Common Uses: Immune stimulant

Adverse Events: Hepatotoxicity, allergic reactions

Drug Interactions: Immunosuppressants; inhibits CYP1A2, −3A4; induces CYP3A4

Comments: D/C ≥2 wk before surgery; cross-sensitivity with chrysanthemum, ragweed, daisy, and aster allergies; kidney disease; immunosuppression; mixed results regarding effectiveness to shorten duration, reduce severity, or prevent colds; should not be taken for >10 d because of concern about immunosuppression

Feverfew

Common Uses: Anti-inflammatory, migraine prophylaxis

Adverse Events: Platelet inhibition, bleeding, GI upset

Drug Interactions: NSAIDs, antiplatelet agents, anticoagulants

Comments: D/C 7 d before surgery, active bleeding; cross-sensitivity with chrysanthemum and daisy; evidence lacking for either indication; minimum of 1-mo trial for migraine prophylaxis suggested

Fish oil (omega-3 fatty acids, *Lovaza*)

Common Uses: Decrease risk of coronary artery and heart disease, hypertriglyceridemia, symptomatic treatment of rheumatoid arthritis, inflammatory bowel disease, asthma, bipolar disorder, schizophrenia and in cases of immunosuppression

Adverse Events: GI upset, dyspepsia, diarrhea, nausea, bleeding, increased ALT and LDL-C

Drug Interactions: Anticoagulants, antiplatelet agents

Comments: Use with caution if allergic to seafood; monitor LFTS, triglycerides, and LDL-C at baseline, then periodically; a 2-mo trial is adequate for hypertriglyceridemia.

Flaxseed oil

Common Uses: Rheumatoid arthritis, asthma, constipation, diabetes, hyperlipidemia, menopausal symptoms, prevention of stroke and CHD, BPH, laxative

Adverse Events: Bleeding, hypoglycemia, hypotension

Drug Interactions: NSAIDs, antiplatelet agents, anticoagulants, insulin and hypoglycemic agents, lithium (mania)

Garlic

Common Uses: HTN, hypercholesterolemia, platelet inhibitor

Adverse Events: Bleeding, GI upset, hypoglycemia

Drug Interactions: NSAIDs, antiplatelet agents, anticoagulants, INH, NNRTIs, protease inhibitors

Comments: D/C 7 d before surgery; effect on lipid lowering modest and of questionable clinical value

Ginger

Common Uses: Antiemetic, anti-inflammatory, dyspepsia

Adverse Events: GI upset, heartburn, diarrhea, irritation of the mouth and throat

Drug Interactions: NSAIDs, antiplatelet agents, anticoagulants

Comments: D/C 7 d before surgery

Ginkgo biloba

Common Uses: Alzheimer's disease, memory, intermittent claudication, macular degeneration, diabetic retinopathy, glaucoma

Adverse Events: Bleeding, nausea, headache, GI upset, diarrhea, anxiety

Drug Interactions: MAOIs (increased effect and toxicity), antiplatelet agents, anticoagulants, NSAIDs

Comments: D/C 36 h before surgery; mixed results in dementia trials; recent trials tend to have negative results

Ginseng

Common Uses: Physical and mental performance enhancer, digestive, diuretic

Adverse Events: HTN, tachycardia, insomnia

Drug Interactions: Antiplatelet agents, anticoagulants, NSAIDs

Comments: D/C 7 d before surgery, kidney failure

Glucosamine

Common Uses: Osteoarthritis, rheumatoid arthritis

Adverse Events: GI distress, anorexia, insomnia, painful and itchy skin, peripheral edema, tachycardia

Drug Interactions: Warfarin

Comments: Knee pain did not respond better to glucosamine alone or in combination with chondroitin compared with placebo in >1500 patients with osteoarthritis. If patients choose a trial of glucosamine alone or in combination, it should be glucosamine sulfate.

Kava kava

Common Uses: Anxiety, sedative

Adverse Events: Sedation, hepatotoxicity, GI upset, headache, dizziness, EPS

Drug Interactions: Anticonvulsants (increased effect), benzodiazepines, CNS depressants

Comments: D/C 24 h before surgery; compared with placebo, kava has demonstrated antianxiety efficacy, but effect small and not robust

Melatonin

Common Uses: Sleep disorders, insomnia, jet lag

Adverse Events: Daytime drowsiness, headache, dizziness

Drug Interactions: Warfarin, ASA, clopidogrel, ticlopidine, dipyridamole (loss of hemostasis), antidiabetic agents (decreased glucose tolerance and insulin sensitivity), CNS depressants

Methyl sulfonyl methane (MSM)
Common Uses: Anti-inflammatory, analgesia, osteoarthritis, chronic pain
Adverse Events: Nausea, diarrhea, fatigue, bloating, insomnia
Comments: A derivative of DMSO that produces less odor

Red yeast rice (*Monascus purpureus*, Xue Zhi Kang)
Common Uses: Coronary heart disease, diabetes mellitus, hypercholesterolemia
Adverse Events: Nausea, vomiting, GI upset, hepatic disorders, myopathy, rhabdomyolysis
Drug Interactions (theoretical): Cyclosporine, CYP3A4 substrates (see **Table 10**), digoxin, statins, niacin
Comments: Use with caution in patients taking other lipid-lowering agents

SAMe (S-adenosyl-methionine)
Common Uses: Depression, fibromyalgia, insomnia, osteoarthritis, rheumatoid arthritis
Adverse Events: GI distress, insomnia, dizziness, dry mouth, headache, restlessness
Drug Interactions: Antidepressants, St. John's wort, NSAIDs, antiplatelet agents, anticoagulants
Comments: Not effective for bipolar depression, hyperhomocysteinemia (theoretical), D/C $\geq$14 d before surgery

Saw palmetto
Common Uses: BPH
Adverse Events: Headache, nausea, GI distress, erectile dysfunction, dizziness
Drug Interactions: Finasteride, a_1-adrenergic agonist properties in vitro may decrease efficacy; may prolong bleeding time so use with caution with antiplatelet agents, anticoagulants, NSAIDs
Comments: Efficacy in BPH did not differ from placebo in an adequately powered, randomized clinical trial

St. John's wort (*Hypericum perforatum*)
Common Uses: Depression, anxiety
Adverse Events: Photosensitivity, hypomania, insomnia, GI upset
Drug Interactions: Potent CYP3A4 inducer (see **Table 10**), finasteride (decreased finasteride concentration and possible effectiveness)
Comments: Wear sunscreen with UVA and UVB coverage; avoid in fair-skinned patients; D/C 5 d before surgery; not effective in severe depression; effects reported to vary from those of conventional antidepressants, yet no more effective than placebo; evaluation of effectiveness may be complicated by product, extraction process, and composition

Valerian
Common Uses: Anxiety, insomnia
Adverse Events: Sedation, benzodiazepine-like withdrawal, headache, GI upset, insomnia
Drug Interactions: Benzodiazepines, CNS depressants
Comments: Taper dose several weeks before surgery

WARFARIN THERAPY

- For anticoagulation in nonacute conditions, initiate therapy by giving warfarin▲ *(Coumadin)* 2–5 mg/d as fixed dose [T: 1, 2, 2.5, 3, 4, 5, 6, 7.5, 10]; reduce dose if INR >2.5 on day 3.
- Half-life is 31–51 h; steady state is achieved on day 5–7 of fixed dose.
- Genetic tests for VKORC1 (modulates sensitivity to warfarin) and CYP2C9 (modulates metabolism of warfarin) are available to help guide dosing for initiation of warfarin therapy; it is unknown if their routine use significantly improves outcomes. Medicare does not cover genetic testing.
- Home INR testing results in similar outcomes (rates of stroke, death, or severe bleeding episodes) compared with monthly testing in an anticoagulation clinic.
- Warfarin therapy is implicated in **many** adverse drug-drug interactions.
- Some drugs that **increase** INR in conjunction with warfarin (type in *italics* = major interaction):
  - alcohol (with concurrent liver disease)
  - amiodarone
  - androgens
  - many antibiotics*
  - APAP (>1.3 g/d for >1 wk)
  - ASA (>3 g/d)
  - *celecoxib*
  - chloral hydrate
  - *cilostazol*
  - cimetidine
  - clofibrate
  - *duloxetine*
  - flu vaccine
  - isoniazid
  - *ketoprofen*
  - *naproxen*
  - propafenone
  - sulindac
  - *tamoxifen*
- Some drugs that **decrease** INR in conjunction with warfarin:
  - barbiturates
  - carbamazepine
  - cholestyramine
  - cyclosporine
  - dicloxacillin
  - griseofulvin
  - nafcillin
  - rifampin *
  - sucralfate
  - vitamin K

* especially fluconazole, itraconazole, ketoconazole, miconazole, ciprofloxacin, erythromycin, *moxifloxacin*, metronidazole, *sulfamethoxazole, trimethoprim*

Table 12. Indications for Warfarin Anticoagulation in the Absence of Active Bleeding or Severe Bleeding Risk

Condition	Target INR	Duration of Therapy
Hip fracture or replacement surgery, major knee surgery	2–3	11–35 d
VTE secondary to reversible risk factor[a]	2–3	3 mo
Idiopathic VTE[a,b]	2–3	At least 3 mo
Recurrent VTE[b]	2–3	Indefinitely
AF with CHADS$_2$ score ≥2[c]	2–3	Indefinitely
Rheumatic mitral valvular disease with hx of systemic embolization, left atrial thrombus, or left atrial diameter >5.5 cm	2–3	Indefinitely
Mitral valve prolapse with documented systemic embolism or recurrent TIAs despite ASA therapy	2–3	Indefinitely

(cont.)

Table 12. Indications for Warfarin Anticoagulation in the Absence of Active Bleeding or Severe Bleeding Risk (cont.)

Condition	Target INR	Duration of Therapy
Bileaflet mechanical or Medtronic Hall tilting disk aortic valve with normal left atrial size and sinus rhythm	2–3	Indefinitely
Tilting-disk or bileaflet mitral mechanical valve; caged ball or caged disk valve	2.5–3.5	Indefinitely
Mechanical heart valve with AF, anterior-apical STEMI, left atrial enlargement, hypercoagulable state, or low EF	2.5–3.5	Indefinitely
Bioprosthetic mitral valve	2–3	3 mo
Peripheral arterial embolectomy	2–3	Indefinitely
Cerebral venous sinus thrombosis	2–3	12 mo
MI with large anterior involvement, significant HF, intracardiac thrombosis, or hx of thromboembolic event	2–3	At least 3 mo

[a] Consider longer treatment in men and in patients with elevated D-dimer level during the third month of warfarin therapy; an elevated D-dimer level 1 mo after cessation of therapy also indicates higher risk of recurrent DVT/PE and should prompt strong consideration of resuming anticoagulation.
[b] Periodically reassess for benefit (decreases annual risk of VTE from about 20% to about 2%) vs risk (increases annual risk of major bleeding from 0% to about 2%) of indefinite anticoagulation.
[c] CHADS$_2$ scoring: 1 point each for age ≥75 yr old, HTN, diabetes mellitus, decreased LVEF, HF; 2 points each for prior stroke, TIA, or systemic embolism. Patients with CHADS$_2$ score = 1 or in whom anticoagulation is contraindicated or not tolerated can be treated with warfarin or ASA 75–325 mg/d; patients with CHADS$_2$ score = 0 should be treated with ASA 75–325 mg/d. Dabigatran or rivaroxaban (see p 52) is an alternative to warfarin in patients with AF.

Table 13. Treatment of Warfarin Overdose

INR	Clinical Situation	Action
≥3.5 and <5	No significant bleeding	Omit next warfarin dose and/or lower dose
≥5 and <9	No significant bleeding	Omit next 1–2 doses of warfarin and restart therapy at lower dose; alternatively, omit 1 dose and give VK 1–2.5 mg po
≥9	No significant bleeding	D/C warfarin and give VK 2.5–5 mg po; give additional VK po if INR is not substantially reduced in 24–48 h. Restart warfarin at lower dose when INR is therapeutic.
Any elevation	Serious bleeding	D/C warfarin; give VK 10 mg by slow IV infusion, supplemented with fresh frozen plasma (FFP), prothrombin complex concentrate (PCC), or recombinant factor VII (rVIIa) depending on urgency of situation; check INR q6h; repeat VK q12h as needed
Any elevation	Life-threatening bleeding	D/C warfarin; give FFP, PCC, or rVIIa supplemented with VK 10 mg by slow IV infusion.

Note: VK = vitamin K

Source: Ansell J, Hirsch J, Hylek E, et al. Pharmacology and management of the vitamin K antagonists: American College of Chest Physicians Evidence-based Clinical Practice Guidelines (8th edition). *Chest* 2008; 133 (6 Suppl):160S–198S.

DVT/PE PROPHYLAXIS, DIAGNOSIS, AND TREATMENT

Prophylaxis

- Most hospitalized patients >60 yr old are considered to be at high risk of postoperative DVT and should receive prophylaxis. See **Table 14** for thromboprophylactic options.
  - Dosages should be lowered when using LMWH or fondaparinux in patients with CrCl <30 mL/min.
  - In patients with clinically overt heparin-induced thrombocytopenia (HIT) and/or positive HIT antibodies, danaparoid, argatroban, or lepirudin should be used for thromboprophylaxis.
- See **Table 15** for DVT/PE prophylaxis dosages for specific surgeries.

DVT Diagnosis

DVT diagnosis is directed by risk score, D-dimer testing, and duplex ultrasound imaging.

- Determine risk score
  - 1 point for each of the following:
    - active cancer
    - paralysis, paresis, or plaster immobilization of lower limb
    - bedridden for 3 d or major surgery in past 12 wk
    - localized tenderness along distribution of deep venous system
    - entire leg swelling
    - calf swelling ≥3 cm over diameter of contralateral calf
    - pitting edema confined to symptomatic leg
    - collateral superficial veins
    - prior DVT
  - −2 points for alternative diagnosis as likely as DVT
- Interpret risk score and further testing
  - ≤0 points = low risk: If D-dimer is negative, DVT is excluded; if D-dimer is positive, obtain duplex ultrasound testing for diagnosis.
  - ≥1 point = moderate/high risk: Obtain duplex ultrasound imaging; if negative, obtain D-dimer. If D-dimer is negative, DVT is excluded; if D-dimer is positive, obtain venogram or repeat ultrasound in 3–7 d.

PE Diagnosis

- Consider PE with any of the following (classic triad of dyspnea, chest pain, and hemoptysis seen in only ≤20% of cases):
  - Chest pain
  - Hemoptysis
  - Hypotension
  - Hypoxia
  - Shortness of breath
  - Syncope
  - Tachycardia

- Calculate clinical probability of PE using clinical decision rule (**Table 16**), then follow evaluation of PE algorithm (**Figure 3**). Clinical probability of PE unlikely: total ≤4 points; clinical probability of PE likely: total >4 points.

Treatment
- See **Table 15** for DVT/PE treatment dosages.
- LMWH or fondaparinux is preferred to unfractionated heparin (UFH) in most patients because of lower risk of hemorrhage and mortality. Reduce dosage when CrCl <30 mL/min.
- If warfarin is part of a long-term anticoagulation plan, it may be started the same day as acute anticoagulant. Specific conditions may require a period of overlap when both agents should be used (eg, for DVT or PE, heparin or similar products should be used a minimum of 5 d, including 1–3 d of overlap with therapeutic INR).
- Acute massive PE (filling defects in ≥2 lobar arteries or the equivalent by angiogram) associated with hypotension, severe hypoxia, or high pulmonary pressures on echocardiogram should usually be treated with thrombolytic therapy within 48 h of onset.

Table 14. DVT/PE Prophylaxis in Older Surgical and Medical Inpatients

DVT/PE Risk	Surgeries or Medical Conditions	Thromboprophylactic Options
Low	Healthy and mobile patients undergoing minor surgery Laparoscopic gynecologic procedures Transurethral or other low-risk urologic procedures Spine surgery Knee arthroscopy	Aggressive early ambulation after procedure
Moderate	Most general surgeries Major vascular procedures Thoracic surgery Open gynecologic and urologic surgery Medical or surgical patients admitted for HF or severe respiratory disease Inpatients at bed rest with active cancer, previous DVT/PE, sepsis, active neurologic disease, or inflammatory bowel disease	Fondaparinux, LMWH, or UFH*
High	Total hip replacement Total knee replacement Hip fracture surgery Trauma Spinal cord injury	Fondaparinux, LMWH, rivaroxaban (hip or knee replacement), or warfarin*

*For patients at high risk of bleeding, acceptable alternative is intermittent pneumatic compression and/or use of graduated compression stockings.

Table 15. Anticoagulants for DVT or PE Prophylaxis and Treatment

Class, Agent	DVT or PE Prophylaxis Dosage by Condition	DVT or PE Treatment Dosage	Comments
Heparin▲			
Unfractionated heparin▲ᵃ *(Hep-Lock)*	Surgery: 5000 U SC 2 h before and q12h after surgery; Medical patients: 5000 U SC q12h	5000 U IV bolus followed by 15 U/kg/h IV; *or* for outpatient treatment of DVT, 333 U/kg SC followed by 250 U/kg SC q12h	Bleeding, anemia, thrombocytopenia, hypertransaminasemia, urticaria (L, K)
LMWH			
Enoxaparinᵃ *(Lovenox)*	THA, HFX: 30 mg SC q12h or 40 mg SC q24h KR: 30 mg SC q12h Other surgeries and medical patients: 40 mg SC q24h	Outpatient treatment of DVT: 1 mg/kg SC q12h; inpatient treatment of DVT ± PE: 1 mg/kg SC q12h or 1.5 mg/kg SC q24h	Bleeding, spinal hematoma if spinal anesthesia, anemia, hyperkalemia, hyper-transaminasemia, thrombocytopenia, thrombocytosis, urticaria, angioedema; lower dosage in renal impairment (L, K)
Dalteparinᵃ *(Fragmin)*	Low-risk THA: 2500–5000 U SC before surgery, 5000 U SC q24h after surgery Other surgeries and medical patients: 5000 U SC q24h	DVT in patients with cancer: 200 U/kg SC q24h × 30 d, followed by 150 U/kg SC q24h for the next 5 mo	Same as above (K)
Tinzaparin *(Innohep)*	NA	175 anti-Xa IU/kg SC q24h	Same as above; contraindicated in older patients with CrCl <30 mL/min (K)
Heparinoid			
Danaparoid *(Orgaran)*	THA, HFX, HIT: 750 anti-Xa U SC q12h	NA	Same as LMWH (K)
Factor Xa Inhibitor			
Fondaparinuxᵃ *(Arixtra)*	2.5 mg/d SC; for surgical patients begin 6–8 h after surgery	Weight <50 kg: 5 mg/d SC; weight 50–100 kg: 7.5 mg/d SC; weight >100 kg: 10 mg/d SC	Lower dosage in renal impairment; contraindicated if CrCl <30 mL/min (K)
Rivaroxaban *(Xarelto)*	THA, KR: 10 mg/d po; begin 6–10 h after surgery	NA	Avoid use if CrCl <30 mL/min (L, K)
Direct Thrombin Inhibitors			
Argatroban	HIT: 2 mcg/kg/min IV infusion	HIT: 2 mcg/kg/min IV infusion	↓ Dosage if hepatic impairment (L)
Desirudin *(Iprivask)*	THA: 15 mg SC q12h starting 5–15 min before surgery	NA	If CrCl = 31–60 mL/min, starting dose is 5 mg; if CrCl <31 mL/min, starting dose is 1.7 mg
Lepirudin *(Refludan)*	HIT: 4 mcg/kg bolus, then 0.15 mg/kg/h	HIT: 4 mcg/kg bolus, then 0.15 mg/kg/h	↓ Bolus to 0.2 mg/kg if CrCl <60 mL/min

Note: THA = total hip arthroplasty (hip replacement); HFX = hip fracture surgery; AS= abdominal surgery; KR = knee replacement; HIT = heparin-induced thrombocytopenia; NA = not applicable
ᵃ Also indicated for anticoagulation in acute coronary syndrome (see **Table 18**).

Table 16. Clinical Decision Rule

Variable	Points
Clinical signs and symptoms of DVT (minimal leg swelling and pain with palpation of the deep veins)	3
Alternative diagnosis less likely than PE	3
Heart rate >100/min	1.5
Immobilization (>3 d) or surgery in the previous 4 wk	1.5
Previous PE or DVT	1.5
Hemoptysis	1
Malignancy (receiving treatment, treated in last 6 mo, or palliative)	1
Total	

Source: Wells PS, Anderson DR, Rodger M, et al. Derivation of a simple clinical model to categorize patients' probability of pulmonary embolism: increasing the model's utility with the SimpliRED D-dimer. *Thromb Haemost* 2000;83(3):416–420. Reprinted with permission.

Figure 3. Evaluation of Suspected Pulmonary Embolism

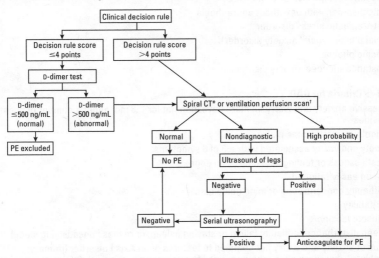

* Multidetector-row CT more sensitive than single-detector CT. Patient must be able to hold breath for 10 sec.
† When unable to use contrast (eg, renal dysfunction), need to avoid ionizing radiation.

DIAGNOSIS

Anxiety disorders as a whole are the most common mental disorders in older adults. Some anxiety disorders (panic attack, OCD) appear to be less prevalent in older than in younger adults. Generalized anxiety disorder (GAD) and new-onset anxiety in older adults are often secondary to physical illness, poorer health-related quality of life, depression, or adverse events of or withdrawal from medications.

DSM-IV recognizes several anxiety disorders:
(Italicized type indicates the most common anxiety disorders in older adults.)
- Acute stress disorder
- Agoraphobia without a history of panic
- *Generalized anxiety disorder (GAD)*
- *Anxiety disorder due to a general medical condition*
- Obsessive-compulsive disorder (OCD)
- Panic disorder, with or without agoraphobia
- Post-traumatic stress disorder
- Social phobia (social anxiety disorder)
- Specific phobia
- Substance-induced anxiety disorder

DSM-IV Criteria for GAD

- Excessive anxiety and worry on more days than not for ≥6 mo, about a number of events or activities
- Difficulty controlling the worry
- Anxiety and worry associated with ≥3 of 6 symptoms:
  ○ restlessness or feeling keyed up or on edge
  ○ being easily fatigued
  ○ difficulty concentrating or mind going blank
  ○ irritability
  ○ muscle tension
  ○ sleep disturbance (difficulty falling or staying asleep, or restless unsatisfying sleep)
- Focus of anxiety and worry not confined to features of an Axis I disorder (primary psychiatric disorder); often, about routine life circumstances; may shift from one concern to another
- Anxiety, worry, or physical symptoms cause clinically significant distress or impairment in social, occupational, or other important areas of functioning
- Disturbance not due to the direct physiologic effects of a drug of abuse or a medication or to a medical condition; does not occur exclusively during a mood disorder, psychotic disorder, or a pervasive development disorder

DSM-IV Criteria for Panic Attack

Discrete period of intense fear or discomfort with ≥4 of the following (also, must peak within 10 min):

- Palpitations, rapid HR
- Sweating
- Feeling dizzy, unsteady, lightheaded, or faint
- Trembling or shaking
- Sensations of shortness of breath or smothering
- Choking feeling
- Chest pain or discomfort
- Nausea or abdominal distress
- Feelings of unreality or being detached from self
- Fear of losing control or going crazy
- Fear of dying
- Paresthesias
- Chills or hot flushes

Differential Diagnosis

- Panic disorder: recurrent, unexpected panic attacks
- Physical conditions producing anxiety
  - Cardiovascular: arrhythmias, angina, MI, HF
  - Endocrine: hyperthyroidism, hypoglycemia, pheochromocytoma
  - Neurologic: movement disorders, temporal lobe epilepsy, AD, stroke
  - Respiratory: COPD, asthma, pulmonary embolism
- Medications producing anxiety
  - Caffeine
  - Corticosteroids
  - Nicotine
  - Psychotropics: antidepressants, antipsychotics, stimulants
  - Sympathomimetics: pseudoephedrine, β-agonists
  - Thyroid hormones: overreplacement
- Withdrawal states: alcohol, sedatives, hypnotics, benzodiazepines, SSRIs
- Depression

EVALUATION

- Past psychiatric hx
- Drug review: prescribed, OTC, alcohol, caffeine
- Mental status evaluation
- Physical examination: Focus on signs and symptoms of anxiety (eg, tachycardia, tachypnea, sweating, tremor).
- Laboratory tests: Consider CBC, blood glucose, TSH, B_{12}, ECG, oxygen saturation, drug and alcohol screening.

MANAGEMENT

Nonpharmacologic

- Cognitive-behavior therapy may be useful for GAD, panic disorder, and OCD; efficacy in both individual and group formats.
- Graded desensitization used in panic and phobia relies on gradual exposure with learning to manage resultant anxiety.

- May be effective alone but mostly used in conjunction with pharmacotherapy.
- Requires a cognitively intact, motivated patient.

Pharmacologic (See **Table 35** for dosing of antidepressants and indication of generic status.)
- Obsessive-compulsive: fluoxetine, fluvoxamine, paroxetine, sertraline; secondary choices include β-blockers and second-generation antipsychotics
- Panic: sertraline, paroxetine; secondary choices include β-blockers and second-generation antipsychotics
- Social phobia: paroxetine, sertraline, venlafaxine XR
- Generalized anxiety: duloxetine, escitalopram, paroxetine, sertraline, venlafaxine XR
- Post-traumatic stress disorder: paroxetine, sertraline
  - Avoid benzodiazepines.
  - For nightmares, prazosin may be helpful (initiate at 1 mg qhs and titrate slowly to avoid orthostatic syncope).

Buspirone▲ (BuSpar):
- Serotonin 1A partial agonist effective in GAD and anxiety symptoms accompanying general medical illness (although geriatric evidence is limited)
- Not effective for acute anxiety, panic, or OCD
- May take 2–4 wk for therapeutic response
- Recommended starting dosage: 7.5–10 mg q12h [T: 5, 10, 15, 30], up to max 60 mg/d
- No dependence, tolerance, withdrawal, or CNS depression
- Risk of serotonin syndrome with SSRIs, MAOIs, TCAs, 5-hydroxytryptamine 1 receptor agonists, ergot alkaloids, lithium, St. John's wort, opioids, dextromethorphan

Benzodiazepines:
- Most often used for acute anxiety, GAD, panic, OCD (**Table 17**)
- Preferred: intermediate–half-life drugs inactivated by direct conjugation in liver and therefore less affected by aging (**Table 17**)
- Avoid long-acting benzodiazepines (eg, flurazepam, diazepam, chlordiazepoxide)
- Linked to cognitive impairment, falls, sedation, psychomotor impairment, delerium
- Problems: dependence, misuse (p 273), tolerance, withdrawal, more so with short-acting benzodiazepines; seizure risk with alprazolam withdrawal
- Potentially fatal if combined with alcohol or other CNS depressants
- Only short-term (60–90 d) use recommended
- Not covered by Medicare Part D (www.medicare.gov/navigation/medicare-basics/medicare-benefits/part-d.aspx or call Medicare at 1-800-633-4227)

Table 17. Benzodiazepines for Anxiety Recommended for Older Adults

Drug	Dosage	Formulations
Lorazepam▲ (Ativan)	0.5–2 mg in 2–3 divided doses	T: 0.5, 1, 2; S: 2 mg/mL; inj: 2 mg/mL
Oxazepam▲ (Serax)	10–15 mg q8–12h	T: 10, 15, 30

Nonbenzodiazepine Hypnotics:
Zolpidem (Ambien), zaleplon (Sonata), eszopiclone (Lunesta), and ramelteon (Rozerem) should not be used for treatment of anxiety disorders. See Sleep Disorders, **Table 113**.

CORONARY ARTERY DISEASE
Calculating Risk
- Risk factors:
  - Previous MI or angina
  - Age
  - Diabetes mellitus
  - Dyslipidemia
  - Family hx
  - HTN
  - Obesity
  - Sedentary lifestyle
  - Smoking
- To calculate 10-yr risk, see http://hp2010.nhlbihin.net/atpiii/calculator.asp?usertype=prof.
- If calculated 10-yr risk is 10%–20%, consider measurement of coronary artery calcification by CT or carotid intima-media thickness by ultrasonography to further clarify risk and direct treatment.
- Consider C-reactive protein testing to guide statin therapy in older adults with a 10%–20% risk of CAD over a 10-yr period (ie, LDL <130 mg/dL; without CAD, DM, CKD, or severe inflammatory conditions; and who are not on lipid-lowering, hormone replacement, or immunosuppressive therapy). If C-reactive protein ≥2 mg/L, statin therapy (eg, rosuvastatin 20 mg/d) may be beneficial.

Diagnostic Cardiac Tests
- Cardiac catheterization is the gold standard; cardiac CT angiography is a less invasive, but less accurate, alternative.
- Stress testing: The heart is stressed either through exercise (treadmill, stationary bicycle) or, if the patient cannot exercise or the ECG is markedly abnormal, with pharmacologic agents (dipyridamole, adenosine, dobutamine). Exercise stress tests can be performed with or without cardiac imaging, while pharmacologic stress tests always include imaging. Imaging can be accomplished by echocardiography or single-photon-emission computed tomography (SPECT).

Acute Coronary Syndrome (ACS)
- ACS encompasses diagnoses of ST segment MI (STEMI), non-ST segment MI (NSTEMI), and unstable angina.
- Suspect ACS with anginal chest pain or anginal equivalent: arm, jaw, or abdominal pain (with or without nausea); acute functional decline.
- Diagnosis is based on symptoms along with cardiac serum markers and ECG findings:
  - STEMI: elevated serum markers, elevated ST segments
  - NSTEMI: elevated serum markers, depressed ST segments or inverted T-waves
  - Unstable angina: nonelevated serum markers, normal or depressed ST segments, normal or inverted T-waves
- Measuring cardiac serum markers:
  - Most protocols call for checking troponins T and I and creatine kinase MB isoenzymes (CK-MB) at presentation and 3, 6, 12, and 24 h later.
  - A single negative enzyme measurement, particularly within 6 h of symptom onset, does not exclude MI.
  - Sensitivity of troponins is improved with use of sensitive or ultrasensitive assays.

- Elevated troponin in the face of normal CK-MB can indicate increased risk of MI in the ensuing 6 mo.
- Troponins are not useful for detecting reinfarction within first wk of an MI. CK-MB is the preferred marker for early reinfarction.
- Both CK-MB and cardiac troponins can have false-positive results due to subclinical ischemic myocardial injury or nonischemic myocardial injury.

Initial Management of ACS

- Bed rest with continuous ECG monitoring
- Oxygen to maintain saturation >90%
- ASA with or without clopidogrel (or prasugrel) (see **Table 18**)
- D/C NSAIDs
- If ischemia is ongoing (based on symptoms or ECG changes), give nitroglycerin▲ 0.4 mg sl q5min for a total of 3 doses
- Nitroglycerin IV is indicated for persistent ischemia, HTN, large anterior infarction, or HF. Begin at 5–10 mcg/min IV and titrate to pain relief, SBP >90 mmHg, or resolution of ECG abnormalities.
- If chest pain persists on nitroglycerin therapy, give morphine sulfate 2–4 mg IV with increments of 2–8 mg IV repeated q5–15 min prn.
- Administer antiplatelet agents, anticoagulants, and glycoprotein IIb/IIIa inhibitors according to reperfusion strategy (see **Table 18**):
  - Thrombolytic therapy: ASA, clopidogrel or ticagrelor, and an anticoagulant
  - Early invasive therapy with planned percutaneous cardiac intervention: ASA, clopidogrel or prasugrel or ticagrelor, an anticoagulant, and a glycoprotein IIb/IIIa inhibitor
  - Medical management: ASA, clopidogrel or ticagrelor, and an anticoagulant; consider adding a glycoprotein IIb/IIIa inhibitor
  - CABG: ASA and unfractionated heparin▲
- Clopidogrel dosing considerations:
  - Some patients may be poor metabolizers of clopidogrel due to low activity of the CYP2C19 liver enzyme. Blood testing for CYP2C19 status is available to theoretically guide clopidogrel dosing, but dosing regimens for patients with low CYP2C19 activity are not established. In patients with known low CYP2C19 activity, alternative antiplatelet agents or higher clopidogrel dosages (eg, second loading dose of 600 mg or maintenance dosage of 150 mg/d) should be considered.
  - It is unclear if PPIs decrease effectiveness of clopidogrel due to inhibition of CYP2C19 function. If GI bleeding prophylaxis is desired with clopidogrel therapy in ACS, consider using an H_2 blocker as an alternative to a PPI.
  - Other medications may interact with clopidogrel through CYP2C19 activity (see **Table 10**).

Table 18. Antithrombotic Therapy in Acute Coronary Syndrome						
		| Treatment Strategy			
Class, Agent	**Dosage**	TT	PCI	MM	CABG
Antiplatelet Agents					
ASA▲	162–325 mg po initially, followed by 75–160 mg po q24h[a]	•	•	•	•

(cont.)

Table 18. Antithrombotic Therapy in Acute Coronary Syndrome (cont.)

Class, Agent	Dosage	TT	PCI	MM	CABG
Clopidogrel *(Plavix)*	300–600 mg po initially, followed by 75 mg po q24h[b]	•		•	
Prasugrel[c] *(Effient)*	60 mg po initially, followed by 10 mg po q24h		○		
Ticagrelor *(Brilinta)*	180 mg po initially, followed by 90 mg po q12h[d]		•	•	
Anticoagulants (see **Table 15**)					
Bivalirudin *(Angiomax)*	0.1 mg/kg bolus, followed by 0.25 mg/kg/h IV	○	•		
Enoxaparin *(Lovenox)*	30 mg IV bolus, followed by 1 mg/kg SC q12h	•	•	•	
Dalteparin *(Fragmin)*	120 IU/kg SC q12h		○		
Fondaparinux *(Arixtra)*	2.5 mg/d SC	○	○	•	
Heparin▲ *(Hep-Lock)*	60–70 U/kg (max 5000 U) IV bolus, followed by 12–15 U/kg/h IV	•	•	○	•
Glycoprotein IIb/IIIa Inhibitors					
Abciximab *(ReoPro)*	0.25 mg/kg IV bolus, followed by 0.125 mcg/kg/min (max 10 mcg/min)		•		
Eptifibatide *(Integrilin)*	180 mcg/kg IV bolus, followed by 2 mcg/kg/min IV		•	○	
Tirofiban *(Aggrastat)*	0.4 mcg/kg/min IV over 30 min, followed by 0.1 mcg/kg/min		•	○	

Note: TT = thrombolytic therapy; PCI = early invasive therapy with planned percutaneous cardiac intervention; CABG = acute coronary syndrome with emergent CABG a likely possibility; MM = conservative therapy with medical management

• = preferred or first-line treatment

○ = alternative or second-line treatment

[a] Use dose of 325 mg if patient is undergoing PCI and has not previously been on chronic ASA therapy; continue at same dose 1–6 mo after PCI before reducing dose. ASA therapy should be lifelong after ACS.

[b] Clopidogrel should also be used in MM if patient is allergic to ASA. In combination with ASA, clopidogrel causes increased risk of bleeding, so it should be used carefully. Clopidogrel should not be used if there is a reasonable possibility that patient will be undergoing CABG within the ensuing 5 days.

[c] Not recommended in patients ≥75 yr old or with hx of TIA or stroke because of increased severe bleeding risk. Consider maintenance dosage of 5 mg/d in patients <60 kg.

[d] Ticagrelor should be used with ASA dosage of 75–100 mg/d.

Ongoing Hospital Management of ACS

- An oral β-blocker should be started within 24 h of symptom onset and continued long term unless there is acute HF, evidence of a low-output state, pronounced bradycardia, or cardiogenic shock.

- An oral ACEI should be started within 24 h of symptom onset for all patients with clinical HF or EF <40% and a systolic BP ≥100 (see **Table 21**). If patient cannot tolerate ACEIs, give oral ARB.

- A statin should be started (if there are no contraindications).

- Lipid-lowering therapy, preferably including the use of a statin, should be instituted with target levels of LDL cholesterol <70–100 mg/dL (see Dyslipidemia, p 40).
- Anticoagulation with dabigatran (see p 52), rivaroxaban (see p 52), or warfarin▲ (see p 24) is indicated in post-MI patients with AF. Warfarin is indicated in post-MI patients with left ventricular thrombosis or large anterior infarction (see **Table 12**).
- Patients with a hematocrit ≤30 and who are not in HF should receive a transfusion to increase hematocrit to >33.
- At time of discharge, prescribe rapid-acting nitrates prn: sublingual nitroglycerin▲ or nitroglycerin spray q5min for max of 3 doses in 15 min. See **Table 19**.
- Longer-acting nitrates should be prescribed if symptomatic angina and treatment will be medical rather than surgical or angioplasty. May be combined with β-blockers or calcium channel blockers, or both. See **Table 19**.
- Calcium channel blockers should be used cautiously for management of angina only in non-Q-wave infarctions without systolic dysfunction and a contraindication to β-blockers.

Table 19. **Nitrate Dosages and Formulations**		
Medication	**Dosage**	**Formulations**
Oral		
Isosorbide dinitrate▲ (Isordil, Sorbitrate)	10–40 mg 3 ×/d (6 h apart)	T: 5, 10, 20, 30, 40; ChT: 5, 10
Isosorbide dinitrate SR (Dilatrate SR)	40–80 mg q8–12h	T: 40
Isosorbide mononitrate▲ (ISMO, Monoket)	20 mg q12h (8 am and 3 pm)	T: 10, 20
Isosorbide mononitrate SR▲ (Imdur)	start 30–60 mg/d; max 240 mg/d	T: 30, 60, 120
Nitroglycerin▲ (Nitro-Bid)	2.5–9 mg q8–12h	T: 2.5, 6.5, 9
Sublingual		
Isosorbide dinitrate▲ (Isordil, Sorbitrate)	1 tab prn	T: 2.5, 5, 10
Nitroglycerin (Nitrostat)	0.4 mg prn	T: 0.15, 0.3, 0.4, 0.6
Oral spray		
Nitroglycerin (Nitrolingual, Nitromist)	1–2 spr prn; max 3/15 min	0.4 mg/spr
Ointment		
Nitroglycerin 2%▲ (Nitro-Bid, Nitrol)	start 0.5–4 inches q4–8h	2%
Transdermal		
Nitroglycerin▲	1 pch 12–14 h/d	(all in mg/h)
(Deponit)		0.2, 0.4
(Minitran)		0.1, 0.2, 0.4, 0.6
(Nitrek)		0.2, 0.4, 0.6
(Nitro-Dur)		0.1, 0.2, 0.3, 0.4, 0.6, 0.8
(Nitrodisc)		0.2, 0.3, 0.4
(Transderm-Nitro)		0.1, 0.2, 0.4, 0.6, 0.8

POST-MI AND CHRONIC STABLE ANGINA CARE

- Unless contraindicated, all post-MI patients should be on ASA, a β-blocker, and an ACEI.
- Give clopidogrel for at least 12 mo in patients receiving drug-eluting stents, and at least 28 d and up to 12 mo in patients who receive a bare metal stent or no stent. Prasugrel or ticagrelor (**Table 18**) can be given as an alternative to clopidogrel. Prasugrel should be considered only in patients <75 yr old without hx of TIA or stroke. When using ticagrelor, concomitant ASA dosage should not exceed 100 mg/d.
- If β-blockers are contraindicated, use long-acting nitrates or long-acting calcium channel blockers for chronic angina.
- For refractory chronic angina despite treatment with β-blocker, calcium channel blocker, or nitrates, consider addition of ranolazine *(Ranexa)* 500–1,000 mg po q12h [T:500]; contraindicated in patients with QT prolongation or on QT-prolonging drugs, with hepatic impairment, or on CYP3A inhibitors, including diltiazem (see p 19).
- Use sublingual or spray nitroglycerin for acute angina.
- Treat HTN (see p 42); goal of <140/90 mmHg or <130/80 mmHg if HF, diabetes mellitus, or kidney failure is present.
- Treat dyslipidemia (see p 40); goals of LDL <70–100 mg/dL and TG <150 mg/dL.
- Treat diabetes mellitus; see p 83 for target goals.
- Weight reduction in obese individuals; goal BMI <25 kg/m^2.
- Aerobic exercise 30–60 min/d, at least intermediate intensity (eg, brisk walking).
- Smoking cessation.
- Increase consumption of oily fish (eg, white canned or fresh tuna, salmon, mackerel, herring) and foods rich in α-linolenic acid (eg, flax-seed, canola, and soybean oils; flax seeds; walnuts). Consider supplementation with fish oil capsules to achieve omega-3 fatty acid intake of 1 g/d; higher dosages are advised in patients with hypertriglyceridemia.
- Strongly consider placement of implantable cardiac defibrillator (see p 58) in patients with LVEF ≤30% at least 40 d after MI or 3 mo after CABG.
- Avoid NSAIDs, especially selective COX-2 inhibitors (see **Table 70**).

HEART FAILURE (HF)

Evaluation and Assessment

- All patients initially presenting with HF should have an echocardiogram to evaluate left ventricular function. An ejection fraction (EF) of <40% indicates systolic dysfunction. HF with an EF ≥40% indicates HF with preserved systolic function (diastolic dysfunction).
  - Echocardiography can also evaluate cardiac dyssynchrony (see **Table 20**) in patients with a wide QRS complex on ECG.
  - Echocardiography with tissue doppler imaging may be helpful in diagnosing diastolic dysfunction.
- Other routine initial assessment: orthostatic blood pressures, height, weight, BMI calculation, ECG, CXR, CBC, electrolytes, creatinine, BUN, lipid profile, fasting glucose, LFTs, TSH, UA, functional status
- Measurement of plasma brain natriuretic peptide (BNP) or N-terminal prohormone brain natriuretic peptide (NT-proBNP) can aid in diagnosis of HF in patients presenting with acute dyspnea.
  - BNP and NT-proBNP levels increase with age.
  - In dyspneic patients >70 yr old:

- HF very unlikely (likelihood ratio negative = 0.1) if BNP <100 pg/mL (22 mmol/L) or if NT-proBNP <300 pg/mL (35 mmol/L)
- HF very likely (likelihood ratio positive = 6) if BNP >500 pg/mL (110 mmol/L) or if NT-proBNP >1,200 pg/mL (140 mmol/L).
  - Other conditions causing increased BNP or NT-proBNP levels include impaired renal function, pulmonary disease, HTN, hyperthyroidism, hepatic cirrhosis with ascites, paraneoplastic syndrome, glucocorticoid use, and sepsis.
- Optional: Radionuclide ventriculography, which measures EF more precisely, provides a better evaluation of right ventricular function, and is more expensive than echocardiography.
- If HF is accompanied by angina or signs of ischemia, coronary angiography should be strongly considered.
- Consider coronary angiography if HF presents with atypical chest pain or in patients who have known or suspected coronary artery disease.
- Consider stress testing if HF presents in patients at high risk (ie, numerous risk factors) for coronary artery disease.

Table 20. Heart Failure Staging and Management

Clinical Profile	ACC/AHA Staging	New York Heart Association Staging	Management[a]
Asymptomatic but at high risk of developing HF (eg, HTN, diabetes mellitus, CAD present)	Stage A	—	RFR, E
Asymptomatic with structural disease: LVH, low EF, prior MI, or valvular disease	Stage B	Class I	RFR, E, ACEI (or ARB if unable to tolerate ACEI), BB
Normal EF; current or prior symptoms (diastolic dysfunction)	Stage C	Class I-IV	RFR, drug therapy for symptomatic HF, control of ventricular rate
Low EF[b]; currently asymptomatic but with hx of symptoms	Stage C	Class I	RFR, E, DW, SR, ACEI (or ARB if unable to tolerate ACEI), BB
Low EF[b]; patient comfortable at rest but symptomatic on normal physical activity	Stage C	Class II	RFR, E, DW, SR, drug therapy for symptomatic HF (below), consider biventricular pacing if cardiac dyssynchrony is present, consider placement of ICD if LVEF ≤35%
Low EF[b]; patient comfortable at rest but symptomatic on slight physical activity	Stage C	Class III	
Low EF[b]; patient symptomatic at rest	Stage C	Class IV	
Refractory symptoms at rest in hospitalized patient requiring specialized interventions (eg, transplant) or hospice care	Stage D	Class IV	Decide on care preference; above measures or hospice as appropriate

[a] RFR = cardiac risk factor reduction, E = exercise (regular walking or cycling), BB = β blocker, DW = measurement of daily weight, SR = salt restriction (≤3 g/d if severe HF)
[b] Low EF = EF <40%

Drug Therapy for Symptomatic HF (AHA Stage C and D, NYHA Class II–IV)

For information on drug dosages and adverse events not listed below, see **Table 24**. Efficacy of different medications may vary significantly across racial and ethnic groups; eg, blacks may require higher doses of ACEIs and β-blockers and may benefit from isosorbide dinitrate combined with hydralazine therapy.

- Systolic dysfunction (low EF):
  - Diuretics if volume overload
  - ACEIs to target doses (see **Table 21**)
  - An angiotensin II receptor blocker is indicated in patients who cannot take ACEIs (see **Table 21**).
  - β-blockers to target doses (see **Table 21**) once volume status is stabilized
  - Add low-dose digoxin▲ *(Lanoxin)* [T: 0.125, 0.25; S: 0.05 mg/mL]; *(Lanoxicaps)* [T: 0.05, 0.1, 0.2], 0.125–0.375 mg/d (target serum levels 0.5–0.8 mg/dL) if HF is not controlled on diuretics and ACEIs. Digoxin may be less effective and even harmful in women.
    - Digoxin concentration must be monitored with concomitant administration of many other medications.
      - The following **increase** digoxin concentration or effect, or both:

amiodarone	hydroxychloroquine	quinine
diltiazem	ibuprofen	spironolactone
erythromycin	indomethacin	tetracycline
esmolol	nifedipine	tolbutamide
flecainide	quinidine	verapamil

      - The following **decrease** digoxin concentration or effect, or both:

aminosalicylic acid	colestipol	sulfasalazine
antacids	kaolin pectin	St. John's wort
antineoplastics	metoclopramide	
cholestyramine	psyllium	

  - Adding an aldosterone antagonist can reduce mortality in patients with NYHA Class II–IV failure. Use either spironolactone▲ *(Aldactone)* 25 mg/d po [T: 25] or eplerenone *(Inspra)* 25–50 mg/d po [T: 25, 50, 100]. Monitor serum potassium carefully and avoid these medications if Cr >2.5 mg/dL in men or >2 mg/dL in women.
  - Adding a combination of isosorbide dinitrate and hydralazine (see **Table 19** and **Table 24**; also available as a single preparation: *BiDil* 1–2 tabs po q8h [T: 20/37.5]) can be helpful for patients with persistent symptoms.
  - Correct iron deficiency using IV iron (see **Table 56**) with or without anemia.
  - Some clinicians recommend anticoagulation in patients with EF <25%.
  - Calcium channel blockers and Class I antiarrhythmics are not indicated.
- HF with preserved systolic function (diastolic dysfunction; normal EF):
  - Diuretics should be used judiciously and only if there is volume overload.
  - There is no agreed-upon primary treatment. β-Blockers, ACEIs, and/or nondihydropyridine calcium channel blockers may be of benefit.
- Avoid thiazolidinediones (see **Table 40**) in patients with HF and diabetes mellitus.

Source: Hunt SA, Abraham WT, Chin MH, Feldman AM, Francis GS, Ganiats TG, Jessup M, Konstam MA, Mancini DM, Michl K, Oates JA, Rahko PS, Silver MA, Stevenson LW, Yancy CW. 2009 Focused update incorporated into the ACC/AHA 2005 guidelines for the diagnosis and management of heart failure in adults: a report of the American College of Cardiology Foundation/American Heart Association Task Force on Practice Guidelines. *Circulation* 2009;119:e391–e479.

Table 21. Target Dosages of ACEIs, Angiotensin II Receptor Blockers, and β-Blockers in Patients with HF and Low EF

Agent	Starting Dosage	Target Dosage
ACEIs		
Benazepril▲	2.5 mg/d	40 mg/d
Captopril▲	6.25 mg q8h	50 mg q8h
Enalapril▲	2.5 mg q12h	10 mg q12h
Fosinopril▲	5 mg/d	40 mg/d
Lisinopril▲	2.5 mg/d	20 mg/d
Perindopril	2 mg/d	8 mg/d
Quinapril▲	5 mg q12h	20 mg q12h
Ramipril▲	1.25 mg/d	10 mg/d
Trandolapril▲	1 mg/d	4 mg/d
Angiotensin II Receptor Blockers		
Candesartan	4 mg/d	32 mg/d
Losartan▲	12.5 mg/d	50 mg q12h
Valsartan	20 mg q12h	160 mg q12h
β-Blockers		
Bisoprolol▲	1.25 mg/d	10 mg/d
Carvedilol▲	3.125 mg q12h	25 mg q12h
Carvedilol ER	10 mg/d	80 mg/d
Metoprolol XR▲	12.5–25 mg/d	200 mg/d
Nebivolol	1.25 mg/d	10 mg/d

DYSLIPIDEMIA

Table 22. Treatment Indications for Dyslipidemia

Risk Category	Conditions	LDL-Cholesterol Goal	Initiate Non-pharmacologic Management	Consider Drug Therapy (see Table 23)
Low	0 or 1 risk factor[a]	<160 mg/dL	≥160 mg/dL	≥190 mg/dL; optional: 160–189 mg/dL
Moderate	≥2 risk factors; 10-yr CAD risk <10%[b]	<130 mg/dL	≥130 mg/dL	≥160 mg/dL
Moderately high	≥2 risk factors; 10-yr CAD risk 10%–20%[b]	<130 mg/dL	≥130 mg/dL	≥130 mg/dL; optional: 100–129 mg/dL
High	CVD[c], DM, or 10-yr CAD risk >20%[b]	<100 mg/dL	≥100 mg/dL	≥100 mg/dL

(cont.)

Table 22. Treatment Indications for Dyslipidemia (cont.)				
Risk Category	Conditions	LDL-Cholesterol Goal	Initiate Non-pharmacologic Management	Consider Drug Therapy (see Table 23)
Very high	DM + CVD[c]; acute coronary syndrome; multiple severe or poorly controlled risk factors	<70 mg/dL	≥100 mg/dL	≥100 mg/dL; optional: 70–99 mg/dL

Note: CVD = cardiovascular disease; DM = diabetes mellitus

[a] Risk factors are cigarette smoking, HTN, HDL <40 mg/dL, family history of premature CAD, male age ≥45 yr, female age ≥55 yr.

[b] Calculation of 10-yr risk of CAD is available at http://hp2010.nhlbihin.net/atpiii/calculator.asp?usertype=prof

[c] CVD refers to CAD, angina, PAD, TIA, stroke, abdominal aortic aneurysm, or 10-yr CAD risk >20%.

Management

Nonpharmacologic: A cholesterol-lowering diet should be considered initial therapy for dyslipidemia and should be used as follows:

• The patient should be at low risk of malnutrition.

• The diet should be nutritionally adequate, with sufficient total calories, protein, calcium, iron, and vitamins, and low in saturated fats (<7% of total calories), trans-fatty acids, and cholesterol.

• The diet should be easily understood and affordable (a dietitian can be very helpful).

• Plant stanol/sterols (2 g/d), found in many fruits, vegetables, vegetable oils, nuts, seeds, cereals, and legumes, can lower LDL.

• Cholesterol-lowering margarines can lower LDL cholesterol by 10% to 15% *(Take Control 1–2 tbsp/d, 45 calories/tbsp; Benecol 3 servings of 1.5 tsp each/d, 70 calories/tbsp)*.

Pharmacologic: Target drug treatment according to type of dyslipidemia (**Table 23**).

Table 23. Medication Regimens for Dyslipidemia			
Condition	Medication	Dosage	Formulations
Elevated LDL, normal TG	Statin (HMG-CoA reductase inhibitor)[a]		
	Atorvastatin *(Lipitor)*	10–80 mg/d	T: 10, 20, 40, 80
	Fluvastatin▲ *(Lescol, Lescol XL)*	20–80 mg/d in PM, max 80 mg	C: 20, 40; T: ER 80
	Lovastatin▲ *(Mevacor, Altoprev)*	10–40 mg/d in PM or q12h	T: 10, 20, 40; T: ER 10, 20, 40, 60
	Pravastatin▲ *(Pravachol)*	10–40 mg/d	T: 10, 20, 40, 80
	ASA/pravastatin *(Pravigard PAC)*	1 tab/d	T: 81/20, 81/40, 81/80, 325/20, 325/40, 325/80
	Rosuvastatin *(Crestor)*	10–40 mg/d	T: 5, 10, 20, 40
	Simvastatin▲ *(Zocor)*	5–40 mg/d in PM	T: 5, 10, 20, 40, 80
	Ezetimibe *(Zetia)*[b]	10 mg/d	T: 10

(cont.)

Table 23. Medication Regimens for Dyslipidemia (cont.)

Condition	Medication	Dosage	Formulations
Elevated TG (>500 mg/dL)	Fenofibrate▲ (Tricor, Lofibra, Antara)	48–200 mg/d	T: 48, 54, 145, 160 C: 43, 67, 130, 134, 200
	Fenofibrate delayed release (Trilipix)	45–135 mg/d	C: 45, 135
	Gemfibrozil▲ (Lopid)	300–600 mg po q12h	T: 600
	Omega-3-acid ethyl esters (Omacor, Lovaza)	4 g/d in single or divided doses	C: 1 g
Combined elevated LDL, low HDL, elevated TG	Fenofibrate, gemfibrozil, or HMG-CoA if TG <300 mg/dL	As above	As above
Alternative for any of above	Niacin▲c	100 mg q8h to start; increase to 500–1000 mg q8h; extended release 150 mg qhs to start, increase to 2000 mg qhs as needed	T: 25, 50, 100, 250, 500; ER 150, 250, 500, 750, 1000 C: TR 125, 250, 400, 500
	Niacin ER▲ (Niaspan)	500–2000 mg/d	T: 500, 750, 1000
Elevated LDL or combined dyslipidemia with inadequate response to one agent	Lovastatin/niacin combinationa,c (Advicor)	20 mg/500 mg qhs to start; max dose 40 mg/2000 mg	T: 20/500, 20/750, 20/1000, 40/1000
	Simvastatin/niacin combinationa,c (Simcor)	20 mg/500 mg qhs to start; max dose 40 mg/2000 mg	T: 20/500, 20/750, 20/1000
	Colesevelam (WelChol)	Monotherapy: 1850 mg po q12h; combination therapy: 2500–3750 mg/d in single or divided doses	T: 625
	Colestipol▲ (Colestid, Colestid Tablets)	5–30 g mixed with liquid in 1 or more divided doses	Packets or scoops: 5 g, 7.5 g T: 1 g

[a] Measure transaminases at baseline, at 3 mo, and then periodically. Watch for statin-induced myopathy, usually presenting as diffuse, symmetric myalgias. If myopathy is suspected (higher risk at higher statin doses or in combination with fenofibrate, gemfibrozil, or niacin), measure CPK and transaminases; CPK levels >10 times the upper limit of normal indicate serious myopathy/rhabdomyolysis. Even if CPK and transaminases are normal, myalgias still may be due to statin; if this is the case, myalgias should disappear within 1 wk of discontinuing statin.

[b] Use as monotherapy only in patients unable to tolerate statins, niacin, or a bile acid sequestrant (colesevelam, colestipol) and who have not reached LDL lowering goal.

[c] Monitor for flushing, pruritus, nausea, gastritis, ulcer. Dosage increases should be spaced 1 mo apart. ASA 325 mg po 30 min before first niacin dose of the day is effective in preventing adverse events.

HYPERTENSION (HTN)

Definition, Classification

JNC 7 defines HTN as SBP ≥140 mmHg or DBP ≥90 mmHg. In older adults, base treatment decisions primarily on the SBP level.

Evaluation and Assessment

- Measure both standing and sitting BP after 5 min of rest.
- Base diagnosis on two or more readings at each of two or more visits. Once diagnosis is made, evaluation includes:
  - Assessment of cardiac risk factors: smoking, dyslipidemia, obesity, and diabetes mellitus are important in older adults.
  - Assessment of end-organ damage: LVH, angina, prior MI, prior coronary revascularization, HF, stroke or TIA, nephropathy, peripheral arterial disease, retinopathy.
  - Routine laboratory tests: CBC, UA, electrolytes, creatinine, fasting glucose, total cholesterol, HDL cholesterol, and ECG.
  - Consider renal artery stenosis (RAS) if new onset of diastolic hypertension, sudden rise in BP in previously well controlled HTN, HTN despite therapy with maximal dosages of 3 antihypertensive agents, or azotemia induced by treatment with ACEI/ARB therapy.
    - RAS diagnostic test options include renal artery duplex ultrasonography, CT angiography, or magnetic resonance angiography.
    - Medical treatment for RAS includes aggressive management of vascular risk factors and antihypertensive regimens that include an ACEI or ARB (monitor creatinine closely).
    - Consider renovascular angioplasty if BP cannot be controlled despite aggressive medical therapy, if HF develops, or if there is progressive decline in renal function.

Aggravating Factors

- Emotional stress
- Excessive alcohol intake
- Excessive salt intake
- Lack of aerobic exercise
- Low potassium intake
- Low calcium intake
- Nicotine
- Obesity

Management

- JNC 7 recommendations: Target is <140/90 mmHg (130/80 mmHg in patients with diabetes mellitus or kidney disease). Lowering BP below 120/80 mmHg is not recommended. Particularly in patients with "white coat" HTN, home monitoring of BP with a properly calibrated machine can produce more reliable readings than office-based measurements.
- In a large trial of HTN treatment in participants ≥80 yr old using a target BP of 150/80 mmHg, stroke, HF, and death were significantly reduced. Thus, for patients ≥80 yr old without coexisting conditions, a reasonable BP goal is <150/80 mmHg.

Nonpharmacologic:

- Adequate calcium and magnesium intake as well as a low-fat diet for optimizing general health.
- Adequate dietary potassium intake; fruits and vegetables are the best sources.
- Aerobic exercise: 30–45 min most days of the week.
- Moderation of alcohol intake: limit to 1 oz of ethanol/d.
- Moderation of dietary sodium: watch for volume depletion with diuretic use. Goal: ≤2.4 g Na+/d, optimal ≤1.5 g Na+/d.
- Smoking cessation
- Weight reduction if obese: even a 10-lb weight loss can significantly lower BP. Goal: BMI <25 kg/m².

Pharmacologic: Table 24 lists commonly used antihypertensives.

- Use antihypertensives carefully in patients with orthostatic BP drop.
- Base treatment decisions on standing BP.

- If no coexisting conditions, a thiazide diuretic, an ACEI, or a calcium channel blocker can be used as a first-line drug.
- If coexisting conditions, therapy should be individualized (see **Table 25**).
- Combination drugs for hypertension are listed in **Table 26**.
- Available dose formulations of oral potassium supplements▲: [T: (mEq) 6, 7, 8, 10, 20; S: (mEq/15 mL) 20, 40; powders (mEq/pk) 15, 20, 25]
- Follow-up BP measurements monthly until target BP is attained; visits may be q3–6mo if BP is stable at target goal.

Hypertensive Emergencies and Urgencies:

- Elevated BP alone without symptoms or target end-organ damage does not require emergent BP lowering.
- Conditions requiring emergent BP lowering include hypertensive encephalopathy, intracranial hemorrhage, unstable angina, acute MI, acute left ventricular failure with pulmonary edema, dissecting aortic aneurysm.
- Most common initial treatment for emergent BP lowering is sodium nitroprusside▲ *(Nipride)* 0.25–10 mg/kg/min as IV infusion.
- Nonemergent (ie, urgent) BP lowering is indicated only in cases in which BP needs to be lowered for procedural evaluation or treatment (such as β blockade before surgery, see p 224) or in asymptomatic people with SBP >210 mmHg or DBP >120 mmHg.
  - Administer standard dose of a recommended antihypertensive orally (see **Table 24**) or an extra dose of patient's usual antihypertensive.
  - If the patient is npo, give **low** dose antihypertensive IV, titrating upward **slowly**. Options include β-blocker (eg, labetalol 20 mg), ACEI (eg, enalaprilat 0.625 mg over 5 min), or diuretic (eg, furosemide 10 mg).

Table 24. Oral Antihypertensive Agents			
Class, Medication	**Geriatric Dosage Range, Total mg/d (times/d)**	**Formulations**	**Comments (Metabolism, Excretion)**
Diuretics			↓ potassium, Na, magnesium levels; ↑ uric acid, calcium, cholesterol (mild), and glucose (mild) levels
Thiazides			
✔ Chlorothiazide▲ *(Diuril)*	125–500 (1)	T: 250, 500	
✔ Chlorthalidone▲ *(Hygroton)*	12.5–25 (1)	T: 15, 25, 50, 100	↑ adverse events at >25 mg/d (L)
✔ HCTZ▲ *(Esidrix, HydroDIURIL, Microzide, Oretic)*	12.5–25 (1)	T: 25, 50, 100; S: 50 mg/mL; C: 12.5	↑ adverse events at >25 mg/d (L)
✔ Indapamide▲ *(Lozol)*	0.625–2.5 (1)	T: 1.25, 2.5	Less or no hypercholesterolemia (L)
✔ Metolazone *(Mykrox)*	0.25–0.5 (1)	T rapid: 0.5	Monitor electrolytes carefully (L)
✔ Metolazone▲ *(Zaroxolyn)*	2.5–5 (1)	T: 2.5, 5, 10	Monitor electrolytes carefully (L)
✔ Polythiazide *(Renese)*	1–4 (1)	T: 1, 2, 4	

✔ = preferred for treating older adults; ♥ = useful in treating HF with low EF   *(cont.)*

Note: Listing of adverse events is not exhaustive, and adverse events are for the drug class except when noted for individual drugs.

Table 24. Oral Antihypertensive Agents (cont.)

Class, Medication	Geriatric Dosage Range, Total mg/d (times/d)	Formulations	Comments (Metabolism, Excretion)
Loop diuretics			
♥ Bumetanide▲ *(Bumex)*	0.5–4 (1–3)	T: 0.5, 1, 2	Short duration of action, no hypercalcemia (K)
♥ Furosemide▲ *(Lasix)*	20–160 (1–2)	T: 20, 40, 80; S: 10, 40 mg/5 mL	Short duration of action, no hypercalcemia (K)
♥ Torsemide▲ *(Demadex)*	2.5–50 (1–2)	T: 5, 10, 20, 100	Short duration of action, no hypercalcemia (K)
Potassium-sparing drugs			
Amiloride▲ *(Midamor)*	2.5–10 (1)	T: 5	(L, K)
Triamterene▲ *(Dyrenium)*	25–100 (1–2)	T: 50, 100	(L, K)
Aldosterone receptor-blockers			
♥ Eplerenone *(Inspra)*	25–100 (1)	T: 25, 50, 100	(L, K)
♥ Spironolactone▲ *(Aldactone)*	12.5–50 (1–2)	T: 25, 50, 100	Gynecomastia (L, K)
Adrenergic Inhibitors			
α₁-Blockers			Avoid as primary therapy for HTN unless patient has BPH; avoid in patients with HF
Doxazosin▲ *(Cardura)*	1–16 (1)	T: 1, 2, 4, 8	(L)
Prazosin▲ *(Minipress)*	1–20 (2–3)	T: 1, 2, 5	(L)
Terazosin▲ *(Hytrin)*	1–20 (1–2)	T: 1, 2, 5, 10; C: 1, 2, 5, 10	(L, K)
Central α₂-agonists and other centrally acting drugs			Sedation, dry mouth, bradycardia, withdrawal HTN
Clonidine▲ *(Catapres, Catapres-TTS)*	0.1–1.2 (2–3) **or** 1 pch/wk	T: 0.1, 0.2, 0.3▲; pch: 0.1, 0.2, 0.3 mg/d	Continue oral for 1–2 d when converting to patch (L, K)
Guanfacine▲ *(Tenex)*	0.5–2 (1)	T: 1, 2	(K)
Methyldopa▲ *(Aldomet)*	250–2500 (2)	T: 125, 250, 500; S: 250 mg/5 mL	(L, K)
Reserpine▲ *(Serpasil)*	0.05–0.25 (1)	T: 0.1, 0.25	Depression, nasal congestion, activation of peptic ulcer (L, K)

(cont.)

✔ = preferred for treating older adults; ♥ = useful in treating HF with low EF

Note: Listing of adverse events is not exhaustive, and adverse events are for the drug class except when noted for individual drugs.

Table 24. Oral Antihypertensive Agents (cont.)

Class, Medication	Geriatric Dosage Range, Total mg/d (times/d)	Formulations	Comments (Metabolism, Excretion)
β-Blockers			Bronchospasm, bradycardia, acute HF, may mask insulin-induced hypoglycemia; less effective for reducing HTN-related endpoints in older vs younger patients; lipid solubility is a risk factor for delirium
✔ Acebutolol▲ *(Sectral)*	200–800 (1)	C: 200, 400	β_1, low lipid solubility, intrinsic sympathomimetic activity (L, K)
✔ Atenolol▲ *(Tenormin)*	12.5–100 (1)	T: 25, 50, 100	β_1, low lipid solubility (K)
✔ Betaxolol▲ *(Kerlone)*	5–20 (1)	T: 10, 20	β_1, low lipid solubility (L, K)
✔ ♥ Bisoprolol▲ *(Zebeta)*	2.5–10 (1)	T: 5, 10	β_1, low lipid solubility (L, K)
✔ Carteolol *(Cartrol)*	1.25–10 (1)	T: 2.5, 5	β_1, low lipid solubility, intrinsic sympathomimetic activity (K)
✔ Metoprolol▲ *(Lopressor)*	25–400 (2)	T: 25, 50, 100	β_1, moderate lipid solubility (L)
✔ ♥ Long-acting▲ *(Toprol XL)*	50–400 (1)	T: 25, 50, 100, 200	(L)
Nadolol▲ *(Corgard)*	20–160 (1)	T: 20, 40, 80, 120, 160	β_1, β_2, low lipid solubility (K)
✔ ♥ Nebivolol *(Bystolic)*	2.5–40 (1)	T: 2.5, 5, 10	β_1, low lipid solubility (L, K)
Penbutolol *(Levatol)*	10–40 (1)	T: 20	β_1, β_2, high lipid solubility, intrinsic sympathomimetic activity (L, K)
Pindolol▲ *(Visken)*	5–40 (2)	T: 5, 10	β_1, β_2, moderate lipid solubility, intrinsic sympathomimetic activity (K)
Propranolol▲ *(Inderal)*	20–160 (2)	T: 10, 20, 40, 60, 80, 90; S: 4 mg/mL, 8 mg/mL, 80 mg/mL	β_1, β_2, high lipid solubility (L)
Long-acting▲ *(Inderal LA, InnoPran XL)*	60–180 (1)	C: 60, 80, 120, 160	β_1, β_2, high lipid solubility (L)
Timolol▲ *(Blocadren)*	10–40 (2)	T: 5, 10, 20	β_1, β_2, low to moderate lipid solubility (L, K)
Combined α- and β-blockers			Postural hypotension, bronchospasm
✔ ♥ Carvedilol▲ *(Coreg)*	3.125–25 (2)	T: 3.125, 6.25, 12.5, 25	β_1, β_2, high lipid solubility (L)
✔ ♥ Extended-release *(Coreg CR)*	10–80 (1)	C: 10, 20, 40, 80	Multiply regular daily dose of carvedilol by 1.6 to convert to CR dose; do not take within 2 h of alcohol ingestion

✔ = preferred for treating older adults; ♥ = useful in treating HF with low EF

(cont.)

Note: Listing of adverse events is not exhaustive, and adverse events are for the drug class except when noted for individual drugs.

Table 24. Oral Antihypertensive Agents (cont.)

Class, Medication	Geriatric Dosage Range, Total mg/d (times/d)	Formulations	Comments (Metabolism, Excretion)
✔ Labetalol▲ (Normodyne, Trandate)	100–600 (2)	T: 100, 200, 300	β_1, β_2, moderate lipid solubility (L, K)
Direct Vasodilators			Headaches, fluid retention, tachycardia
♥ Hydralazine▲ (Apresoline)	25–100 (2–4)	T: 10, 25, 50, 100	Lupus syndrome; used in combination with isosorbide dinitrate for HF in blacks (L, K)
Minoxidil▲ (Loniten)	2.5–50 (1)	T: 2.5, 10	Hirsutism (K)
Calcium Antagonists			
Nondihydropyridines			Conduction defects, worsening of systolic dysfunction, gingival hyperplasia
✔ Diltiazem SR▲ (Cardizem CD, Cardizem SR, Dilacor XR, Tiazac)	120–360 (1–2), max 480	C: 1/d: 120, 180, 240, 300, 360, 420; 2/d: 60, 90, 120; T: 30, 60, 90, 120, ER: 120, 180, 240	Nausea, headache (L)
✔ Verapamil SR▲ (Calan SR, Covera-HS, Isoptin SR, Verelan PM)	120–360 (1–2)	T: SR 120, 180, 240; C: SR 100, 120, 180, 200, 240, 300, 360; T: 40, 80, 120	Constipation, bradycardia (L)
Dihydropyridines			Ankle edema, flushing, headache, gingival hypertrophy
✔ Amlodipine▲ (Norvasc)	2.5–10 (1)	T: 2.5, 5, 10	(L)
✔ Felodipine▲ (Plendil)	2.5–20 (1)	T: 2.5, 5, 10	(L)
✔ Isradipine SR (DynaCirc CR)	2.5–10 (1)	T: 5, 10	(L)
✔ Nicardipine▲ (Cardene)	60–120 (3)	C: 20, 30	(L)
✔ Sustained release (Cardene SR)	60–120 (2)	T: 30, 45, 60	(L)
✔ Nifedipine SR▲ (Adalat CC, Procardia XL)	30–60 (1)	T: 30, 60, 90	(L)
✔ Nisoldipine▲ (Sular)	10–40 (1)	T: ER 10, 20, 30, 40	(L)

✔ = preferred for treating older adults; ♥ = useful in treating HF with low EF

(cont.)

Note: Listing of adverse events is not exhaustive, and adverse events are for the drug class except when noted for individual drugs.

Table 24. **Oral Antihypertensive Agents (cont.)**

Class, Medication	Geriatric Dosage Range, Total mg/d (times/d)	Formulations	Comments (Metabolism, Excretion)
ACEIs*			Cough (common), angioedema (rare), hyperkalemia, rash, loss of taste, leukopenia
✔ ♥ Benazepril▲ *(Lotensin)*	2.5–40 (1–2)	T: 5, 10, 20, 40	(L, K)
✔ ♥ Captopril▲ *(Capoten)*	12.5–150 (2–3)	T: 12.5, 25, 50, 100	(L, K)
✔ ♥ Enalapril▲ *(Vasotec)*	2.5–40 (1–2)	T: 2.5, 5, 10, 20	(L, K)
✔ ♥ Fosinopril▲ *(Monopril)*	5–40 (1–2)	T: 10, 20, 40	(L, K)
✔ ♥ Lisinopril▲ *(Prinivil, Zestril)*	2.5–40 (1)	T: 2.5, 5, 10, 20, 30, 40	(K)
✔ Moexipril▲ *(Univasc)*	3.75–30 (1)	T: 7.5, 15	(L, K)
✔ ♥ Perindopril▲ *(Aceon)*	4–8 (1–2)	T: 2, 4, 8	(L, K)
✔ ♥ Quinapril▲ *(Accupril)*	5–40 (1)	T: 5, 10, 20, 40	(L, K)
✔ ♥ Ramipril▲ *(Altace)*	1.25–20 (1)	T: 1.25, 2.5, 5, 10	(L, K)
✔ ♥ Trandolapril▲ *(Mavik)*	1–4 (1)	T: 1, 2, 4	(L, K)
Angiotensin II Receptor Blockers (ARBs)*			Angioedema (very rare), hyperkalemia
✔ ♥ Candesartan *(Atacand)*	4–32 (1)	T: 4, 8, 16, 32	(K)
✔ Eprosartan *(Teveten)*	400–800 (1–2)	T: 400, 600	(biliary, K)
✔ Irbesartan *(Avapro)*	75–300 (1)	T: 75, 150, 300	(L)
✔ ♥ Losartan▲ *(Cozaar)*	12.5–100 (1–2)	T: 25, 50, 100	(L, K)
✔ Olmesartan *(Benicar)*	20–40 (1)	T: 5, 20, 40	(F, K)
✔ Telmisartan *(Micardis)*	20–80 (1)	T: 20, 40, 80	(L)
✔ ♥ Valsartan *(Diovan)*	40–320 (1)	T: 40, 80, 160, 320; C: 80, 160	(L, K)
Renin Inhibitor			
Aliskiren *(Tekturna)*	150-300 (1)	T: 150, 300	Monitor electrolytes in patients with renal disease; contraindicated in patients with DM who are also taking an ACEI or ARB

✔ = preferred for treating older adults; ♥ = useful in treating HF with low EF
* See **Table 21** for target dosages in treating HF.
Note: Listing of adverse events is not exhaustive, and adverse events are for the drug class except when noted for individual drugs.
Source: Data in part from The seventh report of the Joint National Committee on Prevention, Detection, Evaluation, and Treatment of High Blood Pressure: The JNC 7 report. *JAMA* 2003;289:2560–2572.

Table 25. Choosing Antihypertensive Therapy on the Basis of Coexisting Conditions

Condition	Appropriate for Use	Avoid or Contraindicated
Angina	β, D, non-D	
Atrial tachycardia and fibrillation	β, non-D	
Bronchospasm		β, αβ
Chronic kidney disease	AA, ACEI[a]	
Diabetes mellitus	ACEI, ARB, β, T[b]	T[b]
Dyslipidemia		β, T[c]
Essential tremor	β	
HF	AA, ACEI, ARB, β, αβ, L	D, non-D[d]
Hyperthyroidism	β	
MI	β, AA, ACEI, ARB	non-D
Osteoporosis	T	
Prostatism (BPH)	α	
Urge UI	D, non-D	L, T

Note: AA = aldosterone antagonist; α = α-blocker; β = β-blocker; αβ = combined α- and β-blocker; ARB = angiotensin receptor blocker; D = dihydropyridine calcium antagonist; non-D = nondihydropyridine calcium antagonist; L = loop diuretic; T = thiazide diuretic

[a] Use with great caution in renovascular disease.

[b] Low-dose diuretics probably beneficial in type 2 diabetes; high-dose diuretics relatively contraindicated in types 1 and 2.

[c] Low-dose diuretics have a minimal effect on lipids.

[d] May be beneficial in HF caused by diastolic dysfunction.

Table 26. Combination Medications Containing an Antihypertensive Agent

Combination Type	Fixed-dose Combination (mg)*	Trade Name
ACEIs and calcium channel blockers	Amlodipine/benazepril hydrochloride▲ (2.5/10, 5/10, 5/20, 10/20)	*Lotrel*
	Enalapril maleate/felodipine (5/2.5, 5/5)	*Lexxel*
	Trandolapril/verapamil (2/180, 1/240, 2/240, 4/240)	*Tarka*
ACEIs and diuretics	Benazepril/HCTZ▲ (5/6.25, 10/12.5, 20/12.5, 20/25)	*Lotensin HCT*
	Captopril/HCTZ▲ (25/15, 25/25, 50/15, 50/25)	*Capozide*
	Enalapril maleate/HCTZ▲ (5/12.5, 10/25)	*Vaseretic*
	Lisinopril/HCTZ▲ (10/12.5, 20/12.5, 20/25)	*Prinzide, Zestoretic*
	Moexipril hydrochloride/HCTZ▲ (7.5/12.5, 15/12.5, 15/25)	*Uniretic*
	Quinapril hydrochloride/HCTZ▲ (10/12.5, 20/12.5, 20/25)	*Accuretic*
ARB and calcium channel blockers	Amlodipine/valsartan (5/160, 10/160, 5/320, 10/320)	*Exforge*
	Amlodipine/olmesartan (5/20, 5/40, 10/20, 10/40)	*Azor*
	Amlodipine/telmisartan (5/40, 5/80, 10/40, 10/80)	*Twynsta*
ARB, calcium channel blocker, and diuretic	Amlodipine/valsartan/HCTZ (5/160/12.5, 10/160/12.5, 5/160/25, 10/160/25, 10/320/25)	*Exforge HCT*

(cont.)

Table 26. Combination Medications Containing an Antihypertensive Agent (cont.)

Combination Type	Fixed-dose Combination (mg)*	Trade Name
ARBs and diuretic	Candesartan cilexetil/HCTZ (16/12.5, 32/12.5)	*Atacand HCT*
	Eprosartan mesylate/HCTZ (600/12.5, 600/25)	*Teveten HCT*
	Irbesartan/HCTZ (150/12.5, 300/12.5, 300/25)	*Avalide*
	Losartan potassium/HCTZ (50/12.5, 100/12.5, 100/25)	*Hyzaar*
	Olmesartan/HCTZ (20/12.5, 40/12.5, 40/25)	*Benicar HCT*
	Telmisartan/HCTZ (40/12.5, 80/12.5, 80/25)	*Micardis HCT*
	Valsartan/HCTZ (80/12.5, 160/12.5, 160/25, 320/12.5, 320/25)	*Diovan HCT*
β-Blockers and diuretics	Atenolol/chlorthalidone▲ (50/25, 100/25)	*Tenoretic*
	Bisoprolol fumarate/HCTZ▲ (2.5/6.25, 5/6.25, 10/6.25)	*Ziac*
	Propranolol LA/HCTZ▲ (40/25, 80/25)	*Inderide*
	Metoprolol tartrate/HCTZ▲ (50/25, 100/25, 100/50)	*Lopressor HCT*
	Nadolol/bendroflumethiazide▲ (40/5, 80/5)	*Corzide*
Calcium channel blocker and statin	Amlodipine/atorvastatin (2.5/10, 2.5/20, 2.5/40, 5/10, 5/20, 5/40, 5/80, 10/10, 10/20, 10/40, 10/80)	*Caduet*
Centrally acting drug and diuretic	Methyldopa/HCTZ▲ (250/15, 250/25, 500/30, 500/50)	*Aldoril*
	Reserpine/chlorothiazide▲ (0.125/250, 0.25/500)	*Diupres*
	Reserpine/HCTZ▲ (0.125/25, 0.125/50)	*Hydropres*
Direct vasodilator and nitrate	Isosorbide dinitrate/hydralazine (20/37.5)	*BiDil*
Diuretic and diuretic	Amiloride hydrochloride/HCTZ▲ (5/50)	*Moduretic*
	Spironolactone/HCTZ▲ (25/25, 50/50)	*Aldactazide*
	Triamterene/HCTZ▲ (37.5/25, 50/25, 75/50)	*Dyazide, Maxzide*
Direct renin inhibitor and diuretic	Aliskiren/HCTZ (150/12.5, 150/25, 300/12.5, 300/25)	*Tekturna HCT*

*Some drug combinations are available in multiple fixed doses. Each drug dose is reported in mg.

PULMONARY ARTERIAL HYPERTENSION (PAH)

Evaluation and Assessment

• PAH can be primary (unexplained) or secondary to underlying conditions.

• Almost all cases in older adults are secondary, most commonly associated with chronic pulmonary and/or cardiac disease, including COPD, interstitial lung disease, obstructive sleep apnea, pulmonary emboli, HF, and mitral valvular disease.

• Early symptoms are often nonspecific and include dyspnea on exertion, fatigue, and vague chest discomfort.

• Late symptoms include severe dyspnea on exertion, cyanosis, syncope, chest pain, HF, arrhythmias.

• Physical examination findings relate to manifestations of the associated conditions mentioned above.

- Diagnostic tests:
  - ECG may show right-axis deviation, right atrial and ventricular hypertrophy, T-wave changes
  - CXR may show large right ventricle, dilated pulmonary arteries
  - Echocardiography estimates pulmonary arterial pressure and evaluates possible valvular disease
  - Right heart catheterization is gold standard, with PAH defined as mean pulmonary arterial pressure >25 mmHg at rest or >30 mmHg during exercise.
- Additional tests (eg, pulmonary function tests, sleep study) may clarify severity of coexisting conditions.

Management
- Correct/optimize underlying conditions.
- Supplemental oxygen for chronic hypoxemia
- Diuretics for volume overload from HF
- Avoid calcium channel blockers unless they have been shown to be of benefit from a right heart catheterization vasodilator challenge study.
- Other agents have been studied mainly in primary PAH and are of uncertain effectiveness and safety in secondary PAH:
  - Warfarin (see p 24)
  - Prostacyclins: epoprostenol *(Flolan)* by continuous IV infusion, treprostinil *(Remodulin)* by continuous subcutaneous infusion, iloprost *(Ventavis)* by inhalation
  - Endothelial receptor antagonists: bosentan *(Tracleer)* 62.5 mg q12h × 4 wk, then 125 mg q12h; ambrisentan *(Letairis)* 5–10 mg/d
  - Sildenafil *(Revatio, Viagra)* po 20–25 mg q8h

ATRIAL FIBRILLATION (AF)
Evaluation and Assessment
Causes:
- Cardiac disease: cardiac surgery, cardiomyopathy, HF, hypertensive heart disease, ischemic disease, pericarditis, valvular disease
- Noncardiac disease: alcoholism, chronic pulmonary disease, infections, pulmonary emboli, thyrotoxicosis

Standard testing: ECG, CBC, electrolytes, creatinine, BUN, TSH, echocardiogram

Management
- Correct precipitating cause.
- Patients presenting with AF and hypotension, severe angina, or advanced HF should be strongly considered for acute direct-current cardioversion.
- For acute management of AF with rapid ventricular response in patients who do not receive or respond to cardioversion, ventricular rate should be acutely lowered with one or more of the following medications:
  - β-Blockers, eg, metoprolol▲ 2.5–5 mg IV bolus over 2 min; may repeat twice
  - Diltiazem▲, 0.25 mg/kg IV over 2 min
  - Verapamil▲, 0.075–0.15 mg/kg IV over 2 min

- For patients with minimal symptoms or in whom sinus rhythm cannot be easily achieved, rate control plus antithrombotic therapy is the preferred treatment strategy.
  - Rate control (target <110 bpm) can be achieved with oral metoprolol or other β-blocker, diltiazem, or verapamil.
  - Digoxin▲ can be used as a third-line agent for rate control.
  - For symptomatic patients in whom ventricular rate does not respond to pharmacologic therapy, AV node ablation with pacemaker placement can effectively control rate.
  - Antithrombotic therapy (ASA, dabigatran, rivaroxaban, or warfarin) is based on the $CHADS_2$ scoring system for stroke risk: 2 points for prior stroke, TIA, or systemic embolism; 1 point for each of the following: age ≥75 yr, hx of DM, hx of HF, hx of HTN.
    - If $CHADS_2$ score is ≥2, anticoagulate with dabigatran, rivaroxaban, or warfarin (see below for dosing information).
    - If $CHADS_2$ score = 1, anticoagulate with dabigatran, rivaroxaban, or warfarin, or use antiplatelet therapy with ASA.
    - If $CHADS_2$ score = 0, use antiplatelet therapy with ASA.
  - For stroke prevention and bleeding risk, warfarin is as effective and safe as dabigatran or rivaroxaban when INR is in the therapeutic range at least 67–72% of the time.
  - Antithrombotic therapy dosing:
    - ASA 81–325 mg/d
    - Dabigatran (*Pradaxa*): 150 mg po q12h [T: 75, 150]; reduce dosage to 75 mg po q12h if CrCl 15–30 mL/min. Use with caution in adults aged ≥75 due to possible increased bleeding risk. There is no antidote to dabigatran; bleeding episodes should be treated with fresh frozen plasma and/or prothrombin complex concentrate (see **Table 13**).
    - Rivaroxaban (*Xarelto*): 20 mg/d po taken in the evening [T: 10, 15, 20] when CrCl is >50 mL/min; 15 mg/d po taken in the evening when CrCl is 15–50 mL/min. There is no antidote for rivaroxaban; prothrombin complex concentrate and/or recombinant factor VIIa may be tried for bleeding episodes, but these treatments have not been evaluated.
    - Warfarin (*Coumadin*): titrate to achieve INR 2–3 [T: 1, 2, 2.5, 3, 4, 5, 6, 7.5, 10].
  - If anticoagulation is contraindicated or not tolerated in patients with $CHADS_2$ scores ≥1, use ASA 81–325 mg/d. Addition of clopidogrel 75 mg/d to ASA lowers stroke risk but also increases risk of major hemorrhage. Both ASA and clopidogrel are less effective for stroke prevention in patients ≥75 yr of age.
- For patients with unpleasant symptoms or decreased exercise tolerance on rate control therapy, rhythm control via direct-current or pharmacologic cardioversion is the preferred treatment strategy.
  - For direct-current cardioversion, three methods may be used:
    - Early cardioversion (<48 h from onset): proceed with cardioversion; use adjunctive anticoagulation based on risk of thromboembolism (eg, $CHADS_2$ score).
    - Delayed cardioversion (≥48 h from onset) with transesophageal echocardiography (TEE): perform TEE to exclude intracardiac thrombus; if no thrombus, begin anticoagulation and cardiovert.
    - Delayed cardioversion (≥48 h from onset) without TEE: anticoagulate for at least 3 wk with INR ≥2 before cardioversion; continue anticoagulation after cardioversion.
  - For pharmacologic cardioversion and rhythm maintenance (recommended only if AF produces symptoms significantly impairing quality of life), rhythm control drugs may be tried (see **Table 27**).

- Unless contraindicated, anticoagulation should be continued indefinitely after cardioversion due to the high risk for recurrent AF.
- In selected patients with symptomatic AF refractory to antiarrhythmic drugs, catheter or surgical AF ablation may be considered.

Table 27. Selected Medications for Rhythm Control in AF

Medication	Dosage	Formulations	Comments (Metabolism)
Amiodarone▲ (Cordarone, Pacerone)	100–400 mg/d	T: 200, 400	Most effective antifibrillatory agent but numerous adverse events, including pulmonary and hepatic toxic effects, neurologic and dermatologic adverse events, hypothyroidism, hyperthyroidism, corneal deposits, warfarin▲ interaction (L)
Propafenone▲ (Rythmol)	150–300 mg q8h	T: 150, 225, 300	Contraindicated in patients with ischemic and structural heart disease; adverse events include VT and HF (L)
Sotalol▲ (Betapace, Betapace AF, Sorine)	80–160 mg q12h	T: 80, 120, 160, 240	Prolongs QT interval; adverse events include torsades de pointes, HF, exacerbation of COPD/bronchospasm (K)

AORTIC STENOSIS (AS)
Evaluation and Assessment
- Presence of symptoms—angina, syncope, HF (frequently diastolic dysfunction)— indicates severe disease and a life expectancy without surgery of <2 yr.
- Echocardiography is essential to measure aortic valve gradient (AVG) and aortic valve area (AVA).
  - Moderate AS is indicated by an AVG of 25–50 mmHg and by an AVA of 1–1.5 cm².
  - Severe AS is indicated by an AVG of 50–80 mmHg and by an AVA <1 cm².
  - Critical AS is indicated by an AVG >80 mmHg and by an AVA <0.5 cm².
- For asymptomatic cases, echocardiography should be repeated annually for moderate AS and q6–12 mo for severe AS.
- ECG and CXR should be obtained initially to look for conduction defects, LVH, and pulmonary congestion.

Treatment
- Aortic valve replacement (AVR)
  - Alleviates symptoms and improves ventricular functioning.
  - In most cases, perform AVR promptly *after* symptoms have appeared.

- Surgical AVR vs transcatheter AVR (a percutaneous procedure in the catheterization lab in which an artificial valve is implanted via a catheter):
  - In low-risk patients (young, no other heart problems or significant comorbidities), AVR surgery is superior to transcatheter AVR.
  - In high-risk surgical patients (older, cardiac and/or other significant comorbidities), surgical AVR results in higher 30-d mortality, major bleeding episodes, and new-onset AF, but lower stroke rate than transcatheter AVR. Death rates after 1 yr are the same for both procedures.
- Avoid vasodilators if possible.

ABDOMINAL AORTIC ANEURYSM (AAA)
- Ultrasound should be performed if aortic diameter is felt to be >3 cm on physical examination.
- Ultrasonographic screening for AAA is recommended once for men between age 65 and 75 if former or current smoker.
- Management is based on diameter of AAA
  - <4.5 cm: ultrasound q12mo
  - 4.5–5.4 cm: ultrasound q3–6mo
  - >5.4 cm: surgical referral
- Endovascular vs open surgical repair
  - Endovascular repair is associated with significantly less perioperative morbidity and 30-day mortality.
  - At 2 yr, mortality rates are similar, and endovascular repair is associated with more secondary interventions.
  - Consider open repair for patients with low risk of perioperative mortality and remaining life expectancy >10 yr (see **Table 7**).
  - Endovascular repair is appropriate for patients with higher comorbidities and shorter life expectancy.

PERIPHERAL ARTERIAL DISEASE (PAD)
Evaluation
Hx should include inquiry regarding the following:
- Lower extremity exertional fatigue or pain, or pain at rest
- Poorly healing or nonhealing wounds
- Cardiac risk factors

Physical examination should include the following:
- Palpation of pulses (brachial, radial, ulnar, femoral, popliteal, posterior tibial, and dorsalis pedis)
- Auscultation for abdominal, flank, and femoral bruits
- Inspection of feet

Diagnosis established by ABI <0.9 or other test (**Table 28**).

Table 28. **Management of PAD**		
Signs and Symptoms	Useful Tests	Treatment (see below)
Asymptomatic; diminished or absent peripheral pulses	ABI[a]	Risk factor reduction
Atypical leg pain	ABI, EABI[b]	Risk factor reduction, antiplatelet therapy
Claudication: exertional fatigue, discomfort, pain relieved by rest	ABI, EABI, Doppler ultrasound, pulse volume recording, segmental pressure measurement	Risk factor reduction, antiplatelet therapy, claudication therapy; consider endovascular or surgical revascularization if symptoms persist
Rest pain, nonhealing wound (see also p 258), gangrene	ABI, Doppler ultrasound, angiography (MRI, CT, or contrast)	Risk factor reduction, antiplatelet therapy, claudication therapy, endovascular or surgical revascularization

[a] Abnormal is <0.9; <0.4 is critical.
[b] Exercise treadmill test with ABI measurement

Treatment
Risk Factor Reduction
- Smoking cessation
- Lipid-lowering therapy (goal LDL <100 mg/dL, <70 mg/dL in those with rest pain or who are at very high risk (see **Table 22** and **Table 23**)
- BP control (goal <140/90 mmHg)
- Diabetes treatment (good foot care, HbA_{1c} <7%)

Antiplatelet Therapy
- ASA▲ 75–325 mg/d
- Clopidogrel *(Plavix)* 75 mg/d (T: 75] if no response or intolerant of ASA

Claudication Therapy
- Walking program (goal: 50 min of intermittent walking 3–5 ×/wk)
- Cilostazol▲ *(Pletal)* 100 mg q12h, 1 h before or 2 h after meals (contraindicated in patients with HF); second-line alternative therapy is pentoxifylline▲ *(Trental)* 400 mg q8h [T: 400]
- If ACEI not contraindicated, routine use is recommended to prevent adverse cardiovascular events in patients with claudication.

Table 29. Classification of Syncope

Cause	Frequency (%)	Features	Increased Risk of Death
Vasovagal	21	Preceded by lightheadedness, nausea, diaphoresis; recovery gradual, frequently with fatigue	No
Cardiac	10	Little or no warning before blackout, rapid and complete recovery	Yes
Orthostatic	9	Lightheaded prodrome after standing, recovery gradual	No
Medication-induced	7	Lightheaded prodrome, recovery gradual	No
Seizure	5	No warning, may have neurologic deficits, slow recovery	Yes
Stroke, TIA	4	Little or no warning, neurologic deficits	Yes
Other causes	8	Preceded by cough, micturition, or specific situation	No
Unknown	37	Any of the above	Yes

Source: Adapted from Soteriades ES, Evans JC, Larson MG, et al. Incidence and prognosis of syncope. *N Engl J Med* 2002;347:878–885.

Evaluation

- Focus hx on events before, during, and after loss of consciousness; hx of cardiac disease (significantly worsens prognosis of syncope of all causes); careful medication review.
- Focus on cardiovascular and neurologic systems in physical examination.
- ECG and orthostatic BP or pulse check for all patients.
- The following characteristics are associated with serious outcomes and likely require urgent/emergent further testing and monitoring: age >90 yr, male sex, abnormal ECG, hx of arrhythmia (ventricular tachycardia, symptomatic supraventricular tachycardia, third-degree or Mobitz II AV block, sinus pause >3 sec, symptomatic bradycardia), hx of HF, dyspnea, abnormal troponin I, SBP <90 mmHg or >160 mmHg.
- Additional testing as suggested by initial evaluation:
  - Ambulatory ECG monitoring for further evaluation of arrhythmia
  - Stress testing to investigate ischemic heart disease
  - Echocardiography to investigate structural heart disease
  - Electrophysiologic studies in patients with prior MI or structural heart disease
  - Tilt-table testing for suspected vasovagal cause
  - Head imaging, electroencephalogram for suspected neurologic cause
  - If suspected orthostatic cause, evaluation for Parkinson disease, autonomic neuropathy, diabetes mellitus, hypovolemia

Management

- Patients with cardiac syncope require immediate hospitalization on telemetry; exclude MI and PE.
- Strongly consider hospital admission for patients with syncope due to neurologic or unknown causes, particularly if concurrent heart disease.

- Patients with syncope due to vasovagal, orthostatic, medication-induced, or other causes can usually be managed as outpatients, particularly if there is no hx of heart disease.
- Treatment is correction of underlying cause.

ORTHOSTATIC (POSTURAL) HYPOTENSION
See also **Table 46**.

Evaluation and Assessment
- Associated with following symptoms usually after standing: lightheadedness, dizziness, syncope, blurred vision, diaphoresis, head or neck pain, decreased hearing
- Diagnosis: ≥20 mmHg drop in SBP or ≥10 mmHg in DBP within 3 min of rising from lying to standing
- Causes
  - Medications, including antihypertensives, phenothiazines, TCAs, MAOIs, anti-Parkinsonian drugs, PDE5 inhibitors (for erectile dysfunction)
  - Autonomic dysregulation (suggested by lack of compensatory rise in heart rate with postural hypotension): age-related decreased baroreceptor sensitivity, Parkinson disease and related disorders, peripheral neuropathy, prolonged bed rest
  - Hypovolemia
  - Anemia

Management
- Correct underlying disorder, particularly by discontinuing medications that could exacerbate hypotension
- Alter movement behavior: educate patients to rise slowly, flex calf and forearm muscles when standing, stand with one foot in front of other, avoid straining, and elevate head of bed
- Dietary changes: avoid alcohol, maintain adequate fluid intake, increase salt and caffeine intake
- Above-the-knee compression stockings (at least medium compression strength, eg, Jobst)
- Pharmacologic interventions:
  - First-line: fludrocortisone▲: 0.1–0.2 mg q8–24h [T: 0.1]; use with caution in patients with HF, cardiac disease, hypertension, renal disease, esophagitis, peptic ulcer disease, or ulcerative colitis
  - Midodrine▲ *(ProAmantine):* 2.5–10 mg q8–24h [T: 2.5, 5]; use with caution in patients with HTN, diabetes, urinary retention, renal disease, hepatic disease, glaucoma, BPH
  - Pyridostigmine▲ *(Mestinon):* 60 mg q24h [T: 60]; can be used in combination with midodrine 2.5–5 mg/d.
  - Caffeine: 1 cup of caffeinated coffee q8–12h; alternatively, caffeine tabs 100–200 mg q8–12h; useful for postprandial hypotension when taken with meals
  - Erythropoietin (see **Table 56**) can be useful for hypotension secondary to anemia if Hb <10 mg/dL

IMPLANTABLE CARDIAC DEFIBRILLATOR (ICD) PLACEMENT

Indications (consider life expectancy and comorbidities)

- Established:
  - Cardiac arrest due to ventricular fibrillation (VF) or ventricular tachycardia (VT)
  - Spontaneous sustained VT with structural heart disease
  - Spontaneous sustained VT without structural heart disease not alleviated by other treatments
  - Unexplained syncope with hemodynamically significant VF or VT inducible by electrophysiologic study when drug therapy is ineffective, not tolerated, or not preferred
  - Nonsustained VT, CAD, and inducible VF by electrophysiologic study that is not suppressed by Class I antiarrhythmic
  - LVEF ≤30%, NYHA Class II or III HF, and CAD ≥40 d after MI
  - ICD + biventricular pacing for advanced HF (NYHA Class III or IV), LVEF ≤35%, and QRS interval ≥120 millisec or mild HF (NYHA Class I or II), LVEF ≤30%, and QRS interval ≥130 millisec
- Less established: Nonischemic cardiomyopathy with LVEF ≤35% and either premature ventricular complexes or nonsustained VT

Contraindications

- Terminal illness with life expectancy <6 mo
- Unexplained syncope without inducible VT or VF and without structural heart disease
- VT or VF due to transient or easily reversible disorder
- End-stage HF (ACC/AHA Stage D) not awaiting cardiac transplant

Complications

- Surgical: infection (1%–2%), hematoma, pneumothorax
- Device-related: lead dislodgement or malfunction, connection problems, inadequate defibrillation threshold
- Therapy-related: frequent shocks (appropriate or inappropriate), acceleration of VT, anxiety and other psychological stress
- End-of-life planning: discuss and document the circumstances in which the patient would desire the ICD to be turned off. ICDs can be turned off by the cardiologist or the device manufacturer's representative.

DIAGNOSIS

Diagnostic Criteria—Adapted from *DSM-IV*

- Disturbed consciousness (ie, decreased attention, environmental awareness)
- Cognitive change (eg, memory deficit, disorientation, language disturbance) or perceptual disturbance (eg, visual illusions, hallucinations)
- Rapid onset (hours to days) and fluctuating daily course
- Evidence of a causal physical condition

Risk Factors

- Dementia greatly increases risk of delirium.
- Advanced age, comorbid physical problems (especially sleep deprivation, immobility, dehydration, pain, sensory impairment).

Evaluation

- Confusion Assessment Method (CAM): **Both** acute onset and fluctuating course **and** inattention **and either** disorganized thinking **or** altered level of consciousness (Inouye SK. *N Engl J Med* 2006;354[11]:1157–1165). For nonverbal patients, use CAM–ICU to assess attention and level of consciousness (Ely EW. *JAMA* 2001;286[21]:2703–2710).
- Assume reversibility unless proven otherwise.
- Thoroughly review prescription and OTC medications, and alcohol usage.
- Exclude infection and other medical causes.
- Laboratory studies may include CBC, electrolytes, LFTs, ammonia, thyroid function tests, renal function tests, serum albumin, B_{12}, serum calcium, serum glucose, UA, oxygen saturation, arterial blood gas levels, CXR, and ECG.
- Brain imaging and EEG typically not helpful unless there is evidence of cerebral trauma, possible stroke, focal neurologic signs, or seizure activity.

CAUSES

(Italicized type indicates the most common causes in older adults.)

Medications (see **Table 30** and **Table 31**)

- *Anticholinergics* (eg, diphenhydramine), TCAs (eg, amitriptyline, imipramine), antipsychotics (eg, chlorpromazine, thioridazine)
- Anti-inflammatory agents, including prednisone
- Benzodiazepines or alcohol—acute toxicity or withdrawal
- Cardiovascular (eg, digitalis, antihypertensives)
- Diuretics
- Lithium
- GI (eg, cimetidine, ranitidine)
- Opioid analgesics (especially meperidine)

Table 30. **Potentially Differentiating Features of Medication-induced Delirium**

Medication type	Early	Late
Anticholinergic	Visual impairment, dry mouth, constipation, urinary retention	↑ HR, mydriasis, ↓ bowel sounds
Serotonin syndrome	Tremor, diarrhea	Hyperreflexia, ↑ bowel sounds, diaphoretic
Neuroleptic malignant syndrome	↑ EPS	Marked rigidity, hyperthermia

Table 31. Anticholinergic Activity of Selected Medications

Low	Moderate	High
Cimetidine	Chlorpromazine	Amitriptyline
Citalopram	Darifenacin	Benztropine
Escitalopram	Desipramine	Clozapine
Fluoxetine	Diphenhydramine	Cyclobenzaprine
Haloperidol	Disopyramide	Dicyclomine
Lithium	Hydroxyzine	Doxepin
Mirtazapine	Fesoterodine	L-Hyoscyamine
Quetiapine	Nortriptyline	Thioridazine
Ranitidine	Olanzapine	Trihexyphenidyl
Temazepam	Oxybutynin	
	Paroxetine	
	Solifenacin	
	Tolterodine	
	Trospium	
	Venlafaxine	

Infections

Respiratory, skin, urinary tract, others

Metabolic Disorders

Acute blood loss, *dehydration, electrolyte imbalance*, end-organ failure (hepatic, renal), hyperglycemia, *hypoglycemia, hypoxia*

Cardiovascular

Arrhythmia, *HF, MI*, shock

Neurologic

CNS infections, head trauma, seizures, stroke, subdural hematoma, TIAs, tumors

Miscellaneous

Fecal impaction, *postoperative state*, sleep deprivation, urinary retention

PREVENTIVE MEASURES

Table 32. Preventive Measures for Delirium[a]

Target for Prevention	Intervention
Cognitive impairment	Orientation protocol: board with names, daily schedule, and reorienting communication Therapeutic activities: stimulating activities 3 times/d
Sleep deprivation	Nonpharmacologic: warm milk/herbal tea, music, massage Noise reduction: schedule adjustments and unit-wide noise reduction
Immobility	Early mobilization: ambulation or range of motion 3 times/d, minimal immobilizing equipment
Visual impairment	Visual aids and adaptive equipment
Hearing impairment	Amplification, cerumen disimpaction, special communication techniques
Dehydration	Early recognition and volume repletion
Infection, HF, hypoxia, pain	Identify and treat medical conditions

[a] May also be valuable for management

MANAGEMENT

Nonpharmacologic

- Ensure safety.
- Use families or sitters as first line.
- Use physical restraints only as last resort to maintain patient safety (eg, to prevent patient from pulling out tubes or catheters).

Pharmacologic

For acute agitation or aggression that impairs care or safety (other than delirium due to alcohol or benzodiazepine withdrawal), choose from one of the following:

- Haloperidol (the most often recommended and studied agent; controls symptoms and may reduce duration and severity of delirium)
  - Because of risk of QT_c prolongation, the IV route is not recommended. *Caution:* If the patient is taking other medications that prolong QT_c (see **Table 11**), D/C all if possible. Even oral or IM dosing may prolong QT_c. Obtain an ECG before the first dose (if possible) or as soon as the patient is calm enough to tolerate the procedure. If QT_c exceeds 500, *do not* administer any antipsychotic; all may prolong QT_c. If $QT_c >460$, correct any deficiency of Mg^{++} and K^+ and recheck.
  - Haloperidol *(Haldol)* 0.5–1 mg po [T: 0.5, 1, 2, 5, 10, 20; S: 2 mg/mL]; evaluate effect in 1–2 hr.
  - If patient is not able to take medications po, haloperidol 0.5–1 mg IM [5 mg/mL] (twice as potent as po, peak effect 20–40 min). Reevaluate q30–60min for continued troublesome agitation.
  - Double the dosage if initial dose is ineffective. Administer additional doses (IM dose q30min or oral dose q60min) until agitation is controlled. Rarely, additional doubling of the dosage is necessary. Most older patients respond to 1–2 mg total dose.
  - Calculate the total dose administered to achieve control of symptoms, and give half the equivalent oral dose the next day, divided for q12h administration. Hold a dose if sedation occurs.
  - Maintain effective dose for 2–3 d.
  - Slowly taper and D/C haloperidol over 3–5 d while monitoring for recurrence of symptoms. If necessary, continue the minimal dose necessary to control symptoms.
  - EPS will develop with prolonged use. If use exceeds 1 wk, switch to a second-generation antipsychotic agent.
- Quetiapine is the drug of choice for patients with Lewy body dementia, Parkinson disease, AIDS-related dementia, or EPS. Initial dosage 12.5–25 mg po daily or q12h, increase q2d as needed to a max of 100 mg/d (50 mg/d in frail older adults). Once symptoms are controlled, administer half the dose needed to control symptoms for 2–3 d; then taper as described above.
- Quetiapine 50 mg q12h with as-needed IV haloperidol may result in faster resolution of delirium and less agitation. Quetiapine may be increased by 50 mg q24h.

When delirium is due to alcohol or benzodiazepine withdrawal, use a benzodiazepine, eg, lorazepam in dosages of 0.5–2 mg IV q30–q60min or po q1–2h and titrated to effect. Validated scales are used to guide dosing of benzodiazepines in alcohol withdrawal (www.chce.research.va.gov/apps/PAWS/content/4.htm). Because these agents themselves may cause delirium, gradual withdrawal and discontinuation are desirable. If delirium is secondary to alcohol, also use thiamine at 100 mg/d (po, IM, or IV).

DEMENTIA

DEMENTIA SYNDROME
Definition
Chronic acquired decline in memory and in at least one other cognitive function (eg, language, visual-spatial, executive) sufficient to affect daily life.

Estimated Frequencies of Causes of Dementia
- AD: 60%–70%
- Other progressive disorders: 15%–30% (eg, vascular, Lewy body, frontotemporal)
- Completely reversible dementia (eg, drug toxicity, metabolic changes, thyroid disease, subdural hematoma, normal-pressure hydrocephalus): 2%–5%

EVALUATION
Although completely reversible dementia (eg, drug toxicity) is rare, identifying and treating secondary physical conditions may improve function.

- Hx: Obtain from family or other caregiver
- Physical and neurologic examination
- Assess functional status (p 286–287)
- Exclude depression (PHQ-9 [p 288], GDS [p 290])
- Evaluate mental status for attention, immediate and delayed recall, remote memory, and executive function. Quick screening tests may include Mini-Cog (p 285), number of animals named in 1 min (18 average; <10 markedly abnormal). If Mini-Cog is positive, use MMSE or Montreal Cognitive Assessment (MoCA [www.mocatest.org]).

Clinical Features Distinguishing AD and Other Types of Dementia
- AD: Memory, language, visual-spatial disturbances, indifference, delusions, agitation
- Frontotemporal dementia: Personality change, executive dysfunction, hyperorality, relative preservation of visual-spatial skills
- Lewy body dementia: visual hallucinations, delusions, EPS, fluctuating mental status, sensitivity to antipsychotic medications
- Vascular dementia: abrupt onset, stepwise deterioration, prominent aphasia, motor signs

Laboratory Testing
CBC, TSH, B_{12}, folate, serum calcium, liver and kidney function tests, electrolytes, serologic test for syphilis (selectively); genetic testing and commercial "Alzheimer blood tests" are not currently recommended for clinical use.

Neuroimaging
The likelihood of detecting structural lesions is increased with:
- Onset age <60 yr
- Focal (unexplained) neurologic signs or symptoms
- Abrupt onset or rapid decline (weeks to months)
- Predisposing conditions (eg, metastatic cancer or anticoagulants)

Neuroimaging may detect the 5% of cases with clinically significant structural lesions that would otherwise be missed.

FDG-PET scans approved by Medicare for atypical presentation or course of AD in which frontotemporal dementia diagnosis is suspected. See www.petscaninfo.com/portals/pat/medicare_guidelines_alzheimers.

DIAGNOSIS OF AD
- Dementia syndrome
- Gradual onset and continuing decline
- Not due to another physical, neurologic, or psychiatric condition or to medications
- Deficits not seen exclusively during delirium
- No validated biomarkers

PROGRESSION OF AD
2011 National Institute on Aging/Alzheimer's Association research criteria identify preclinical stages using PET and CSF biomarkers of $A\beta$ or neuronal injury.

Mild Cognitive Impairment (preclinical)   *MMSE 26–30; CDR 0.5; FAST 3; MoCA <26
- Report by patient or caregiver of memory loss
- Objective signs of memory impairment
- No functional impairment
- Mild construction, language, or executive dysfunction
- 6%–15% annual conversion rate to dementia syndrome
- Some cases of mild cognitive impairment may not progress to AD
- Treating vascular risk factors (hypertension, diabetes, high cholesterol) may reduce risk of progression to AD

Early, Mild Impairment (yr 1–3 from onset of symptoms)   *MMSE 21–25; CDR 1; FAST 4
- Disoriented to date
- Naming difficulties (anomia)
- Recent recall problems
- Mild difficulty copying figures
- Decreased insight
- Social withdrawal
- Irritability, mood change
- Problems managing finances

Middle, Moderate Impairment (yr 2–8)   *MMSE 11–20; CDR 2; FAST 5–6
- Disoriented to date, place
- Comprehension difficulties (aphasia)
- Impaired new learning
- Getting lost in familiar areas
- Impaired calculating skills
- Delusions, agitation, aggression
- Not cooking, shopping, banking
- Restless, anxious, depressed
- Problems with dressing, grooming

Late, Severe Impairment (yr 6–12)   *MMSE 0–10; CDR 3; FAST 7
- Nearly unintelligible verbal output
- Remote memory gone
- Unable to copy or write
- No longer grooming or dressing
- Incontinent
- Motor or verbal agitation

* MMSE = Mini-Mental State Examination; CDR = Clinical Dementia Rating Scale; FAST = Reisberg Functional Assessment Staging Scale (p 292); MoCA = Montreal Cognitive Assessment

Prognosis
- Among nursing-home residents with advanced dementia, 71% die within 6 mo of admission.
- Distressing conditions common in advanced dementia include pressure ulcers, constipation, pain, and shortness of breath.

NONCOGNITIVE SYMPTOMS

Psychotic Symptoms (eg, delusions, hallucinations)
- Seen in about 20% of AD patients
- Delusions may be paranoid (eg, people stealing things, spouse unfaithful)
- Hallucinations (~11% of patients) are more commonly visual

Depressive Symptoms
- Seen in up to 40% of AD patients; may precede onset of AD
- May cause acceleration of decline if untreated
- Suspect if patient stops eating or withdraws

Apathy
- High prevalence and persistence throughout course of AD
- Causes more impairment in ADL than expected for cognitive status
- High overlap with depressive symptoms but lacks depressive mood, guilt, and hopelessness

Agitation or Aggression
- Seen in up to 80% of patients with AD
- A leading cause of nursing-home admission
- Consider superimposed delirium or pain as a trigger

RISK AND PROTECTIVE FACTORS FOR DEMENTIA

Definite Risks	Possible Risks	Possible Protections
Age	Delirium	Antioxidants (eg, vitamin E, beta carotene)
APOE-E4 (whites)	Head trauma	
Atrial fibrillation	Heavy smoking	
Depression	Hypercholesterolemia	
Down syndrome	Hypertension	
Family history	Lower educational level	
	Other genes	
	Postmenopausal hormone therapy	

TREATMENT

Primary goals of treatment are to improve quality of life and maximize functional performance by enhancing cognition, mood, and behavior.

General Treatment Principles
- Identify and treat comorbid physical illnesses (eg, HTN, diabetes mellitus)
- Promote brain health by exercise, balanced diet, stress reduction
- Avoid anticholinergic medications, eg, benztropine, diphenhydramine, hydroxyzine, oxybutynin, TCAs, clozapine, thioridazine
- Set realistic goals
- Limit prn psychotropic medication use
- Specify and quantify target behaviors
- Maximize and maintain functioning

- Establish and maintain alliance with patient and family
- Assess and monitor psychiatric status
- Intervene to decrease hazards of wandering
- Advise patient and family concerning driving
- Advise family about sources of care and support, financial and legal issues
- Consider referral to hospice (FAST = 7 [p 292])
- Identify and examine context of behavior (is it harmful to patient or others) and environmental triggers (eg, overstimulation, unfamiliar surroundings, frustrating interactions); exclude underlying physical discomfort (eg, illnesses or medication); consider nonpharmacologic strategies.

Nonpharmacologic Approaches for Problem Behaviors

To improve function:
- Behavior modification, scheduled toileting, and prompted toileting (see p 133) for UI
- Graded assistance (as little help as possible to perform ADLs), practice, and positive reinforcement to increase independence

For problem behaviors:
- Music during meals, bathing
- Walking or light exercise
- Simulate family presence with video or audio tapes
- Pet therapy
- Speak at patient's comprehension level
- Bright light, "white" noise (ie, low-level, background noise)

Pharmacologic Treatment of Cognitive Dysfunction

- Patients with a diagnosis of mild or moderate AD should receive a trial of a cholinesterase inhibitor; donepezil also approved for severe AD (see **Table 33**).
  - Controlled data for cholinergic drugs compared with placebo for 1 yr show modest symptomatic benefit for cognition, mood, behavioral symptoms, and daily function; open trials demonstrate benefit for 3 yr.
  - Only 10%–25% of patients taking cholinesterase inhibitors show modest global improvement, but many more have less rapid cognitive decline.
  - Initial studies show benefits of these drugs for patients with dementia associated with Parkinson disease, Lewy body dementia, and vascular dementia.
  - Cholinesterase inhibitors have not been demonstrated to slow progression of mild cognitive impairment to dementia, but early treatment may help maintain function at higher level for longer periods.
  - Cholinesterase inhibitors may attenuate noncognitive symptoms and delay nursing-home placement.
  - Adverse events increase with higher dosing. Possible adverse events include nausea, vomiting, diarrhea, dyspepsia, anorexia, weight loss, leg cramps, bradycardia, syncope, insomnia, and agitation.
  - To evaluate response:
    - Elicit caregiver observations of patient's behavior (alertness, initiative) and follow functional status (ADLs [p 286] and IADLs [p 287]).
    - Follow cognitive status (eg, improved or stabilized) by caregiver's report or serial ratings of cognition (eg, Mini-Cog [p 285]; MMSE).

- Memantine *(Namenda)* demonstrated modest efficacy compared with placebo in moderate to severe AD as monotherapy and when combined with donepezil *(Aricept)*.
- D/C cognitive enhancers when FAST = 7 (see p 292).
- Vitamin E at 1000 IU q12h found to delay functional decline in AD (caution in those with cardiovascular disease because ≥400 IU may increase mortality).
- *Ginkgo biloba* is not generally recommended (see p 22).
- *Axona* (medium-chain triglyceride) has insufficient evidence to support its value in preventing or treating AD, and long-term effects are uncertain.

Table 33. Cognitive Enhancers

Medication	Formulations	Dosing (Metabolism)
Donepezil *(Aricept)* [a,b]	T: 5▲, 10▲, 23; ODT: 5, 10; S: 5 mg/mL	Start at 5 mg/d, increase to 10 mg/d after 1 mo (CYP2D6, -3A4); must be on 10 mg/d ≥3 mo to consider increasing to 23 mg/d in moderate to severe AD (L)
Galantamine▲ *(Razadyne)* [a,c]	T: 4, 8, 12; S: 4 mg/mL	Start at 4 mg q12h, increase to 8 mg q12h after 4 wk; recommended dosage 8 or 12 mg q12h (CYP2D6, -3A4) (L)
(Razadyne ER)	C: 8, 16, 24	Start at 1 capsule daily, preferably with food; titrate as above
Rivastigmine▲ *(Exelon)* [a]	C: 1.5, 3, 4.5, 6; S: 2 mg/mL; pch: 4.6, 9.5	Start at 1.5 mg q12h and gradually titrate up to minimally effective dosage of 3 mg q12h; continue up to 6 mg q12h as tolerated; for pch, start at 4.6 mg/d, may be increased after ≥ 4 wk to 9.5 mg/d (recommended effective dosage): retitrate if drug is stopped (K)
Memantine *(Namenda* [NMDA antagonist]) [b]	T: 5, 10	Start at 5 mg/d, increase by 5 mg at weekly intervals to max of 10 mg q12h; if CrCl <30 mL/min, max of 5 mg q12h (K)

[a] Cholinesterase inhibitors. Continue if improvement or stabilization occurs; stopping medications can lead to rapid decline.

[b] Approved by FDA for moderate to severe AD.

[c] Increased mortality found in controlled studies of mild cognitive impairment.

Treatment of Agitation

- Consider nonpharmacologic approaches first before pharmacologic treatment (see **Table 34**).
- Steps to reduce nonverbalized pain (see p 204).
- Cognitive enhancers may slow deterioration, and agitation may worsen if discontinued. Low doses of antipsychotic medications have limited role but may be necessary. Note this use is off-label and increases risk of death compared with placebo in patients with AD. CATIE-AD trial (*NEJM* 2006;355:1525–1538) showed modest treatment benefit compared with placebo for olanzapine and risperidone that was mitigated by greater EPS, sedation, and confusion. In this trial, quetiapine did not appear to be efficacious compared with placebo but caused greater sedation. See also **Table 95** and **Table 96**.
- CATIE-AD reported second-generation antipsychotics cause weight gain, particularly in women treated with olanzapine or quetiapine; olanzapine treatment was also associated with decreased HDL cholesterol.

Treatment of Apathy

- Assess and treat underlying depression.
- Cholinesterase inhibitors help.
- Methylphenidate (5–20 mg/d), very limited data, may cause agitation and psychosis.

Table 34. Pharmacologic Treatment of Agitation

Symptom	Medication	Dosage	Formulations
Agitation in context of psychosis	Aripiprazole[a] *(Abilify)*	2.5–12.5 mg/d	T: 5, 10, 15, 20, 30
	Olanzapine[a] *(Zyprexa) (Zydis)*	2.5–10 mg/d	T: 2.5, 5, 7.5, 10, 15, 20; ODT: 5, 10, 15, 20
	Quetiapine[a] *(Seroquel)*	12.5–100 mg/d	T: 25, 100, 200, 300
	Risperidone▲[a] *(Risperdal)*	0.25–3 mg/d	T: 0.25, 0.5, 1, 2, 3, 4; S: 1 mg/mL
Agitation in context of depression	SSRI, eg, citalopram▲ *(Celexa)*	10–30 mg/d	T: 20, 40; S: 2 mg/mL
Anxiety, mild to moderate irritability	Buspirone▲ *(BuSpar)*	15–60 mg/d[b]	T: 5, 7.5, 10, 15, 30
	Trazodone▲ *(Desyrel)*	50–100 mg/d[c]	T: 50, 100, 150, 300
Agitation or aggression unresponsive to first-line treatment	Carbamazepine▲ *(Tegretol)*	300–600 mg/d[d]	T: 200; ChT: 100; S: sus 100/5 mL
	Divalproex sodium▲ *(Depakote, Epival)*	500–1500 mg/d[e]	T: 125, 250, 500; S: syr 250 mg/mL; sprinkle capsule: 125
	Olanzapine[a,f] *(Zyprexa IntraMuscular)*	2.5–5 mg IM	Inj
Sexual aggression, impulse-control symptoms in men	Second-generation antipsychotic or divalproex▲	See dosages above	
	If no response, estrogen▲ *(Premarin)* **or**	0.625–1.25 mg/d	T: 0.3, 0.625, 0.9, 1.25, 2.5
	medroxyprogesterone▲ *(Depo-Provera)*	100 mg IM/wk	Inj

[a] Increased risk of mortality and cerebrovascular events compared with placebo; use with particular caution in patients with cerebrovascular disease or hypovolemia.

[b] Can be given q12h; allow 2–4 wk for adequate trial.

[c] Small divided daytime dosage and larger bedtime dosage; watch for sedation and orthostasis.

[d] Monitor serum levels; periodic CBCs, platelet counts secondary to agranulocytosis risk. Beware of drug-drug interactions.

[e] Can monitor serum levels; usually well tolerated; check CBC, platelets for agranulocytosis, thrombocytopenia risk in older adults.

[f] For acute use only; initial dose 2.5–5 mg, second dose (2.5–5 mg) can be given after 2 h, max of 3 injections in 24 h (max daily dose 20 mg); should not be administered for >3 consecutive days.

CAREGIVER ISSUES

- Over 50% develop depression.
- Physical illness, isolation, anxiety, and burnout are common.
- Intensive education and support of caregivers may delay institutionalization.
- Adult day care for patients and respite services may help.
- Alzheimer's Association offers support, education services (eg, Safe Return); chapters are located in major cities throughout US (see p 295 for telephone, Web site).
- Family Caregiver Alliance offers support, education, information for caregivers (see p 295 for telephone, Web site).

ADDITIONAL REFERENCE

Blennow K, deLeon MJ, Zetterberg H. Alzheimer's disease. *Lancet* 2006; 368(9533):387–403.

EVALUATION AND ASSESSMENT

Recognizing and diagnosing late-life depression can be difficult. Older adults may complain of lack of energy or other somatic symptoms, attribute symptoms to old age or other physical conditions, or neglect to mention them to a health care professional.

Consider screening with Patient Health Questionnaire 2 (PHQ-2):

• Over the past 2 wk, have you often had little interest or pleasure in doing things?

• Over the past 2 wk, have you often been bothered by feeling down, depressed, or hopeless?

Score each item: 0 = not at all, 1 = several days, 2 = more than half the days, 3 = nearly every day; a score ≥3 indicates high probability of depressive disorder.

Follow-up and/or assess treatment with structured self-assessment scale such as the GDS (see p 290) or the PHQ-9 (see p 288).

Medical Evaluation

TSH, B_{12}, calcium, liver and kidney function tests, electrolytes, UA, CBC

DSM-IV Criteria for Major Depressive Episode (Abbreviated)

Five or more of the following symptoms have been present during the same 2-wk period and represent a change from previous functioning; at least one of the symptoms is either depressed mood *or* loss of interest or pleasure.

• Depressed mood

• Loss of interest or pleasure in activities

• Significant weight loss or gain (not intentional), or decrease or increase in appetite

• Insomnia or hypersomnia

• Psychomotor agitation or retardation

• Fatigue or loss of energy

• Feelings of worthlessness or excessive or inappropriate guilt

• Diminished ability to think or concentrate, or indecisiveness

• Recurrent thoughts of death; suicidal ideation, attempt, or plan

The *DSM-IV* criteria are not specific for older adults; cognitive symptoms may be more prominent.

Subsyndromal Depression

In older adults, subsyndromal depression may actually reflect major depression not diagnosed by current diagnostic criteria and may require pharmacologic and nonpharmacologic intervention. Subsyndromal depression does not meet full criteria for major depressive disorder and may include adjustment disorders and milder depression with anxiety symptoms but can be serious and associated with functional impairment.

MANAGEMENT

Treatment should be individualized on the basis of hx, past response, and severity of illness as well as concurrent illnesses.

Nonpharmacologic

For mild to moderate depression or in combination with pharmacotherapy: cognitive-behavioral therapy, interpersonal therapy, problem-solving therapy, or repetitive transcranial magnetic stimulation (rTMS) (see p 72).

For severe or psychotic depression, consider electroconvulsive therapy (ECT) (see p 71).

Pharmacologic

For mild, moderate, or severe depression: the duration of therapy should be at least 6–12 mo after remission for patients experiencing their first depressive episode. Most older adults with major depression require maintenance antidepressant therapy. Ensure adequate initial trial of 4–6 wk after titrating up to therapeutic dosage; if inadequate response, consider switching to a different first-line agent or second-line therapy or psychiatric referral/consult. Combining antidepressants can lead to significant adverse effects. SSRIs may increase acute stroke risk; low initial dosages and monitoring is recommended, especially in patients at risk of stroke.

Choosing an Antidepressant (see **Table 35** and list on p 71)

First-line Therapy: SSRI

Second-line Therapy: Consider venlafaxine▲, duloxetine, mirtazapine▲, or bupropion▲.

Third-line Therapy: Consider augmentation of first- or second-line antidepressants with aripiprazole or quetiapine, or SSRI with buspirone▲ or bupropion▲.

Table 35. Antidepressants Used for Older Adults

Class, Medication	Initial Dosage	Usual Dosage	Formulations	Comments (Metabolism, Excretion)
SSRIs				*Class adverse events:* EPS, hyponatremia, increased risk of upper GI bleeding, suicide (early in treatment), lower BMD and fragility fractures, risk of toxicity if methylene blue or linezolid co-administered (L, K [10%])
Citalopram▲ *(Celexa)*	10–20 mg qam	20 mg/d	T: 20, 40, 60; S: 5 mg/10 mL	20 mg/d is max dosage in adults >60 yr old
Escitalopram *(Lexapro)*	10 mg/d	10–20 mg/d	T: 10, 20	
Fluoxetine▲ *(Prozac)*	5 mg qam	5–60 mg/d	T: 10; C: 10, 20, 40; S: 20 mg/5 mL; C: SR 90 (weekly dose)	Long half-lives of parent and active metabolite may allow for less frequent dosing; may cause more insomnia than other SSRIs; CYP2D6, -2C9, -3A4 inhibitor (L)
Fluvoxamine▲ *(Luvox)*	25 mg qhs	100–300 mg/d	T: 25, 50, 100	Not approved as an antidepressant in US; greater likelihood of GI adverse events; CYP1A2, -3A4 inhibitor (L)
Paroxetine▲ *(Paxil)*	5 mg	10–40 mg/d	T: 10, 20, 30, 40	Helpful if anxiety symptoms are prominent; increased risk of withdrawal symptoms (dizziness); anticholinergic adverse events; CYP2D6 inhibitor (L)

(cont.)

DEPRESSION 69

| Table 35. Antidepressants Used for Older Adults (cont.) |

Class, Medication	Initial Dosage	Usual Dosage	Formulations	Comments (Metabolism, Excretion)
(Paxil CR)	12.5 mg/d	12.5–37.5 mg/d	T: ER 12.5, 25, 37.5; S: 10 mg/5 mL	Increase by 12.5 mg/d no faster than once a week (L)
Sertraline▲ *(Zoloft)*	25 mg qam	50–200 mg/d	T: 25, 50, 100; S: 20 mg/mL	Greater likelihood of GI adverse events (L)
Additional Medications				
Bupropion▲ *(Wellbutrin)*	37.5–50 mg q12h	75–150 mg q12h	T: 75, 100	Consider for SSRI, TCA nonresponders; safe in HF; may be stimulating; can lower seizure threshold (L)
(Wellbutrin SR▲, Zyban▲)	100 mg q12h or q24h	100–150 mg q12h	T:100, 150, 200	
(Wellbutrin XL)	150 mg/d	300 mg/d	T: 150, 300	
Methylphenidate▲ *(Ritalin)*	2.5–5 mg at 7 AM and noon	5–10 mg at 7 AM and noon	T: 5, 10, 20	Short-term treatment of depression or apathy in physically ill older adults; used as an adjunct (L)
Mirtazapine▲ *(Remeron)*	15 mg qhs	15–45 mg/d	T: 15, 30, 45	May increase appetite; sedating; oral disintegrating tab (SolTab) available (L)
Vilazodone *(Viibryd)*	10 mg/d for 7 d, then 20 mg/d	40 mg/d	T: 10, 20, 40	Metabolized by CYP3A4; limited geriatric data; adverse events: diarrhea and nausea
TCAs				
◆Desipramine▲ *(Norpramin)*	10–25 mg qhs	50–150 mg/d	T: 10, 25, 50, 75, 100, 150	Therapeutic serum level >115 ng/mL (L)
◆Nortriptyline▲ *(Aventyl, Pamelor)*	10–25 mg qhs	75–150 mg/d	C: 10, 25, 50, 75; S: 10 mg/5 mL	Therapeutic window (50–150 ng/mL) (L)
SNRIs				
◆Duloxetine *(Cymbalta)*	20 mg/d, then 20 mg q12h	40–60 mg q24h or 30 mg q12h	C: 20, 30, 60	Most common adverse events: nausea, dry mouth, constipation, diarrhea, urinary hesitancy; reduce dosage if CrCl 30–60 mL/min; contra-indicated if CrCl <30 mL/min (L)

(cont.)

Table 35. Antidepressants Used for Older Adults (cont.)

Class, Medication	Initial Dosage	Usual Dosage	Formulations	Comments (Metabolism, Excretion)
Venlafaxine▲ *(Effexor)*	25–50 mg q12h	75–225 mg/d in divided doses	T: 25, 37.5, 50, 75, 100	Low anticholinergic activity; minimal sedation and hypotension; may increase BP and QT_C; may be useful when somatic pain present; EPS, withdrawal symptoms, hyponatremia (L)
(Effexor XR)	75 mg qam	75–225 mg/d	C: 37.5, 75, 150	Same as above
Desvenlafaxine *(Pristiq)*	50 mg/d	50 mg; max 400 mg	SR tab: 50, 100	Active metabolite of venlafaxine; adjust dosage when CrCl <30 mL/min (L, K 45%)

◆ = Also has primary indication for neuropathic pain.

Antidepressants to Avoid in Older Adults

- Amitriptyline▲ (eg, *Elavil):* anticholinergic, sedating, hypotensive
- Amoxapine▲ *(Asendin):* anticholinergic, sedating, hypotensive; also associated with EPS, tardive dyskinesia, and neuroleptic malignant syndrome
- Doxepin▲ (eg, *Sinequan):* anticholinergic, sedating, hypotensive
- Imipramine▲ *(Tofranil):* anticholinergic, sedating, hypotensive
- Maprotiline▲ *(Ludiomil):* seizures, rashes
- Protriptyline▲ *(Vivactil):* very anticholinergic; can be stimulating
- St. John's wort: drug interactions, photosensitivity, hypomania
- Trimipramine *(Surmontil):* anticholinergic, sedating, hypotensive

Electroconvulsive Therapy (ECT)

Generally safe and very effective. Potential complications include temporary confusion, arrhythmias, aspiration, falls.

Indications: Severe depression when a rapid onset of response is necessary; when depression is resistant to drug therapy; for patients who are unable to tolerate antidepressants, have previous response to ECT, have psychotic depression, severe catatonia, or depression with Parkinson disease.

Evaluation: Before ECT, perform CXR, ECG, serum electrolytes, and cardiac examination. Additional tests (eg, stress test, neuroimaging, EEG) are used selectively.

Contraindications:

- Increased intracranial pressure
- Intracranial tumor
- MI within 3 mo (relative)
- Stroke within 1 mo (relative)

Consider Maintenance ECT:

- Hx of ECT-responsive illness
- Resistance or intolerance to medications alone
- Serious medical comorbidity
- More effective than pharmacotherapy after successful ECT

Repetitive Transcranial Magnetic Stimulation (rTMS)

- Series of magnetic pulses directed to brain at frequency of 1–20 stimulations per sec. Each treatment session lasts ~30 min, and a full course of treatment may be as long as 30 sessions.
- Placebo-controlled studies have demonstrated moderate effect sizes for treatment-resistant depression in younger adults and appears safe with minimal adverse effects.
- Limited experience with rTMS in treatment-resistant late-life depression; rTMS treatment parameters may need to be optimized to address age-related changes such as prefrontal cortical atrophy.

Depression and Parkinson Disease

Patients with Parkinson disease and depression may benefit more from nortriptyline than SSRIs. Pramipexole may also reduce depressive symptoms independent of effect on motor symptoms. See also p 192.

Psychotic Depression

- Psychosis accompanying major depression; increased disability and mortality
- ECT treatment of choice
- Olanzapine 15–20 mg/d added to sertraline 150–200 mg/d significantly improves remission rate vs placebo.

BIPOLAR DISORDER

See **Table 36**.

- 5%–19% of mood disorders in older adults.
- Usually begins in early adulthood, family hx.
- 10% may develop after age 50.
- Distinct period of abnormally and persistently elevated, expansive, or irritable mood for longer than 1 wk.
- Symptoms may include racing thoughts, pressured speech, decreased need for sleep, distractibility, grandiose delusions.
- A single manic episode is sufficient for a diagnosis if secondary causes are excluded.
- Late-onset mania may be secondary to head trauma, stroke, delirium, other neurologic disorders, alcohol abuse, or medications (eg, corticosteroids, L-dopa, thyroxine).
- Use aripiprazole, olanzapine, quetiapine, risperidone▲, or ziprasidone for acute mania (see **Table 95**) and D/C antidepressants if taking.
- If depression emerges in bipolar disorder, lamotrigine▲ may be helpful.
- Initiate long-term treatment (see **Table 37**) as soon as patient is able to comply with oral therapy.

Table 36. Medications for Management of Bipolar Disorders

Medication	Mania		Depression	
	Acute	*Maintenance*	*Acute*	*Maintenance*
Second-generation antipsychotics	All +	Aripiprazole + Olanzapine +/−	Quetiapine + Olanzapine +/−	Olanzapine +/−
Mood stabilizers				
Lithium▲	+	+	+	+
Valproate▲	+	+/−	−	+/−
Lamotrigine▲	−	+/−	+	+
Carbamazepine▲	+	+/−	?	+/−
Antidepressants				
SSRIs	Avoid	Avoid	+	+
TCAs	Avoid	Avoid	−	−

Note: + = evidence to support use; +/− = some evidence to support use; − = evidence does not support use; ? = has not been studied

Table 37. Long-term Treatment of Bipolar Disorders*

Medication	Initial Dosage	Usual Dosage	Formulation	Comments
Lithium▲ *(Eskalith, Eskalith CR, Lithobid)*	150 mg/d	300–900 mg/d Levels 0.4–0.8 mEq/L	T: 300; T: ER 300; C: 150, 300, 600; syr 300 mg/mL	Risk of CNS toxicity; cognitive impairment; hypothyroidism; interactions with diuretics, ACEIs, calcium channel blockers, NSAIDs
Carbamazepine▲ *(Tegretol, Tegretol XR)*	100 mg q12h	800–1200 mg/d Levels 4–12 mcg/L	T: 100, 200, 400	Many drug interactions; may cause SIADH; risk of leukopenia, neutropenia, agranulocytosis, thrombocytopenia; monitor CBC; drowsiness, dizziness
Valproic acid▲ *(Depacon, Depakene, Depakote)*	125 mg q12h	750 mg/d in divided doses Levels 50–125 mcg/L	T: 125, 250, 500	Can cause weight gain, tremor, several drug interactions; risk of hepatotoxicity, pancreatitis, neutropenia, thrombocytopenia; monitor LFTs and platelets
Lamotrigine▲ *(Lamictal)*	25 mg/d	100–200 mg/d	T: 25, 100, 150, 200	D/C if rash; interaction with valproate (when used together, begin at 25 mg q48h, titrate to 25–100 mg q12h); prolongs PR interval; somnolence, headache common

*Limited evidence base in older adults. See www.healthquality.va.gov. (See also **Table 79**.)

DERMATOLOGIC CONDITIONS

DERMATOLOGIC CONDITIONS COMMON IN OLDER ADULTS

For numerous dermatologic images, see http://hardinmd.lib.uiowa.edu/derm.html.

Actinic Keratosis

Erythematous, flat, rough, scaly papules 2–6 mm; may be easier felt than seen; precancerous (can develop into squamous or basal cell carcinoma); cutaneous horn may develop; affects sun-exposed areas, including lips (actinic cheilitis)

Risk Factors: UV light exposure (amount and intensity), increased age, fair coloring, immunosuppression

Prevention: Limit UV light exposure, use sunscreen with UVA and UVB coverage, wear protective clothing

Treatment

- Cryosurgery
- Topical 5-fluorouracil *(Carac* crm 0.5% daily × 4 wk, *Efudex* crm 5% q12h × 2–4 wk, *Fluoroplex* crm 1% q12h × 2–6 wk) to entire area affected
- Aminolevulinic acid *(Levulan Kerastick* 20%) applied to lesions with blue light illumination after 14–18 h, repeat in 8 wk
- Curettage with or without electrosurgery
- Chemical peels, dermabrasion, laser treatments

Basal Cell Carcinoma

Can affect any body surface exposed to the sun, most often head and neck

Types

- Nodular: pearly papule or nodule over telangiectases with a rolled border; may contain melanin
- Superficial: scaly erythematous patch or plaque, may contain melanin
- Morpheaform: indurated, whitish, scar-like plaque with indistinct margins

Risk Factors

- Exposure to UV radiation, especially intense intermittent exposure during childhood or adolescence
- Physical factors: fair skin, light eye color, red or blonde hair
- Exposure to ionizing radiation, arsenic, psoralen, UV-A radiation, smoking
- Immunosuppression (eg, after solid-organ transplant)

Prevention: Avoid sun exposure, use sunscreen with UVA and UVB coverage, wear protective clothing

Treatment: (localized control)

- Surgical: Mohs micrographic surgery, cryosurgery, excision, curettage and electrodessication
- Nonsurgical: radiotherapy, imiquimod 5% crm *(Aldara)* applied daily 5 d/wk × 6 wk (not for use on face, hands, or feet); photodynamic therapy

Candidiasis

Erythema, pustules, or cheesy, whitish matter in body folds; satellite lesions

Treatment: See intertrigo; antifungal powders (see **Table 38**)

Cellulitis

Ill-defined erythema, pain, blisters and exudates; most often affects lower dermis and subcutaneous tissue, commonly the legs; group A streptococci and *Staphylococcus aureus* most frequent pathogens

Treatment

- Antistaphylococcal penicillin, amoxicillin-clavulanate▲ × 10 d
- Macrolide (eg, erythromycin▲), 1st-generation cephalosporin (eg, cephalexin▲), or tetracycline▲ if penicillin allergy

Erysipelas

Bright red, edematous, and tender with unilateral distribution; orange peel appearance; well-demarcated border with vesicles and bullae; affects lower dermis and subcutaneous tissue, face and legs

Treatment: Penicillin; erythromycin or cephalosporin if penicillin allergy

Folliculitis

Multiple small, erythematous papules and pustules surrounding a hair; most often affects areas with coarse, short hair, ie, neck, beard, buttocks, thighs

Treatment

- Mild localized cases—topical antibiotic: mupirocin 2%▲ *(Bactroban)*, erythromycin, or clindamycin
- Extensive or severe cases—oral antistaphylococcal penicillin, amoxicillin-clavulanate, or erythromycin

Impetigo

Very contagious; nonbullous and bullous variants; honey-colored crusts on face around nose and mouth

Treatment

- Small, localized lesions: topical mupirocin 2%▲ *(Bactroban)* q8h × 7–10 d, topical retapamulin 1% oint *(Altabax)* q12h × 5 d
- Widespread: oral antistaphylococcal penicillin, erythromycin, or a cephalosporin × 10 d

Intertrigo

Moist, erythematous lesions with local superficial skin loss; satellite lesions caused by *Candida*; can affect any place two skin surfaces rest against one another (eg, under breasts, between toes)

Treatment

- Keep area dry.
- Topical antifungals, absorbent pwd, 1%–2% hydrocortisone▲ or 0.1% triamcinolone▲ crm q12h × 1–2 d if inflamed

Melanoma

Less common than nonmelanoma lesions; usually asymptomatic

Clinical Features

Asymmetry: a line down the center of the lesions does not create a mirror image

Border: irregular, ragged, fuzzy, or scalloped

Color: nonuniform throughout the lesion

Diameter: >6 mm (considered relatively insensitive as an independent factor)

Types

- Lentigo maligna: most often located on atrophic, sun-damaged skin; irregular-shaped tan or brown macule; slow growing
- Superficial spreading: occur anywhere; irregular-shaped macule, papule, or plaque; coloration varies
- Nodular: a rapidly growing, often black or gray papule or nodule
- Acral lentiginous: located on the palms, soles, or nail beds; dark brown or black patch; more common in Hispanic, black, and Asian individuals

Risk Factors

- Very fair skin type
- Family hx
- Dysplastic or numerous nevi
- Sun exposure; blistering sunburns as a child

Prevention: Avoid sun exposure, use sunscreen with UVA and UVB coverage, wear protective clothing

Treatment: Surgical excision

Neurodermatitis

Generalized or localized itching, redness, scaling; can affect any skin surface

Treatment: Mid- to higher-potency topical corticosteroids (**Table 39**); exclude other causes, eg, allergies, irritants, xerosis

Onychomycosis

Thickening and discoloration; affects nails *(Tinea unguium)*

Treatment: Obtain nail specimens for laboratory culture to confirm diagnosis before prescribing itraconazole or terbinafine.

- Itraconazole▲ *(Sporanox* [C: 100; S: 100 mg/mL]), contraindicated in HF (L)
  - Toenails: 200 mg po q24h × 3 mo—23% complete cure rate (negative mycologic analysis and normal nail) reported with this regimen, or 200 mg po q12h × 1 wk/mo × 3 mo
  - Fingernails: 200 mg po q12h × 1 wk/mo × 2 mo
- Fluconazole▲ *(Diflucan* [T: 50, 100, 150, 200; S: 10, 40 mg/mL]) (L)
  - Toenails: 150 or 300 mg po/wk × 6–12 mo
  - Fingernails: 150 or 300 mg po/wk × 3–6 mo
- Terbinafine▲ *(Lamisil* [T: 250]), avoid if CrCl <50 mL/min
  - Toenails: 250 mg po q24h × 12 wk—48% complete cure rate reported with this regimen
  - Fingernails: 250 mg po q24h × 6 wk
- Ciclopirox▲ *(Loprox, Penlac):* Toenails and fingernails—apply lacquer q12h to nails and adjacent skin; remove with alcohol q7d—8% complete cure rate reported with this regimen
- Mentholatum (eg, *Vicks VapoRub)* applied 2–3 ×/d for several months has been reported as a treatment for fungal infections of the nail but has not been compared with marketed treatments or placebo.

Psoriasis

Well-defined, erythematous plaques covered with silver scales; severity varies; can affect all skin areas, nails (pitting)

Treatment

- Topical corticosteroids, UV light, PUVA, methotrexate, cyclosporine, etretinate, sulfasalazine, anthralin preparations and tar + 1%–4% salicylic acid
- Calcipotriene for nonfacial areas

Rosacea

Vascular and follicular dilatation; mild to moderate; can accompany seborrhea; can affect face (nose, chin, cheeks, forehead) or eyes (dryness, blepharitis, conjunctivitis)

Prevention: Avoid triggers (stress, prolonged sun exposure and exercise, hot and humid environment, alcohol, hot drinks, spicy foods); may be worsened by vasodilators, niacin, or topical corticosteroids. Wear sunscreen with UVA and UVB coverage (SPF ≥15) or sunblock with titanium and zinc oxide. See www.rosacea.org.

Treatment

- Topical (for mild cases and maintenance)
  - Azelaic acid 15% gel *(Finacea)* q12–24 h or 20% crm *(Azelex, Finevin)* q12h
  - Benzoyl peroxide 2.5, 5, 10% crm, gel, wash, soap q12–24h
  - Metronidazole 0.75% crm▲ *(MetroCream)* q12h or 1% crm or gel *(Noritate, MetroGel)* q24h
  - Sodium sulfacetamide 10% + sulfa 5% (*Rosula* aqueous gel, *Clenia* crm, foaming wash) q12–24h, avoid if sulfa allergy or kidney disease (K)
  - Erythromycin 2% sol▲ q12h
  - Tretinoin▲ 0.025% crm or liq, 0.01% gel qhs
- Oral (for moderate to severe papular-pustular rosacea)
  - Tetracycline▲ 500 mg q8–12h × 6–12 wk
  - Doxycycline▲ 50–100 mg q12–24h × 6–12 wk
  - Minocycline▲ 50–100 mg q12h × 6–12 wk
  - Clarithromycin▲ 250–500 mg q12h × 6–12 wk
  - Metronidazole▲ 200 mg q12–24h × 4–6 wk
  - Erythromycin▲ 250–500 mg q12–24h × 6–12 wk
  - Azithromycin▲ 250–500 mg q24h × 6–12 wk

Scabies

Burrows, erythematous papules or rash, dry or scaly skin, pruritus (worse at night); spread by close, skin-to-skin or sexual contact; can affect interdigital webs, flexor aspects of wrists, axillae, umbilicus, nipples, genitalia

Treatment

- Infestation can result in epidemics; treat all contacts and treat environment
- Oatmeal baths, topical corticosteroids, or emollient creams for symptom relief
- Apply topical products from head to toe:
  - Permethrin 5% crm▲ *(Elimite)*, wash off after 8–14 h, repeat in 7–10 d if symptomatic or if live mites were found.
  - Lindane 1% crm▲ *(K-well, Scabene)*, wash off after 8–12 h
  - Crotamiton 10% crm *(Eurax)*, less effective, leave on 48 h, repeat in 7–10 d if necessary
  - Ivermectin *(Stromectol)* 200 mcg/kg po, may repeat once in 1 or 2 wk [T: 3, 6]

Seborrheic Dermatitis

Greasy, yellow scales with or without erythematous base; common in Parkinson disease and in debilitated patients; can affect nasal labial folds, eyebrows, hairline, sideburns, posterior auriculare and midchest

Treatment
- Hydrocortisone 1% or 2% crm▲ q12h or triamcinolone 0.1% oint q12h × 2 wk
- Scalp: shampoo containing selenium sulfide, zinc, or tar
- Ketoconazole 2% crm▲ for severe conditions if *Pityrosporum orbiculare* infection suspected

Skin Maceration
Erythema; abraded, excoriated skin; blisters; white and silver patches; can affect any area constantly in contact with moisture, covered by occlusive dressing or bandage; skin folds, groin, buttocks

Prevention and Treatment
- Eliminate cause of moisture.
  - Toileting program for incontinence (p 134)
  - Condom catheter
  - Indwelling catheter (reserve for most intractable conditions)
  - Fecal incontinence collector
- Protect skin from moisture.
  - Clean gently with mild soap after each incontinent episode.
  - Apply moisture barrier (eg, *Vaseline, Proshield, Smooth and Cool, Calmoseptine*).
  - Use disposable briefs that wick moisture from the skin; use linen incontinence pads when disposable briefs worsen perineal dermatitis.

Urticaria
Hives
- Uniform, red edematous plaques surrounded by white halos, can affect any skin surface
- Treatment
  - Identify cause.
  - Oral H$_1$ antihistamines (see **Table 102**) or oral H$_2$ antihistamines (see **Table 47**)
  - Oral glucocorticoids (eg, prednisone 40 mg q24h)
  - Doxepin▲ (po or topical *Zonalon* 5%) for refractory cases

Angioedema
- Larger, deeper than hives; can affect lips, eyelids, tongue, larynx, GI tract
- Treatment
  - Oral H$_1$ antihistamines (see **Table 102**)
  - Oral glucocorticoids
  - For severe reactions, epinephrine 0.3 mL of a 1:1000 dilution *(EpiPen)* SC

Cholinergic
- Round, red papular wheals; can affect any skin surface
- Treatment
  - Hot shower may relieve itching
  - Oral H$_1$ antihistamines (see **Table 102**) 1 h before exercise

Xerosis
Dull, rough, flaky, cracked; nummular; can affect all skin surfaces
Treatment
- Increase humidity

- Avoid excess bathing and use of bath oils, which can lead to falls from slippery feet
- Tepid water in baths or showers
- Oatmeal baths
- Apply emollient oint (eg, *Aquaphor)* or crm (eg, *Eucerin)* immediately after bathing
- Hydrocortisone 1% oint

DERMATOLOGIC MEDICATIONS

Table 38. Topical Antifungal Medications

Medication	Formulation	Dermatologic Indications	Dosing Frequency
Butenafine *(Lotrimin ultra*, Mentax)*	1% crm	*Tinea pedis, T cruris, T corpis, T versicolor*	q24h × 2–4 wk
Ciclopirox▲ *(Loprox, Penlac)*	0.77% crm, gel, lot, sus; 1% shp; 8% lacquer	*Tinea pedis, T cruris, T corpis, T versicolor;* candidiasis; scalp seborrhea; onychomycosis	2 times/wk × 4 wk; shp 3 ×/wk; lacquer qhs
Clotrimazole▲* *(Cruex, Mycelex, others)*	1% crm, sol	Candidiasis, dermatophytoses; superficial mycoses	q12h
Econazole▲ nitrate *(Spectazole)*	1% crm	Candidiasis; *Tinea cruris, T corpis, T versicolor*	q24h × 2–4 wk
Ketoconazole▲ *(Nizoral, Nizoral A-D*)*	2% crm, 1% shp	Candidiasis; seborrhea; *Tinea cruris, T corpis, T versicolor*	q12–24h; shp 2 ×/wk
Miconazole▲* (eg, *Micatin, Monistat-Derm)*	2% crm, lot, pwd, spr, tinc	*Tinea cruris, T corpis, T pedis*	q12h × 2–4 wk
Naftifine *(Naftin)*	1% crm, gel	*Tinea cruris, T corpis, T pedis*	crm; gel q12h
Nystatin▲ *(Mycostatin, Nilstat, Nystex)*	100,000 units/g crm, oint, pwd	Mucocutaneous candidiasis	q8–12h up to 4 wk
Oxiconazole *(Oxistat)*	1% crm, lot	*Tinea corpis, T cruris, T pedis, T versicolor*	q12–24h × 2–4 wk
Sertaconazole *(Ertaczo)*	2% crm	*Tinea pedis*	q12h × 4 wk
Sulconazole *(Exelderm)*	1% crm, sol	*Tinea corpis, T cruris,*	q12–24h × 3–4 wk
Terbinafine▲ *(Lamisil, LamisilAT*)*	1% crm▲, sol	*Tinea cruris, T corpis, T pedis, T versicolor*	q12h × 1–4 wk
Tolnaftate▲* *(Absorbine Jr. Antifungal, Tinactin, others)*	1% crm▲, gel, S▲, pwd▲, spr	*Tinea cruris, T corpis, T pedis*	q12h × 2–4 wk
Triacetin *(Myco–Nail*)*	25% sol	*Tinea pedis*	q12h, continue for 7d after symptoms have resolved
Undecylenic acid *(Fungi–Nail*)*	25% sol	*Tinea pedis*, ringworm (except nails and scalp)	q12h × 4 wk

*OTC

Table 39. Topical Corticosteroids

Medication	Strength and Formulations	Frequency of Application
Lowest Potency		
Hydrocortisone▲*	0.5%, 1%, 2.5% crm, oint, lot, sol	q6–8h
Low Potency		
Alclometasone dipropionate▲* (Aclovate)	0.05% crm, oint	q8–12h
Desonide▲ (DesOwen, Tridesilon)	0.05% crm, oint	q6–12h
Fluocinolone acetonide▲ (Synalar)	0.01% crm, sol	q6–12h
Mid-potency		
Betamethasone dipropionate▲ (Diprosone)	0.05% lot	q6–12h
Betamethasone valerate▲ (Valisone)	0.1% crm	q6–12h
Clocortolone pivalate▲ (Cloderm)	0.1% crm	q6–24h
Desoximetasone▲ (Topicort)	0.05% crm	q12h
Fluocinolone acetonide▲ (Synalar)	0.025% crm, oint	q6–12h
Flurandrenolide (Cordran)	0.05% crm, oint, lot, tape	q12–24h
Fluticasone propionate▲ (Cutivate)	0.05% crm, 0.005% oint	q12h
Hydrocortisone butyrate (Locoid)	0.1% oint	q12–24h
Hydrocortisone valerate▲ (Westcort)	0.2% crm, oint	q6–8h
Mometasone furoate▲* (Elocon)	0.1% crm, lot, oint	q24h
Prednicarbate▲ (Dermatop)	0.1% crm, lot	q12h
Triamcinolone acetonide▲ (Aristocort, Kenalog)	0.025%, 0.1% crm, oint, lot	q8–12h
Higher Potency		
Amcinonide▲ (Cyclocort)	0.1%, crm, oint, lot	q8–12h
Betamethasone dipropionate▲ (Diprolene AF)	0.05% augmented crm	q6–12h
Betamethasone dipropionate▲ (Diprosone)	0.05%, crm, oint	q6–12h
Betamethasone valerate▲ (Valisone)	0.1% oint	q6–12h
Desoximetasone▲ (Topicort)	0.25% crm, oint; 0.05% gel	q12h
Diflorasone diacetate▲ (Florone, Maxiflor)	0.05%, crm, oint	q6–12h
Fluocinonide▲ (Lidex)	0.05% crm, oint, gel	q6–12h
Halcinonide▲ (Halog)	0.1% crm, oint	q8–24h
Triamcinolone acetate▲	0.5% crm, spr	q8–12h
Super Potency		
Betamethasone dipropionate▲ (Diprolene)	0.05% oint, lot, gel (augmented)	q6–12h
Clobetasol propionate (Temovate)	0.05% crm▲, oint▲, lot, gel▲, shp	q12h
Diflorasone diacetate▲ (Psorcon)	0.05% optimized oint	q8–24h
Halobetasol propionate▲ (Ultravate)	0.05% crm, oint	q12h

* Hydrocortisone (all forms), alclometasone, and mometasone are nonfluorinated.

HYPOTHYROIDISM

Common Causes
- Autoimmune (primary thyroid failure)
- Following therapy for hyperthyroidism
- Pituitary or hypothalmic disorders (secondary thyroid failure)
- Medications, especially amiodarone (rare after first 18 mo of therapy) and lithium

Evaluation
TSH, free T_4

Pharmacologic Therapy
- Treatment of subclinical hypothyroidism (TSH 5–10 mIU/L, normal free T_4 concentration, and no overt symptoms) is controversial.
- Levothyroxine▲ (T_4 *[Eltroxin, Levo-T, Levothroid, Levoxyl, Synthroid]* [T: 25, 50, 75, 88, 100, 112, 125, 137, 150, 175, 200, 300 mcg]) given on empty stomach and waiting for 1 hr before eating or at bedtime (more potent). Start at 25 mcg and increase by 12- to 25-mcg intervals q6wk with repeat TSH testing until TSH is in normal range. Prescribe product from same manufacturer for individual patients for consistent bioavailability.
- For myxedema coma: Load T_4 400 mcg IV or 100 mcg q6–8h for 1 d, then 100 mcg/d IV (until patient can take orally) and give stress doses of corticosteroids (see p 90); then start usual replacement regimen.
- Thyroid USP is not recommended. To convert thyroid USP to thyroxine: 60 mg USP = 50 mcg thyroxine.
- If patients are npo and must receive IV thyroxine, dose should be half usual po dose.
- Monitor TSH level at least q12mo (ATA) in patients on chronic thyroid replacement therapy.

HYPERTHYROIDISM

Common Causes
- Graves' disease
- Toxic nodule
- Toxic multinodular goiter
- Medications, especially amiodarone (can occur any time during therapy)

Evaluation
TSH, free T_4
- If TSH is low and free T_4 is normal, recheck TSH in 4–6 wk; if TSH is still low, check free T_3.
- If TSH is low and free T_4 or free T_3 is high, check radioactive iodine uptake and thyroid scan.

Pharmacologic Therapy
- Radioactive iodine ablation is usual treatment of choice, but surgery or medical therapy are options.
- Methimazole▲ *(Tapazole* [T: 5, 10]*)*: First-line drug therapy; start 5–20 mg po q8h, then adjust.

- Propylthiouracil (PTU [T: 50]): Use only if allergic to or intolerant of methimazole; can cause serious liver injury; start 100 mg po q8h, then adjust up to 200 mg po q8h prn.
- When dose has stabilized, follow TSH per hypothyroid monitoring.
- Adjunctive therapy with β-blockers (see **Table 24**) or calcium antagonists (see **Table 24**) may improve symptoms.
- In older adults, treat both symptomatic hyperthyroidism and subclinical hyperthyroidism (low TSH and normal serum free T_4 and T_3 concentrations) if TSH <0.1 mIU/L or if TSH 0.1–0.5 mIU/L and low BMD.

EUTHYROID SICK SYNDROME
Definition
Abnormal thyroid function tests in nonthyroidal illness

Evaluation
- Do not assess thyroid function in acutely ill patients unless thyroid dysfunction is strongly suspected.
- Low T_3, high reverse T_3, low T_4, low or high TSH may be seen.
- If TSH is very low (<0.1 mIU/L in high sensitivity assays), then hyperthyroidism is likely.
- If TSH is very high (>20 mIU/L), then hypothyroidism is likely.
- If thyroid disease is not strongly suspected, recheck in 3–6 wk.

SOLITARY THYROID NODULE
Evaluation
- Ultrasound of thyroid
- If TSH is normal, do fine-needle aspirate.
- If TSH is low, do radionuclide scan; if "cold," do fine-needle aspirate.

Management
- Benign nodules: follow clinically and with ultrasound q6–12mo initially
- "Hot" nodules: radioactive iodine or surgery
- Malignant nodules: surgery
- Inconclusive biopsy of nodules: follow clinically and with ultrasound, and repeat fine-needle aspirate.

DIABETES MELLITUS
Definition and Classification (ADA)
Diabetes mellitus is a group of metabolic diseases characterized by hyperglycemia resulting from defects in insulin secretion, insulin action, or both.
Type 1: Caused by an absolute deficiency of insulin secretion.
Type 2: Caused by a combination of resistance to insulin action and an inadequate compensatory insulin secretory response. Type 2 diabetes is a progressive disorder requiring higher dosages or additional medications over time.
Screening—Screen asymptomatic older adults if BMI >25 kg/m² with HbA_{1c}, fasting plasma glucose or OGTT; repeat at 3-yr intervals.

Criteria for Diagnosis—One or more of the following:
- Symptoms of diabetes (eg, polyuria, polydipsia, unexplained weight loss) plus casual plasma glucose concentration $\geq$200 mg/dL
- Fasting (no caloric intake for $\geq$8 h) plasma glucose $\geq$126 mg/dL
- 2-h plasma glucose $\geq$200 mg/dL during an OGTT.
- Unless hyperglycemia is unequivocal, diagnosis should be confirmed by repeat testing.
- HbA_{1c} >6.5

Pre-diabetes—Any of the following:
- Impaired fasting glucose: defined as fasting plasma glucose $\geq$100 and <126 mg/dL
- Impaired glucose tolerance: 2-h plasma glucose 140–199 mg/dL
- HbA_{1c} 5.7%–6.4%

Prevention/Delay of Type 2 Diabetes in Patients with Pre-diabetes
- Lifestyle modification (most effective)
  - Weight loss (target 7%) if overweight
  - Reduction in total and saturated dietary fat
  - High dietary fiber (14 g fiber/1000 kcal) and whole grains
  - Exercise (at least 150 min/wk of moderate activity, such as walking)
- Pharmacologic
  - Metformin (850 mg q12h) (less effective than lifestyle modification)
  - Valsartan (beginning 80 mg/d and increased to 160 mg/d after 2 wk as tolerated) slightly reduces risk of developing diabetes but does not reduce rate of cardiovascular events.
  - Acarbose (100 mg q8h) (less effective than lifestyle modification)

Management of Diabetes
Evaluate for Comorbid Conditions (AGS, ADA): Depression (see p 68), polypharmacy (see p 14), cognitive impairment (see p 285), urinary incontinence (see p 132), falls (see p 101), pain (see p 203) (AGS), PAD (claudication history and assessment of pedal pulses) (see p 54) (ADA), stress test screening for CAD is of no benefit in asymptomatic patients (see p 33).

Goals of Treatment (ADA, AGS):
- Outpatient: An HbA_{1c} goal of <7.5% in healthier older adults may be more appropriate than the ADA goal of <7%. Average preprandial capillary blood glucose 80–120 mg/dL, average bedtime capillary blood glucose 100–140 mg/dL, and HbA_{1c} <7% (ADA) (<8% if frail; life expectancy <5 yr; or high risk of hypoglycemia, polypharmacy, or drug interaction) (AGS). Intensive control of diabetes to HbA_{1c} <6.5% reduces the likelihood of nephropathy but does not improve macrovascular events, causes more hypoglycemia, and may increase mortality.
- Inpatient: If critically ill, 140–180 mg/dL; if noncritically ill, there are no clear evidence-based guidelines, but fasting <140 mg/dL and random <180 mg/dL are suggested (might be relaxed if severe comorbidities [ADA]). Scheduled basal and prandial insulin doses with correction doses with rapid-acting analog (aspart, glulisine, or lispro) is preferred over sliding-scale insulin regimens.

Nonpharmacologic Interventions:

- Individualize medical nutrition therapy to achieve treatment goals (diet plus exercise is more effective than diet alone)
- Lifestyle (eg, regular exercise for ≥150 min/wk, resistance training 3 ×/wk if not contraindicated, alcohol and smoking cessation)
- Weight loss if overweight or obese
- Limit saturated fat to <7% of total calories
- Minimize intake of trans fat
- Low-carbohydrate, low-fat calorie-restricted; or Mediterranean diet
- Limit protein intake to ≤0.8 g/kg/d if any chronic kidney disease
- For younger and healthier older adults with BMI >35 kg/m^2 who have type 2 diabetes that is difficult to control with lifestyle and pharmacologic therapy, consider bariatric surgery.
- High-fiber diet (25 g insoluble and 25 g soluble/d)
- Limit alcohol intake to <1 drink/d in women and <2 drinks/d in men
- Patient and family education for self-management (reimbursed by Medicare)
- Psychosocial assessment and care

Pharmacologic Interventions for Type 2:

If diet and exercise have not achieved target HbA$_{1c}$ in 6 mo, begin drug treatment.

- Management of glycemia: stepped therapy* (ADA), see **Table 40**.

  Step 1: Metformin▲ (unless CrCl <60 mL/min) beginning 500 mg q12h or q24h; can titrate up q5–7d to max of 2000 mg/d if no adverse events and blood glucose uncontrolled.

  Step 2: Add one of the following:

  ○ Basal insulin (intermediate at bedtime or long-acting at bedtime or morning) 10 U or 0.2 U/kg; can increase by 2–4 U q3d depending on fasting blood glucose. When fasting blood glucose is 70–130 mg/dL, recheck HbA$_{1c}$ in 2–3 mo. If hypoglycemia or fasting blood glucose <70 mg/dL, reduce dose by 4 U or 10%, whichever is greater. If above target HbA$_{1c}$, check pre-lunch, dinner, and bedtime blood glucose concentrations and add rapid- or intermediate-acting insulin (see **Table 41**).

    ▪ Use 4-mm, 32-gauge needle if BMI <40 kg/m^2.

    ▪ Injection sites for human insulin: fastest onset is abdomen and slowest onset is thigh.

    ▪ Timing for prandial insulin: if blood glucose is in 100s, give 10 min before eating; if blood glucose is in 200s, give 20 min before eating; if blood glucose is in 300s, give 30 min before eating.

  ○ Sulfonylurea

  ○ Less well-validated *Step 2* therapies

    ▪ Pioglitazone

    ▪ GLP-1 agonists

  Step 3: Combine *Step 2* agents. D/C sulfonylureas and metglitinides when insulins are started.

  Step 4: Other agents (**Table 41**) may be appropriate for selected patients.

  *Reinforce lifestyle modifications at every visit.

- Management of treatment-associated hypoglycemia

  ○ If conscious, patients should have fast-acting carbohydrate (eg, glucose tabs, hard candy, paste (Instant Glucose), or instant fruit that provides 15–20 g.

  ○ Effects may last only 15 min, so need to eat and recheck blood glucose.

- If hypoglycemia is severe (patient unconscious or cannot ingest carbohydrate), then glucagon 0.5–1 mg SC or IM.
  - In medical settings, 25–50 g of D50 IV restores glucose quicker.
- Manage HTN (BP goal <130/80 mmHg; also see HTN, p 42) beginning with ACEI or ARB. Tighter control (systolic BP <120 mmHg) confers no additional benefit.
- Treat lipid disorders (see p 40) as CHD risk equivalent. If no overt heart disease, statin therapy to reduce LDL with goal of LDL <100 mg/dL; if overt heart disease, LDL goal of <70 mg/dL, using a high-dose statin, is an option (ADA). Triglyceride goal is <150 mg/dL, and HDL goal is >40 mg/dL in men and >50 mg/dL in women. Statins should be used as primary prevention against macrovascular complications in patients with type 2 diabetes and other cardiovascular risk factors (ACP). Adding fenofibrate to statin therapy does not reduce cardiovascular risk beyond a statin alone.
- ACEI or angiotensin II receptor blocker if albuminuria, HTN, or another cardiovascular risk factor. Check kidney function and serum potassium within 1–2 wk of initiation of therapy, with each dosage increase, and at least yearly.
- ASA 75–162 mg/d if hx of heart disease but value in primary prevention is uncertain; consider using if 10-yr risk of CAD >10% (see http://hp2010.nhlbihin.net/atpiii/calculator. asp?usertype=prof); if allergic, clopidogrel 75 mg/d
- Pneumococcal vaccination
- Annual influenza vaccination
- Smoking cessation

Table 40. Non-insulin Agents for Treating Diabetes Mellitus

Medication	Dosage	Formulations	Comments (Metabolism)
Oral Agents			
Biguanide			Decrease hepatic glucose production; lower HbA$_{1c}$ by 1.0%–2.0%; do not cause hypoglycemia
Metformin▲ *(Glucophage)*	500–2550 mg divided	T: 500, 850, 1000	Avoid in patients with eGFR <30 mL/1.73 m^2, HF, COPD, ↑ LFTs; hold before contrast radiologic studies; may cause weight loss (K)
(Glucophage XR)▲	1500–2000 mg/d	T: ER 500, 750	
2nd-Generation Sulfonylureas			Increase insulin secretion; lower HbA$_{1c}$ by 1.0%–2.0%; can cause hypoglycemia and weight gain
Glimepiride▲ *(Amaryl)*	4–8 mg once (begin 1–2 mg)	T: 1, 2, 4	Numerous drug interactions, long-acting (L, K)
Glipizide▲ (generic or *Glucotrol*)	2.5–40 mg once or divided	T: 5, 10	Short-acting (L, K)
(Glucotrol XL)	5–20 mg once	T: ER 2.5, 5, 10	Long-acting (L, K)

(cont.)

Table 40. Non-insulin Agents for Treating Diabetes Mellitus (cont.)

Medication	Dosage	Formulations	Comments (Metabolism)
Glyburide▲ (generic or *Diaβeta, Micronase*)	1.25–20 mg once or divided	T: 1.25, 2.5, 5	Long-acting, ↑ risk of hypoglycemia; not recommended for use in older adults (L, K)
Micronized glyburide *(Glynase)*	1.5–12 mg once	T: 1.5, 3, 4.5, 6	Long-acting, ↑ risk of hypoglycemia; not recommended for use in older adults (L, K)
α-Glucosidase Inhibitors			Delay glucose absorption; lower HbA_{1c} by 0.5%–1%; can cause hypoglycemia and weight gain
Acarbose▲ *(Precose)*	50–100 mg q8h, just before meals; start with 25 mg/d	T: 25, 50, 100	GI adverse events common, avoid if Cr >2 mg/dL, monitor LFTs (gut, K)
Miglitol *(Glyset)*	25–100 mg q8h, with 1st bite of meal; start with 25 mg/d	T: 25, 50, 100	Same as acarbose but no need to monitor LFTs (L, K)
DPP–4 Enzyme Inhibitors			Protect and enhance endogenous incretin hormones; lower HbA_{1c} by 0.5%–1%; do not cause hypoglycemia, weight neutral
Linagliptin *(Tradjenta)*	5 mg	T: 5 mg	L
Sitagliptin *(Januvia)*	100 mg once daily as monotherapy or in combination with metformin or a thiazolidinedione; 50 mg/d if CrCl 31–50 mL/min; 25 mg/d if CrCl <30 mL/min	T: 25, 50, 100	
Saxagliptin *(Onglyza)*	5 mg; 2.5 mg if CrCl <50 mL/min	T: 2.5, 5	K
Meglitinides			Increase insulin secretion; lower HbA_{1c} by 1.0%–2.0%; can cause hypoglycemia and weight gain
Nateglinide▲ *(Starlix)*	60–120 mg q8h	T: 60, 120	Give 30 min before meals
Repaglinide *(Prandin)*	0.5 mg q6–12h if HbA_{1c} <8% or previously untreated; 1–2 mg q6–12h if HbA_{1c} ≥8% or previously treated	T: 0.5, 1, 2	Give 30 min before meals, adjust dosage at weekly intervals, potential for drug interactions, caution in hepatic, renal insufficiency (L)

(cont.)

Table 40. **Non-insulin Agents for Treating Diabetes Mellitus (cont.)**

Medication	Dosage	Formulations	Comments (Metabolism)
Thiazolidinediones			Insulin resistance reducers; lower HbA$_{1c}$ by 0.5%–1.5%; ↑ risk of HF; avoid if NYHA Class III or IV cardiac status; D/C if any decline in cardiac status; weight gain
			Check LFTs at start, q2mo during 1st yr, then periodically; avoid if clinical evidence of liver disease or if serum ALT levels >2.5 times upper limit of normal; may increase risk of fractures in women (L, K)
Pioglitazone *(Actos)*	15 or 30 mg/d; max 45 mg/d as monotherapy, 30 mg/d in combination therapy	T: 15, 30, 45	
Rosiglitazone *(Avandia)*	4 mg q12–24h	T: 2, 4, 8	*Restricted access:* Because of data suggesting higher cardiovascular risk, people with type 2 diabetes who are not currently taking rosiglitazone can be prescribed the medication only if glycemic control cannot be achieved with an alternative medication. Rosiglitazone will continue to be available to those who are currently taking it only if they appear to be benefiting and understand the risks.
Combinations			
Glipizide and metformin▲ *(METAGLIP)*	2.5/250 mg once; 20/2000 in 2 divided doses	T: 2.5/250, 2.5/500, 5/500	Avoid in patients >80 yr, Cr >1.5 mg/dL in men, Cr >1.4 mg/dL in women; see individual drugs (L, K)
Glyburide and metformin▲ *(Glucovance)*	1.25/250 mg initially if previously untreated; 2.5/500 mg or 5/500 mg q12h with meals; max 20/2000/d	T: 1.25/250, 2.5/500, 5/500	Starting dose should not exceed total daily dose of either drug; see individual drugs (L, K)
Pioglitazone and metformin *(ACTO plus met)*	15/850 mg q12–24h	T: 15/850	See individual drugs.
Repaglinide and metformin *(PrandiMet)*	1/500 mg to 4/1000 mg twice q12h or q8h before meals; max 10/2500 mg/d	T: 1/500, 2/500	See individual drugs.

(cont.)

Table 40. Non-insulin Agents for Treating Diabetes Mellitus (cont.)

Medication	Dosage	Formulations	Comments (Metabolism)
Rosiglitazone and glimepiride *(Avandaryl)*	1 or 2 tab/d; max 8 mg/4 mg	T: 4/1, 4/2, 4/4, 8/2, 8/4	See individual drugs.
Rosiglitazone and metformin *(Avandamet)*	4/1000– 8/2000 mg in 2 divided doses	T: 1/500, 2/500, 4/500, 2/1000, 4/1000	Avoid in patients >80 yr, Cr >1.5 mg/dL in men, Cr >1.4 mg/dL in women; see individual drugs (L, K)
Pioglitazone and glimepiride *(Duetact)*	30/2 mg initially; max 45/8 mg	T: 30/2, 30/4	See individual drugs.
Saxagliptin and metformin *(Kombiglyze XR)*	5/1000–2000 mg once	T: ER 5/500, 5/1000, 2.5/1000	See individual drugs.
Sitagliptin and metformin *(Janumet)*	Begin with current doses; max 100/2000 mg in 2 divided doses	T: 50/500, 50/1000	See individual drugs.
Injectable Agents			Hypoglycemia common if combined with sulfonyl urea or insulin
Exenatide *(Byetta)*	5–10 mcg SC twice daily with meals	1.2-, 2.4-mL pre-filled syringes	Incretin mimetic; lowers HbA$_{1c}$ by 0.4%–0.9%; nausea and hypoglycemia common; less weight gain than insulin; avoid if CrCl <30 mL/min (K)
Liraglutide *(Victoza)*	0.6–1.8 mg SC once daily	0.6, 1.2, 1.8 (6 mg/mL) in pre-filled, multidose "pen"	Glucagon-like peptide-1 (GLP-1) receptor agonist; lowers HbA$_{1c}$ by 1%; risks include acute pancreatitis and possibly medullary thyroid cancer
Pramlintide *(Symlin)*	60 mcg SC immediately before meals	0.6 mg/mL in 5-mL vial	Amylin analog; lowers HbA$_{1c}$ by 0.4%–0.7%; nausea common; reduce pre-meal dose of short-acting insulin by 50% (K)

Table 41. Insulin Preparations

Preparation	Onset	Peak	Duration	Number of Injections/d
Rapid-acting				
Insulin glulisine *(Apidra)*	20 min	0.5–1.5 h	3–4 h	3
Insulin lispro *(Humalog)*	15 min	0.5–1.5 h	3–4 h	3
Insulin aspart *(NovoLog)*	30 min	1–3 h	3–5 h	3
Regular (eg, *Humulin, Novolin*) [a]	0.5–1 h	2–3 h	5–8 h	1–3
Intermediate or long-acting				
NPH (eg, *Humulin, Novolin*) [a]	1–1.5 h	4–12 h	24 h	1–2
Insulin detemir *(Levemir)*	3–4 h	6–8 h	6–24 h depending on dose	1–2
Insulin glargine *(Lantus)* [b]	1–2 h	—	24 h	1
Isophane insulin and regular insulin inj, premixed *(Novolin 70/30)*	30 min	2–12 h	24 h	1–2

[a] Also available as mixtures of NPH and regular in 50:50 proportions.
[b] To convert from NPH dosing, give same number of units once a day. For patients taking NPH q12h, decrease the total daily units by 20%, and titrate on basis of response. Starting dosage in insulin-naive patients is 10 U once daily hs.

Monitoring

- Self-monitor blood glucose (SMBG) >3 ×/d if multiple daily injections or using insulin pump
- The value of SMBG in type 2 diabetes is unclear. For older adults treated with medications that do not cause hypoglycemia, SMBG may be unnecessary and there is no consensus about the frequency of monitoring patients on medications that may cause hypoglycemia.
- BP evaluation at each visit
- Annual comprehensive foot examination, including monofilament testing at 4 plantar sites (great toe and base of first, third, and fifth metatarsals), plus testing any one of: tuning fork, pinprick sensation, ankle reflexes, or vibration perception threshold; assessment of foot pulses; and inspection. Insensate feet should be inspected q3–6mo; well-fitted walking or athletic shoes may be of benefit; refer those with sensory and structural abnormalities to foot care specialists.
- Initial screen for PAD by checking pedal pulses and asking about claudication (see p 54)
- Initial screen for signs and symptoms of cardiovascular autonomic neuropathy
- HbA$_{1c}$ twice/yr in patients with stable glycemic control; quarterly, if poor control
- Comprehensive dilated eye and visual examinations by an ophthalmologist or optometrist who is experienced in management of diabetic retinopathy at time of diagnosis and annually
- Lipid profiles q1–2yr depending on whether values are in normal range
- Annual test for microalbuminuria by measuring albumin:creatinine ratio in a random spot collection
- Annual serum creatinine

ADRENAL INSUFFICIENCY

Common Causes

Secondary (more common; mineralocorticoid function is preserved, no hyperkalemia or hyperpigmentation, dehydration is less common)

- Abrupt discontinuation of chronic glucocorticoid administration
- Megestrol acetate
- Brain irradiation
- Traumatic brain injury
- Pituitary tumors

Primary (less common)

- Autoimmune
- Tuberculosis

Evaluation

- Basal (morning) plasma cortisol >18 mcg/dL excludes adrenal insufficiency, and <3 mcg/dL is diagnostic.
- ACTH stimulation test: tetracosactin *(Synacthen Depot)* 250 mcg IV; best administered in the morning; peak value at 30–60 min >18 mcg/dL is normal, <15 mcg/dL is diagnostic.
- If adrenal insufficiency is diagnosed with high ACTH (eg, >100 pg/mL), then insufficiency is primary.

Pharmacologic Therapy

For corticosteroid dose equivalencies, see **Table 42**. Hydrocortisone preferred for adrenal insufficiency (10–25 mg/m²/d) in 2 or 3 divided doses. If primary adrenal insufficiency, add fludrocortisone▲ to glucocorticoids.

Management

Stress doses of corticosteroids for patients with severe illness, injury, or undergoing surgery: In emergency situations, do not wait for test results. Give hydrocortisone 100 mg IV bolus (or if patient has not been previously diagnosed, dexamethasone 4 mg IV bolus). Also treat with IV fluids (eg, saline). For less severe stress (eg, minor illness), double or triple usual oral replacement dosage for 3 d.

- For minor surgery (eg, hernia repair), hydrocortisone 25 mg/m²/d on day of surgery and return to usual dosage on following day.
- For moderate surgical stress (eg, cholecystectomy, joint replacement), total 50–75 mg/d on the day of surgery and the first postoperative day, then usual dosage on the second postoperative day.
- For major surgical procedures (eg, cardiac bypass), total 100–150 mg/d given in divided doses for 2–3 d, then return to usual dosage.

Medication	Approx Equivalent Dose (mg)	Relative Anti-inflammatory Potency	Relative Mineralo-corticoid Potency	Biologic Half-life (h)	Formulations
Betamethasone▲ (Celestone)	0.6–0.75	20–30	0	36–54	T: 0.6; S: 0.6 mg/5 mL
Cortisone▲ (Cortone)	25	0.8	2	8–12	T: 5; S: 50 mg/mL
Dexamethasone▲ (Decadron, Dexone, Hexadrol)	0.75	20–30	0	36–54	T: 0.25, 0.5, 0.75, 1, 1.5, 2, 4; S: elixir 0.5 mg/5 mL; inj
Fludrocortisone▲ (Florinef)*	NA	10	4	12–36	T: 0.1
Hydrocortisone▲ (Cortef, Hydrocortone)	20	1	2	8–12	T: 5, 10, 20; S: 10 mg/5 mL; inj
Methylprednisolone▲ (eg, Medrol, Solu-Medrol, Depo-Medrol)	4	5	0	18–36	T: 2, 4, 8, 16, 24, 32; inj
Prednisolone▲ (eg, Delta-Cortef, Prelone Syrup, Pediapred)	5	4	1	18–36	S: 5 mg/5 mL; syr 5, 15 mg/5 mL
Prednisone▲ (Deltasone, Liquid Pred, Meticorten, Orasone)	5	4	1	18–36	T: 1, 2.5, 5, 10, 20, 50; S: 5 mg/5 mL
Triamcinolone (eg, Aristocort, Kenacort, Kenalog)	4	5	0	18–36	T: 1, 2, 4, 8; S: syr 4 mg/5 mL

Note: NA = not available

* Usually given for orthostatic hypotension at 0.1 mg q8–24h and at 0.05–0.2 mg/d for primary adrenal insufficiency.

VISUAL IMPAIRMENT

Definition

Visual acuity 20/40 or worse; severe visual impairment (legal blindness) 20/200 or worse

Evaluation

• Acuity testing

  ○ Near vision: check each eye independently with glasses using handheld Rosenbaum card at 14" or Lighthouse Near Acuity Test at 16". *Note:* Distance must be accurate.

  ○ Far vision: Snellen wall chart at 20'

• Visual fields (by confrontation)

• Ophthalmoscopy

• Emergent referral for acute change in vision

Prevention

Biennial full eye examinations for people >65 yr old, annually for people with diabetes.

SPECIFIC CONDITIONS ASSOCIATED WITH VISUAL IMPAIRMENT

Refractive Error

The most common cause of visual impairment.

Cataracts

Lens opacity on ophthalmoscopic examination. Risk factors: age, sun exposure, smoking, corticosteroids, diabetes mellitus, alcohol, low vitamin intake.

Nonpharmacologic Treatment:

• Reduce UV light exposure.

• Surgery (American, Canadian, and Royal [British] Academies of Ophthalmology):

  ○ if visual function no longer meets the patient's needs and cataract surgery is likely to improve vision

  ○ if clinically significant disparity between eyes due to cataract

  ○ when cataract removal will treat another lens-induced disease (eg, glaucoma)

  ○ when cataract coexists with retinal disease requiring unrestricted monitoring (eg, diabetic retinopathy)

Age-related Macular Degeneration (AMD)

Atrophy of cells in the central macular region of retinal pigmented epithelium; on ophthalmoscopic examination, white-yellow patches (drusen) or hemorrhage and scars in advanced stages. Risk factors: age, smoking, sun exposure, family hx, white race. AMD has "wet" and "dry" forms.

• Dry AMD: Accounts for ~90% of cases, is characterized by abnormalities in the retinal pigment with focal drusen, and has a natural history of slow gradual loss of vision.

• Wet AMD: Only 10% of cases are wet or neovascular, which is characterized by often rapid visual loss. Early intervention when the dry form converts to the wet form saves vision.

Nonpharmacologic Treatment:

• Monitor daily for conversion from dry to wet form using Amsler grid.

• Patients with large drusen most at risk of conversion to wet AMD.

- Thermal laser photocoagulation may be appropriate for select patients with extrafoveal choroidal neovascularization.
- Dietary modification reduces risk of progression to neovascular AMD: high intake of beta-carotene, vitamin C, zinc, n-3 long-chain polyunsaturated fatty acids, and fish.

Pharmacologic Treatment of Wet AMD:

- Vascular endothelial growth factor (VEGF) inhibitors reduce neovascularization, eg, bevacizumab *(Avastin)* or ranibizumab *(Lucentis)* intravitreal monthly for up to 2 yr maintains vision in the majority and improves it in a significant minority. As-needed drug administration (ie, only when signs of exudation are present) is as effective as monthly injections. Complications of the intraocular injections include retinal detachment or endophthalmitis and visual loss in 1%–2% of patients.
- Photodynamic therapy: verteporfin *(Visudyne)* infused IV and activated by infrared light q3mo until vessel leaks stop, occludes abnormal vessels and reduces severe visual loss.

Pharmacologic Treatment of Dry AMD: In intermediate or more advanced stages, zinc oxide 80 mg, cupric oxide 2 mg, beta-carotene 15 mg, vitamin C 500 mg, and vitamin E 400 IU taken in divided doses q12h reduces risk of progression (eg, *Ocuvite PreserVision* 2 tabs po q12h). Not recommended for smokers (beta-carotene) or for people with CAD (vitamin E).

Diabetic Retinopathy

Microaneurysms, dot and blot hemorrhages on ophthalmoscopy with proliferative retinopathy ischemia and vitreous hemorrhage. Risk factors: chronic hyperglycemia, smoking.

Nonpharmacologic Treatment:

Laser treatment of proliferative retinopathy or macular edema

Pharmacologic Treatment:

Glycemic control to HbA_{1c} of 7 vs 9 improves visual outcomes at 7–10 yr (see Diabetes, p 82). BP control to a mean of 144/80 mmHg improves visual outcomes compared with higher BPs. Control of lipids and use of antiplatelet agents do not affect visual outcomes.

Glaucoma

Characteristic optic cupping and nerve damage, and loss of peripheral visual fields. Risk factors: black race, age, family hx, increased ocular pressures. Most common cause of blindness in black Americans. Primary open-angle glaucoma is most common, a chronic disease of older adults. Angle-closure glaucoma is an acute disease requiring emergent management.

Glaucoma Surgery:

- Open angle—laser trabeculoplasty, surgical trabeculectomy (most effective but higher complication rates), canuloplasty, aqueous shunt
- Angle closure—laser iridotomy with or without iridoplasty
- Used primarily when pressures or optic nerve damage are poorly controlled by topicals.

Pharmacologic Treatment:

Treat when there is optic nerve damage or visual field loss (see **Table 43**).

Therapy reduces intraocular pressure. Instill one drop under lower lid, close eye for at least 1 min to reduce systemic absorption; repeat if a second drop is needed. Systemic absorption is further reduced by teaching the patient to compress the lacrimal sac for 15–30 sec after instilling a drop. Always wait 5 min before instilling a second type of drop.

Table 43. Medications for Treating Glaucoma

Medication	Strength	Dosage	Comments (Metabolism)
α_2-Agonists (bottles with purple caps)			*Class adverse events:* low BP, fatigue, drowsiness, dry mouth, dry nose (unknown)
Brimonidine▲ *(Alphagan)*	0.2%	1 drop q8–12h	
(Alphagan P)	0.1%, 0.15%	1 drop q8–12h	
α-β Agonist			
Dipivefrin▲ *(AKPro, Propine)*	0.1%	1 drop q12h	HTN, headache, tachycardia, arrhythmia (eye, L)
β-Blockers (bottles with blue or yellow caps)			*Class adverse events:* hypotension, bradycardia, HF, bronchospasm, anxiety, depression, confusion, hallucination, diarrhea, nausea, cramps, lethargy, weakness, masking of hypoglycemia, sexual dysfunction. Avoid in patients with asthma, bradycardia, COPD (L)
✔Betaxolol *(Betoptic▲, Betoptic-S)*	0.25%, 0.5%	1–2 drops q12h	
✔Carteolol▲ *(Ocupress)*	1%	1 drop q12h	
✔Levobunolol▲ *(AKBeta, Betagan)*	0.25%, 0.5%	1 drop q12h	
✔Metipranolol▲ *(OptiPranolol)*	0.3%	1 drop q12h	
✔Timolol drops▲ *(Betimol, Timoptic)*	0.25%, 0.5%	1 drop q12h	Not all formulations available as generic
Cholinergic Agonists (bottles with green caps)			*Class adverse events:* brow ache, corneal toxicity, red eye, retinal detachment
Pilocarpine gel *(Pilopine HS)* *(Ocusert)*	4% 20, 40 mcg/h	1/2" qhs weekly	Systemic cholinergic effects are rare (tissues, K)
Pilocarpine▲ *(Adsorbocarpine, Akarpine, Isopto Carpine, Pilagan, Pilocar, Piloptic, Pilostat)*	0.25%–10%	1 drop q6h	
Miotic, Cholinesterase Inhibitor (bottle with green cap)			*Class adverse events:* cholinomimetic effects (sweating, tremor, headache, salivation), confusion, high or low BP, bradycardia, bronchoconstriction, urinary frequency, cramps, diarrhea, nausea
Echothiophate *(Phospholine)*	0.03%–0.25%	1 drop q12h	

(cont.)

Table 43. Medications for Treating Glaucoma (cont.)

Medication	Strength	Dosage	Comments (Metabolism)
Carbonic Anhydrase Inhibitors (bottles with orange caps)			
Topical			Caution in kidney failure and after corneal transplant (K)
✔Brinzolamide *(Azopt)*	1%	1 drop q8h	
✔Dorzolamide▲ *(Trusopt)*	2%	1 drop q8h	
Oral			*Class adverse events:*
Acetazolamide▲ (eg, *Diamox*)	125–500 mg, SR 500 mg	250–500 mg q6–12h, SR 500 mg q12h	fatigue, weight loss, bitter taste, paresthesias, depression, COPD exacerbation, cramps, nausea, diarrhea, kidney failure, blood dyscrasias, hypokalemia, myopia, renal calculi acidosis; not recommended in kidney failure (K)
Methazolamide▲ (eg, *Neptazane*)	25–50 mg	50–100 mg q8–12h	(L, K)
Prostaglandin Analogs			First-line therapy *Class adverse events:* change in eye color and periorbital tissues, hyperemia, itching
✔Bimatoprost *(Lumigan)*	0.03%	1 drop qhs	(L, K, F)
✔Latanoprost▲ *(Xalatan)*	0.005%	1 drop qhs	(L)
✔Travoprost *(Travatan)*	0.004%	1 drop qhs	(L)
Combinations			
Dorzolamide/timolol *(Cosopt)*	0.05%/0.2%	1 drop q12h	See individual agents (K, L)
Brimonidine/timolol *(Combigan)*	0.2%/0.5%	1 drop q12h	See individual agents (K, L)

✔ = preferred for treating older adults
Note: Patients may not know names of drugs but instead refer to them by the color of the bottle cap. The usual colors are listed above.

ADDITIONAL CONSIDERATIONS IN MANAGEMENT OF EYE DISORDERS

Topical Steroid Treatment
Patients on topical steroids for ocular inflammatory disease require periodic monitoring by an ophthalmologist. Serious and potentially vision-threatening adverse effects can occur from chronic topical corticosteroid use, including glaucoma and cataract or superinfection. Patients on chronic topical steroids should be followed by an ophthalmologist and there should be a legitimate indication for continued treatment.

Low-vision Services
• Address the full range of functional visual impairment from blindness to partial sight. Refer patients with uncompensated visual loss that reduces function.

- Recommend optical aids:
  - Electronic video magnifiers
  - Spectacle-mounted telescopes for distance vision
  - Closed-circuit television to enlarge text
  - A variety of high-technology devices are available (see www.lighthouse.org).
  - Optical aids (like the above) may improve mood unlike traditional aids such as talking books, Braille watches, etc, which do not.
- Environmental modifications that improve function include color contrast, floor lamps to reduce glare, motion sensors to turn on lights, talking clocks, spoken medication reminders.
- Many states have "Services for the Visually Impaired" through the health department.

Dual Sensory Impairment (DSI)
- 9%–21% of adults >70 yr old have loss of both vision and hearing.
- Compared with single-sensory impairment, DSI is more often associated with depression, poor self-rated health, reduced social participation, IADL, and cognitive impairment.
- Management currently limited to vibrating devices such as alarm clocks, door bells, smoke alarms, etc.

RED EYE

The "red eye" is an eye with vascular congestion: some conditions that cause this pose a threat to vision and warrant prompt ophthalmologic referral. See **Figure 4**. Acute conjunctivitis and allergic conjunctivitis are common causes of red eye. Diagnosis and treatment of those conditions are discussed below (see p 98).

Figure 4. Red Eye Decision Tree

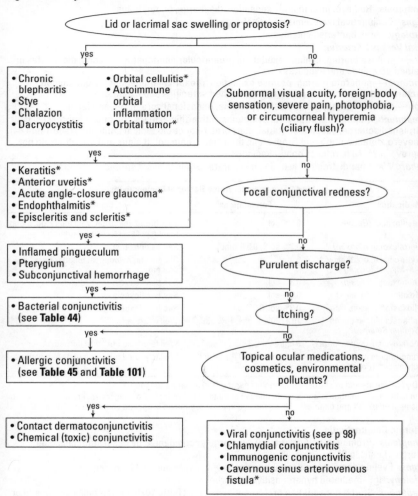

Lid or lacrimal sac swelling or proptosis?

yes

- Chronic blepharitis
- Stye
- Chalazion
- Dacryocystitis
- Orbital cellulitis*
- Autoimmune orbital inflammation
- Orbital tumor*

no

Subnormal visual acuity, foreign-body sensation, severe pain, photophobia, or circumcorneal hyperemia (ciliary flush)?

yes

- Keratitis*
- Anterior uveitis*
- Acute angle-closure glaucoma*
- Endophthalmitis*
- Episcleritis and scleritis*

no

Focal conjunctival redness?

yes

- Inflamed pingueculum
- Pterygium
- Subconjunctival hemorrhage

no

Purulent discharge?

yes

- Bacterial conjunctivitis (see **Table 44**)

no

Itching?

yes

- Allergic conjunctivitis (see **Table 45** and **Table 101**)

no

Topical ocular medications, cosmetics, environmental pollutants?

yes

- Contact dermatoconjunctivitis
- Chemical (toxic) conjunctivitis

no

- Viral conjunctivitis (see p 98)
- Chlamydial conjunctivitis
- Immunogenic conjunctivitis
- Cavernous sinus arteriovenous fistula*

*Potentially dangerous; requires prompt referral to ophthalmology.
Source: Trobe JD. *Physician's Guide to Eye Care, 2nd ed.* American Academy of Ophthalmology, 2001. Reproduced with permission.

Acute Conjunctivitis

Symptoms: Red eye, foreign body sensation, discharge, photophobia

Signs: Conjunctival hyperemia and discharge

Etiology: Viral, bacterial, chlamydial

Viral Versus Bacterial:

Viral—profuse tearing, minimal exudation, preauricular adenopathy common, monocytes in stained scrapings and exudates

Bacterial—moderate tearing, profuse exudation, preauricular adenopathy uncommon, bacteria and polymorphonuclear cells in stained scrapings and exudates

Both—minimal itching, generalized hyperemia, occasional sore throat and fever

Treatment: Majority are viral; treat symptoms with artificial tears and cool compresses. If purulent discharge, suspect bacterial; start broad-spectrum topical antibiotics (see **Table 44**). If severe, obtain culture and Gram stain, then start treatment. If signs and symptoms do not improve in 24–48 h, refer to ophthalmologist.

Other: Wash hands frequently and use separate towels to avoid spread.

Table 44. Treatment for Acute Bacterial Conjunctivitis[a]

Medication	Formulations[b]	Comments
Besifloxacin *(Besivance)*	0.6% sol	Very broad spectrum, well tolerated, a first choice in severe cases, expensive
Ciprofloxacin *(Ciloxan)*	0.3% sol▲, 0.3% oint	See besifloxacin
Erythromycin ophthalmic▲ *(AK-Mycin, Ilotycin)*	5 mg/g oint	Good if staphylococcal blepharitis is present
Gatifloxacin *(Tequin)*	0.3% sol	See besifloxacin
Moxifloxacin *(Avelox)*	0.5% sol	See besifloxacin
Ofloxacin▲ *(Floxin, Ocuflox)*	0.3% sol, 0.3% oint	See besifloxacin; generic available
Sulfacetamide sodium▲ *(Sodium Sulamyd)*	10%, 30% drops, 10% oint	Well tolerated
Tobramycin *(AKTob, Tobrex)*	3 mg/g oint, 3 mg/mL sol▲	Well tolerated but more corneal toxicity
Trimethoprim and polymyxin▲ *(Polytrim)*	1 mg/mL, 10,000 IU/mL sol	Well tolerated but some gaps in coverage

[a] Do not use steroid or steroid-antibiotic preparations in initial treatment.

[b] In mild cases, solution is applied q6h and gel or ointment q12h for 5–7 d. In more severe cases, solution is applied q2–3h and ointment q6h; as the eye improves, solution is applied q6h and ointment q12h.

Allergic Conjunctivitis

Symptoms: Prominent itching, watery discharge accompanied by nasal stuffiness (see allergic rhinitis, p 243)

Signs: Eyelid edema, conjunctival bogginess, and hyperemia (all bilateral)

Etiology: IgE–mediated hypersensitivity to airborne pollen

Treatment: Start a nonsedating oral H$_1$ antihistamine (**Table 102**); if symptoms persist, add or substitute a topical H$_1$ antihistamine or topical mast cell stabilizer/antihistamine (**Table 45**). If these are ineffective, try topical ketorolac (**Table 45**). Nasal steroids reduce ocular symptoms to some degree (**Table 102**). If the above do not relieve symptoms, refer to an ophthalmologist (topical steroids [p 95] may be necessary but should be prescribed only by an ophthalmologist). Oral mast cell stabilizers are not used in the treatment of acute ocular allergies (see **Table 45**). The OTC vasoconstrictor/antihistamines are for short-term use only.

Table 45. Topical Therapy for Allergic Conjunctivitis

Category/Medication	Formulation and Dosing	Adverse Events[a]
H, Antihistamines		
Alcaftadine *(Lastacaft)*	0.25%, 1 gtt OU q24h	Itching, erythema
Azelastine▲ *(Optivar)*	0.05%, 1 gtt OU q6h	Headache, rhinitis
Bepotastine *(Bepreve)*	1.5%, 1 gtt OU q12h	Dysgeusia
Emedastine *(Emadine)*	0.05%, 1 gtt OU q12h	
Epinastine *(Elastat)*	0.5%, 1 gtt OU q12h	
Ketotifen▲* *(Zaditor, Alaway)*	0.025%, 1 gtt OU q8–12h	
Olopatadine *(Patanol)*	0.1%, 1 gtt OU q12h	
Olopatadine *(Pataday)*	0.2%, 1 gtt OU q24h	Cold syndrome, dysgeusia, headache, keratitis
NSAID		
Ketorolac▲ *(Acular)*	0.5%, 1 gtt OU q6h	Ocular irritation, burning
Mast cell stabilizers[b]		
Lodoxamide *(Alomide)*	0.1%, 1–2 gtt OU q6h	Ocular irritation, burning
Nedocromil *(Alocril)*	2%, 1–2 gtt OU q12h	Headache, ocular irritation, burning
Pemirolast *(Alamast)*	0.1%, 1–2 gtt OU q6h	Headache, rhinitis, flu-like symptoms, ocular irritation, burning
Vasoconstrictor/Antihistamine combinations		
Pheniramine maleate 0.315%/ naphazoline hydrochloride 0.02675% *(Opcon-A)*	1–2 gtt up to q6h for no more than a few days	Caution in heart disease, HTN, BPH, narrow angle glaucoma; chronic use can cause follicular reactions or contact dermatitis
Pheniramine maleate 0.3%/ naphazoline hydrochloride 0.025% *(Naphcon-A)*	1–2 gtt up to q6h for no more than a few days	Same as above

[a] Any may cause stinging, which can by reduced by refrigerating drops.
[b] Not used in acute allergy; use when allergen exposure can be predicted, and use well in advance of exposure.

DRY EYE SYNDROME

Symptoms: Itchy or sandy eyes (foreign body sensation)

Etiology: Altered tear film composition, reduced tear production, poor lid function, environment, drug-induced causes (eg, anticholinergics, estrogens, SSRIs), or diseases such as Sjögren's syndrome; refer to ophthalmology for diagnostic assistance.

Therapy:
- Artificial tear formulations (eg, *HypoTears*) administer q1–6h prn. Preservatives may cause eye irritation. Preservative-free preparations, available in single-dose vials, are expensive. Ointment preparations can be used at night or also during the day in severe cases.
- *Lacrisert* is an insert that gradually releases hydroxypropylcellulose after placement in the inferior conjunctival sac.
- Environmental strategies: room humidifiers, frequent blinking, and swim goggles or moisture chambers fit to eye glasses are all helpful.

- Cyclosporine ophthalmic emulsion 0.05% *(Restasis)* 1 gtt OU q12h. Indicated when tear production is suppressed by inflammation. May take 4–6 wk to achieve results. Does not increase tears in people using topical anti-inflammatories or punctal plugs. Adverse events: burning, hyperemia, discharge, pain, blurring. Patients should have a complete ophthalmologic examination before receiving a prescription.
- Temporary or permanent punctal plugs

SYSTEMIC MEDICATIONS WITH OCULAR ADVERSE EVENTS (SYMPTOMS, SIGNS)
- Amiodarone: halos, blurred vision, corneal changes, optic neuropathy
- Anticholinergics: blurry near vision, angle-closure glaucoma (rare)
- Bisphosphonates: scleritis (and perhaps uveitis), ocular pain, red eye, blurred vision
- Carbamazepine and phenytoin: at toxic levels, blurred vision, diplopia, nystagmus
- Cisplatin: optic neuritis, papilledema, retrobulbar neuritis, cortical blindness
- Corticosteroids: cataracts, glaucoma
- Digoxin: yellowish orange vision; snowy, flickering vision
- Ethambutol or INH: loss of color vision, visual acuity, visual field
- Hydroxychloroquine or chloroquine: loss of color vision, visual acuity, visual field
- Minocycline: increased intracranial pressure, papilledema, blurred vision, visual loss
- Niacin: decreased visual field, maculopathy
- Sildenafil: color tinge in vision, increased sensitivity to light, blurred vision. Nonarteritic ischemic optic neuropathy has been reported in association with PDE5 inhibitors.
- Tamoxifen: retinopathy with cumulative dose of 100 g or as little as 7 g (blurred vision, macular edema)
- Topiramate: acute angle-closure glaucoma (ocular pain, blurred vision, red eye)
- Vincristine: sixth cranial nerve palsy (ptosis, diplopia, abduction deficits)

DEFINITION

An event whereby an individual unexpectedly comes to rest on the ground or another lower level without known loss of consciousness (AGS/BGS Clinical Practice Guideline: Prevention of Falls in Older Persons, 2009). Excludes falls from major intrinsic event (eg, seizure, stroke, syncope) or overwhelming environmental hazard.

ETIOLOGY

Typically multifactorial. Composed of intrinsic (eg, poor balance, weakness, chronic illness, visual or cognitive impairment), extrinsic (eg, polypharmacy), and environmental (eg, poor lighting, no safety equipment, loose carpets) factors. Commonly a nonspecific sign for one of many acute illnesses in older adults.

RISK FACTORS

Focus on most common risk factors, which include hx of falls, fear of falling, gait deficit, balance deficit. Other risk factors include muscle weakness, use of assistive devices, visual deficit, arthritis, impaired ADLs, depression, cognitive impairment, age >80 yr old, ≥2 pain locations, higher pain severity, pain interference with activities.

MEDICATIONS ASSOCIATED WITH FALLS

- Antipsychotics (especially phenothiazines)
- Sedatives, hypnotics (including benzodiazepines)
- Antidepressants (including MAOIs, SSRIs, TCAs)
- Antiarrhythmics (Class 1A)
- Anticonvulsants
- Anxiolytics
- Antihypertensives
- Diuretics
- Systemic glucocorticoids

EVALUATION

Exclude acute illness or underlying systemic or metabolic process (eg, infection, electrolyte imbalance as indicated by hx, examination, and laboratory studies). Determine if fall is syncopal or nonsyncopal (see Syncope, p 56).
See **Figure 5** for recommended assessment and management.

History

- Circumstances of fall (eg, activity at time of fall, location, time)
- Associated symptoms (eg, lightheadedness, vertigo, syncope, weakness, confusion, palpitations)
- Relevant comorbid conditions (eg, prior stroke, parkinsonism, cardiac disease, diabetes mellitus, seizure disorder, depression, anxiety, hyperplastic anemia, sensory deficit, osteoarthritis, osteoporosis, cognitive or visual impairment, hyperthyroidism, glucocorticoid excess, GI or chronic renal disease, myeloma)
- Previous falls
- Medication review, including OTC medications and alcohol use; note recent changes in medications (see p 14)
- Ask about person's ability to complete ADLs: bathing, dressing, transferring, continence (see p 286)
- Ask about difficulties with walking or balance and fear related to falling

Figure 5. Assessment and Management of Falls

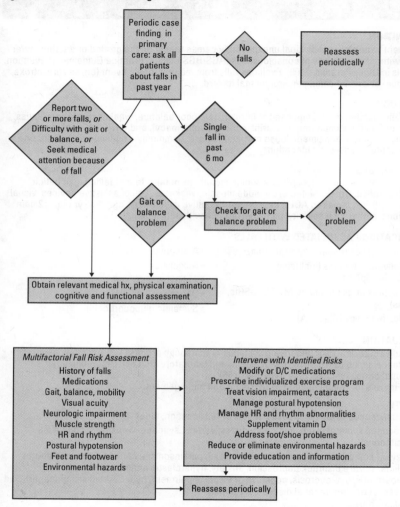

Sources: American Geriatrics Society and British Geriatrics Society. *Clinical Practice Guideline for the Prevention of Falls in Older Persons.* New York: American Geriatrics Society; 2010; www.medcats.com/FALLS/frameset.htm; and Pighills AC, Torgerson DJ, Sheldon TA, et al. Environmental assessment and modification to prevent falls in older people. *J Am Geriatr Soc* 2011; 59:26–33.

Physical Examination

Look for:

- Vital signs: postural pulse and BP changes within 3 min of rising from lying to standing, fever, hypothermia
- Head and neck: visual impairment (especially poor acuity, reduced contrast sensitivity, decreased visual fields, cataracts), motion-induced imbalance (Dix-Hallpike test), bruit, nystagmus
- Musculoskeletal: arthritic changes, motion or joint limitations (especially lower extremity joint function), postural instability, skeletal deformities, podiatric problems, muscle strength
- Neurologic: slower reflexes, altered proprioception, altered mental status, focal deficits, peripheral neuropathy, gait or balance disorders, muscle weakness (especially leg), instability, tremor, rigidity
- Cardiovascular: heart arrhythmias, cardiac valve dysfunction

Diagnostic Tests

- Laboratory tests for people at risk: CBC, serum electrolytes, BUN, Cr, glucose, B_{12}, thyroid function, 25-hydroxy vitamin D
- Bone densitometry in all women >65 yr old, all men >70 yr old
- Echocardiography for those with cardiac conditions impairing blood flow to brain
- Imaging: neuroimaging if head injury or new, focal neurologic findings on examination or if a CNS process is suspected; spinal imaging to exclude cervical spondylosis or lumbar stenosis in patients with abnormal gait, neurologic examination, or lower extremity spasticity or hyperreflexia
- Ambulatory cardiac monitoring rarely helpful
- Arrhythmic evaluation only if clinical evidence of this diagnosis (eg, hx of cardiac events or abnormal ECG)
- Drug concentrations for anticonvulsants, antiarrhythmics, TCAs, and high-dose ASA

Gait, Balance, and Mobility Assessment

- Functional gait: observe patient rising from chair, walking (stride, length, velocity, symmetry), turning, sitting (Get Up and Go test, POMA, p 285)
- Balance: side-by-side, semi-tandem, and full tandem stance; Functional Reach test; POMA, p 285; Berg Balance Scale (especially retrieve object from floor)
- Mobility: observe patient's use and fit of assistive device (eg, cane, walker) or personal assistance, extent of ambulation, restraint use, footwear evaluation
  - Cane fitting: top of the cane should be at the top of the greater trochanter or at the break of the wrist; when the patient holds the cane, there is approximately a 15-degree bend at the elbow. Canes are most often used to improve balance but can also be used to reduce weight-bearing on the opposite leg.
  - Walker fitting: walkers are prescribed when a cane does not offer sufficient stability. Four-wheeled walkers allow a more natural gait and are easier for cognitively impaired patients to use. Rolling walkers (rollators) have the advantage for a smoother faster gait, but require more coordination because of the brakes; however, they are good for outside walking because the larger wheels move more easily over sidewalks.
- ADLs: complete ADL skill evaluation, including use of adaptive equipment and mobility aids as appropriate

PREVENTION

Goal is to minimize risk of falling without compromising mobility and functional independence. Recommendations are primarily based on studies of community-dwelling older adults with limited evidence from randomized controlled trials regarding single or multifactorial interventions in the long-term–care setting and in cognitively impaired.

- Assess risk of falling as part of routine primary health care visit (at least annually). Risk of falling significantly increases as number of risk factors increases. Falling is more frequent in ambulatory residents in long-term care.

  ○ Screen for fall risk in nursing home (Morse Fall Scale; Morse JM, Morse RM, Tylko S. Development of a scale to identify the fall-prone patient. *Can J Aging*. 1989;8:366–377.)

- Assess for risk factors using a multidisciplinary approach, including PT and OT if problems with gait, balance, or lower extremity strength identified.
- Complete environmental assessment, including home safety, and mitigate identified hazards.
- Diagnose and treat underlying cause.
- Begin fall prevention program targeting interventions for risk factors (see **Table 46**).

Table 46. Preventing Falls: Selected Risk Factors and Suggested Interventions

Factors	Suggested Interventions
General Risk	
	Offer exercise program to include combination of resistance (strength) training, gait, balance, and coordination training
	medical assessment before starting
	tailor to individual capabilities
	initiate with caution in those with limited mobility not accustomed to physical activity
	prescribed by qualified healthcare provider
	regular review and progression
	Education and information, cognitive-behavioral intervention to decrease fear of falling and activity avoidance
	Recommend daily supplementation of vitamin D (at least 800 IU) to achieve 25-hydroxy level >30 (see Osteoporosis, p 198).
Medication-related Factors	
Use of benzodiazepines, sedative-hypnotics, antidepressants, or antipsychotics	Consider agents with less risk of falls
	Taper and D/C medications, as possible
	Address sleep problems with nonpharmacologic interventions (see p 267)
	Educate regarding appropriate use of medications and monitoring for adverse events
Recent change in dosage or number of prescription medications *or* use of ≥4 prescription medications *or* use of other medications associated with fall risk	Review medication profile and reduce number and dosage of all medications, as possible
	Monitor response to medications and to dosage changes

(cont.)

Table 46. Preventing Falls: Selected Risk Factors and Suggested Interventions (cont.)

Factors	Suggested Interventions
Mobility-related Factors	
Presence of environmental hazards (eg, improper bed height, cluttered walking surfaces, lack of railings, poor lighting)	Improve lighting, especially at night
	Remove floor barriers (eg, loose carpeting)
	Replace existing furniture with safer furniture (eg, correct height, more stable)
	Install support structures, especially in bathroom (eg, railings, grab bars, elevated toilet seats)
	Use nonslip bathmats
Impaired gait, balance, or transfer skills	Refer to PT for comprehensive evaluation and rehabilitation
	Refer to PT or OT for gait training, transfer skills, use of assistive devices, balancing, strengthening and resistance training, and evaluation for appropriate footwear
Impaired leg or arm strength or range of motion, or proprioception	Refer to PT or OT
Medical Factors	
Parkinson disease, osteoarthritis, depressive symptoms, impaired cognition, carotid sinus hypersensitivity, other conditions associated with increased falls	Optimize medical therapy
	Monitor for disease progression and impact on mobility and impairments
	Determine need for assistive devices
	Use bedside commode if frequent nighttime urination
	Cardiac pacing in patients with carotid sinus hypersensitivity who experience falls due to syncope
Postural hypotension: drop in SBP ≥20 mmHg (or ≥20%) with or without symptoms, within 3 min of rising from lying to standing	See orthostatic postural hypotension, p 57
Visual (see Eye Disorders, p 92)	Cataract extraction
	Avoid wearing multifocal lenses while walking, particularly up stairs

DYSPHAGIA

See also p 221.

Presentation/Patient Complaints

Structural:

• Pocketing of food in cheeks, on hard palate, or under tongue

• Food gets stuck after swallowing

• Speech abnormalities: slurring, gurgly voice

• Orofacial changes: facial weakness, abnormal tongue movements

Functional:

• Inability to initiate a swallow

• Impaired ability to transfer food from mouth to esophagus

• Nasal regurgitation

• Coughing (aspiration)

• Drooling or excessive secretions

• Reluctance to eat specific foods or foods of certain consistency, or to eat at all

Common Causes

• Cerebrovascular accident/stroke

• Parkinson disease

• Oropharyngeal tumors

• Zenker's diverticulum

• Cervical osteophytes

• GERD

• Multifactorial (eg, transfer dysphagia)

• Poor-fitting dentures

Evaluation

• Physical examination

  ○ Oral cavity, head, neck, and supraclavicular region

  ○ All cranial nerves with emphasis on nerves V, VII, IX, X, XI, XII

• Review medications for those that can decrease saliva production (eg, anticholinergics)

• Referral to speech-language pathologists

• Diagnostic tests (as indicated)

  ○ Modified barium swallow or videofluoroscopy to assess swallowing mechanism; may document aspiration

  ○ Upper endoscopy

  ○ Fiberoptic nasopharyngeal laryngoscopy provides detailed evaluation of lesions in oropharynx, hypopharynx, larynx, and proximal esophagus; also visualizes pooled secretions or food

  ○ Esophageal manometry often used in combination with barium radiography; more useful for assessment of esophageal dysphagia

Treatment

• Identify and treat underlying cause (eg, endoscopic dilation, cricopharyngeal myotomy, botulinum toxin injection in cricopharyngeal muscle)

• Dietary modifications based on recommendation of speech pathologist, occupational therapist, or dietitian

- Swallowing rehabilitation, eg, multiple swallows, tilt head back and place bolus on strong side, or chin tuck
- Avoid rushed or forced feeding
- Sit upright at 90 degrees
- Elevate head of the bed at 30 degrees
- Review medications and administration for unsafe practices, eg, crushing enteric-coated or ER formulations
- Symptomatic presbyesophagus responds to esophageal dilatation

Food Consistencies
- Pureed: thick, homogenous textures; pudding-like
- Ground/minced: easily chewed without coarse texture; excludes most raw foods except mashed bananas
- Soft or easy to chew: soft foods prepared without a blender; tender meats cut to ≤1-cm pieces; excludes nuts, tough skins, and raw, crispy, or stringy foods
- Modified general: soft textures that do not require grinding or chopping

Fluid Consistencies and Thickening Agents
- Thin: regular fluids
- Nectar-like: thin enough to be sipped through a straw or from a cup, but still spillable (eg, eggnog, buttermilk); 2–3 tsp of thickening powder to ½ cup (4 fl oz) of liquid
- Honey-like: thick enough to be eaten with a spoon, too thick for a straw, not able to independently hold its shape (eg, yogurt, tomato sauce, honey); 3–5 tsp of thickening powder to ½ cup (4 fl oz) of liquid
- Spoon-thick: pudding-like, must be eaten with a spoon (eg, thick milk pudding, thickened applesauce); 5–6 tsp of thickening powder to ½ cup (4 fl oz) of liquid

GASTROESOPHAGEAL REFLUX DISEASE (GERD)

Evaluation and Assessment
Empiric treatment is appropriate when hx is typical for uncomplicated GERD.
- Endoscopy (if symptoms are chronic or persist despite initial management, atypical presentation)
- Ambulatory pH testing

Risk Factors
- Obesity
- Hiatal hernia
- Use of estrogen, nitroglycerin, tobacco

Symptoms Suggesting Complicated GERD and Need for Evaluation
- Dysphagia
- Bleeding
- Weight loss
- Anemia
- Choking, cough, shortness of breath, hoarseness
- Chest pain
- Pain with swallowing

Management

- Antacids
- Avoid alcohol and fatty foods
- Avoid lying down for 3 h after eating
- Avoid tight-fitting clothes
- Change diet (avoid pepper, spearmint, chocolate, spicy or acidic foods, carbonated beverages)
- Drink 6–8 oz water with all medications
- Elevate head of the bed (6–8 in)
- Lose weight (if overweight)
- Stop drugs that may promote reflux or can induce esophagitis
- Stop smoking
- Consider surgery

Table 47. Pharmacologic Management of GERD

Medication	Initial Oral Dosage	Formulations (Metabolism, Excretion)
PPIs[a]		
Dexlansoprazole *(Dexilant)*	30 mg/d × 4 wk	C: ER 30, 60 (L)
✔ Esomeprazole *(Nexium)*	20 mg/d × 4 wk	C: ER 20, 40 (L)
✔ Lansoprazole▲* *(Prevacid)*	15 mg/d × 8 wk	C: ER 15, 30; granules for susp: 15, 30/packet (L)
✔ Omeprazole▲* *(Prilosec)*	20 mg/d × 4–8 wk	C: ER 10, 20,[b] 40; T: enteric-coated 20 (L)
✔ Pantoprazole *(Protonix)*	40 mg/d × 8 wk	T: enteric-coated 20, 40; inj (L)
✔ Rabeprazole *(AcipHex)*	20 mg/d × 4–8 wk; 20 mg/d maintenance, if needed	T: ER enteric-coated 20 (L)
H₂ Antagonists (for less severe GERD)		
Cimetidine▲*c *(Tagamet HB 200)*	400 or 800 mg q12h	S: 200 mg/20 mL, 300 mg/5 mL with alcohol 2.8%; T: 100, 200,[b] 300, 400, 800; inj (K, L)
✔ Famotidine▲* *(Pepcid)*	20 mg q12h × 6 wk	S: oral sus 40 mg/5 mL; T: film-coated 10,[b] 20, 40; ODT 20, 40; C (gel): 10;[b] ChT: 10;[b] inj (K)
✔ Nizatidine▲ *(Axid)*	150 mg q12h	C: 150, 300; T: 75 (K)
Ranitidine▲* *(Zantac)*	150 mg q12h	Pk: gran, effervescent (EFFERdose) 150 mg; S: syr 15 mg/mL; T: 75,[b] 150, 300; T: effervescent (EFFERdose) 150; inj (K, F)
Mucosal Protective Agent		
Sucralfate▲ *(Carafate)*	1 g q6h, 1 h ac, and hs	S: oral sus 1 g/10 mL; T: 1 g (F, K)
Prokinetic Agents		
✔ Domperidone[d]	10 mg 15–30 min ac and hs	T: 10 mg (L)
Metoclopramide▲e *(Reglan)*	5 mg q6h, ac, and hs	S: syr, sugar-free 5 mg/5 mL, conc 10 mg/mL; T: 5, 10; inj (K, F)

✔ = preferred for treating older adults

* Available OTC

[a] Associated with osteopenia/osteoporosis; can inhibit CYP2C19 and -3A4 (see **Table 10** and p 34); prolonged exposure may increase risk of fractures, community-acquired pneumonia, hospital-acquired *Clostridium difficile* diarrhea, hypomagnesemia; reduce vitamins C and B₁₂ concentrations

[b] OTC strength

[c] Inhibits CYP1A2, -2D6, -3A4 (see **Table 10**)

[d] Available in the United States only through an Investigational New Drug application for compassionate use in patients refractory to other treatments (see www.fda.gov); domperidone is approved in Canada as a treatment for upper GI motility disorders associated with gastritis and diabetic gastroparesis, and for prevention of GI symptoms associated with use of dopamine-agonist anti-Parkinson agents.

[e] Risk of EPS high in people >65 yr old.

Source: Data from DeVault KR, Castell DO. Updated guidelines for the diagnosis and treatment of gastroesophageal reflux disease. *Am J Gastroenterol* 2005;100(1):190–200.

PEPTIC ULCER DISEASE

Causes
Helicobacter pylori is the major cause. NSAIDs are the second most common cause.

Diagnosis of *H pylori*
- Endoscopy with biopsy
- Serology
- Urea breath test
- Fecal antigen test

Initial Treatment Options
- Empiric anti-ulcer treatment for 6 wk
- Definitive diagnostic evaluation by endoscopy
- Noninvasive testing for *H pylori* and treatment with antibiotics for those that test positive (see **Table 48** for regimens)
- Review patient's chronic medications for drug interactions before selecting regimen; many potential drug interactions and adverse drug events.

Table 48. Pharmacotherapeutic Management of *H pylori* Infection

Regimen	Duration	Comments
Triple Therapy		Preferred if no previous macrolide exposure
PPI[a] q12h[b] *plus* Clarithromycin 500 mg q12h *plus* Amoxicillin 1000 mg q12h	10–14 d	Example: *PrevPac* (includes lansoprazole 30 mg)
PPI[a] q12h[b] *plus* Clarithromycin 500 mg q12h *plus* Metronidazole 500 mg q12h	10–14 d	Preferred if penicillin allergy or unable to tolerate bismuth quadruple therapy
Second-line Triple Therapy		
PPI[a] q24h *plus* Amoxicillin 1 g *plus* Metronidazole 500 mg q12h	7–14 d	
Quadruple Therapy		
PPI[a] q12h[b] or H$_2$ antagonist *plus* Bismuth subsalicylate 525 mg q6h *plus* Metronidazole 250 mg q24h *plus* Tetracycline 500 mg q24h *(Helidac)*	10–14 d	
PPI[a] q12h[b] or H$_2$ antagonist *plus* Bismuth subcitrate 425 mg q24h *plus* Metronidazole 250 mg q24h *plus* Tetracycline 500 mg q24h *(Pylera)*	10–12 d	Consider if penicillin allergy or previous macrolide exposure, *or as* second-line if triple therapy fails

[a] Associated with osteopenia/osteoporosis; can inhibit CYP2C19 and -3A4 (see **Table 10** and p 34); prolonged exposure may increase risk of fractures, community-acquired pneumonia, hospital-acquired *Clostridium difficile* diarrhea; reduce vitamins C and B$_{12}$ concentrations

[b] Esomeprazole is dosed 40 mg q24h.

Source: Adapted from Chey WD, Wong BC. Practice Parameters Committee of the American College of Gastroenterology. American College of Gastroenterology guideline on the management of *Helicobacter pylori* infection. *Am J Gastroenterol.* 2007;102(8):1808–1825.

Medications

Bismuth subsalicylate▲ *(Pepto-Bismol)* [T: 324; ChT: 262; S: sus 262 mg/15 mL, 525 mg/15 mL]
Antibiotics: (for complete information, see **Table 65**)
Amoxicillin▲ *(Amoxil)* [C: 250, 500; ChT: 125, 250; S: oral sus 125 mg/5 mL, 250 mg/5 mL]
Clarithromycin▲ *(Biaxin)* [T: film-coated 250, 500; S: oral sus 125 mg/5 mL, 250 mg/5 mL]
Metronidazole▲ *(Flagyl)* [T: 250, 500, 750; C: 375]
Tetracycline▲ *(Achromycin, Sumycin)* [T: 250, 500; S: oral sus 125 mg/5 mL]
PPIs: See **Table 47**.

STRESS-ULCER PREVENTION IN HOSPITALIZED OLDER ADULTS
Risk Factors (in order of prevalence in older adults)
- Hx of GI ulceration or bleed in past year
- Sepsis
- Multiple organ failure
- Hypotension
- Mechanical ventilation for >48 h
- Kidney failure
- Major trauma, shock, or head injury
- Coagulopathy (platelets <50,000/μL, INR >1.5, or PTT >2 × control)
- Burns over >25% of body surface area
- Hepatic failure
- Intracranial hypertension
- Spinal cord injury
- Quadraplegia

Prophylaxis
- H_2 antagonists (see **Table 47**)
- PPIs (see **Table 47**)
- Sucralfate▲ (see **Table 47**)
- Antacids
- Enteral feedings

Discontinue H_2 antagonists, proton-pump inhibitors, and other treatments for stress-ulcer prevention before transfer or discharge from hospital.

Key Points
- Prophylaxis has not been shown to reduce mortality.
- No one regimen has shown superior efficacy.
- Choice of regimen depends on access to and function of GI tract and presence of nasogastric suction.

IRRITABLE BOWEL SYNDROME (IBS)
Signs and Symptoms
Symptoms should be present ≥12 wk.
Consistent with IBS:
- Abdominal pain
- Bloating
- Constipation
- Diarrhea

Not Consistent with IBS:
- Weight loss
- First onset after age 50
- Nocturnal diarrhea
- Family hx of cancer or inflammatory bowel disease
- Rectal bleeding or obstruction
- Laboratory abnormalities
- Presence of fecal parasites

Diagnosis (of exclusion)

Exclude ischemia, diverticulosis, colon cancer, inflammatory bowel disease by physical examination and testing (colonoscopy, CT scan, or small-bowel series)

Treatment

- Reassurance; not life threatening; focus on relief of physical and emotional symptoms
- Dietary modification
  - Avoid foods that trigger symptoms or produce excess gas or bloating
  - Consider a trial of a lactose-free diet
- Behavioral interventions: hypnosis, biofeedback, psychotherapy have been shown to be more effective than placebo
- Fiber supplements (see **Table 49**)
  - Synthetic: polycarbophil▲ *(FiberCon* [caplet: 625], others), methylcellulose▲ *(Citrucel, Fiber Ease* [C, sus, pwd])
  - Natural: psyllium▲ *(Metamucil* [C, T, wafer, pwd], others)
- Antispasmodics (short-term use only)
  - Dicyclomine *(Bentyl* [C: 10▲; T: 20▲; syr: 10 mg/5 mL; inj]) 10–20 mg po q6h prn (L)
  - Hyoscyamine▲ *(Anazpaz, Levsin, Levsin/SL,* others [T (sl): 0.125, 0.15; T ER, C: 0.375; inj: 125 sol]) 0.125–0.25 mg po/sl q6–8h prn (L, K)
- Antidiarrheals: may be helpful for diarrhea but not for global IBS symptoms, abdominal pain, or constipation
  - Loperamide▲ *(Imodium A-D* [C, T: 2; sol 1 mg/5 mL]) 4 mg × 1, then 2 mg after each loose bowel movement; max 16 mg/24 h
- Antidepressants
  - TCAs and SSRIs may be beneficial for patients with diarrhea or pain. See Depression, p 68, for dosing.
- Serotonin agent
  - Alosetron *(Lotronex* [T: 0.5, 1]): serotonin 3 antagonist; treatment of women with severe diarrhea-predominant IBS who have not responded to conventional therapy; 0.5 mg po q12h × 4 wk, increase to 1 mg q12h × 4 wk, stop if no response (K, L)

CONSTIPATION

Definition

Frequency of bowel movements <2–3 times/wk, straining at defecation, hard feces, or feeling of incomplete evacuation. Clinically, large amount of feces in rectum on digital examination and/or colonic fecal loading on abdominal radiograph.

Medications That Constipate

- Analgesics—opioids
- Antacids with aluminum or calcium
- Anticholinergic drugs
- Antidepressants, lithium
- Antihypertensives
- Antipsychotics
- Barium sulfate
- Bismuth
- Calcium channel blockers
- Diuretics
- Iron

Conditions That Constipate

- Colon tumor or mechanical obstruction
- Dehydration
- Depression
- Diabetes mellitus
- Hypercalcemia
- Hypokalemia
- Hypothyroidism
- Immobility
- Low intake of fiber
- Panhypopituitarism
- Parkinson disease
- Spinal cord injury
- Stroke
- Uremia

Management of Chronic Constipation

Step 1: Stop all constipating medications, when possible.

Step 2: Increase dietary fiber to 6–25 g/d, increase fluid intake to ≥1500 mL/d, and increase physical activity; or add bulk laxative (**Table 49**), provided fluid intake is ≥1500 mL/d. If fiber exacerbates symptoms or is not tolerated, or patient has limited mobility, go to Step 3.

Step 3: Add an osmotic (eg, 70% sorbitol solution, polyethylene glycol *[Miralax]*).

Step 4: Add stimulant laxative (eg, senna, bisacodyl), 2–3 times/wk. (Alternative: saline laxative, but avoid if CrCl <30 mL/min.)

Step 5: Use tap water enema or saline enema 2 times/wk.

Step 6: Use oil-retention enema for refractory constipation.

Table 49. Medications That May Relieve Constipation

Medication	Onset of Action	Starting Dosage	Site and Mechanism of Action
Bulk laxatives—not useful in managing opioid-induced constipation			
Methylcellulose▲ (Citrucel) *	12–24 h (up to 72 h)	2–4 caplets or 1 heaping tbsp with 8 oz water q8–24h	Small and large intestine; holds water in feces; mechanical distention
Psyllium▲ (Metamucil) *a	12–24 h (up to 72 h)	1–2 capsules, packets, or tsp with 8 oz water or juice q8–24h	Small and large intestine; holds water in feces; mechanical distention
Polycarbophil▲ (FiberCon, others) a	12–24 h (up to 72 h)	1250 mg q6–24h	Small and large intestine; holds water in feces; mechanical distention
Chloride channel activator			
Lubiprostone (Amitiza)		24 mcg q12h with food C: 8, 24 mcg	Enhances chloride-ion intestinal fluid secretion; does not affect serum Na+ or K+ concentrations. For idiopathic chronic constipation.
Opioid antagonists			
Alvimopan (Entereg)	NA	Initial: 12 mg po 30 min to 5 h before surgery Maintenance: 12 mg po q12h the day after surgery × 7 d max	Hospital use only; for accelerating time to recovery after partial large- or small-bowel resection with primary anastomosis; contraindicated if >7 consecutive days of therapeutic opioids (L, K, F)
Methylnaltrexone (Relistor)	30–60 min	Weight-based dosing: <38 kg: 0.15 mg/kg 38 to <62 kg: 8 mg 62–114 kg: 12 mg >114 kg: 0.15 mg/kg (all SC q48hr); if CrCl <30 mL/min, decrease dosage 50%	Peripheral-acting opioid antagonist for the treatment of opioid-induced constipation in palliative care patients who have not responded to conventional laxatives (L, K, F)

(cont.)

Table 49. Medications That May Relieve Constipation (cont.)

Medication	Onset of Action	Starting Dosage	Site and Mechanism of Action
Osmotic laxatives			
Lactulose▲ *(Chronulac)*	24–48 h	15–30 mL q12–24h	Colon; osmotic effect
Polyethylene glycol▲ *(Miralax)* *	48–96 h	17 g pwd q24h (~1 tbsp) dissolved in 8 oz water	GI tract; osmotic effect
Sorbitol 70%▲*	24–48 h	15–30 mL q12–24h; max 150 mL/d	Colon; delivers osmotically active molecules to colon
Saline laxatives			*Class effect:* potential hyperphosphatemia in patients with renal insufficiency
Magnesium citrate▲ *(Citroma)* *	30 min–3 h	120–240 mL × 1; 10 oz q24h or 5 oz q12h followed by 8 oz water × ≤5 d	Small and large intestine; attracts, retains water in intestinal lumen
Magnesium hydroxide▲ *(Milk of Magnesia)* *	30 min–3 h	30 mL q12–24h 311-mg tab (130 mg magnesium); 400, 800 mg/5 mL sus	Osmotic effect and increased peristalsis in colon
Sodium phosphate/ biphosphate emollient enema▲ *(Fleet)* *	2–15 min	14.5-oz enema × 1, repeat prn	Colon; osmotic effect
Stimulant laxatives			
Bisacodyl tablet▲ *(Dulcolax)* *	6–10 h	5–15 mg × 1	Colon; increases peristalsis
Bisacodyl suppository▲ *(Dulcolax)* *	15 min–1 h	10 mg × 1	Colon; increases peristalsis
Senna▲ *(Senokot)* *	6–10 h	1–2 tabs or 1 tsp qhs	Colon; direct action on intestine; stimulates myenteric plexus; alters water and electrolyte secretion
Surfactant laxative (fecal softener)			
Docusate▲ *(Colace)* *	24–72 h	100 mg q12–24h	Small and large intestine; detergent activity; facilitates admixture of fat and water to soften feces (effectiveness questionable); does not increase frequency of bowel movements

* Available OTC

ª Psyllium caplets and packets contain ≥3 g dietary fiber and 2–3 g soluble fiber each. A teaspoonful contains ~3.8 g dietary fiber and 3 g soluble fiber.

NAUSEA AND VOMITING

Causes

- CNS disorders (eg, motion sickness, intracranial lesions)
- Drugs (eg, chemotherapy, NSAIDs, opioid analgesics, antibiotics, digoxin)
- GI disorders (eg, mechanical obstruction; inflammation of stomach, intestine, or gallbladder; pseudo-obstruction; motility disorders; dyspepsia; gastroparesis)
- Infections (eg, viral or bacterial gastroenteritis, hepatitis, otitis, meningitis)
- Metabolic conditions (eg, uremia, acidosis, hyperparathyroidism, adrenal insufficiency)
- Psychiatric disorders

Evaluation

- If patient is not seriously ill or dehydrated, can probably wait 24–48 h to see if symptoms resolve spontaneously.
- If patient is seriously ill, dehydrated, or has other signs of acute illness, hospitalize for further evaluation.
- If symptoms persist, evaluate on the basis of the most likely causes.

Pharmacologic Management

- If analgesic drug is suspected, decrease dosage, consider adding antiemetic until tolerance develops, or change to a different analgesic drug.
- Drugs that are useful in the management of nausea and vomiting are listed in **Table 50**.

Table 50. Antiemetic Therapy

Class/Site of Action	Dosage (Metabolism)	Formulation
Dopamine antagonists/CTZ[a] vomiting center		
Haloperidol▲	IM, po: 0.5–1 mg q6h (L, K)	See page 239.
Metoclopramide▲ *(Reglan)*	PONV[b]: 5–10 mg IM near the end of surgery Chemotherapy (IV): 1–2 mg/kg 30 min before and q2–4h or q4–6h (K)	T: 5, 10 S: 10 mg/mL; syr (sugar-free): 5 mg/mL Inj: 5 mg/mL
Prochlorperazine▲ *(Compazine)*	IM, po: 5–10 mg q6–8 h, usual max 40 mg/d IV: 2.5–10 mg, max 10 mg/dose or 40 mg/d; may repeat q3–4h prn (L)	T: 5, 10, 25 mg C: 10, 15, 30 mg Syr: 5 mg/5 mL Inj: 5 mg/mL Sp: 2.5, 10, 25
Serotonin (5-HT$_3$) antagonists/CTZ, gut		
✔Ondansetron▲ *(Zofran)*	PONV: 16 mg po 1 h before anesthesia IM, IV: 4 mg immediately before anesthesia; repeat if needed (L) Radiation therapy: 8 mg po 1–2 h before, then 8 mg po q8h × 1–2 d	T: 4, 8, 24 mg ODT: 4, 8 mg S: 4 mg/5 mL Inj: 2 mg/mL
Granisetron *(Kytril)*	PONV: 1 mg IV before anesthesia or anesthesia reversal Chemotherapy: 2 mg/d po (L, K) Radiation therapy: 2 mg po 1 h before	T: 1 mg S: 2 mg/10 mL Inj: 1 mg/mL Pch: 3.1 mg/24 h
Dolasetron *(Anzemet)*	PONV: 100 mg po 2 h before surgery; 12.5 mg IV 15 min before stopping anesthesia (L)	T: 50, 100 mg Inj: 20 mg/mL
Antimuscarinic/H$_1$ antagonist/vestibular apparatus		
Diphenhydrinate▲ *(Dramamine)* *	IM, IV, po: 50–100 mg q4–6h; max 400 mg/d (L)	T, ChT: 50 mg S: 12.5 mg/4 mL, 16.62 mg/5 mL Inj: 10 mg/mL
Meclizine▲ *(Antivert)* *	Motion sickness: 12.5–25 mg 1 h before travel, repeat dose q12–24h if needed Vertigo: 25–100 mg/d in divided doses (L)	T: 12.5, 25, 50 mg ChT: 25 mg C: 25, 30 mg
Scopolamine *(Transderm Scop)*	Motion sickness: apply 1 pch behind ear ≥4 h before travel/exposure; change q3d (L)	Pch: 1.5 mg

✔ = preferred for treating older adults
* Available OTC
[a] Chemoreceptor trigger zone
[b] Postoperative nausea and vomiting
Note: All have potential CNS toxicity. Metoclopramide associated with EPS and tardive dyskinesia.

DIARRHEA

Causes
- Drugs (eg, antibiotics [see **Table 65** and below], laxatives, colchicine)
- Fecal impaction
- GI disorders (eg, irritable bowel syndrome, malabsorption, inflammatory bowel disease)
- Infections (eg, viral, bacterial, parasitic)
- Lactose intolerance

Evaluation
- If patient is not seriously ill or dehydrated and there is no blood in the feces, can probably wait 48 h to see if symptoms resolve spontaneously.
- If patient is seriously ill, dehydrated, or has other signs of acute illness, hospitalize for further evaluation.
- If diarrhea persists, evaluate on the basis of the most likely causes.

Pharmacologic Management
Drugs that are useful in the management of diarrhea are listed in **Table 51**.

Table 51. Antidiarrheals		
Drug	**Dosage (Metabolism)**	**Formulations**
✔ Attapulgite *(Kaopectate)* *	1200–1500 mg after each loose bowel movement or q2h; 15–30 mL up to 9 × /d, up to 9000 mg/24 h (not absorbed)	S: oral conc 600, 750 mg/15 mL; T: 750; ChT: 300, 600
✔ Bismuth subsalicylate▲* *(Pepto-Bismol)*	2 tabs or 30 mL q30–60min prn up to 8 doses/24 h (L, K)	S: 262 mg/15 mL, 525 mg/15 mL; T: 324; ChT: 262
Diphenoxylate with atropine▲ *(Lomotil)* [a]	15–20 mg/d of diphenoxylate in 3–4 divided doses; maintenance 5–15 mg/d in 2–3 divided doses (L)	S: oral, diphenoxylate hydrochloride 2.5 mg + atropine sulfate 0.025 mg/5 mL; T: diphenoxylate hydrochloride 2.5 mg + atropine sulfate 0.025 mg
✔ Loperamide▲ *(Imodium A-D)* *	Initial: 4 mg followed by 2 mg after each loose bowel movement, up to 16 mg/d (L)	Caplet: 2; C: 2; T: 2; S: oral, 1 mg/5 mL

✔ = preferred for treating older adults
* Available OTC
[a] Anticholinergic, potential CNS toxicity

ANTIBIOTIC-ASSOCIATED DIARRHEA
(Antibiotic-associated pseudomembranous colitis [AAPMC])

Definition
A specific form of *Clostridium difficile* pseudomembranous colitis

Risk Factors

- Almost any oral or parenteral antibiotic and several antineoplastic agents, including cyclophosphamide, doxorubicin, fluorouracil, methotrexate
- Advanced age
- Duration of hospitalization
- PPI

Prevention

Probiotic products containing *Lactobacillus caseia*, *Streptococcus thermophilus*, and *L bulgaricus* are not recommended to prevent primary infection.

Presentation

- Abdominal pain, cramping
- Dehydration
- Diarrhea (can be bloody)
- Fecal leukocytes
- Fever (100–105°F)
- Hypoalbuminemia
- Hypovolemia
- Leukocytosis

Symptoms appear a few days after starting to 10 wk after discontinuing the offending agent.

Evaluation and Empiric Management

- D/C unnecessary antibiotics, and agents that can slow gastric motility such as opioids and antidiarrheal agents.
- Initiate empiric treatment if severe or complicated *C difficile* suspected.
- Perform *C difficile* toxin test on 2 separate bowel movements. If suspicion remains after 2 negative tests, a third toxin test can be performed. Some laboratories perform *C difficile* A and B toxin DNA testing, which is highly sensitive; repeat testing is unnecessary unless symptoms or clinical situation change.
- Place patient in contact isolation and observe infection control procedures. Hand washing is crucial and must be done with soap and water to remove spores. Hand sanitizers do not kill or remove spores.
- Provide adequate fluid and electrolyte replacement.
- Consider empiric metronidazole (see **Table 52** for dosing).

Diagnosis

Isolation of *C difficile* or its toxin from symptomatic patient. At least two negative fecal examinations are needed to exclude diagnosis.

Treatment

Table 52. Treatment of Suspected or Confirmed *Clostridium difficile* Infection		
Clinical Definition	**Supportive Clinical Data**	**Treatment**
Toxin negative on 2 specimens		D/C contact isolation D/C metronidazole/vancomycin Begin antidiarrheal agent Evaluate other causes
Initial episode, mild or moderate	Leukocytosis (WBC ≤15,000 cells/μL), serum Cr <1.5 times premorbid level	Metronidazole 500 mg po q8h × 10–14 d Fidaxomicin* 200 mg po q12h × 10 d
Initial episode, severe	Leukocytosis (WBC >15,000 cells/μL), which signifies colonic inflammation; serum Cr ≥1.5 times premorbid level, which signifies dehydration	Vancomycin 125 mg po q6h × 10–14 d
Initial episode, severe, complicated	Hypotension or shock, ileus, megacolon	Vancomycin 500 mg po or NG tube q6h plus metronidazole IV 500 mg q8h; if complete ileus, vancomycin pr is an option.
First recurrence		Same as initial episode
Second recurrence		Vancomycin in a tapered and/or pulsed regimen

Source: Adapted from Cohen SH, Gerding DN, Johnson S, et al. Clinical practice guidelines for *Clostridium difficile* infection in adults: 2010 Update by the Society for Healthcare Epidemiology of America (SHEA) and the Infectious Diseases Society of America (IDSA). *Infect Control Hosp Epidemiol* 2010;31(5):431–455.
*Fidaxomicin *(Dificid)* [T: 200 mg; 92% F, minimal systemic absorption]. Clinical trials did not include patients with life-threatening or fulminant *C difficile* infection, toxic megacolon, or with >1 *C difficile* infection in the previous 3 mo. Fidaxomicin is not in the SHEA/IDSA guideline.

HEMORRHOIDS
Contributing Factors
- Constipation
- Prolonged straining
- Exercise
- Gravity
- Low-fiber diet
- Pregnancy
- Increased intra-abdominal pressure
- Irregular bowel habits
- Age

Classification
- External: distal to the dentate line and painful on thrombosis, itchy
- Internal: proximal to the dentate line without sensitivity to pain, touch, or temperature; mucous discharge; feeling of incomplete evacuation
  - Grade
    - First-degree: no prolapse, may bleed after defecation, only seen via anoscope
    - Second-degree: prolapse outside anal canal with defecation and retract spontaneously

- Third-degree: prolapse and require manual reduction
- Fourth-degree: prolapsed, nonreducible

Treatment
Diet and Lifestyle Changes
- High-fiber diet (20–35 g/d) or psyllium, methylcellulose, or calcium polycarbophil
- Increased fluid intake
- Avoid prolonged time on commode
Topical Treatments
- Sitz baths (40°C)
- Protectants plus vasoconstrictor, eg, light mineral oil, petrolatum, shark liver oil *plus* phenylephrine *(Preparation H*, Annucort*, Cortifoam*)*, or with hydrocortisone [oint, crm, gel, foam, supp, wipes]; apply/insert up to 4 times/d.
Procedures
- Office-based
  - Rubber band ligation: for first-, second-, or third-degree internal hemorrhoids
    - Contraindicated in patients who are anticoagulated
    - D/C antiplatelet drugs (including aspirin) for 5–7 d before and after banding
  - Sclerotherapy
  - Bipolar diathermy
  - Infrared photocoagulation
- Surgical
  - Open (Millgan-Morgan) hemorrhoidectomy
  - Closed (Ferguson) hemorrhoidectomy
  - Doppler-guided transanal hemorrhoidal ligation
  - Circular stapled hemorrhoidopexy (for prolapsed hemorrhoids)
- Postoperative complications
  - Bleeding
  - Urinary retention
  - Wound infection

DRUG-INDUCED LIVER DISEASE
Risk Factors
- Advanced age
- Sex (drug-specific)
- Alcohol use
- Genetic predisposition

Diagnosis: Clinical features consistent with acute hepatitis or cholestatic liver disease

Classification

- Intrinsic hepatotoxicity (predictable): dose-related, short-term exposure; eg, APAP overdose
- Idiosyncratic hepatotoxicity (unpredictable):
  - Allergic (hypersensitivity): clinical features—fever, rash, eosinophilia, recurrence with rechallenge; usual timeframe 1–5 wk
  - Nonallergic (idiosyncratic) clinical features—allergic features absent; usual timeframe weeks to months

Table 53. Presentation and Management of Drug-induced Liver Disease

Condition	Liver Enzymes/Presentation	Management and Prognosis
Acute Hepatitis		
Hepatocellular necrosis (APAP, halothane, labetalol, methyldopa, herbals, hydralazine, INH, NSAIDs)	ALT >2 × upper limit of normal or ALT:alk phos ratio >5 Asymptomatic to jaundice, fatigue, anorexia, nausea, coagulopathy, ascites	Withdrawal of drug, supportive care; *N*-acetylcysteine for APAP toxicity; mortality rate 10%–50% if jaundice present
Cholestatic (amoxicillin ± clavulanate, erythromycin, dicloxacillin, methyldopa, herbals, hydralazine, sulindac, naproxen)	ALT >2 × upper limit of normal or ALT:alk phos ratio <2; increased GGT Jaundice, pruritus, pale feces, dark urine, abdominal pain, fever, chills	Withdrawal of drug, resolves in a few weeks
Mixed hepatocellular-cholestatic (captopril, herbals, sulindac, nabumetone, naproxen, carbamazepine, phenytoin)	Jaundice, resembles biliary obstruction without pain and fever	Withdrawal of drug, resolves in a few weeks
Acute hyperbilirubinemia (rifampin, anabolic steroids)	Increased indirect bilirubin, increased direct bilirubin	
Chronic Hepatitis		
(nitrofurantoin, HMG-CoA reductase inhibitors, herbals)	Increased ALT, PT; prolonged drug exposure, women more likely to be affected than men; increased serum globulin concentration; autoantibodies (ANA); enlarged liver, splenomegaly, ascites, cirrhosis, fibrosis, jaundice, anorexia, fatigue	Withdrawal of drug, resolves in a few weeks

Note: alk phos = alkaline phosphatase; GGT = gamma glutamyl transferase

HEARING IMPAIRMENT

DEFINITION
The most common sensory impairment in old age. To quantify hearing ability, the necessary intensity (decibel = dB) and frequency (Hertz) of the perceived pure-tone signal must be described.

Importance: Hearing impairment is strongly correlated with depression and decreased quality of life.

EVALUATION
Screening and Evaluation

- Note problems during conversation.
- Ask the question: Do you feel you have hearing loss? A "yes" response should prompt referral to audiology.
- Test with handheld audioscope or whisper test. Refer patients who screen positive for audiologic evaluation.

- Whisper test: stand behind patient at arm's length from ear, cover untested ear, fully exhale, whisper a combination of 3 numbers and letters (eg, 6-K-2) and ask patient to repeat the set; if patient unable to repeat all 3, whisper a second set. Inability to repeat at least 3 of 6 is positive for impairment.

Audiometry

- Documents the dB loss across frequencies
- Determines the pattern of loss (see Classification, below)

- Determines if loss is unilateral or bilateral and assesses speech discrimination.

CLASSIFICATION
See **Table 54**. Mixed hearing disorders are quite common, particularly involving features of age-related presbycusis and conductive loss. Central auditory processing disorders become clinically important when superimposed on other ear pathology.

Table 54. Classification of Hearing Disorders			
	Sensorineural Hearing Loss	Conductive Hearing Loss	Central Auditory Processing Disorder
Pathologic process	Cochlear or retrocochlear (cranial nerve VIII) pathology	Impaired transmission to inner ear from external or middle ear pathology	CNS change interfering with ability to discriminate speech, particularly when background noise is present
Weber test findings	Lateralizes away from impaired ear	Lateralizes toward impaired ear	Normal
Rinne test findings	Normal	Abnormal in impaired ear	Normal

(cont.)

	Sensorineural Hearing Loss	Conductive Hearing Loss	Central Auditory Processing Disorder
Audiogram/ Audiometry findings	Air and bone conduction thresholds equal	Air conduction thresholds greater than bone conduction thresholds	Normal for pure tone audiometry; impaired for speech discrimination
Common causes	Age-related presbycusis (high frequency loss, problems with speech discrimination) most common Excessive noise exposure Acoustic neuroma Ménière disease (both high- and low-frequency loss) Ototoxic drugs	Cerumen impaction Otosclerosis Rheumatoid arthritis Paget disease	Dementia Stroke Presbycusis

MANAGEMENT

Remove Ear Wax

Ear wax causes conductive loss and further reduces hearing. Soft wax can be flushed with a syringe, removed with a cerumen scoop, or suctioned. Dry or recurrent impactions benefit from softening.

Fill ear canal with 5–10 gtt water and cover with cotton q12h × ≥4 d. Liquid must stay in contact with ear for ≥15 min. Hearing may worsen as cerumen expands. Water is as effective as commercial preparations (eg, *Debrox, Cerumenex, Colace*). Use of any of the commercial preparations for >4 d may cause ear irritation.

Table 55. Rehabilitation of Hearing Loss, by Level of Loss

Level of Loss (dB)	Difficulty Understanding	Need for Hearing Technology
0–24	None	None
25–40 (mild)	Normal speech	Hearing aid or AMEI in specific situations
41–55 (moderate)	Loud speech	Hearing aid or AMEI in many situations
56–69 (severe)	Anything but amplified speech	Hearing aid, AMEI, or EAS for all communication
70–79 (severe)	Even amplified speech	EAS or cochlear implent, or combined cochlear implant and hearing aid
≥80 (profound)	Even amplified speech	Cochlear implant and/or speech reading, aural rehabilitation, sign language

Note: AMEI = active middle ear implant; EAS = electric acoustic stimulation

Hearing Technology

Hearing Aids: Digital devices enhance select frequencies for each ear. Amplification in both ears (binaural) provides best speech understanding; unilateral aid may be appropriate if hearing loss is asymmetrical, if hearing-aid care is challenging, or if cost is a factor. Features that enhance sound and speech quality include directional microphones, open-fit hearing aids, ear-to-ear wireless coordination, and in the canal extended-wear aids *(Lyric)*.

Cochlear Implants: Bypass the middle ear, directly innervate auditory nerve. Results after age 65 comparable to those in younger people. Failure rate <1%, but patient selection important. Selection criteria:

- Severe to profound bilateral sensorineural hearing loss
- <40% correct on sentence recognition test in best aided ear
- Benefit from aids less than that expected from implant
- No external or middle ear pathology
- No medical contraindication to general anesthesia
- No contraindication to surgical placement of device
- Family support, motivation, appropriate expectations

Active Middle Ear Implants: A fully implantable ossicular stimulator; all components (including battery) are implanted under the skin; for adults who cannot wear hearing aids for medical (eg, collapsed ear canal, inability to handle device) or personal (ie, cosmetic) reasons.

Electric Acoustic Stimulation: Use of a cochlear implant and hearing aid in the same ear; for patients who have ≥60 dB hearing loss at frequencies >1000 Hz, even though they may have mild to moderate hearing loss at frequencies ≤1000 Hz. The hearing aid amplifies residual hearing at low frequencies, while the cochlear implant provides electric stimulation to the high frequencies. Users still perform well when using the implant without the hearing aid.

Assistive Devices: Microphone placed close to sound source transmits to headphones or earpiece. Transmission is by wire or wireless (FM or infrared); these systems increase signal-to-noise ratio, which is useful for people with central auditory processing disorder. Personal pocket devices (eg, *Pocket Talker)* are relatively inexpensive; every care setting should have one. Also consider recommending flashing fire alarms, amplified telephones, closed captioning.

Telephone Device for the Deaf (TDD): Receiver is a keyboard that allows the hearing-impaired person to respond.

Tips for Communication with Hearing-impaired People

- Ask the person how best to communicate
- Stand 2–3 ft away
- Have the person's attention
- Have the person seated in front of a wall, which helps reflect sound
- Speak toward the better ear
- Use lower-pitched voice
- Speak slowly and distinctly; don't shout
- Rephrase rather than repeat
- Pause at the end of phrases or ideas
- Ask the person to repeat what was heard

TINNITUS

Definition

The perception of sound in the absence of external acoustic stimulation; may be ringing, crackling, or whistling; may be continuous or intermittent

Objective Tinnitus

Noise heard by both patient and examiner (rare); usually due to abnormal blood flow in or around ear (normal anatomic variants or a pathologic condition)

Subjective Tinnitus

- Cannot be heard externally by others (common)
- Normal tinnitus lasts <5 min, <once/week
- Pathologic tinnitus lasts >5 min, >weekly (usually in people with hearing loss)

Evaluation

- Auscultate the head and neck near ear orbits, mastoids for objective tinnitus.
  - If pulsatile, obtain CT/MRA for vascular cause.
  - If continuous, obtain MRI looking for patulous Eustachian tube; other causes include palatal myoclonus, stapedial muscle spasm.
  - Refer to otolaryngology
- Examine ear canals for cerumen, otitis externa or interna; treat and reassess.
- Assess hearing (as above); unilateral hearing loss and tinnitus suggest acoustic neuroma; obtain MRI.
- Audiometry (see p 120)
- Check medication list for drugs associated with tinnitus, eg, NSAIDs, ASA, antibiotics (especially erythromycin), loop diuretics (especially furosemide), chemotherapy, quinine.

Treatment

- Objective tinnitus: refer to otolaryngology.
- Subjective tinnitus without distress:
  - Normal tinnitus (see p 122): reassure patient.
  - Pathologic tinnitus (see p 122): educate patient, encourage amplification for those with hearing impairment.
- Subjective tinnitus with distress: warrants referral to otolaryngology.
  - Severe complaints about tinnitus are often a sign of depression; treat if indicated (see p 68).
  - Treatment may include tinnitus control instruments and desensitization therapy.
- Tinnitus retraining therapy (a form of desensitization, combined with counseling) may be the most effective approach (www.tinnitus-pjj.com).

ANEMIA
Evaluation
- Hematopoietic reserve capacity declines with age, eg, slower return of Hb to normal after phlebotomy.
- Evaluate people >65 yr old when Hb <13.
- Evaluate if Hb falls >1 g/dL in 1 yr.
- Physical examination and laboratory tests for kidney or liver disease.
- Evaluate GI and GU source if iron deficient.
- Check WBC and peripheral blood smear; pursue suspected causes as appropriate.
- Combined deficiencies are common in older adults; reasonable to check B_{12}, folate, and iron in all cases. MCV is not reliable in combined deficiency states.
- Check reticuloctye count and reticulocyte index.
  - Reticuloctye count or index high: adequate response, suspect blood loss or RBC destruction
  - Reticulocyte count or index normal or low: evaluate for possible B_{12} or folate deficiency (see **Figure 6**), and possible iron deficiency (see **Figure 7**)

Common Anemias of Later Life: Diagnosis and Treatment
Iron deficiency anemia: Usual laboratory values (iron, TIBC, ferritin) less reliable in presence of inflammatory conditions (see **Figure 7**). Begin with oral iron using the steps outlined in **Table 57**.

Anemia of inflammation (also known as anemia of chronic inflammation or chronic disease):
- Most common causes in older adults:
  - Acute and chronic infection
  - Chronic inflammation
  - Malignancy
  - Protein calorie malnutrition
  - Unidentified chronic disease
- Laboratory tests: usually low iron, low or normal TIBC, ferritin >100 ng/mL, low soluble transferrin receptor (sTfR)
- Type determines treatability:
  - "Rheumatoid arthritis type" responds to erythropoietin at usual dosages (see **Table 56**).
  - "Cancer type" may respond to erythropoietin at high dosages (see **Table 56**).
- Restoring Hb to 10–11 g/dL improves quality of life, function, and possibly survival.

Combined iron deficiency and anemia of inflammation:
- Anemia often more severe than in chronic inflammation alone.
- Ferritin ≤100 mg/mL.
- Iron, transferrin, and saturation reduced.
- Give iron trial and check reticulocyte count in 2 wk (see **Table 57**).

Figure 6. Evaluation of Hypoproliferative Anemia Due to Possible B₁₂ or Folate Deficiency

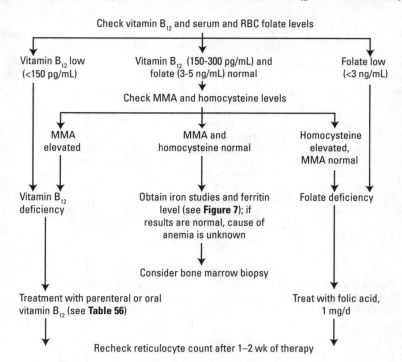

Source: Balducci L. Epidemiology of anemia in the elderly: Information on diagnostic evaluation. *J Amer Geriatr Soc* 2003; 51(3 Suppl):S2–9. Reprinted with permission.

Figure 7. Evaluation of Hypoproliferative Anemia Due to Possible Iron Deficiency

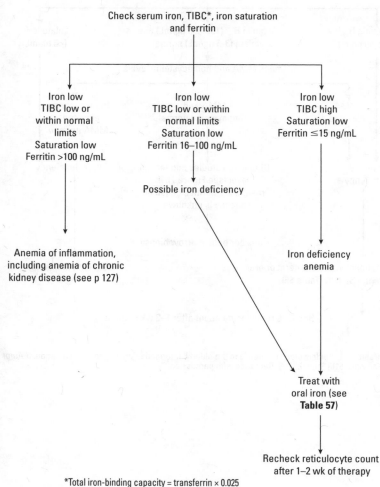

Check serum iron, TIBC*, iron saturation and ferritin

- Iron low
  TIBC low or within normal limits
  Saturation low
  Ferritin >100 ng/mL
  → Anemia of inflammation, including anemia of chronic kidney disease (see p 127)

- Iron low
  TIBC low or within normal limits
  Saturation low
  Ferritin 16–100 ng/mL
  → Possible iron deficiency → Treat with oral iron (see **Table 57**)

- Iron low
  TIBC high
  Saturation low
  Ferritin ≤15 ng/mL
  → Iron deficiency anemia → Treat with oral iron (see **Table 57**)

Treat with oral iron (see **Table 57**) → Recheck reticulocyte count after 1–2 wk of therapy

*Total iron-binding capacity = transferrin × 0.025

Anemia of chronic kidney disease:

- Caused by decreased erythropoietin production; check erythropoietin level and iron studies.
- Restoring Hb levels decreases transfusions and fatigue but doubles stroke risk in people with diabetes, chronic kidney disease, and anemia. Until new guidelines are developed in 2012 (www.kdigo.org), therapy should be individualized and patients informed of the modest benefits and potential risks before starting or continuing therapy. If treatment is deemed necessary, an approach to treatment is outlined below:
- Treatment is erythropoietin and iron replacement when Hb <10 g/dL (see **Table 56**). Keep transferrin saturation 20%–50% and ferritin 100–500 ng/mL. Oral iron absorption is poor in chronic kidney disease; parenteral replacement often needed.
  - Begin erythropoietin based on body weight (see **Table 56**); check Hb q2wk with target increase of 0.5–1 g/dL/wk, not more. Adjust erythropoietin dosage q4wk; increase or decrease by 25% to reach goal. Some patients will not respond to usual dosages, and it may be that risk of cardiovascular events are a result of high dosages. No target Hb is recommended; rather, treat only to reduce or eliminate the need for transfusion. Erythropoietin dosages should probably not exceed those recommended in **Table 56**.

Anemia of B_{12} and folate deficiency:

- Laboratory tests: anemia or pancytopenia, macrocytosis
- B_{12} deficiency definite at concentrations <150 pg/mL, possible at concentrations of 150–300 pg/mL; check MMA or give trial of B_{12} replacement (see **Figure 6**)
- Treatment: see **Table 56**

Anemia of unknown cause:

- No evidence of B_{12} or folate deficiency, iron studies all normal, CrCl >30 mL/min
- Prevalence: 17% of all anemias after age 65
- May be age-related decline in hematopoietic reserve, low erythropoietin, or poor response to endogenous erythropoietin

Hemolytic anemia:

- Hallmark is high reticulocyte count.
- Causes if Coombs' test positive: chronic lymphocytic leukemia, medications, lymphoma, collagen vascular disease, idiopathic
- Causes if Coombs' test negative: vascular, intrinsic

Table 56. Treatment of Anemias Associated with Deficiency

Treatment	Formulation and Dosage	Comments
B$_{12}$	1000 mcg IM daily × 5 days, then weekly × 4 wk, then 1000 mcg IM every mo or 1000 mcg/d po or 2500 mcg sl once daily or nsal spray *(Nascobal)* 500 mcg intranasally in one nostril once weekly (nasal spray should be administered ≥1 h before or after ingestion of hot foods or liquids)	Monitor K$^+$ in first wk of treatment
Folate	1 mg/d po for 1–4 mo or until complete hematologic recovery	
Iron (oral)	See **Table 57**.	
(parenteral)	Iron sucrose *(Venofer)*: 200 mg IV, injected undiluted over 2–5 min on 5 different occasions within 14-d period (total cumulative dose of 1000 mg) Other recommended dosing options: • 100 mg, dilute to max of 100 mL in NS and infuse over ≥15 min • 300 mg, dilute to max of 250 mL in NS and infuse over 1.5 h • 400 mg, dilute to max of 250 mL in NS and infuse over 2.5 h Ferumoxytol *(Feraheme)*: 510 mg IV × 1 dose followed by 510 mg 3–8 d later	
Erythropoiesis-stimulating agents		*Caution:* Raise Hb only to avoid need for transfusion; higher Hb increases cardiovascular events.
	Epoetin alfa *(Epogen, Procrit)* usual dosage 50–150 U/kg SC q2–4wk in chronic kidney disease; 40,000–60,000 U/wk in chemotherapy	Monitor BP, adjust dosage q4–6wk based on response. Use in cancer patients not on chemotherapy increases risk of death. Use in patients on chemotherapy reduces need for transfusion but increases risk of thromboembolic events
	Epoetin beta *(Micera)* 40–80 U/kg q2–4 wk in kidney disease Darbepoetin alfa *(Aranesp)* 2.25–4.5 mcg/kg/wk in chemotherapy; 0.4–0.6 mcg/kg/wk in renal disease; dose q2–4wk when Hb stable.	

Table 57. Steps in Oral Iron Replacement		
Step 1: Estimate iron replacement dose based on Hb	**Hb (g/dL)**	**Elemental iron total replacement dose (mg)**
	>11	5,000
	9–11	10,000
	<9	15,000
Step 2: Select an oral iron preparation (only 10% of oral iron is absorbed)	**Preparation**	**Number of tablets to achieve 5000-mg elemental iron replacement**
	Ferrous sulfate (324-mg tab, 65 mg elemental iron)	75
	Ferrous gluconate (300-mg tab, 36 mg elemental iron)	140
	Ferrous fumarate (100-mg tab, 33 mg elemental iron)	150
	Iron polysaccharide (150-mg tab, 150 mg elemental iron)	33
Step 3: Decide on dosing frequency	Many patients cannot tolerate more than a single tablet daily. Iron is best absorbed on an empty stomach. Assess tolerance after 1 wk (phone call); if not tolerating, adjust dose, interval, or formulation.	
Step 4: Recheck Hb and ferritin after each 5000-mg cycle	Give additional 5000-mg cycles as needed.	

Note: 1 unit packed RBCs replaces 500 mg iron, or approximately the same as is absorbed from a 5000-mg cycle of oral iron. Reticulocytosis should occur in 7–10 d. Lack of correction with replacement suggests nonadherence, malabsorption, or ongoing blood loss. H_2-blockers, antacids, and PPIs reduce absorption. Enterically coated preparations are less well absorbed.

PANCYTOPENIA

Unless due to B_{12} deficiency or drug-induced, bone marrow aspirate is indicated; causes include cancer, fibrosis, myelodysplasia, sideroblastic anemia

Aplastic Anemia

• Hematopoietic stem cell failure; in 78%, cause is idiopathic
• Diagnosis: hypocellular bone marrow
• Treatment: 50% respond to antithymocyte globulin and cyclosporine, or stem cell transplant

Myelodysplasia

A group of stem cell disorders with decreased production of blood elements

• Anemia (with or without ringed sideroblasts), macrocytosis, mild leukopenia, normal or increased platelets
• Cytogenetic abnormalities in >55%, most often 5q deletion
• Treatment mainly supportive. Several primary therapies available all have limited effectiveness.
• DiGugleilmo's syndrome related to myelodysplasia; red cell, white cell, and platelet dysplasia often evolves to erythroleukemia

PRIMARY MYELOPROLIFERATIVE DISORDERS

Polycythemia Vera
- Diagnosis: elevated RBC mass with normal arterial oxygen saturation and splenomegaly
- If no splenomegaly, 2 of the following: leukocytosis, increased leukocyte alkaline phosphatase, or increased B_{12}; or genetic testing showing JAK-2
- Treatment: phlebotomy to achieve iron deficiency and hematocrit ≤45, and ASA 325 mg/d

Essential Thrombocytosis
- Platelet count >600,000/μL on two occasions ≥1 mo apart; Hb <13 mg/dL or normal RBC mass
- Normal iron marrow stores and no splenomegaly; exclude reactive thrombocytosis
- No Philadelphia or *bcr-abl* gene rearrangements or myelofibrosis in marrow
- Treatment: For patients at high risk of thrombohemorrhagic events, use low-dose ASA and hydroxyurea. Anagrelide is less effective at preventing thrombosis.

Chronic Myelogenous Leukemia
- Leukocytosis with early myeloid forms evenly distributed in peripheral blood
- Philadelphia chromosome in >95% of cases
- Leukocyte alkaline phosphatase score low
- Treatment: chronic and acute phases—imatinib *(Gleevec)*; acute-phase treatment for select patients is stem cell transplantation.

Myelofibrosis
- Pancytopenia, splenomegaly, and other extramedullary hematopoiesis
- Marrow fibrosis (dry tap) and peripheral blood: leukoerythroblastosis, tear-drop cells
- Acute leukemia develops in 5%–20%
- Treatment for patients with symptomatic anemia: androgens, steroids, transfusion; erythropoietin probably has limited effectiveness.

MONOCLONAL GAMMOPATHY AND MULTIPLE MYELOMA

Monoclonal Gammopathy of Undetermined Significance (MGUS)
- Definition: monoclonal immunoglobulin concentration in serum ≤3 g/dL; no lytic bone lesions, anemia, hypercalcemia, or renal insufficiency; plasma cells in marrow ≤10%
- Prevalence increases with age: 3.2% at ≥50 yr; 6.6% at ≥80 yr.
- Evaluation: SPEP, serum immunofixation, and serum κ:λ light-chain ratio.
  - If initial monoclonal protein is <1.5 g/dL and no other risk factors (see below), repeat laboratory testing at 6 mo and q2–3 yr thereafter if stable.
  - If initial monoclonal protein is ≥1.5 g/dL or any other of the below risk factors is abnormal, obtain bone marrow biopsy and skeletal survey, and repeat laboratory testing at 6 mo and annually.
  - If monoclonal protein is IgM, obtain abdominal CT to exclude a lymphoproliferative process.

- 0.4%–1%/yr progress to multiple myeloma. Risk of progression to myeloma increases with increasing number of these risk factors: monoclonal protein ≥1.5 g/dL, monoclonal immunoglobulin other than IgG, abnormal serum free light chain ratio ($\kappa \cdot \lambda$ light chains) of <0.26 or >1.65.
- Increased risk of vertebral fracture; bone turn-over markers are normalized with use of bisphosphonates.

Multiple Myeloma
- Definition: an incurable clonal B-cell malignancy; most have MGUS years before diagnosis
- Median age at diagnosis is 68 yr; incidence in black Americans is double that in whites
- Smoldering myeloma (asymptomatic stage)
  - Initial evaluation: SPEP, 24-h urine with electrophoresis, serum λ:κ ratio, serum calcium, Cr, and CBC. Also obtain bone marrow biopsy and skeletal survey. Repeat serum calcium, CBC at 2–3 mo to check for stability.
  - Diagnosis: marrow plasmacytosis >10%, and serum or urine (or both) monoclonal protein ≥3 g/dL; bisphosphonates reduce skeletal events but not disease progression.
- Symptomatic stage: above plus evidence of end-organ damage, hypercalcemia, lytic lesions, renal failure, anemia, or recurrent infection
- Treat symptomatic patients. First, determine eligibility for stem cell transplant:
  - If eligible, induction with thalidomide, dexamethasone, and bortezemide, followed by autologous transplant.
  - If not eligible, melphalan, prednisone, plus bortezemib improves survival and time to progression in patients >75 yr old.
  - Zoledronic acid (not all bisphosphonates) started at the time of diagnosis reduces skeletal events and improves overall survival independent of skeletal events. This effect was seen whether patients received transplant or oral agents.
  - Adverse effects of bisphosphonates include hypocalcemia, fever, and in 1/163 osteonecrosis of the jaw. Risk of osteonecrosis of jaw is reduced with good oral hygiene and prophylactic antibiotics if oral surgery is required.
- Patients at all stages are at risk of venous and possibly also arterial thrombosis related to both the disease and its treatment (eg, thalidomide).
- Supportive care for all patients with advanced disease
  - Anemia may require transfusion. Erythropoietin is generally reserved for patients on chemotherapy with Hb <10 g/dL.
  - IV immunoglobulins monthly for recurrent bacterial infections and hypogammaglobulinemia; administer pneumococcal but not varicella vaccine.
  - Radiation to specific symptomatic bone lesions, or vertebroplasty or kyphoplasty.
  - Maintain hydration with at least 2 L/d and avoid NSAIDs and contrast because of renal dysfunction.
  - Provide adequate analgesia.

URINARY INCONTINENCE (UI)

UI is not a normal part of aging. It is a loss of urine control due to a combination of:

- Genitourinary pathology
- Age-related changes
- Comorbid conditions and medications
- Functional impairments

Like other geriatric syndromes, UI often has more than one cause in older adults. Effective treatment requires addressing more than one factor.

Classification of UI

Transient and Functional Causes of Incontinence: UI caused or exacerbated by factors outside the lower urinary tract (eg, comorbidities, medications, mobility). However, UI from these sources is transient only if they are recognized and addressed, and these same factors are frequent contributors to UI in patients with urge, stress, and other persistent causes of UI.

Urge UI: Leakage occurs with a compelling and often sudden need to void due to uninhibited bladder contractions. The cause may be idiopathic or associated with CNS lesions or bladder irritation from infection, stones, or tumors. Detrusor hyperactivity with impaired contractility (DHIC) is urge incontinence with a weak detrusor muscle.

Stress UI: Leakage occurs with increased intra-abdominal pressure (eg, cough or sneeze) due to failure of sphincter mechanisms to remain closed during bladder filling (often due to insufficient pelvic support in women and to trauma from prostate surgery in men).

Overflow UI: Leakage is continual, and postvoid residual urine is increased. Causes are impaired detrusor contractility or bladder outlet obstruction. Impaired contractility may result from chronic outlet obstruction, diabetes mellitus, vitamin B_{12} deficiency, tabes dorsalis, alcoholism, or spinal disease. Outlet obstruction in men is most often due to BPH, cancer, or stricture, and in women to prior incontinence surgery or a large cystocele.

Mixed UI: Leakage occurs with both urgency and increases in intra-abdominal pressure.

Other (rare): Bladder-sphincter dyssynergia, fistulas, reduced detrusor compliance

Overactive Bladder: Frequency and urgency without UI; treatment is the same as for urge UI.

Evaluation

History

- Onset, frequency, volume, timing, precipitants (eg, caffeine, diuretics, alcohol, cough, physical activity, medications)
- "Red flag" symptoms that require prompt evaluation include sudden onset of UI, pelvic pain (constant, worsened, or improved with voiding), and hematuria.
- Lower urinary tract symptom review: frequency, nocturia, slow stream, hesitancy, interrupted voiding, terminal dribbling
- Medical condition status and medications used to treat them, reviewed in association with onset or worsening of UI
- Ask "How does UI affect your life?" and also ask about the presence of fecal incontinence.

Physical Examination
- Functional status (eg, mobility, dexterity)
- Mental status
- Findings:
  - Bladder distention
  - Cord compression (interosseus muscle wasting, Hoffmann's or Babinski's signs)
  - Rectal mass or impaction
  - Sacral root integrity (anal sphincter tone, anal wink, perineal sensation)
  - Volume overload, edema

Male GU
Prostate consistency; symmetry; if uncircumcised, check phimosis, paraphimosis, balanitis

Female GU
Atrophic vaginitis (see p 256); pelvic support (cystocele, rectocele, prolapse; see p 280)

Testing
- **Bladder Diary:** Record time and volume of incontinent and continent voids, activities and time of sleep; knowing oral intake is sometimes helpful.
- **Standing Full Bladder Stress Test (for patients with symptoms of stress UI):** Relax perineum and cough once—immediate loss suggests stress, several seconds delay suggests urge UI.
- **Postvoid Residual:** If available, bladder ultrasound after voiding is preferred to catheterization. If >100 mL, repeat; still >100 mL suggests detrusor weakness, neuropathy, medications, fecal impaction, outlet obstruction, or DHIC. Even if postvoid residual is not available, begin treatment steps as shown in **Figure 8**.
- **Laboratory:** UA to check for hematuria or glycosuria; urine C&S if onset of UI or worsening of UI is acute; serum glucose and calcium if polyuric; renal function tests and B_{12} if urinary retention; urine cytology if hematuria or pain.
- **Urodynamic Testing:** Usually not needed; indicated before corrective surgery, when diagnosis is unclear, when empiric therapy is ineffective, or if postvoid residual volume >200–300 mL (possibly lower in men).

Management in a Stepped Approach (see Figure 8)
Contributing Factors
- Environment: ensure adequate access
- Mentation: If the patient is cognitively impaired, recommend prompted toileting (ask if patient needs to void, take him or her to toilet) starting at 2- to 3-h intervals during day; encourage patients to report continence status; praise patient when continent and responds to toileting.
- Manual dexterity: compensate for deficits, eg, by adapting clothing
- Medical conditions: optimize treatment for HF, COPD, or chronic cough
- Medications: eliminate or minimize those with adverse effects (see **Table 58**)
- Mobility: improve mobility or adapt environment

Lifestyle Factors
- Caffeine and diuretic (including carbonated) beverages produce rapid bladder filling
- Fluid intake: avoid extremes of fluid intake, reduce fluids after supper time to avoid nocturia
- Constipation: produces urethral obstruction or places pressure on bladder

- Weight loss: 60% UI reduction with large weight loss (≥16 kg); 30% decrease in odds for stress UI with 3.5 kg loss
- Smoking: produces chronic cough, encourage patient to quit

Behavioral Therapy

- Efficacy for behavioral therapy: >35% reduction in UI; 50% greater patient perception of cure.
- Two components of bladder training for urge UI:

    1) Voiding on schedule during the day (start q2h) to keep bladder volume low. When no incontinence for 2 d, increase voiding interval by 30–60 min until voiding q3–4h.

    2) Urge suppression (see **Figure 9**), which retrains the CNS and pelvic mechanisms to inhibit contractions and leakage.
- Therapy for stress UI involves timed toileting (as above) and also pelvic muscle (Kegel) exercises—isolate pelvic muscles (avoid thigh, rectal, buttocks contraction); perform slow velocity contraction, sustained for 6–8 sec in sets of 8–12 contractions, 3–4 d/wk for at least 15–20 wk. Handout alone can reduce leakage by 50% (see www.healthinaging.org/public_education/tools/UItool10.pdf). Biofeedback can help with teaching; covered by Medicare if patient unsuccessful after 4 wk of conventional teaching (refer to PT).
- Therapy for post-prostatectomy UI
    - Pelvic floor electrical stimulation and biofeedback begun soon after catheter removal in post-prostatectomy patients improves early recovery of continence.
    - Even for those with UI ≥1 yr after prostatectomy, pelvic floor exercises and urge control (**Figure 9**) reduces the number of incontinence episodes by more than half. Send patients to an experienced continence specialist for training (nurse practitioner or PT).
- DHIC is first treated with behavioral methods; may add detrusor muscle-relaxing medications but follow postvoid residual; clean intermittent self-catheterization if needed.

Figure 8. Stepwise Evaluation and Treatment of UI

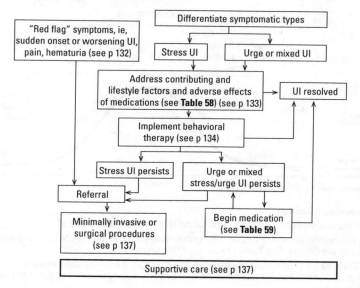

Differentiate symptomatic types

→ Stress UI

→ Urge or mixed UI

"Red flag" symptoms, ie, sudden onset or worsening UI, pain, hematuria (see p 132)

Address contributing and lifestyle factors and adverse effects of medications (see **Table 58**) (see p 133) → UI resolved

Implement behavioral therapy (see p 134)

Stress UI persists

Urge or mixed stress/urge UI persists

Referral

Minimally invasive or surgical procedures (see p 137)

Begin medication (see **Table 59**)

Supportive care (see p 137)

Figure 9. Urge Suppression

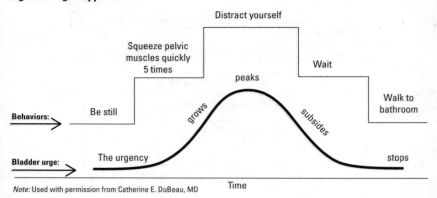

Note: Used with permission from Catherine E. DuBeau, MD

Pharmacologic Therapy

- Eliminate medications causing/exacerbating UI if possible (see **Table 58**).
- Data suggesting benefit of topical postmenopausal estrogen therapy in urge and possibly stress UI are limited. See **Table 119** for available preparations.
- See **Table 59** for antimuscarinics for urge and mixed UI. All have shown equal efficacy in randomized controlled clinical trials. No oral agent is clearly superior in terms of cognitive adverse events.

Table 58. Medications Commonly Associated with UI	
Medication/Class	**Adverse Effects**
Alcohol	Frequency, urgency, sedation, immobility
α-Adrenergic agonists	Outlet obstruction (men)
α-Adrenergic blockers	Stress leakage (women)
Anticholinergics	Impaired emptying, delirium, fecal impaction
Antidepressants/antipsychotics	Anticholinergic effects, sedation, immobility
Calcium channel blockers	Impaired detrusor contraction, edema with nocturnal diuresis
Estrogen (oral)	Stress and mixed UI (women)
GABA-ergics (gabapentin, pregabalin)	Edema, nocturnal diuresis
Loop diuretics	Polyuria, frequency, urgency
NSAIDs/thiazolidinediones	Edema, nocturnal diuresis
Sedative hypnotics	Sedation, delirium, immobility
Opioid analgesics	Constipation, sedation, delirium

Table 59. Antimuscarinic Agents to Treat Urge or Mixed Urinary Incontinence

Medication	Dosage	Formulations	Adverse Events (Metabolism)
			Class adverse events: dry mouth, blurry vision, dry eyes, delirium/confusion, constipation
Oxybutynin *(Ditropan▲, Ditropan XL▲, Gelnique Oxytrol)*	2.5–5 mg q8–12h 5–20 mg/d 1 g gel topically q24h 3.9 mg/d (apply pch 2 ×/wk)	T: 5; S: 5 mg/5 mL SR: 5, 10, 15 10% gel, unit dose (1.14 mL) Transdermal pch 39 cm²	Dry mouth and constipation less with XL than immediate release Gel: rotate sites to reduce skin irritation Pch: adverse events similar to those of placebo; may irritate skin (L)
Tolterodine *(Detrol, Detrol LA)*	2 mg q12h 4 mg/d	T: 1, 2 C: ER 2, 4	Least constipating of oral agents; P450 interactions (L, CYP3A4 and CYP2D6)
Trospium *(Sanctura, Sanctura XR)*	20 mg q12–24h (on empty stomach) 60 mg/d (XR)	T: 20 C: ER 60	Dyspepsia, headache; caution in liver dysfunction; dose once daily at hs in patients ≥75 yr old or with CrCl <30 mL/min; XR formulation not recommended if CrCl <30 mL/min (L, K)
Darifenacin *(Enablex)*	7.5–15 mg/d	T: 7.5, 15	Gastric retention; not recommended in severe liver impairment (L, CYP3A4 and CYP2D6)
Solifenacin *(VESIcare)*	5–10 mg/d	T: 5, 10	Same as darifenacin; max dose 5 mg if CrCl <30 mL/min or moderate liver impairment (L, CYP3A4)
Fesoterodine *(TOVIAZ)*	4–8 mg/d	T: 4, 8	Max dose 4 mg if CrCl <30 mL/min (L, CYP3A4, CYP2D6)

Note: For prostate obstruction UI, see benign prostatic hyperplasia, p 233.

Minimally Invasive Procedures

- Sacral nerve neuromodulation can be effective for refractory urge UI and urinary retention (both idiopathic and neurogenic). Electrode is implanted to stimulate S3; done as a trial before permanent device.
- Pessaries may benefit women with vaginal (see p 280) or uterine prolapse who experience retention and stress or urge UI.
- Botulinum toxin is also effective for refractory urge UI (not FDA approved for this purpose), but patients must be willing to perform self-catheterization because risk of retention is high.

Surgical Therapy

- Consider for the 50% of women whose stress UI does not respond adequately to behavioral treatment and exercise.
- Type of surgery depends on type of urethral function impairment, patient-related factors, and coexisting conditions (eg, prolapse).

Supportive Care

- Pads and protective garments should be chosen on the basis of gender and volume of urine loss. Medicaid (some states) covers pads; Medicare does not.
- Because of expense, patients may not change frequently enough.

Nocturnal Frequency in the Absence of HF

- Two voidings per night is probably normal for older adults.
- Exclude sleep difficulties (see Sleep Disorders, p 267); then consider if the condition is due to excessive output or urinary tract dysfunction.
- Bladder diary with measured voided volumes can be very helpful. Voiding more than ⅓ of total 24-h output between bedtime and awakening is excessive nocturnal fluid excretion.
- All patients should restrict fluid intake 4 h before bedtime.
- If stasis edema is present, have patient wear pressure-graded stockings during the day.
- If no stasis edema, a potent, short-acting loop diuretic can be used in the afternoon or early evening to induce a diuresis before bedtime, eg, bumetanide 0.5–1.5 mg titrated to achieve a brisk diuresis.
- Evaluate for other factors contributing to volume overload or diuresis (eg, HF, poorly controlled diabetes).

UI in Nursing-home Residents

- Rather than bladder diaries, observe toileting patterns and UI episodes over several days.
- Trial of prompted toileting in patients who are able to state their name and transfer with assist of no more than one. Continue prompted schedule; ability to toilet at least 75% of the time during a 3-d trial is considered success.
- Consider use of antimuscarinics in patients with urge UI who succeed with prompted toileting and still have UI episodes.
- Do not neglect evaluation for stress UI and outlet obstruction.

Catheter Care

- Use catheter **only** for chronic urinary retention, to protect pressure ulcers, and when requested by patients or families to promote comfort (eg, at end of life).
- Leakage around catheter can be caused by large Foley balloon, too large catheter diameter, constipation, impaction.
- Bacteriuria is universal; treat only if symptoms (eg, fever, inanition, anorexia, delirium) or if bacteriuria persists after catheter removal.
- Suprapubic catheters reduce meatal and penile trauma but not infection. Condom catheters are less painful and have a somewhat lower complication rate.
- Replace catheter if symptomatic bacteriuria develops, then culture urine from new catheter.
- Nursing-facility patients with catheters should reside in separate rooms.
- For acute retention, catheterize for 7–10 d, then do voiding trial after catheter removal.

Replacing Catheter: Routine replacement not necessary. Changing q4–6wk is reasonable to prevent blockage. Patients with recurrent blockage need increased fluid intake, possibly acidification of urine, or change of catheter q7–10d.

FECAL INCONTINENCE (FI)

Definition

Involuntary or inappropriate passing of feces that impacts social functioning or hygiene

Prevalence

After age 65: 2% of community-dwelling, 14% of hospitalized, 54% of nursing-home residents

Risk Factors
Constipation, age >80 yr, female sex, UI, impaired mobility, dementia, neurologic disease

Age-related Factors
Decreased strength of external sphincter and weak anal squeeze; increased rectal compliance, decreased resting tone in internal sphincter, and impaired anal sensation

Causes: FI is commonly multifactorial.
- Overflow: from colonic distention by excessive feces, causing continuous soiling
- Loose feces: caused by medications, neoplasia, colitis, lactose intolerance
- Functional incontinence: associated with poor mobility
- Dementia related: uninhibited rectal contraction, often have UI
- Anorectal incontinence: weak external sphincter (surgery, multiparity, etc)
- Comorbidity: stroke, diabetes mellitus (autonomic neuropathy), sacral cord dysfunction

Evaluation
History
- Description of FI (eg, diarrhea, hard feces, etc), including usual bowel habit, change in habit, usual fecal consistency
- Frequency, urgency, ability to delay, difficulty wiping, post-defecation soiling, ability to distinguish feces and flatus
- Evacuation difficulties: straining, incomplete emptying, rectal prolapse or pain
- Functional: communication of needs, need for assistance, toilet access
- Other: bowel medications, other medications, UI, prior treatment (eg, pads)
Examination
- Examine/palpate abdomen for colonic distention, and visually inspect anus.
- Check for prolapse while patient seated on commode.
- Perform rectal examination for tone, volume, and consistency of feces; heme test.
- Observe gait, mobility, dressing, hygiene, mental status.
Laboratory
- TSH, electrolytes, calcium
Bowel investigations
- Abdominal radiograph: may identify colonic distention by excessive feces
- Colonoscopy: only when pathology suspected (unexplained loose feces, bleeding)
- Anorectal physiology tests: not generally needed for treatment

Treatment: Multiple interventions may be required.
Main approach is to simulate the patient's usual bowel pattern.
- Use rectal evacuants to stimulate evacuation and to establish a bowel pattern.
- Use evacuants in the following order: glycerine suppository, bisacodyl suppository, microenemas (eg, *Enemeez*, docusate 5 mL), phosphate or tap water enemas; digital stimulation.
- Use antidiarrheals to slow an overactive bowel or to enable planned evacuation with rectal preparations.
Constipation (see p 111): often plays a role; evaluate (if needed) and treat

Modify fecal consistency to achieve soft, formed feces.
- Loose feces: use fiber or loperamide titrated to effect, sometimes as little as q48h.
- Hard feces: modify diet; add MgSO or MgOH at low dosages. In poorly mobile people, bran and fiber may exacerbate constipation.

Patient education
- Respond promptly on urge to defecate, heed the gastrocolic reflex.
- Take loperamide 2–4 mg 45 min before meal or social event to prevent evacuation.
- Use coffee to stimulate the gut.
- Position on toilet with back support, foot stool to achieve squat position.
- Exercise to improve bowel motility.
- Those who are able may be taught rectal sphincter exercises (tighten rectal sphincter for 10 sec 50 times/d) or may use biofeedback.

Rectal evacuation and toilet training
- Following a regimen improves bowel control.
- When no spontaneous bowel action, stimulate with suppositories or enemas (see **Table 49**); those with incompetent sphincters may not retain usual enemas.
- Bed pans should not be used; bedside commodes are not as good as toilets.

Nursing-home residents and very disabled older adults: FI is most often due to colonic loading and overflow. Treat as follows:
- Daily enemas until no more results.
- Add a daily osmotic laxative (see **Table 49**) and follow bowel training (above).
- Fecal transit can be stimulated with abdominal massage in direction of colonic transit.

Other therapies
- Manual evacuation may be appropriate in some patients.
- Skin care: Wet wipes better than dry; commercial preparations better than soap and water; toilet tongs and bottom wipers help those with shoulder disease.
- Surgery:
  ○ Full-thickness rectal prolapse usually requires surgery using a transanal approach.
  ○ Denervation of the sphincter can be repaired, but long-term results are often unsatisfactory.
  ○ Division of the external anal sphincter or anal fissure can be repaired, but long-term results are less than satisfactory.
  ○ Selected patients have improved quality of life through creation of a stoma.
- Sacral nerve stimulation for patients with both intact and defective rectal sphinters is FDA-approved for chronic fecal incontinence in patients who cannot tolerate more conservative treatment or in whom such treatment has not been effective. Patients must show appropriate response to a trial of stimulation and must be able to operate the device.

ANTIMICROBIAL STEWARDSHIP: PRINCIPLES FOR PRESCRIBERS
• Collaborate with local antimicrobial stewardship teams and efforts.
• Be familiar with formulary restrictions and preauthorization requirements.
• Participate in educational offerings on antimicrobials and antimicrobial stewardship.
• Streamline or de-escalate empirical antimicrobial therapy based on C&S results.
• Optimize and individualize antimicrobial dose.
• Switch eligible patients from IV to oral antimicrobials.

Based on: Dellit TH, Owens RC, McGowan JE Jr, et al. Infectious Diseases Society of America and the Society for Healthcare Epidemiology of America Guidelines for Developing an Institutional Program to Enhance Antimicrobial Stewardship. *Clin Infect Dis*. 2007;44:159–177.
See also www.cdc.gov/getsmart/healthcare.

PNEUMONIA
Presentation
Can range from subtle signs such as lethargy, anorexia, dizziness, falls, and delirium to septic shock or acute respiratory distress syndrome. Pleuritic chest pain, dyspnea, productive cough, fever, chills, or rigors are not consistently present in older adults.

Evaluation and Assessment
• Physical examination: Respiratory rate >20 breaths/min; low BP; chest sounds may be minimal, absent, or consistent with HF; 20% are afebrile.
• CXR: Infiltrate may not be present on initial film if the patient is dehydrated.
• Sputum: Gram's stain and culture (optional per ATS guidelines)
• CBC with differential: Up to 50% of patients have a normal WBC count, but 95% have a left shift.
• BUN, creatinine, electrolytes, glucose
• Blood culture × 2
• Oxygenation: arterial blood gas or oximetry
• Test for *Mycobacterium tuberculosis* with acid-fast bacilli stain and culture in selected patients.
• Test for *Legionella* spp in patients who are seriously ill without an alternative diagnosis, are immunocompromised, are nonresponsive to β-lactam antibiotics, have clinical features suggesting this diagnosis, or in outbreak setting. Urinary antigen testing is highly specific for serotype 1 but lacks specificity for other serotypes. Value and use vary by geographic region.
• Thoracentesis (if moderate to large effusion)

Aggravating Factors (* indicates modifiable)
• Age-related changes in pulmonary reserve
• Alcoholism
• Altered mental status
• Aspiration
• Comorbid conditions that alter gag reflexes or ciliary transport
• COPD or other lung disease
• Heart disease

- Heavy sedation* or paralytic agents
- Hyperglycemia*
- Intubation, mechanical ventilation (orotracheal intubation and orogastric tubation preferred)
- Malnutrition
- Medications*: immunosuppressants, sedatives, anticholinergic or other agents that dry secretions, agents that increase gastric pH
- Nasogastric tubes
- Oral care* (manual brushing plus rinse with fluoride/chlorhexidine 0.12% × 30 sec/d)
- Poor compliance with infection control* (eg, hand disinfection)
- Supine positioning* (semi-recumbent, 30–45 degrees preferred)
- Swallowing* (eat/feed upright at 90 degrees over 15–20 min)

Predominant Organisms by Setting

Community-acquired:
- *Streptococcus pneumoniae*
- *Legionella* spp
- Respiratory viruses
- *Haemophilus influenzae*
- Gram-negative bacteria
- *Chlamydia pneumoniae*
- *Moraxella catarrhalis*
- *M tuberculosis*
- Endemic fungi
- Anaerobes

Nursing-home–acquired:
- *Strep pneumoniae*
- Gram-negative bacteria
- *Staphylococcus aureus* (including methicillin-resistant *S aureus*)
- Anaerobes
- *H influenzae*
- Group B streptococci
- *Chlamydia pneumoniae*

Hospital-acquired:
- Gram-negative bacteria
- Anaerobes
- Gram-positive bacteria
- Fungi

Supportive Management
- Chest percussion
- Inhaled β-adrenergic agonists
- Mechanical ventilation (if indicated)
- Oxygen as indicated
- Rehydration

Empiric Antibiotic Therapy (see Table 65)

Table 60. Treatment of Community-acquired Pneumonia for Immunocompetent Patients by Clinical Circumstances or Setting	
Clinical Circumstances or Setting	**Treatment Options**
Outpatient, previously healthy and no antibiotic therapy in past 3 mo	Azithromycin, clarithromycin, or erythromycin Alternative: doxycycline
Outpatient, with comorbidities[a] or antibiotic therapy in past 3 mo[c]	A fluoroquinolone[b] alone *or* Azithromycin, clarithromycin, or erythromycin *plus* amoxicillin (high dose) or amoxicillin-clavulanate Alternative β-lactams: ceftriaxone, cefpodoxime, or cefuroxime Alternative to a macrolide: doxycycline
Hospitalized patient	A fluoroquinolone[b] alone *or* Azithromycin or clarithromycin *plus* cefotaxime, ceftriaxone, or ampicillin Alternative β-lactam: ertapenem Alternative to a macrolide: doxycycline

(cont.)

Clinical Circumstances or Setting	Treatment Options
Hospitalized patient, intensive care unit	
No concern about *Pseudomonas*	Cefotaxime, ceftriaxone, or ampicillin-sulbactam *plus* azithromycin or a fluoroquinolone[b]
No concern about *Pseudomonas* but β-lactam allergy	A fluoroquinolone[b] *plus* aztreonam
Concern about *Pseudomonas*	Piperacillin-tazobactam, imipenem, meropenem, or cefepime *plus* ciprofloxacin or levofloxacin; *or* Piperacillin-tazobactam, imipenem, meropenem, or cefepime *plus* an aminoglycoside *and* azithromycin, ciprofloxacin, or levofloxacin
Concern about *Pseudomonas* and β-lactam allergy	Aztreonam *plus* ciprofloxacin or levofloxacin *plus* an aminoglycoside
Nursing-home patient[d,e]	A fluoroquinolone[c] alone *or* Azithromycin, clarithromycin, or erythromycin *plus* amoxicillin (high dose) or amoxicillin-clavulanate

[a] Comorbidities: chronic heart, lung, liver, or kidney disease; diabetes mellitus; alcoholism; malignancies; asplenia; immunosuppressing conditions or drugs

[b] Fluoroquinolones (respiratory): moxifloxacin, levofloxacin, or gemifloxacin

[c] Choice of antibiotic should be from a different class

[d] Patients being treated in the nursing home; for treatment of nursing-home patients who are hospitalized, see hospitalized patient or intensive care unit.

[e] Because of the incidence of gram-negative and atypical bacterial pneumonia in nursing-home patients, experts in geriatric infectious disease often recommend expanded gram-negative antibiotic coverage.

Source: Mandell LA, Wunderink RG, Anzueto A, et al. Infectious Disease Society of America/American Thoracic Society consensus guidelines on the management of community-acquired pneumonia in adults. *Clin Infect Dis* 2007;44:S27–72.

Nursing-home or Hospital-acquired Pneumonia Requiring Parenteral Treatment: Alternative Recommendations

Antipseudomonal cephalosporin (cefepime or ceftazadime) *or*
Antipseudomonal carbepenem (imipenem or meropenem) *or*
β-Lactam/β-lactamase inhibitor (piperacillin-tazobactam)

plus

Antipseudomonal fluoroquinolone (ciprofloxacin or levofloxacin) *or*
Aminoglycoside (amikacin, gentamicin, or tobramycin)

plus

Linezolid or vancomycin (if risk factors for methicillin-resistant *S aureus* are present or if local incidence is high)

For both sets of empiric therapy guidelines, the choice of combination depends on local bacteriologic patterns.

Source: Adapted from: ATS and IDSA Guidelines for the management of adults with hospital-acquired, ventilator-associated, and healthcare-associated pneumonia. *Am J Resp Crit Care Med* 2005;171:388–416.

Duration of Treatment

Inpatient—until clinical indicators have been reached:

- Temperature <100°F (37.8°C)
- SBP >90 mmHg
- HR <100 bpm
- O_2 saturation >90%
- Respiratory rate <25/min
- Ability to maintain oral intake

Switch from parental to oral antibiotics when patient is hemodynamically stable, shows clinical improvement, is afebrile for 16 h, and can tolerate oral medicatons; total duration of treatment 7–14 d depending on clincial response.

Outpatient and long-term care facility—usually 10–14 d

Note: The empiric use of vancomycin should be reserved for patients with a serious allergy to β-lactam antibiotics or for patients from environments in which methicillin-resistant *S aureus* is known to be a problem pathogen. For all cases, antimicrobial therapy should be individualized once Gram's stain or culture results are known.

URINARY TRACT INFECTION OR UROSEPSIS

Definition

Bacteriuria is the presence of a significant number of bacteria in the urine without reference to symptoms.

- **Symptomatic bacteriuria** usually has signs of dysuria and increased frequency of urination; fever, chills, nausea may be present; >10^5 cfu/mL of the same organism from a single specimen supports the diagnosis of UTI, counts ≥10^3 cfu/mL are diagnostic for specimens obtained by in and out catheterization. New onset or worsening of urinary incontinence may be the only symptom.
- **Asymptomatic bacteriuria** is seen when there is an absence of symptoms, including absence of fever (<100.4°F [38°C]) plus:
  - the same organism(s) (≥10^5 cfu/mL) is found on 2 consecutive cultures in women
  - one bacterial species (≥10^5 cfu/mL) in a single clean-catch specimen in men
  - one bacterial species (≥10^2 cfu/mL) in a catheterized specimen in men and women

Risk Factors

- Abnormalities in function or anatomy of the urinary tract
- Female gender
- Limited functional status
- Catheterization or recent instrumentation
- Comorbid conditions (eg, diabetes mellitus, BPH)

Assessment and Evaluation

Choice is based on presenting symptoms and severity of illness.

- Urinalysis with culture (do not obtain sample from catheter bag)
- BUN, creatinine, electrolytes
- CBC with differential
- Blood culture × 2

Expected Organisms

Noncatheterized Patients: Most common: *Escherichia coli, Proteus* spp, *Klebsiella* spp, *Providencia* spp, *Citrobacter* spp, *Enterobacter* spp, *Gardenerella vaginalis*, group B streptococci, and *Pseudomonas aeruginosa* if recent antibiotic exposure, known colonization, or known institutional flora

Nursing-Home–Catheterized Patients: *Enterobacter* spp and gram-negative bacteria

Empiric Antibiotic Treatment

- Routine treatment of asymptomatic bacteriuria is not recommended.
- Empiric regimens should be changed based on culture and sensitivity results, patient factors, and treatment costs.
- Treatment duration should be at least 7–10 days.

Community-Acquired or Nursing-Home–Acquired Cystitis or Uncomplicated UTI (oral route): TMP/SMZ DS, cephalexin, ampicillin, or amoxicillin. Amoxicillin-clavulanate should be reserved for patients with sulfa allergy and for settings with known β-lactam resistance. Fluoroquinolones should be reserved for patients with allergies to sulfa or β-lactams, or for settings with known resistance.

Suspected Urosepsis (IV route): Third-generation cephalosporin plus aminoglycoside, aztreonam, or fluoroquinolone ± aminoglycoside.

Vancomycin should be reserved for patients with a serious allergy to β-lactam antibiotics.

UTI Prophylaxis

- Leads to antibiotic resistance regardless of patient's catheter status or duration of catheterization; generally not recommended. Noncatheterized women with a hx of UTI, especially if caused by *E coli*, may benefit from prophylaxis with cranberry juice (250–300 mL/d). Time to benefit may be ≥ 2 mo.
- Vaginal atrophy due to estrogen depletion may predispose women to recurrent UTIs. Local topical estrogen replacement may be indicated (see **Table 119**).

HERPES ZOSTER ("SHINGLES")

Definition
Cutaneous vesicular eruptions followed by radicular pain secondary to the recrudescence of varicella zoster virus.

Prevention
Zoster vaccine live *(Zostavax)* for individuals ≥50 yr who are immunocompetent and without contraindication to the vaccine. (See **Table 92**.)

Clinical Manifestations

- Abrupt onset of pruritus or pain along a specific dermatome (see **Figure 1**)
- Macular, erythematous rash that becomes vesicular and pustular (Tzanck cell test positive) after ~3 d, crusts over and clears in 10–14 d
- Complications: post-herpetic neuralgia, visual loss or blindness if ophthalmic involvement

Pharmacologic Management

When started within 72 h of the rash's appearance, antiviral therapy (see **Table 61**) decreases the severity and duration of the acute illness and possibly shortens the duration and reduces the risk of post-herpetic neuralgias. Corticosteroids can also decrease the risk and severity of post-herpetic neuralgias. (See p 197 for treatment of post-herpetic neuralgia.)

Table 61. Antiviral Treatments for Herpes Zoster

Medication, Route	Dosage	Formulations	Comment
Acyclovir▲ *(Zovirax)*			
Oral	800 mg 5 ×/d for 7–10 d	T: 400, 800; C: 200; S: 200 mg/5 mL	Reduce dosage when CrCl[a] <25 mL/min
IV[b]	10 mg/kg q8h for 7–10 d	500 mg/10 mL	Reduce dosage when CrCl[a] <50 mL/min
Famciclovir▲ *(Famvir)*			
Oral	500 mg q8h for 7 d	T: 125, 250, 500	Reduce dosage when CrCl[a] <60 mL/min
Valacyclovir▲c *(Valtrex)*			
Oral	1000 mg q8h for 7 d	C: 500, 1000	Reduce dosage when CrCl[a] <50 mL/min

[a] The CrCl listed is the threshold below which the dosage (amount or frequency) should be reduced. See package insert for detailed dosing guidelines.

[b] Use IV for serious illness, ophthalmic infection, or patients who cannot take oral medication.

[c] Preferred to po acyclovir; prodrug of acyclovir with serum concentrations equal to those achieved with IV administration.

INFLUENZA

Vaccine Prevention (ACIP Guidelines)

Yearly vaccination is recommended for all adults ≥65 yr old and all residents and staff of nursing homes, or residential or long-term–care facilities. Nursing-home residents admitted during the winter months after the vaccination program has been completed should be vaccinated at admission if they have not already been vaccinated. The influenza vaccine is contraindicated in people who have an anaphylactic hypersensitivity to eggs or any other component of the vaccine. Dose: 0.5 mL IM once in the fall for those living in the northern hemisphere.

Pharmacologic Prophylaxis and Treatment with Antiviral Agents
Indications:

- Prevention (during an influenza outbreak): people who are not vaccinated, are immunodeficient, or may spread the virus
- Prophylaxis: during 2 wk required to develop antibodies for people vaccinated after an outbreak of influenza A
- Reduction of symptoms, duration of illness when started within the first 48 h of symptoms
- During epidemic outbreaks in nursing homes
- Resistance to antivirals and the emergence of specific strains of influenza (eg, H1N1) have led to frequent updates of recommendations for prophylaxis and treatment. Check the CDC Web site for the most current information and guidance (www.cdc.gov/flu/professionals/antivirals/).

Duration: Treatment of symptoms: 3–5 d or for 24–48 h after symptoms resolve. Prophylaxis during outbreak: min 2 wk or until ~1 wk after outbreak ends.

Table 62. Antiviral Treatment of Influenza

Agent	Formulation	Dosage
Amantadine▲ *(Symmetrel)* [a]	C: 100 mg S: 50 mg/5 mL	100 mg/d po[b]
✔ Oseltamivir *(Tamiflu)* [c]	C: 75 mg S: 12 mg/mL	Treatment: 75 mg po q12h × 5 d (75 mg/d po if CrCl 10–30 mL/min); not recommended if CrCl <10 mL/min Prophylaxis: 75 mg/d po × ≥7 d up to 6 wk (75 mg po q48h if CrCl 10–30 mL/min); not recommended if CrCl <10 mL/min
Rimantadine *(Flumadine)* [a]	T▲: 100 mg S: 50 mg/5 mL	100 mg/d po for frail older adults and nursing-home residents 200 mg/d po for other adults, including those ≥65 yr old Decrease dose to 100 mg if adverse events appear
Zanamivir *(Relenza)* [c,d]	Inh: 5 mg/blister	2 × 5-mg inhalations q12h × 5 d Give doses on first day ≥2 h apart Prophylaxis: 2 × 5-mg inhalations q24h; household setting—start 36 h after onset of signs and symptoms of initial case, duration 10 d; community—begin within 5 d of outbreak, duration 30 d.

✔ = preferred for treating older adults

[a] No longer recommended for prophylaxis.

[b] Dosage adjustments for kidney function, CrCl (mL/min): ≥30 = 100 mg/d; 20–29 = 200 mg 2 ×/wk; 10–19 = 100 mg 3 × /wk; <10 = 200 mg alternating with 100 mg q7d.

[c] Must be started within 2 d of symptom onset.

[d] Do not use in patients with COPD or asthma.

TUBERCULOSIS (TB)

TB in older adults may be the reactivation of old disease or a new infection due to exposure to an infected individual. Treatment recommendations differ; if a new infection is suspected or the patient has risk factors for resistant organisms, then bacterial sensitivities must be determined.

Risk or Reactivating Factors

- Chronic institutionalization
- Corticosteroid use
- Diabetes mellitus
- Malignancy
- Malnutrition
- Kidney failure

Risk Factors for Resistant Organisms

- HIV infection
- Homelessness, institutionalization (other than a nursing home)
- IV drug abuse
- Origin from geographic regions with a high prevalence of resistance (New York, Mexico, Southeast Asia)
- Exposure to INH-resistant TB or history of ineffective chemotherapy
- Previous treatment for TB
- AFB-positive sputum smears after 2 mo of treatment
- Positive cultures after 4 mo of treatment

Diagnosis

- Mantoux tuberculin skin test (TST): 0.1 mL of tuberculin purified protein derivative (PPD) intradermal injection into the inner surface of the forearm
- Read 48–72 h after injection (see **Table 63** for interpretation).

- Repeat ("booster") 1–2 wk after initial skin testing can be useful for nursing-home residents, healthcare workers, and others who are retested periodically to reduce the likelihood of misinterpreting a boosted reaction to subsequent TSTs.

Treatment
Latent Infection: See Table 63 and Table 64.

Table 63. Identification of Patients at High Risk of Developing TB Who Would Benefit from Treatment of Latent Infection

Population	Minimum Induration Considered a Positive Test
Considered positive in any person, including those considered low risk	15 mm
Residents and employees of hospitals, nursing homes, and long-term facilities for older adults, residential facilities for AIDS patients, and homeless shelters	10 mm
Recent immigrants (<5 yr) from countries where TB prevalence is high	10 mm
Injectable-drug users	10 mm
People with silicosis; diabetes mellitus; chronic kidney failure; leukemia; lymphoma; carcinoma of the head, neck, or lung; weight loss of ≥10%; gastrectomy or jejunoileal bypass	10 mm
Recent contact with TB patients	5 mm
Fibrotic changes on CXR consistent with prior TB	5 mm
Immunosuppressed (receiving the equivalent of prednisone at ≥15 mg/d for ≥1 mo), organ transplant recipients, patients receiving TNF-α inhibitors	5 mm
HIV-positive patients	5 mm

Table 64. Treatment of Latent Tuberculosis

Drug	Dosage and Duration
INH▲*	5 mg/kg/d (max 300 mg/d) for 6 or 9 mo; or 15 mg/kg/d (max 900 mg/d) 2 × /wk with directly observed therapy for 6 or 9 mo
RIF▲	10 mg/kg/d (max 600 mg/d) for 4 mo

Note: INH = isoniazid; RIF = rifampin

*The preferred treatment for patients not infected with HIV.

Source: Data from: American Thoracic Society. Targeted tuberculin testing and treatment of latent tuberculosis. *Am J Respir Crit Care Med* 2000;161:S221–S247 (also available at www.atsjournal.org). *MMWR* 2003;52:735–739.

Active Infection:
Refer to CDC guidelines at www.cdc.gov/mmwr/preview/mmwrhtml/rr5211a1.htm#tab2.

HUMAN IMMUNODEFICIENCY VIRUS (HIV)
Reasons for increase in HIV infection in adults ≥50 yr old:

- Increased survival of people with HIV
- Age-associated decrease in immune function with resultant increased susceptibility
- Treatments for erectile dysfunction leading to more sexual activity
- Difficulty with condom use secondary to erectile dysfunction
- Less condom use by partners of postmenopausal women

Presentation

Many symptoms that may delay diagnosis are common in older adults:

- Anorexia
- Arthralgias
- Earlier, more symptomatic menopause
- Fatigue
- Flu-like symptoms
- Forgetfulness
- Hypogonadism
- Insomnia
- Myalgias
- Pain in hands or feet (neuropathy)
- Recurrent pneumonia
- Sexual disorders
- Weight loss

Comorbidities common in older adults that can occur earlier in people with HIV:

- Cancers (eg, anal, liver, lung)
- Cirrhosis
- Coronary artery disease
- Diabetes
- HTN
- Obstructive lung disease
- Osteoporosis
- Vascular disease

Laboratory Abnormalities

- Anemia
- Leukopenia
- Low cholesterol
- Transaminitis

Screening

Routine screening of adults ≥65 yr old is not recommended.
Screening is recommended regardless of age if:

- Starting treatment for TB
- Treating a sexually transmitted disease
- Other HIV risk factors are present: unprotected sex and multiple partners, hazardous alcohol or illicit drug use
- Unexplained anemia
- Peripheral neuropathy
- Oral candidiasis
- Herpes zoster (widespread infection)
- Recurrent bacterial pneumonia
- Unexplained weight loss or pronounced fatigue

Treatment

For complete guidelines on antiretroviral regimens, see
http://aidsinfo.nih.gov/contentfiles/AA_Tables.pdf.
Treatment-naive patients:

- Non-nucleoside reverse transcriptase inhibitor + 2 Nucleos(t)ide reverse transcriptase inhibitors (NRTIs), *or*
- Protease inhibitor with retonavir (preferred) + 2 NRTIs, *or*
- Integrase strand transfer inhibitor + 2 NRTIs

Complications of Pharmacotherapy

- Increased cholesterol (accelerated atherosclerosis)
- Glucose intolerance
- Drug-drug interactions (see **Table 9**)
- Drug toxicity

Table 65. Antibiotics				
Antimicrobial Class, *Subclass*	**Dosage**	**Adjust When CrCl[a] Is: (mL/min)**	**Formulations**	**Route of Elimination (%)**
β-Lactams *Penicillins*				
Amoxicillin▲ *(Amoxil)*	po: 250 mg–1 g q8h	<50	T: film coated 500, 875 C: 250, 500 ChT: 125, 200, 250, 400 S: 125, 200, 250, 400 mg/5 mL	K (80)
Ampicillin▲	po: 250–500 mg q6h IM/IV: 1–2 g q4–6h	<30	C: 250, 500 S: 125, 250 mg/5 mL Inj	K (90)
Penicillin G▲	IV: 3–5 × 10⁶ U q4–6h IM: 0.6–2.4 × 10⁶ U q6–12h	<30	Inj procaine for IM	K L (30)
Penicillin VK▲	po: 125–500 mg q6h	b	T: 250, 500 S: 125, 250 mg/5 mL	K, L
Antipseudomonal Penicillin				
Piperacillin▲ *(Pipracil)*	IM: 1–2 g q8–12h IV: 2–4 g q6–8h	<40	Inj	K, F (10–20)
Antistaphylococcal Penicillins				
Dicloxacillin▲ *(Dycill, Pathocil)*	po: 125–500 mg q6h	NA	C: 125, 250, 500 S: 62.5 mg/5 mL	K (56–70)
Nafcillin▲	IM: 500 mg q4–6h IV: 500 mg–2 g q4–6h	NA	Inj	L
Oxacillin▲ *(Bactocill)*	po: 500 mg–1 g q4–6h IM, IV: 250 mg–2 g q6–12h	<10	C: 250, 500 S: 250 mg/5 mL Inj	K
Monobactam (antipseudomonal)				
Aztreonam *(Azactam)*	IM: 500 mg–1 g q8–12h IV: 500 mg–2 g q6–12h	<30	Inj	K (70)
Carbapenems				
Doripenem *(Doribax)*	IV: 500 mg q8h	<50	Inj	K (>70)
Ertapenem *(Invanz)*	IM, IV: 1 g q24h × 3–14 d IM × 7 d max IV × 14 d max	<30	Inj	K (80), F (10)
Imipenem-cilastatin *(Primaxin)*	IM: 500 mg–1 g q8–12h IV: 500 mg–2 g q6–12h	<70	Inj	K (70)
Meropenem *(Merrem IV)*	IV: 1 g q8h	≤50	Inj	K (75), L (25)

(cont.)

Table 65. **Antibiotics** (cont.)				
Antimicrobial Class, *Subclass*	**Dosage**	**Adjust When CrCl[a] Is: (mL/min)**	**Formulations**	**Route of Elimination (%)**
Penicillinase-resistant Penicillins				
Amoxicillin–clavulanate▲ *(Augmentin)*	po: 250 mg q8h, 500 mg q12h, 875 mg q12h	<30	T: 250, 500, 875 ChT: 125, 200, 250, 400 S: 125, 200, 250, 400 mg/5 mL	K (30–40), L
Ampicillin–sulbactam▲ *(Unasyn)*	IM, IV: 1–2 g q6–8h	<30	Inj	K (85)
Penicillinase-resistant and Antipseudomonal Penicillins				
Piperacillin–tazobactam▲ *(Zosyn)*	IV: 3.375 g q6h	<40	Inj	K (70), F (10–20)
Ticarcillin–clavulanate *(Timentin)*	IV: 3 g q4–6h	<60	Inj	K, L
First-generation Cephalosporins				
Cefadroxil▲ *(Duricef)*	po: 500 mg–1 g q12h	<50	C: 500 T: 1 g S: 125, 250, 500 mg/5 mL	K (90)
Cefazolin▲ *(Ancef, Kefzol)*	IM, IV: 500 mg–2 g q12h	<55	Inj	K (80–100)
Cephalexin▲ *(Keflex)*	po: 250 mg–1 g q6h	<40	C: 250, 500 T: 250, 500; 1 g S: 125, 250 mg/5 mL	K (80–100)
Cephalothin▲ *(Keflin)*	IM, IV: 500 mg–2 g q4–6h	<50	Inj	K (50–75)
Cephradine *(Anspor)*	po, IM, IV: 500 mg–2 g q6h	<20	C: 250, 500 T: 1 g S: 125, 250 mg/5 mL Inj	K (80–90)
Second-generation Cephalosporins				
Cefaclor▲ *(Ceclor)*	po: 250–500 mg q8h	<50	C: 250, 500 S: 125, 187, 250, 375 mg/5 mL T: ER 375, 500	K (80)
Cefotetan▲ *(Cefotan)*	IM, IV: 1–3 g q12h or 1–2 g q24h (UTI)	<30	Inj	K (80)
Cefoxitin▲ *(Mefoxin)*	IM, IV: 1–2 g q6–8h	<50	Inj	K (85)
Cefprozil▲ *(Cefzil)*	po: 250–500 mg q12–24h	<30	T: 250, 500 S: 125, 250 mg/5 mL	K (60–70)
Cefuroxime axetil▲ *(Ceftin)*	po: 125–500 mg q12h IM, IV: 750 mg–1.5 g q6h	<20	T: 125, 250, 500▲ S: 125, 150 mg/5 mL Inj▲	K (66–100)

(cont.)

Table 65. Antibiotics (cont.)				
Antimicrobial Class, *Subclass*	Dosage	Adjust When CrCl[a] Is: (mL/min)	Formulations	Route of Elimination (%)
Third-generation Cephalosporins				
Cefdinir▲ *(Omnicef)*	po: 300 mg q12h or 600 mg/d × 10 d	<30	C: 300 S: 125 mg/5 mL	K
Cefditoren *(Spectracef)*	po: 400 mg q12h × 10 d (bronchitis) 400 mg q12h × 14 d (pneumonia) 200 mg q12h × 10 d (soft tissue or skin)	<50	T: 200	K
Cefixime *(Suprax)*	po: 400 mg/d	<60	T: 200, 400 S: 100 mg/5 mL	K (50)
Cefotaxime▲ *(Claforan)*	IM, IV: 1–2 g q6–12h	<20	Inj	K, L
Cefpodoxime▲ *(Vantin)*	po: 100–400 mg q12h	<30	T: 100, 250▲ S: 50, 100 mg/5 mL	K (80)
Ceftazidime▲ *(Ceptaz, Fortaz)*	IM, IV: 500 mg–2 g q8–12h UTI: 250–500 mg q12h	<50	Inj	K (80–90)
Ceftibuten *(Cedax)*	po: 400 mg/d	<50	C: 400 S: 100, 200 mg/5 mL	K (65–70)
Ceftizoxime *(Cefizox)*	IM, IV: 500 mg–2 g q4–12h	<80	Inj	K (100)
Ceftriaxone▲ *(Rocephin)*	IM, IV: 1–2 g q12–24h	NA	Inj	K (33–65)
Fourth-generation Cephalosporins				
Cefepime▲ *(Maxipime)*	IV: 500 mg–2 g q12h	<60	Inj	K (85)
Fifth-generation Cephalosporin				
Ceftaroline fosamil *(Tefloro)*	400–600 mg q12h	≤50	IV: 400, 600 mg	K (88)
Aminoglycosides				
Amikacin▲ *(Amikin)*	IM, IV: 15–20 mg/kg/d divided q12–24h; 15–20 mg/kg q24–48h	<60, TDM	Inj	K (95)
Gentamicin▲ *(Garamycin)*	IM, IV: 2–5 mg/kg/d divided q12–24h; 5–7 mg/kg q24–48h	<60, TDM	Inj ophth sus, oint	K (95)
Streptomycin▲	IM, IV: 10 mg/kg/d not to exceed 750 mg/d	<50	Inj	K (90)
Tobramycin▲ *(Nebcin)*	IM, IV: 2–5 mg/kg/d divided q12–24h; 5–7 mg/kg q24–48h	<60, TDM	Inj ophth sus, oint	K (95)

(cont.)

Table 65. Antibiotics (cont.)				
Antimicrobial Class, *Subclass*	**Dosage**	**Adjust When CrCl[a] Is: (mL/min)**	**Formulations**	**Route of Elimination (%)**
Macrolides				
Azithromycin▲ *(Zithromax)*	po: 500 mg day 1, then 250 mg/d IV: 500 mg/d	NA	C: 250 S: 100, 200 mg/5 mL,▲ 1 g (single-dose pk) T: 600▲ Inj▲	L
Clarithromycin▲ *(Biaxin, Biaxin XL)*	po: 250–500 mg q12h ER: 1000 mg/d	<30	S: 125, 250 mg/5 mL T: 250, 500 ER: 500	L, K (20–30)
Erythromycin▲	po: Base: 333 mg q8h Stearate or base: 250–500 mg q6–12h Ethylsuccinate: 400–800 mg q6–12h IV: 15–20 mg/kg/d divided q6h	NA	Base: C, T: 250, 333, 500 Stearate: T: 250, 500 Ethylsuccinate: S: 100, 200, 400 mg/5 mL T: 400 ChT: 200 Inj	L
Fidaxomycin *(Dificid)*			T: 200 mg	F (92)
Ketolide				
Telithromycin *(Ketek)*	po: 800 mg/d × 5–10 d	<30	T: 800	L, K
Quinolones				
Ciprofloxacin▲ *(Cipro)*	po: 250–750 mg q12h ophth: see **Table 44** IV: 200–400 mg q12h	po: <50 IV: <30	T: 100, 250, 500, 750▲ S: 250 mg/5 mL, 500 mg/5 mL Ophth sol:▲ 3.5 mg/5 mL Inj	K (30–50), L, F (20–40)
(Cipro XR)			XR: 500	
Gemifloxacin *(Factive)*	po: 320 mg/d	≤40	T: 320 mg	K, L, F
Levofloxacin▲ *(Levaquin)*	po, IV: 250–500 mg/d	<50	T: 250, 500	K
Moxifloxacin *(Avelox)*	po: 400 mg/d	NA	T: 400	L (~55), F (25), K (20)
Norfloxacin *(Noroxin)*	po: 400 mg q12h ophth: see **Table 44**	<30	T: 400 Ophth: 0.3%	K (30), F (30)
Ofloxacin▲ *(Roxin)*	po, IV: 200–400 mg q12–24h ophth: see **Table 44**	<50	T: 200, 300, 400▲ Ophth: 0.3%▲ Inj	K

(cont.)

Table 65. Antibiotics (cont.)				
Antimicrobial Class, *Subclass*	**Dosage**	**Adjust When CrCl[a] Is: (mL/min)**	**Formulations**	**Route of Elimination (%)**
Tetracyclines				
Doxycycline▲ (eg, *Vibramycin*)	po, IV: 100–200 mg/d given q12–24h	NA	C: 50, 100 T: 50, 100 S: 25, 50 mg/5 mL Inj	K (25), F (30)
Minocycline▲ *(Minocin)*	po, IV: 200 mg once, then 100 mg q12h	NA	C: 50, 100 S: 50 mg/5 mL Inj	K
Tetracycline▲	po, IV: 250–500 mg q6–12h	NA	C: 100, 250, 500 T: 250, 500 S: 125 mg/5 mL Inj Ophth: oint, sus Topical: oint, sol	K (60)
Glycycline				
Tigecycline *(Tygacil)*	IV: 100 mg once, then 50 mg q12h × 5–14 d	NA	Inj	K (33), F (59), L
Other Antibiotics				
Chloramphenicol▲ *(Chloromycetin)*	po, IV: 50 mg/kg/d given q6h; max: 4 g/d	NA	C: 250 Topical Ophth Inj	L (90)
Clindamycin▲ *(Cleocin)*	po: 150–450 mg q6–8h; max: 1.8 g/d IM, IV: 1.2–1.8 g/d given q8–12h; max: 3.6 g/d	NA	C: 75, 150, 300▲ S: 75 mg/5 mL▲ Vaginal crm: 2% Topical gel: 1%▲ Inj▲	L (90)
Co-trimoxazole▲ (TMP/SMZ, *Bactrim*)	Doses based on the trimethoprim component: po: 1 double-strength tab q12h; IV: sepsis: 20 TMP/kg/d given q6h	≤30	T: SMZ 400, TMP 80 double-strength: SMZ 800, TMP 160 S: SMZ 200, TMP 40 mg/5 mL Inj	K, L
Daptomycin *(Cubicin)*	IV: 4 mg/kg/d × 7–14 d	<30	Inj	K (78), L (6)
Fosfomycin *(Monurol)*	Complicated UTI: Women—po: 3 g in 90–120 mL water × 1 dose Men—po: 3 g in 90–120 mL water q2–3d × 3 doses Prostate—po: 3 g in 90–120 mL water q3d × 21 d		pwd: 3 g/packet	K, F
Linezolid *(Zyvox)*	po: 600 mg q12h IV: 600 mg q12h	NA	T: 600 S: 100 mg/5 mL Inj	L (65), K (30)

(cont.)

Table 65. Antibiotics (cont.)

Antimicrobial Class, *Subclass*	Dosage	Adjust When CrCl[a] Is: (mL/min)	Formulations	Route of Elimination (%)
Metronidazole▲ *(Flagyl, MetroGel)*	po: 250–750 mg q6–8h Topical: apply q12h Vaginal: 1 applicator full (375 mg) qhs or q12h	≤10	T: 250, 500▲ ER: 750 C: 375▲ Topical gel: 0.75%▲ (30 g) Vaginal gel: 0.75%▲ (70 g) Inj▲	L (30–60), K (20–40), F (6–15)
Nitrofurantoin▲ *(Macrobid, Macrodantin)*	po: 50–100 mg q6h	Do not use if <40	C: 25, 50, 100▲ S: 25 mg/5 mL	L (60), K (40)
Quinupristin-dalfopristin *(Synercid)*	Vancomycin-resistant *E faecium*: IV: 7.5 mg/kg q8h Complicated skin or skin structure infection: 7.5 mg/kg q12h	NA	Inj	L, B, F (75), K (15–19)
Telavancin *(Vibativ)*	IV: 10 mg/kg q24h × 1–2 wk	≤50	Inj	K (76)
Vancomycin *(Vancocin)*	po: *C difficile*: 125–500 mg q6–8h IV: 500 mg–1 g q8–24h Peak: 20–40 mcg/mL Trough: 5–10 mcg/mL	<60	C: 125, 250 Inj▲	K (80–90)

Antifungals (see also **Table 38**)
Amphotericin

Amphotericin B▲ *(Fungizone)*	IV: test dose: 1 mg infused over 20–30 min; if tolerated, initial therapeutic dosage is 0.25 mg/kg; the daily dosage can be increased by 0.25-mg/kg increments on each subsequent day until the desired daily dosage is reached Maintenance dosage: IV: 0.25–1 mg/kg/d or 1.5 mg/kg q48h; do not exceed 1.5 mg/kg/d	c	Topical: crm, lot, oint: 3% Inj	K
Amphotericin B Lipid Complex *(Abelcet)*	2.5–5 mg/kg/d as a single infusion	c	Inj	K
Amphotericin B Liposomal *(AmBisome)*	3–6 mg/kg/d infused over 1–2 h	c	Inj	K

(cont.)

Antibiotics – INFECTIOUS   155

Table 65. Antibiotics (cont.)				
Antimicrobial Class, *Subclass*	**Dosage**	**Adjust When CrCl[a] Is: (mL/min)**	**Formulations**	**Route of Elimination (%)**
Amphotericin B Cholestreyl Sulfate Complex *(Amphotec)*	3–4 mg/kg/d infused at 1 mg/kg/h; max dosage 7.5 mg/kg/d	c	Inj	K
Azoles				
Fluconazole▲ *(Diflucan)*	po, IV: first dose 200–800 mg, then 100–400 mg q24h for 14 d–12 wk, depending on indication Vaginal candidiasis: 150 mg as a single dose	<50	T: 50, 100, 150, 200 S: 10 and 40 mg/mL Inj	K (80)
Itraconazole *(Sporanox)*	po: 200–400 mg/d; dosages >200 mg/d should be divided. Life-threatening infections: loading dose: 200 mg q8h should be given for the first 3 d of therapy IV: 200 mg q12h × 4 d, then 200 mg/d	<30	C: 100▲ S: 100 mg/10 mL Inj	L
Ketoconazole▲ *(Nizoral)*	po: 200–400 mg/d shp: 2/wk × 4 wk with ≥ 3 d between each shp Topical: apply q12–24h	NA	T: 200 shp: 2% crm: 2%	L, F
Miconazole▲ *(Monistat IV)*	IT: 20 mg q1–2d IV: initial: 200 mg, then 1.2–3.6 g/d divided q8h for up to 2 wk	NA	Inj	L, F
Voriconazole *(VFEND)*	IV: loading dose 6 mg/kg q12h for 2 doses, then 4 mg/kg q12h po: >40 kg: 200 mg q12h; ≤40 kg: 100 mg q12h If on phenytoin, IV: 5 mg/kg q12h, and po: >40 kg: 400 mg q12h; ≤40 kg: 200 mg q12h	<50 (IV only)	Inj T: 50, 200 mg	L

(cont.)

Table 65. Antibiotics (cont.)				
Antimicrobial Class, *Subclass*	**Dosage**	**Adjust When CrCl[a] Is: (mL/min)**	**Formulations**	**Route of Elimination (%)**
Echinocandins				
Anidulafungin *(Eraxis)*	Esophageal candidiasis: 100 mg on day 1, then 50 mg/d × ≥13 d and 7 d after symptoms resolve	NA	Inj	L, F (30)
Caspofungin *(Cancidas)*	Initial: 70 mg infused over 1 h; esophageal candidiasis: 50 mg/d; dosage with concurrent enzyme inducers: 70 mg/d	NA	Inj	L (50), F (35)
Micafungin *(Mycamine)*	Esophageal candidiasis: 150 mg/d; prophylaxis in stem cell transplant: 50 mg/d	NA	Inj	L, F (71), K (<15)
Other Antifungals				
Flucytosine *(Ancobon)*	po: 50–150 mg/kg/d divided q6h	<40	C: 250, 500	K (75–90)
Griseofulvin▲ *(Fulvicin P/G, Grifulvin V)*	po: Microsize: 500–1000 mg/d in single or divided doses Ultramicrosize: 330–375 mg/d in single or divided doses Duration based on indication	NA	Microsize: S: 125 mg/5 mL▲ T: 250, 500 Ultramicrosize:▲ T: 125, 165, 250, 330	L
Terbinafine▲ *(Lamisil)*	po: 250 mg/d × 6–12 wk for superficial mycoses; 250–500 mg/d for up to 16 mo Topical: apply q12–24h for max of 4 wk	<50	T: 250 mg▲ crm: 1%▲ Topical S: 1%	L, K (70–75)

Note: NA = not applicable; TDM = adjust dose on basis of therapeutic drug monitoring principles and institutional protocols

[a] The CrCl listed is the threshold below which the dosage (amount or frequency) should be adjusted. See package insert for detailed dosing guidelines.

[b] Dosage should not exceed 250 mg q6h in kidney impairment.

[c] Adjust dosage if decreased kidney function is due to the medication, or give every other day.

ACUTE KIDNEY FAILURE

Definition

An acute deterioration in kidney function defined by decreased urine output or increased values of kidney function tests, or both

Precipitating and Aggravating Factors (Italicized type indicates most common.)

• *Acute tubular necrosis* due to hypoperfusion or nephrotoxins
• Medications (eg, aminoglycosides, radiocontrast materials, NSAIDs, ACEIs), including those causing allergic interstitial nephritis (eg, NSAIDs, penicillins and cephalosporins, sulfonamides, flouroquinolones, allopurinol, rifampin, PPIs)
• Multiple myeloma
• Obstruction (eg, BPH)
• Vascular disease (thromboembolic, atheroembolic)
• *Volume depletion* or redistribution of ECF (eg, cirrhosis, burns)

Evaluation

• Review medication list
• Catheterize bladder, determine postvoid residual
• UA (see **Table 66** for likely diagnoses)
• Renal ultrasonography
• Renal biopsy in selected cases

• If patient is not on diuretics, determine fractional excretion of sodium (FENa):

$$FENa = \left[\frac{urine\ Na/plasma\ Na}{urine\ creatinine/plasma\ creatinine} \right] \times 100$$

FENa $<1\%$ indicates prerenal cause; FENa $>2\%$ generally indicates acute tubular necrosis; FENa $1\%–2\%$ is nondiagnostic. Note that some older adults who have prerenal cause may have FENa $\geq 1\%$ because of age-related changes in sodium excretion.

• If patient is receiving diuretics, determine fractional excretion of urea (FEUrea):

$$FEUrea = \left[\frac{urine\ urea\ nitrogen/BUN}{urine\ creatinine/plasma\ creatinine} \right] \times 100$$

FEUrea $\leq 35\%$ indicates prerenal azotemia; FEUrea $>50\%$ indicates acute tubular necrosis; FEUrea $36\%–50\%$ is nondiagnostic.

| Table 66. Likely Diagnoses Based on UA Findings ||
Findings	Diagnoses
Hematuria, RBC casts, heavy proteinuria	Glomerular disease or vasculitis
Granular and epithelial cell casts, free epithelial cells	Acute tubular necrosis
Pyuria, WBC casts, granular or waxy casts, little or no proteinuria	Acute interstitial nephritis, glomerulitis, vasculitis, obstruction, renal infarction
Normal UA	Prerenal disease, obstruction, hypercalcemia, myeloma, acute tubular necrosis

Prevention of Radiocontrast-induced Acute Kidney Failure in High-risk Patients
(Cr >1.5 mg/dL, GFR <60 mL/min/1.73 m² body surface area)

- Hold NSAIDs and diuretics for 24 h and metformin for 48 h before administration
- Use low osmolal or iso-osmolal contrast agents in low doses
- Avoid closely spaced repeat studies (eg, <48 h apart)
- Intravenous hydration
  - 0.9% saline IV 1 mL/kg/h for 24 h beginning 2–12 h before administration and continuing 6–12 h after procedure, *or*
  - Sodium bicarbonate (154 mEq/L) 3 mL/kg/h for 1 h before procedure and 1 mL/kg/h for 6 h after procedure, especially if insufficient time for hydration before procedure
- Oral acetylcysteine *(Mucomyst)* (100, 200/mL) 1200 mg po q12h the day before and the day of procedure (controversial)
- Repeat serum creatinine 24–48 h after administration

Treatment

- D/C medications that are possible precipitants; avoid contrast dyes.
- If prerenal pattern, treat HF (see p 37) if present. Otherwise, volume repletion. Begin with fluid challenge 500–1000 mL over 30–60 min. If no response (increased urine output), give furosemide 100–400 mg IV.
- If obstructed, leave urinary catheter in place during evaluation and while specific treatment is implemented.
- If acute tubular necrosis, monitor weight daily, record intake and output, and monitor electrolytes frequently. Fluid replacement should be equal to urinary output plus other drainage plus 500 mL/d for insensible losses.
- If acute interstitial nephritis (except if NSAID-induced) and does not resolve with 3–7 d, then glucocorticoids (eg, prednisone 1 mg/kg/d) for a minimum 1–2 wk and gradual taper when Cr has returned near baseline for a total duration of 2–3 mo.
- Dialysis is indicated when severe hyperkalemia, acidosis, or volume overload cannot be managed with other therapies or when uremic symptoms (eg, pericarditis, coagulopathy, or encephalopathy) are present.

CHRONIC KIDNEY FAILURE
Classification (Kidney Disease Outcomes Quality Initiative)
Stage 1: GFR >90 mL/1.73 m² and persistent albuminuria
Stage 2: GFR 60–89 mL/1.73 m² and persistent albuminuria
Stage 3: GFR 30–59 mL/1.73 m²
Stage 4: GFR 15–29 mL/1.73 m²
Stage 5: GFR <15 mL/1.73 m² or end-stage renal disease
If stage 3–5, refer to a nephrologist for co-management.

Evaluation

- Hx and physical examination: assess for diabetes mellitus, HTN, vascular disease, HF, NSAIDs, contrast dye exposure, angiographic procedures with possible cholesterol embolization, glomerulonephritis, myeloma, BPH or obstructive cancers, current or previous treatment with a nephrotoxic drug, hereditary kidney disease (eg, polycystic)
- Blood tests (CBC, comprehensive metabolic profile, phosphorus, cholesterol, ESR, serum protein immunoelectrophoresis)

- Progression to kidney failure can be predicted by age, sex, eGFR, urine albumin:creatinine ratio, serum calcium, serum phosphate, serum bicarbonate, and serum albumin using equation:
  http://www.qxmd.com/calculate-online/nephrology/kidney-failure-risk-equation.
- Estimate CrCl or GFR (see p 1). CrCl is usually about 20% higher than true GFR. eGFR based on the MDRD equation and true GFR are very close when the GFR is <60 mL/1.73 m^2, but true GFR exceeds eGFR by a small amount when GFR is >60 mL/1.73 m^2. Older people with eGFR 45–59 mL/1.73 m^2 may have normal kidney function for their age.
- If GFR 15–59 mL/min, then measure iPTH; if iPTH >100 pg/mL, then measure serum 25-hydroxy vitamin D
- UA and quantitative urine protein (protein:Cr ratio or 24-h urine for protein and Cr); urine immunoelectrophoresis, if indicated; at all stages, heavier proteinuria is predictive of mortality, ESRD, and doubling of serum Cr
- Renal ultrasound (large kidneys suggest tumors, infiltrating disease, cystic disease; small kidneys suggest chronic kidney disease; can also identify cysts, stones, masses, and hydronephrosis)
- Exclude renal artery stenosis with MRI angiography, spiral CT with CT angiography, or duplex Doppler ultrasound if acute rise in Cr shortly after beginning treatment with ACEI or ARB
- Renal biopsy in selected cases

Treatment

- Attempt to slow progression of kidney failure
  - Control BP (target $<125/75$ if proteinuria or increased Cr); most important
  - If diabetes or proteinuria, begin ACEI or ARB (see **Table 21**) regardless of whether or not patient has HTN. Combining ACEI and ARB is of uncertain benefit.
  - Diabetes control, HbA$_{1c}$ <7
  - Treat hyperlipidemia (p 40)
  - Moderate dietary protein restriction, 0.8–1 g/kg/d, especially if diabetic nephropathy; if stage 4 or 5 chronic kidney disease, consider low-protein (0.6 g/kg/d) diet.
  - Smoking cessation
  - Reduction of proteinuria to <1 g/d, if possible and at least to <60% of baseline
- Prevent and treat symptoms and complications
  - Treat hyperkalemia if present (p 164).
  - Sodium bicarbonate (daily dosage of 0.5–1 mEq/kg) therapy to maintain serum bicarbonate concentration >23 mEq/L.
  - Normalize serum calcium with calcium carbonate▲ (500 mg elemental calcium q6–24h) or calcium acetate *(Phoslo)* (3 or 4 tabs q8h with meals); if hypocalcemia is refractory, consider calcitriol *(Rocaltrol)* 0.25 mcg/d.
  - Normalize serum phosphate if not on dialysis and maintain between 3.5 and 5.5 mg/dL if on dialysis; restrict dairy products and cola to phosphate intake <900 mg/d. When hyperphosphatemia is refractory, begin:
    - If serum calcium is low, calcium carbonate▲ (1250–1500 mg q8h with meals) or calcium acetate *(PhosLo)* (3 or 4 tabs q8h with meals).

- If serum calcium is normal or calcium supplementation is ineffective:
  - Sevelamer hydrochloride *(Renagel)* [T: 400, 800; C: 403] or sevelamer carbonate *(Renvela)* [0.8 g packet, T: 800], which does not lower bicarbonate 800–1600 mg po q8h with each meal
  - Lanthanum carbonate *(Fosrenol)* [ChT: 250, 500] at initial dosage of 250–500 mg po q8h with each meal, then titrate in increments of 750 mg/d at intervals of 2–3 wk to max of 3750 mg/d.
- Treating vitamin D insufficiency improves biochemical markers but the effect on clinical outcomes is uncertain. Use vitamin D$_2$ (ergocalciferol) 50,000 U/mo or oral vitamin D with calcitriol 25 mcg/d if 25(OH) vitamin D is <30 ng/mL. Stop if corrected serum calcium is >10.2 mg/dL.
- Treat anemia with iron (if iron-deficient) to maintain transferrin saturation >20% and serum ferritin >100 ng/L and, if necessary, erythropoietin-darbopoetin (see **Table 56**) to maintain a target Hb goal of ≤11 g/dL.
- Manage volume overload (see HF, p 37).
- Prevent and treat cardiovascular disease (see p 33) with target LDL goal <100 mg/dL. The value of statins for patients on maintenance dialysis is questionable.
- Treat secondary hyperparathyroidism; increased PTH can be treated with calcitriol as mentioned above.
- Immunize with *Pneumovax* and, before dialysis, hepatitis B vaccines if hepatitis B surface antigen and antibody are negative.
- Prepare for dialysis or transplant. Educate patients regarding options of hemodialysis, peritoneal dialysis, and kidney transplantation. If estimated GFR <25 mL/min, recommend referral for arteriovenous fistula access. If estimated GFR <20 mL/min, patients can be listed for cadaveric kidney transplant.
- Dialysis is indicated when severe hyperkalemia, acidosis, or volume overload cannot be managed with other therapies or when uremic symptoms (eg, pericarditis, coagulopathy, or encephalopathy) are present.

VOLUME DEPLETION (DEHYDRATION)
Definition
Losses of sodium and water that may be isotonic (eg, loss of blood) or hypotonic (eg, nasogastric suctioning)

Precipitating Factors
- Blood loss
- Diuretics
- GI losses
- Kidney or adrenal disease (eg, renal sodium wasting)
- Sequestration of fluid (eg, ileus, burns, peritonitis)
- Age-related changes (impaired thirst, sodium wasting due to hyporeninemic hypoaldosteronism, and free water wasting due to renal insensitivity to antidiuretic hormone)

Evaluation
Clinical Symptoms
- Anorexia
- Nausea and vomiting
- Orthostatic lightheadedness
- Delirium
- Weakness

Clinical Signs
- Dry tongue and axillae
- Oliguria
- Orthostatic hypotension
- Elevated heart rate
- Weight loss

Laboratory Tests

- Serum electrolytes
- Urine sodium (usually <10 mEq/L) and FENa (usually <1% but may be higher because of age-related sodium wasting)
- Serum BUN and creatinine (BUN:creatinine ratio often >20)

Management

- Weigh daily; monitor fluid losses and serum electrolytes, BUN, creatinine.
- If mild, oral rehydration of 2–4 L of water/d and 4–8 g Na diet; if poor oral intake, give IV D5W1/2 NS with potassium as needed.
- If hemodynamically unstable, give IV 0.9% saline 1–2 L as quickly as possible until SBP ≥100 mmHg and no longer orthostatic. Then switch to D5W1/2 NS. Monitor closely in patients with a hx of HF.

HYPERNATREMIA

Causes

- Pure water loss
  - Insensible losses due to sweating and respiration
  - Central (eg, post-traumatic, CNS tumors, meningitis) diabetes insipidus or nephrogenic (eg, hypercalcemia, lithium) diabetes insipidus
- Hypotonic sodium loss
  - Renal causes: osmotic diuresis (eg, due to hyperglycemia), postobstructive diuresis, polyuric phase of acute tubular necrosis
  - GI causes: vomiting and diarrhea, nasogastric drainage, osmotic cathartic agents (eg, lactulose)
- Hypertonic sodium gain (eg, treatment with hypertonic saline)
- Impaired thirst (eg, delirious or intubated) or access to water (eg, functionally dependent) may sustain hypernatremia

Evaluation

- Measure intake and output.
- Obtain urine osmolality:
  - >800 mOsm/kg suggests extrarenal (if urine Na <25 mEq/L) or remote renal water loss or administration of hypertonic Na^+ salt solutions (if urine Na >100 mEq/L).
  - <250 mOsm/kg and polyuria suggest diabetes insipidus.

Treatment

- Treat underlying causes.
- Correct slowly over at least 48–72 h using oral (can use pure water), nasogastric (can use pure water), or IV (D5W, 1/2 or 1/4 NS) fluids; correct at rate of no more than 1 mmol/L/h if acute (eg, developing over hours) and at no more than 10 mmol/L/d if of longer duration.
- Correct with NS only in cases of severe volume depletion with hemodynamic compromise; once stable, switch to hypotonic solution.
- When repleting fluids, use the following formula to estimate the effect of 1 L of any infusate on serum Na:

$$\text{Change in serum Na} = \frac{\text{infusate Na} - \text{serum Na}}{\text{total body water} + 1}$$

- ◦ Infusate Na (mmol/L): D5W = 0; 1/4 NS = 34; 1/2 NS = 77; NS = 154
- ◦ Calculate total body water as a fraction of body weight (0.5 kg in older men and 0.45 kg in older women).
- Divide treatment goal (usually 10 mmol/L/d) by change in serum Na/L (from formula) to determine amount of solution to be given over 24 h.
- Compensate for any ongoing obligatory fluid losses, which are usually 1–1.5 L/d.
- Divide amount of solution for repletion plus amount for obligatory fluid losses by 24 to determine rate per hour.

HYPONATREMIA

Causes

- With increased plasma osmolality: hyperglycemia (1.6 mEq/L decrement for each 100 mg/dL increase in plasma glucose)
- With normal plasma osmolality (pseudohyponatremia): severe hyperlipidemia, hyperproteinemia (eg, multiple myeloma)
- With decreased plasma osmolality:
  - ◦ With ECF excess: kidney failure, HF, hepatic cirrhosis, nephrotic syndrome
  - ◦ With decreased ECF volume: renal loss from salt-losing nephropathies, diuretics, cerebral salt wasting, osmotic diuresis; extrarenal loss due to vomiting, diarrhea, skin losses, and third-spacing (usually urine Na <20 mEq/L, FENa <1%, and uric acid >4 mg/dL)
  - ◦ With normal ECF volume: primary polydipsia (urine osmolarity <100 mOsm/kg), hypothyroidism, adrenal insufficiency, SIADH (urine Na >40 mEq/L and uric acid <4 mg/dL)

Management

Treat underlying cause. Specific treatment only if symptomatic (eg, altered mental status, seizures) or severe acute hyponatremia (eg, <120 mEq/L).

- If initial volume estimate is equivocal, give fluid challenge of 0.5–1 L of isotonic (0.9%) saline.
- If volume depletion, give saline IV (corrects ~1 mEq/L for every liter given) or oral salt tablets.
- If edematous states, SIADH, or chronic renal failure, fluid restriction to below the level of urine output is the primary therapy.
- Hypovolemic hyponatremia is almost always chronic (except for cerebral salt wasting and after diuretic initiation), and hypertonic saline is seldom indicated.
- Euvolemic hyponatremia if acute (<48 h duration) should be corrected promptly with hypertonic (3%) saline; initial infusion rate: body weight (kg) × desired rate of increase in Na (mEq/h); correct 2–4 mEq/L in first 2–4 h if symptomatic.
- Goal is <10 mEq/L/24 h, <18 mEq/L/48 h, and <20 mEq/L/72 h rise in Na (more rapid correction can result in central pontine myelinolysis).
- Monitor Na closely and taper treatment when >120 mEq/L or symptoms resolve.
- Arginine vasopressin receptor antagonists
  - ◦ Conivaptan *(Vasprisol)* is effective in euvolemic hyponatremia in hospitalized patients; 20 mg IV over 30 min once, followed by continuous infusion of 20–40 mg over 24 h for 4 d max (L) (CYP3A4 interactions).
  - ◦ Tolvaptan *(Samsca)* 15–60 mg/d [T:15, 30]: initiate in hospital and monitor blood sodium concentration closely.

SYNDROME OF INAPPROPRIATE SECRETION OF ANTIDIURETIC HORMONE (SIADH)

Definition

Hypotonic hyponatremia (<280 mOsm/kg) with:

- Less than maximally dilute urine (usually >100 mOsm/kg)
- Elevated urine sodium (usually >40 mEq/L)
- Normal volume status
- Normal kidney, adrenal, and thyroid function

Precipitating Factors, Causes

- Medications (eg, SSRIs, venlafaxine, chlorpropamide, carbamazepine, oxcarbazepine, NSAIDs, barbiturates)
- Neuropsychiatric factors (eg, neoplasm, subarachnoid hemorrhage, psychosis, meningitis)
- Postoperative state, especially if pain or nausea
- Pulmonary disease (eg, pneumonia, tuberculosis, acute asthma)
- Tumors (eg, lung, pancreas, thymus)

Evaluation

- BUN, creatinine, serum cortisol, TSH
- CXR
- Review of medications
- Neurologic tests as indicated
- Urine sodium and osmolality

Management

Acute Treatment: See euvolemic hyponatremia management, p 163.
Chronic Treatment:

- D/C offending medication or treat precipitating illness.
- Restrict water intake to <800 mL/d with goal of Na ≥130 mEq/L.
- Liberalize salt intake or give salt tablets.
- Demeclocycline▲ *(Declomycin)* 150–300 mg q12h [T: 150, 300] (may be nephrotoxic in patients with liver disease) only if symptomatic and above steps do not work.
- Tolvaptan *(Samsca)* 15–60 mg/d [T:15, 30]: initiate in hospital and monitor blood sodium concentration closely only if symptomatic and above steps do not work.

HYPERKALEMIA

Causes

- Kidney failure
- Addison's disease
- Hyporeninemic hypoaldosteronism
- Renal tubular acidosis
- Acidosis
- Diabetic hyperglycemia
- Hemolysis, tumor lysis, rhabdomyolysis
- Medications (potassium-sparing diuretics, ACEIs, trimethoprim-sulfamethoxazole, β-blockers, NSAIDs, cyclosporine, tacrolimus, pentamidine, heparin, digoxin toxicity)
- Pseudohyperkalemia from extreme thrombocytosis or leukocytosis
- Transfusions of stored blood
- Constipation

Evaluation
- ECG; peaked T waves typically occur when K^+ exceeds 6.5 mEq/L. ECG changes are more likely with acute increases of K^+ than with chronic increases.

Treatment
Minor elevations
- K^+ <6 mEq/L without ECG changes:
  - Low-potassium diet (restrict orange juice, bananas, potatoes, cantaloupe, honeydew, tomatoes)
  - Oral diuretics (eg, oral torsemide or bumetanide, combined oral loop and thiazide-like diuretics; metolazone is the most K^+ wasting); avoid hypovolemia
  - Oral $NaHCO_3$ (650–1300 mg q12h)
  - Reduce or D/C medications that increase K^+
- K^+ 6–6.5 mEq/L without ECG changes: above treatments plus sodium polystyrene sulfonate▲ *(SPS, Kayexelate)* 15–30 g po q6–24h, or prn as enema 30–50 g in 100 mL of dextrose; full effect takes 4–24 h.
- K^+ 6.5 mEq/L with peaked T waves but no other ECG changes; hospitalization is decided case-by-case based on acuteness of onset, cause, and other patient factors.

Absolute indications for hospitalization
- K^+ >8 mEq/L
- ECG changes other than peaked T waves (eg, prolonged PR, loss of P waves, widened QRS)
- Acute deterioration of kidney function

Inpatient management of hyperkalemia
- Antagonism of cardiac effects of hyperkalemia (most rapid-acting acute therapy; use only for severe hyperkalemia with significant ECG changes when too dangerous to wait for redistribution therapies to take effect)
  - 10% calcium gluconate IV infused over 2–3 min (20–30 min if on digoxin) with ECG monitoring; effect lasts 30–60 min, may repeat if needed
- Reduction of serum K^+ by redistribution into cells (acute therapy; can be used in combination with calcium gluconate, and different redistribution therapies can be combined depending on severity of hyperkalemia)
  - Insulin (regular) 10 U in 500 mL of 10% dextrose over 30–60 min or bolus insulin (regular) 10 U IV followed by 50 mL of 50% dextrose
  - Albuterol 0.5 mg in 100 mL of 5% dextrose given over 10–15 min or nebulized 10–20 mg in 4 mL of NS over 10 min (should not be used as single agent)
  - Sodium bicarbonate use is controversial.
- Removal of potassium from body (definitive therapy; work more slowly)
  - Diuretics (eg, oral torsemide or bumetanide, IV furosemide, combined oral loop and thiazide-like diuretics; metolazone is the most K^+ wasting). Avoid hypovolemia.
  - Fludrocortisone▲ 0.1–0.3 mg/d
  - Sodium polystyrene sulfonate▲ *(SPS, Kayexalate)* 15–30 g po q6–24h or prn as enema 30–50 g in 100 mL of dextrose; full effect takes 4–24 h; if packaged in sorbitol *(SPS)*, may cause intestinal necrosis.
  - Dialysis

MALNUTRITION

DEFINITION
There is no uniformly accepted definition of malnutrition in older adults. Some commonly used definitions include the following:

Community-dwelling Older Adults
- Involuntary weight loss (eg, $\geq$10 lb over 6 mo, $\geq$4% over 1 yr)
- BMI <22 kg/m^2
- Hypoalbuminemia (eg, $\leq$3.8 g/dL)
- Hypocholesterolemia (eg, <160 mg/dL)
- Overweight (BMI 25–29.9 kg/m^2)
- Obesity (BMI $\geq$30 kg/m^2)
- Specific vitamin or micronutrient deficiencies (eg, vitamin B$_{12}$)
- Cancer-related anorexia/cachexia syndrome: a hypercatabolic state (increased resting energy expenditure) with high levels of tumor-activated or host-produced immune responses (eg, proinflammatory cytokines) to the tumor
- Sarcopenia age-related loss of muscle mass (eg, 2 standard deviations below mean for young healthy adults) with loss of strength and performance; contributors include decreased sex hormones, increased insulin resistance, increased inflammatory cytokines, decreased physical activity, inadequate protein intake, and spinal cord changes (decreased motor units)

Hospitalized Patients
- Dietary intake (eg, <50% of estimated needed caloric intake)
- Hypoalbuminemia (eg, <3.5 g/dL)
- Hypocholesterolemia (eg, <160 mg/dL)

Nursing-home Patients (Triggered by the Minimum Data Set)
- Weight loss of $\geq$5% in past 30 d; $\geq$10% in 180 d
- Dietary intake <75% of most meals

EVALUATION
Multidimensional Assessment
In the absence of valid nutrition screening instruments, clinicians should focus on whether the following issues may be affecting nutritional status:
- Economic barriers to securing food
- Availability of sufficiently high-quality food
- Dental problems that preclude ingesting food
- Medical illnesses that:
  - interfere with digestion or absorption of food
  - increase nutritional requirements
  - require dietary restrictions (eg, low-sodium diet or npo)
- Functional disability that interferes with shopping, preparing meals, or feeding
- Food preferences or cultural beliefs that interfere with adequate food intake

- Poor appetite
- Depressive symptoms

Anthropometrics

Weight on each visit and yearly height (see p 1)

Evaluation for Comorbid Medical Conditions

- CBC, ESR, and comprehensive metabolic panel (if none abnormal, then likelihood ratio for cancer is 0.2)
- CXR
- TSH

Biochemical Markers

Serum Proteins: All may drop precipitously because of trauma, sepsis, or major infection.
- Albumin (half-life 18–20 d) has prognostic value in all settings.
- Transferrin (half-life 7 d)
- Prealbumin (half-life 48 h) may be valuable in monitoring nutritional recovery.

Serum Cholesterol (Low or Falling Levels): Has prognostic value in all settings but may not be nutritionally mediated.

MANAGEMENT

Universal Recommendations

All older adults should receive calcium 1200 mg/d and vitamin D 800 IU/d. The appropriate use of 25-hydroxy vitamin D levels to detect and monitor vitamin D therapy has not been determined. If low, vitamin D should be replaced to levels of ≥30 ng/mL. See Osteoporosis, p 198.

Calculating Basic Energy (Caloric) and Fluid Requirements

- WHO energy estimates for adults 60 yr old and older:
  - Women (10.5) (weight in kg) + 596
  - Men (13.5) (weight in kg) + 487
- Harris-Benedict energy requirement equations:
  - Women: 655 + (9.6) (weight in kg) + (1.7) (height in cm) − (4.7) (age in yr)
  - Men: 66 + (13.7) (weight in kg) + (5) (height in cm) − (6.8) (age in yr)
- Fluid requirements for older adults without heart or kidney disease are ~30 mL/kg/d. Depending on activity and physiologic stress levels, these basic requirements may need to be increased (eg, 25% for sedentary or mild, 50% for moderate, and 100% for intense or severe activity or stress).

Obesity and Overweight Management

- Overweight probably does not increase mortality risk; however, weight loss in obese older adults may decrease mortality risk.
- In younger overweight and obese patients, no particular combination of protein, carbohydrate, and fat in weight loss diets offers any advantage in losing weight.
- Moderate exercise at 90 min/wk and a caloric prescription to produce a deficit of 750 calories per day can lead to loss of 4–9 kg, but this has not been confirmed in older adults.

Undernutrition Management

- If possible, remove disease-specific (eg, for hypercholesterolemia) dietary restrictions.
- Refeeding syndrome caused by the glucose-induced acute transcellular shift of phosphate typically occurs in malnourished patients who have had poor oral intake and then receive IV glucose-containing fluids, or enteral or parenteral nutrition. Symptoms occur most commonly within 2–4 d of refeeding and include hypophosphatemia, hyperglycemia, and hyperinsulinemia, which may be accompanied by hypokalemia, hypomagnesemia, and fluid retention. Supplementing IV fluids with potassium phosphate or oral phosphate and potassium may help prevent this syndrome.
- Post-hospitalization home visits by a dietitian may be valuable.

Appetite Stimulants

- No medications are FDA approved to promote weight gain in older adults.
- Dronabinol and megestrol acetate (not covered by Medicare Part D) have been effective in promoting weight gain in younger adults with specific conditions (eg, AIDS, cancer). Small clinical trials of megestrol in select groups (eg, after hospitalization, nursing home) have shown benefit for some nutritional markers (eg, prealbumin, weight) but not for clinical outcomes.
- A minority of patients receiving mirtazapine▲ report appetite stimulation and weight gain.
- All medications used for appetite have substantial potential adverse events.

Nutritional Supplements

- Protein and energy supplements in older adults at risk of malnutrition appear to have beneficial effects on weight gain and mortality, and shorten length of stay in hospitalized patients. Among those who are well nourished at baseline, the benefit is less clear. Supplements should be given between rather than with meals.
- For ICU patients, enteral nutrition is preferred over parenteral nutrition and should be started within the first 24–48 h after admission. Absence of bowel sounds and evidence of bowel function (eg, passing flatus or feces) are not contraindications to beginning tube feeding.
- Many formulas are available (see **Table 67** and **Table 68**). Read the content labels and choose on the basis of calories/mL, protein, fiber, lactose, and fluid load.
  - Oral: Many (eg, *Carnation Instant Breakfast, Health Shake*) are milk-based and provide ~1–1.5 calories/mL.
  - Enteral: Commercial preparations have between 0.5 and 2 calories/mL; most contain no milk (lactose) products. For patients who need fluid restriction, the higher concentrated formulas may be valuable, but they may cause diarrhea. Because of reduced kidney function with aging, some recommend that protein should contribute no more than 20% of the formula's total calories. If formula is sole source of nutrition, consider one that contains fiber (25 g/d is optimal).

Table 67. Examples of Lactose-free Oral Products

Product	Kcal/mL	mOsm	Protein (g/L)	Water (mL/L)	Na (mEq/L)	K (mEq/L)	Fiber (g/L)
Routine use formulations							
Boost Drink [a]	1.00	625	42.2	850	27.5	49.6	0
Boost Plus	1.50	630–670	59.1	780	31.2	41.0	0

(cont.)

Table 67. Examples of Lactose-free Oral Products (cont.)

Product	Kcal/mL	mOsm	Protein (g/L)	Water (mL/L)	Na (mEq/L)	K (mEq/L)	Fiber (g/L)
Ensure [b]	1.06	590	38.0	840	36.7	39.9	0
Ensure Plus	1.50	680	54.9	760	42.2	47.6	0
Carnation Instant Breakfast lactose-free	1.00	480–490	35.0	850	38.0	32.0	0
Carnation Instant Breakfast lactose-free Plus	1.50	620	52.0	780	50.5	48.1	0
Low volume (packaged as 45-mL supplement; nutrients are provided per serving)							
Resource Benecalorie	330	NA	7.0	0	0	0	0
Clear liquid							
Resource Breeze	1.06	750	38.0	830	14.8	0.5	0
Ensure Enlive	1.01	796	35.3	800	7.7	4.5	0
Diabetes formulations							
Boost Glucose Control	1.06	400	67.5	870	32.9	7.2	14.8
Glucerna shake[c]	0.93	530	41.8	850	38.5	39.9	10.1

NA = not available

[a] Also has "pudding" product that has 160 Kcal/5 oz and 0 fiber

[b] Also has "pudding" product that has 170 Kcal/4 oz and 1.0 g fiber/serving

[c] Institutional formulation (also available in 8-oz retail bottle with 200 Kcal, 5 g fiber, 10 g protein/serving)

Table 68. Examples of Lactose-free Enteral Products

Product	Kcal/mL	mOsm	Protein (g/L)	Water (mL/L)	Na (mEq/L)	K (mEq/L)	Fiber (g/L)
Diabetes formulations							
Diabetisource AC	1.20	450	28.7	840	28.7	28.3	15.0
Glucerna 1.0 Cal [a]	1.00	355	41.8	850	40.4	39.9	14.3
Low residue							
Isosource HN [b]	1.20	490	53.0	820	48.0	49.0	0
Osmolite 1 Cal [a]	1.06	300	44.3	840	40.5	40.1	0
Nutren 1.0 [c]	1.00	370	40.0	840	38.0	32.0	0
Low volume							
Nutren 2.0	2.00	745	80.0	700	56.5	49.2	0
TwoCal HN	2.00	725	84.0	700	63.3	62.4	5.1
High fiber							
Jevity 1 Cal [a]	1.06	300	44.3	840	40.4	40.2	14.4
Fibersource HN	1.20	490	54.0	810	52.0	51.0	10.0
Nutren 1.0 with fiber	1.00	410	40.0	840	38.0	32.0	14.0

[a] Also has 1.2 and 1.5 calorie formulations

[b] Also has 1.5 calorie formulation with 8 g fiber/L

[c] Also has 1.5 calorie formulation

Important Drug-enteral Interactions

- Soybean formulas increase fecal elimination of thyroxine; time administration of thyroxine and enteral nutrition as far apart as possible.
- Enteral feedings reduce absorption of phenytoin, levodopa, levofloxacin, and ciprofloxacin; administer these medications at least 2 h after a feeding and delay feeding at least 2 h after medication is administered; monitor levels (if taking phenytoin) and adjust dosages, as necessary.

- Check with pharmacy about suitability and best way to administer sustained-release, enteric-coated, and micro-encapsulated products (eg, omeprazole, lansoprazole, diltiazem, fluoxetine, verapamil).

Gastrostomy/Jejunostomy Tube Feeding

- Chronic artificial nutrition and hydration is not a basic intervention and is associated with uncertain benefit and considerable risks and discomfort.
- Artificial nutrition and hydration should be used only for specific medical indications, not to increase patient comfort.
- Randomized trials have not shown benefit in stroke patients with dysphagia.

Tips for Successful Tube Feeding

- Gastrostomy tube feeding may be either intermittent or continuous.
- Jejunostomy tube feedings must be continuous.
- Continuous tube feeding is associated with less frequent diarrhea but with higher rates of tube clogging.
- To prevent clogging and to provide additional free water, flushing with at least 30–60 mL of water q4–6h is recommended. Do not allow formula bags to run dry, fully crush medications, do not give more than one medication at a time, and flush before and after medication administration. Papain and chymopapain are more effective at clearing clogged tubes than sugar-free carbonated beverages or cranberry juice. Commercial devices (eg, Clog-Zapper) may be effective.
- Diarrhea, which develops in 5%–30% of people receiving enteral feeding, may be related to the osmolality of the formula, the rate of delivery, high sorbitol content in liquid medications (eg, APAP, lithium, oxybutynin, furosemide), or other patient-related factors such as antibiotic use or impaired absorption.
- To help prevent aspiration, maintain 30- to 45-degree elevation of the head of the bed during continuous feeding and for at least 2 h after bolus feedings.
- Do not administer bulk-forming laxatives (eg, methylcellulose or psyllium) through feeding tubes.
- Check gastric residual volume before each bolus feeding. Gastric residual volumes in the range of 200–500 mL should raise concern and lead to the implementation of measures to reduce risk of aspiration, but automatic cessation of feeding should not occur for gastric residual volumes <500 mL in the absence of other signs of intolerance. If needed, naloxone *(Narcan)* 8 mg q6h per nasogastric tube, metoclopramide▲ *(Reglan)* 10 mg, or erythromycin 250 mg IV [5 mg/5 mL] q6h may be useful for problems with high gastric residual volume once mechanical obstruction has been excluded.

Parenteral Nutrition

- Indicated in those with digestive dysfunction precluding enteral feeding.
- In ICU settings, if enteral nutrition is not feasible, should wait 8 days to begin parenteral nutrition.
- Delivers protein as amino acids, carbohydrate as dextrose (D5 = 170 kcal/L; D10 = 340 kcal/L), and fat as lipid emulsions (10% = 1100 kcal/L; 20% = 2200 kcal/L).

Peripheral Parenteral Nutrition: For short-term use; requires rotation of peripheral IV site q72h; solution osmolarity of <900 mOsm/L is recommended to reduce risk of phlebitis.

Total Parenteral Nutrition: Must be administered through a central catheter, which may be inserted peripherally.

SHOULDER PAIN: DIFFERENTIAL DIAGNOSIS AND TREATMENT

Rotator Cuff Tendinitis, Subacromial Bursitis, or Rotator Tendon Impingement on Clavicle

Dull ache radiating to upper arm. Painful arc (on abduction 60–120 degrees and external rotation) is characteristic. Also can be distinguished by applying resistance against active range of motion while immobilizing the neck with hand.

May cause shoulder impingement syndrome (insidious onset of anterolateral acromial pain frequently radiating to lateral mid-humerus). Pain is worse at night, exacerbated by lying on the involved shoulder or sleeping with the arm overhead. Active and passive range of motion are normal. Lidocaine injection will result in normal strength and temporary pain relief. See **Table 69**.

Table 69. Use of Lidocaine Injections to Distinguish Different Shoulder Pain Syndromes[a]

	Response to Lidocaine Injection	
Cause of shoulder pain	*Strength/Range of Motion*	*Pain*
Tendinitis, bursitis	Normal	Temporary relief
Rotator cuff tear	Persistent weakness	Temporary relief
Frozen shoulder	No change in range of motion	

[a] Insert a 1½-inch, 22-gauge needle 1½ inches below the midpoint of the acromion to a depth of 1 to 1½ inches. The angle of entry parallels the acromion. One mL of lidocaine is injected into the deltoid, and 1–2 mL into the subacromial bursa. Dramatic relief of pain and improvement of function by injection into subacromial bursa effectively excludes glenohumeral joint process.

Treatment: Identify and eliminate provocative, repetitive injury (eg, avoid overhead reaching). A brief period of rest and immobilization with a sling may be helpful. Pain control with APAP or a short course of NSAIDs (**Table 70**), home exercises or PT (especially assisted range of motion and wall walking), and corticosteroid injections (see p 178) may be useful.

Rotator Cuff Tears

Mild to complete; characterized by diminished shoulder movement. If severe, patients do not have full range of active or passive motion. The "drop arm" sign (the inability to maintain the arm in an abducted 90-degree position) indicates supraspinatus and infraspinatus tear. Weakness of external rotation (elbows flexed, thumbs up with examiner's hands outside patient's elbows; patient is asked to resist inward pressure) is common. Lidocaine injection will result in persistent weakness despite pain relief. See **Table 69**. MRI or ultrasound when performed by experienced operators establishes diagnosis.

Treatment: If due to injury, a brief period of rest and immobilization with a sling may be helpful. Pain control with APAP or a short course of NSAIDs (**Table 70**), home exercises or PT (especially assisted range of motion and wall walking) may be useful. Subacromial glucocorticoid injections may provide short-term pain relief, but multiple injections may be deleterious to healthy tendons. If no improvement after 6–8 wk of conservative measures, consider surgical repair.

Bicipital Tendinitis

Pain felt on anterior lateral aspect of shoulder, tenderness in the groove between greater and lesser tuberosities of the humerus. Pain is elicited on resisted flexion of shoulder, flexion of the elbow, or supination (external rotation) of the hand and wrist with the elbow flexed at the side.

Treatment: Identify and eliminate provocative, repetitive activities (eg, avoid overhead reaching). A period of rest (at least 7 d with no lifting) and corticosteroid injections (see p 178) are major components of therapy. After rest period, PT should focus on stretching biceps tendon (eg, putting arm on doorframe and hyperextending shoulder, with some external rotation). Tendon sheath injection with corticosteroids may be helpful.

Frozen Shoulder (Adhesive Capsulitis)

Loss of passive external (lateral) rotation, abduction, and internal rotation of the shoulder to <90 degrees. Usually follows three phases: painful (freezing) phase lasting wks to a few mo; adhesive (stiffening) phase lasting 4–12 mo; resolution phase lasting 6–24 mo. Lidocaine injection does not restore range of motion. See **Table 69**.

Treatment: Avoid rest and begin PT and home exercises for stretching the arm in flexion, horizontal adduction, and internal and external rotation. Corticosteroid injections (see p 178) may reduce pain and permit more aggressive PT. Consider surgical manipulation under anesthesia or arthroscopic dilation of capsule.

BACK PAIN: DIFFERENTIAL DIAGNOSIS AND TREATMENT

Acute Lumbar Strain (Low Back Pain Syndrome)

Acute pain frequently precipitated by heavy lifting or exercise. Pain may be central or more prominent on one side and may radiate to sacroiliac region and buttocks. Pain is aggravated by motion, standing, and prolonged sitting, and relieved by rest. Sciatic pain may be present even when neurologic examination is normal.

Treatment: Most can continue normal activities. If a patient obtains symptomatic relief from bed rest, generally 1–2 d lying in a semi-Fowler position or on side with the hips and knees flexed with pillow between legs will suffice. Treat muscle spasm with the application of ice, preferably in a massage over the muscles in spasm. APAP or a short course of NSAIDs (**Table 70**) can be used to control pain. Spinal manipulation is also effective for uncomplicated low back pain. As pain diminishes, encourage patient to begin isometric abdominal and lower-extremity exercises. Symptoms often recur. Education on back posture, lifting precautions, and abdominal muscle strengthening may help prevent recurrences.

Acute Disk Herniation

Over 90% of cases have herniation at L4–L5 or L5–S1 levels, resulting in unilateral impairment of ankle reflex, toe and ankle dorsiflexion, and pain (commonly sciatic) on straight leg raising (can be tested from sitting position by leg extension). Pain is acute in onset and varies considerably with changes in position.

Treatment: Initially same as acute lumbar strain (above). If unresponsive, administer epidural injection of a combination of a long-acting corticosteroid with an epidural anesthetic. Consider surgery if recurrence or neurologic signs persist beyond 6–8 wk after conservative treatment. The value of epidural injections and surgery for pain without neurologic signs is controversial. Surgery for severe sciatica provides faster pain relief and perceived recovery rates but no difference in perceived recovery and disability at 1 yr compared with conservative management. (See **Table 2** and **Table 3**.)

Osteoarthritis and Chronic Disk Degeneration

Characterized by aching pain aggravated by motion and relieved by rest. Occasionally, hypertrophic spurring in a facet joint may cause unilateral radiculopathy with sciatica.

Treatment: Identify and eliminate provocative activities. Education on back posture, lifting precautions, and abdominal muscle strengthening. APAP or a short course of NSAIDs (**Table 70**). Corticosteroid injections may be useful. Acupuncture and sham acupuncture may provide benefit. Consider opioids and other pain treatment modalities for chronic refractory pain (see p 203).

Unstable Lumbar Spine

Severe, sudden, short-lasting, frequently recurrent pain often brought on by sudden, unguarded movements. Pain is reproduced when moving from the flexed to the erect position. Pain is usually relieved by lying supine or on side. Impingement on nerve roots by spurs from facet joints or herniated disks can cause similar complaints, although symptoms in these conditions usually worsen over time. Symptoms can mimic disk herniation or degeneration, or osteoarthritis. Lumbar flexion radiographs can be diagnostic.

Treatment: Abdominal and paraspinal exercises, lumbrosacral corset. Surgery only in severe cases.

Lumbar Spinal Stenosis

Symptoms increase on spinal extension (eg, with prolonged standing, walking downhill, lying prone) and decrease with spinal flexion (eg, sitting, bending forward while walking, lying in the flexed position). Only symptom may be fatigue or pain in buttocks, thighs, and legs when walking (neurogenic or pseudoclaudication). May have immobility of lumbar spine, pain with straight leg raises, weakness of muscles innervated by L4 through S1 (see **Table 3**). Over 4 yr, 15% improve, 15% deteriorate, and 70% remain stable.

Treatment: APAP or a short course of NSAIDs (**Table 70**) and exercises to reduce lumbar lordosis (eg, bicycling) are sometimes beneficial. Corticosteroid injections may be useful. Surgical decompression (laminectomy and partial fascectomy) is more effective than conservative treatment in relieving moderate or severe symptoms; if spondylolithesis or scoliosis, then fusion may be better than simple decompression. Simple and complex fusion have more complications and higher costs than decompression alone. However, recurrence of pain several years after surgery is common. Depression, comorbidity influencing walking capacity, cardiovascular comorbidity, and scoliosis predict worse surgical outcome. Male gender, younger age, better walking ability and self-rated health, less comorbidity, and more pronounced canal stenosis predict better surgical outcome. Intraspinous spacer insertion may be effective if no spondylolithesis. Short-term data support the effectiveness of interspinous distraction surgery, which is less invasive.

Vertebral Compression Fracture

Immediate onset of severe pain; worse with sitting or standing; sometimes relieved by lying down.

Treatment: See Osteoporosis, p 198. Bed rest, analgesia, and mobilization as tolerated. Bracing is unproved except for traumatic vetebral fractures. Calcitonin or pamidronate (30 mg/d IV for 3 consecutive days) may provide symptomatic improvement. May require hospitalization to control symptoms. Percutaneous vertebroplasty (injection of cement into the vertebral body) has not been beneficial in clinical trials. The value of kyphoplasty is unproved. Avoid muscle relaxants.

Nonrheumatic Pain (eg, Tumors, Aneurysms)

Gradual onset, steadily expanding, often unrelated to position and not relieved by lying down. Night pain when lying down is characteristic. Upper motor neuron signs may be present. Involvement is usually in thoracic and upper lumbar spine.

HIP PAIN: DIFFERENTIAL DIAGNOSIS AND TREATMENT

Trochanteric Bursitis

Pain in lateral aspect of the hip that usually worsens when patient sits on a hard chair, lies on the affected side, or rises from a chair or bed; pain may improve with walking. Local tenderness over greater trochanter is often present, and pain is often reproduced on resisted abduction of the leg or internal rotation of the hip. However, trochanteric bursitis does not result in limited range of motion, pain on range of motion, pain in the groin, or radicular signs.

Treatment: Identify and eliminate provocative activities. Position pillow posterolaterally behind involved side to avoid lying on bursae while sleeping. Check for leg length discrepancy, prescribe orthotics if appropriate. Injection of a combination of a long-acting corticosteroid with an anesthetic is most effective treatment.

Osteoarthritis

"Boring" quality pain in the hip, often in the groin, and sometimes referred to the back or knee with stiffness after rest. Passive motion is restricted in all directions if disease is fairly advanced. In early disease, pain in the groin on internal rotation of the hip is characteristic.

Treatment: See also Osteoarthritis, p 177. Elective total hip replacement is indicated for patients who have radiographic evidence of joint damage and moderate to severe persistent pain or disability, or both, that is not substantially relieved by an extended course of nonsurgical management.

Guideline for the Management of Pain in Osteoarthritis, Rheumatoid Arthritis, and Juvenile Chronic Arthritis, 2nd ed., American Pain Society, 2002.

Hip Fracture

Sudden onset, usually after a fall, with inability to walk or bear weight, frequently radiating to groin or knee. If hip radiograph is negative and index of suspicion is high, repeat radiograph with hip at 15%–20% internal rotation or obtain MRI. Fractures are 45% femoral neck, 45% intertrochanteric, and 10% subtrochanteric.

Treatment: Treatment is surgical with open reduction and internal fixation (ORIF), hemiarthroplasty, or total hip replacement (THR), depending on site of fracture and amount of displacement. Sliding hip screws may have lower complication rates than intramedullary nails for extracapsular fractures. Displaced femoral neck fractures are generally treated with hemiarthroplasty or THR. Subtrochanteric fractures can be treated with intramedullary nails.

Perioperative Care:

- Timing of surgery: Early surgery (within 48 h) is associated with better outcomes but may be due to more comorbidity in those with delayed surgery.
- Regional anesthesia if possible
- Antibiotics: Perioperative antibiotics (cefazolin or vancomycin) should be given beginning within 1 h of surgery.
- Pressure-reducing rather than standard mattress; if high risk of pressure sore, use large cell, alternating pressure air mattress.
- Oximetry for at least 48 h with supplemental oxygen as needed.
- Graduated compression stockings as soon as possible after admission.
- DVT prophylaxis: Give preoperatively if surgery delay is expected to be >48 h; otherwise begin 12–24 h after surgery. Best evidence is for fondaparinux, rivaroxaban (if THR), or LMWH, but warfarin is commonly used (see Anticoagulation, p 24, for regimens). Recommended duration is 11–35 d but at least 10 d and probably 1 mo if patient is inactive or has comorbidities.

- Adequate pre- and postoperative analgesia (eg, three-in-one femoral nerve block, intrathecal morphine).
- Avoid indwelling urinary catheters.
- Nutritional supplements if undernourished.
- Transfuse only if symptomatic or Hb <8 g/dL.
- Begin assisted ambulation within 48 h.
- Monitor for development of delirium, malnutrition, and pressure sores.
- Weightbearing: Usually as tolerated for hemiarthroplasty or THR; toe-touch if ORIF or intertrochanter fracture.
- Hip precautions: No adduction past midline; no hip flexion beyond 90%; no internal rotation (toes upright in bed).
- Treat osteoporosis: Wait 2 wk before starting bisphosphonates; make sure vitamin D is replete (see Osteoporosis, p 198).
- Falls prevention: See Falls, p 101.

For patients who were nonambulatory before the fracture, conservative management is an option.

Nonrheumatic Pain
Referred pain from viscera, radicular pain from the lower spine, avascular necrosis, Paget disease, metastasis. Treatment based on identified etiology.

KNEE PAIN: DIFFERENTIAL DIAGNOSIS AND TREATMENT
Osteoarthritis
Pain usually related to activity (eg, climbing stairs, arising from chair, walking long distances). Morning stiffness lasts <30 min. Crepitation is common. Examination should attempt to exclude other causes of knee pain such as hip arthritis with referred knee pain (decreased hip range of motion), chondromalacia patellae (tenderness only over patellofemoral joint), iliotibial band syndrome (tenderness is lateral to the knee at site of insertion in fibular head or where courses over lateral femoral condyle), anserine bursitis (tenderness distal to knee over medial tibia), and determination of malalignment varus (bowlegged) or valgus (knock-kneed).

Treatment: See osteoarthritis treatment, p 177.

COMMON FOOT DISORDERS
Bunion: prominent and dorsal medial eminence of the first metatarsal; associated with hallux valgus

Calluses and corns: diffuse thickening of the stratum corneum in response to repeated friction or pressure (calluses); corns are similar but have a central, often painful core and are often found at pressure points, especially caused by ill-fitting shoes or gait abnormalities

Equinus: tight Achilles tendon

Hallux valgus (ie, bunion): deviation of the tip of the great toe, or main axis of the toe, toward the outer or lateral side of the foot

Hammertoe (digiti flexus): muscle tendon imbalance causing contraction of the proximal or distal interphalangeal joint, or both

Pes cavus: higher than normal arch that can result in excessive pressure, usually placed on the metatarsal heads, and cause pain and ulceration

Tarsal tunnel syndrome: an entrapment neuropathy of the posterior tibial nerve

Treatment:

- Calluses and corns are treated with salicylic acid plaster 40%, available OTC (eg, Mediplast, Sal-acid plaster) after paring skin with a #15 scalpel blade. Remove dead skin with metal nail file or pumice stone each night before replacing the patch. Do not use in patients with peripheral neuropathy.

- Orthoses can be placed either on the foot or into the shoe to accommodate for a foot deformity or to alter the function of the foot to relieve physical stress on a certain portion of the foot. OTC devices made of lightweight polyethylene foam, soft plastics, or silicone are available for a certain size of foot. Custom-made orthoses are constructed from an impression of a person's foot.

- If conservative methods fail, refer to podiatry or orthopedics for consideration of surgery.

PLANTAR FASCIITIS

Definition

Strain or inflammation in plantar fascia causing foot pain that is worse when beginning to walk; 80% resolve spontaneously within 1 yr.

Causes/Risk Factors

- Jumping
- Running
- Rheumatic diseases
- Obesity
- Flat feet
- Plantar spurs

Evaluation

Examiner should dorsiflex toes and then palpate plantar fascia to elicit pain points; posterior heel pain is uncommon and suggests other diagnosis.

Treatment

Nonpharmacologic

- Rest and icing
- Exercises (calf plantar fascia stretch, foot/ankle circles, toe curls)
- Avoid walking barefoot or in slippers
- Prefabricated silicone heel inserts
- Shoes (running, arch support, crepe sole)
- Short-leg walking cast
- Surgery (rarely needed)

Pharmacologic

- NSAIDs (short duration, 2–3 wk)
- Corticosteroid (eg, methylprednisolone 20–40 mg) and analgesic (eg, 1% lidocaine) injection of fascia; use only if conservative measures fail

CARPAL TUNNEL SYNDROME

Definition

Painful tingling or hypoesthesia, or both, in one or both hands in distribution innervated by median nerve

Causes

- Repetitive activities
- Diabetes mellitus
- Thyroid disease
- Amyloidosis
- Rheumatoid arthritis
- Space-occupying lesions (eg, lymphoma)
- Trauma (eg, Colles' fracture)

Evaluation and Assessment
Physical Examination
- Decreased sensation in palm, thumb, index finger, middle finger, and thumb side of ring finger
- Weak handgrip
- Tapping over median nerve at wrist causes pain to shoot from wrist to hand (Tinel's sign)
- Acute flexion of wrist for 60 sec (Phalen's test) should also cause pain

Laboratory Studies
- Fasting glucose
- TSH
- Nerve conduction velocity testing confirms diagnosis

Treatment
Nonpharmacologic
- Modify work or leisure activities to avoid repetitive movements
- Carpal tunnel mobilization (moving bones in wrist through PT or OT) may provide some symptom relief
- Splinting in neutral position, especially at night
- Surgery (more effective than splinting)

Pharmacologic
- Injectable corticosteroids, eg, methylprednisolone 15 mg (more effective than oral)
- Oral corticosteroids, eg, prednisone 20 mg/d for 1 wk followed by 10 mg/d for a second wk

OSTEOARTHRITIS
Classification
- Noninflammatory: pain and disability are generally the only complaints; findings include tenderness, bony prominence, and crepitus.
- Inflammatory: may also have morning stiffness lasting ≥30 min and night pain; findings may include joint effusion on examination or radiograph, warmth, and synovitis on arthroscopy.

Nonpharmacologic Approaches
- Superficial heat: hot packs, heating pads, paraffin, or hot water bottles (moist heat is better)
- Deep heat: microwave, shortwave diathermy, or ultrasound
- Biofeedback and transcutaneous electrical nerve stimulation
- Acupuncture and simulated or sham acupuncture have demonstrated benefit for chronic low back pain compared with usual care.
- Exercise (especially water-based), PT, OT: strengthening, stretching, range of motion, functional activities
- Weight loss: especially for low back, hip, and knee arthritis
- Splinting: Avoid splinting for long periods of time (eg, >6 wk) because periarticular muscle weakness and wasting may occur. For base-of-thumb osteoarthritis, use of a custom-made neoprene splint worn only at night results in decreased pain and disability at 12 mo. Bracing (eg, neoprene sleeves over the knee, valgus brace) to correct malalignment is often helpful.

- Assistive devices: Cane should be used in the hand contralateral to the affected knee or hip. Cane length should be to the level of the wrist crease. Use walker if moderate or severe balance impairment, bilateral weakness, or unilateral weakness requiring support of >15%–20% of body weight.
- Surgical intervention (eg, debridement, meniscal repair, prosthetic joint replacement).
- Acupuncture as an adjunct to NSAIDs or analgesics for knee osteoarthritis or chronic low back pain.

Pharmacologic Intervention (see Figure 10)

Topical Analgesics: Liniments containing methylsalicylates (see **Table 88**), capsaicin cream, lidocaine 5% pch *(Lidoderm)*, diclofenac gel or patch (see **Table 70**).

Intra-articular, Bursal, and Trigger-point Injections:
- Corticosteroids (eg, methylprednisolone acetate, triamcinolone acetonide, and triamcinolone hexacetonide [longest acting]) may be particularly effective if monoarticular symptoms. Typical doses for all these drugs:
  - 40 mg for large joints (eg, knee, ankle, shoulder)
  - 30 mg for wrists, ankles, and elbows
  - 10 mg for small joints of hands and feet

Often mixed with lidocaine 1% or its equivalent (some experts recommend giving equal volume with corticosteroids, whereas others give 3–5 times the corticosteroid volume depending on size of joint) for immediate relief. Effect typically lasts 1–2 mo. Usually given no more often than 3 times per year.

- Hyaluronic acid preparations *(Euflexxa, Hyalgan, Orthovisc, Synvisc, Supartz)* 3–5 injections 1 wk apart for knee osteoarthritis. A formulation *(Synvisc-One)* is available that requires only one injection. Benefit is usually modest but may last ≥6 mo.

Nutriceuticals: Glucosamine sulfate (500 mg q8h) with chondroitin (400 mg q8h) has been effective for some patients. Results of clinical trials have been variable, and a recent meta-analysis has shown no benefit for knee or hip osteoarthritis.

APAP: First choice for mild/moderate pain. Fewer adverse events although less effective than NSAIDs.

NSAIDs: Often provide pain relief but have higher rates of adverse events than APAP (see **Table 70**). Not recommended for long-term use. Misoprostol▲ *(Cytotec)* 100–200 mg q6h with food [T: 100, 200], or a PPI (see **Table 47**) may be valuable prophylaxis against NSAID-induced ulcers in high-risk patients. Selective COX-2 inhibitors have lower likelihood of causing gastroduodenal ulcers than nonselective NSAIDs but increase risk of MI more than nonselective NSAIDs. All may increase INR in patients receiving warfarin.

Oral Opioids: Use requires careful risk-benefit analysis (see **Table 86**).

Other:
- Colchicine (0.6 mg q12h) may be of benefit in inflammatory osteoarthritis with recurrent symptoms.
- Duloxetine *(Cymbalta)* [C: 20, 30, 60], beginning at 30 mg/d and increasing to 60 mg/d after 1 wk, may have benefit in chronic low-back pain and osteoarthritis.

Figure 10. Pharmacologic Management of Osteoarthritis*

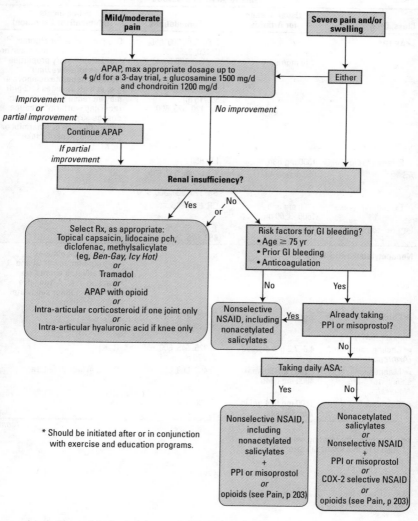

* Should be initiated after or in conjunction with exercise and education programs.

Source: Adapted from original material courtesy of Catherine MacLean, MD, PhD. Reprinted with permission.

Table 70. APAP and NSAIDs

Class, Drug	Usual Dosage for Arthritis	Formulations	Comments (Metabolism, Excretion)
✔APAP▲	650 mg q4–6h (q8h if CrCl <10 mg/mL)	T: 80, 325, 500, 650; C: 160, 325, 500; S: elixir 120/5 mL, 160/5 mL, 167/5 mL, 325/5 mL; S: 160/5 mL, 500/15 mL; Sp: 120, 325, 600	Drug of choice for chronic musculoskeletal conditions; no anti-inflammatory properties and less effective than NSAIDs; hepatotoxic above 4 g/d; at high dosages (≥2 g/d) may increase INR in patients receiving warfarin▲; reduce dosage 50%–75% if liver or kidney disease or if harmful or hazardous alcohol intake (L, K)
Extended release	1300 mg q8h	ER: 650	
ASA▲	650 mg q4–6h	T: 81, 325, 500, 650, 975; Sp: 120, 200, 300, 600	(K)
Extended release▲	1300 mg q8h or 1600–3200 mg q12h	CR: 650, 800	
Enteric-coated▲*	1000 mg q6h	T: 81, 162, 325, 500, 650, 975	
Nonacetylated Salicylates			Do not inhibit platelet aggregation; fewer GI and renal adverse events; no reaction in ASA-sensitive patients; monitor salicylate concentrations
✔Choline magnesium salicylate▲ *(Tricosal, Trilisate, CMT)*	3 g/d in 1, 2, or 3 doses	T: 500, 750, 1000; S: 500 mg/5 mL	(K)
✔Choline salicylate▲ *(Arthropan)*	4.8–7.2 g/d divided	T: 325, 545, 600, 650 S: 870 mg/5 mL	(L, K)
✔Magnesium salicylate▲* (eg, *Novasal)*	2 tabs q6–8h, max 4800 mg q24h	T: 467, 600, 650	Avoid in kidney failure
✔Salsalate▲	1500 mg to 4 g/d in 2 or 3 doses	T: 500, 750	(K)

(cont.)

✔ = preferred for treating older adults
* Also OTC in a lower tab strength

Table 70. APAP and NSAIDs (cont.)			
Class, Drug	Usual Dosage for Arthritis	Formulations	Comments (Metabolism, Excretion)
Nonselective NSAIDs			
Diclofenac▲ (Cataflam, Voltaren)	50–150 mg/d in 2 or 3 doses	T: 50, 75; 50, enteric coated	(L)
(Voltaren-XR)	100 mg/d	T: ER 100	(L)
(Zipsor)	25 mg up to q6h	C: 25	(L)
(Pennsaid)	apply 40 gtt per knee q6h	sol: 1.5%	(L)
✔Enteric coated (Arthrotec 50)	1 tab q8–12h	50 mg with 200 mcg misoprostol	(L)
(Arthrotec 75)	1 tab q12h	75 mg with 200 mcg misoprostol	(L)
✔Gel (Voltaren Gel)	2–4 g q6h	1%	(L)
✔Patch (Flector)	1 q12h	1.3%	(L)
Diflunisal▲ (Dolobid)	500–1000 mg/d in 2 doses	T: 500	(K)
✔Etodolac▲ (Lodine)	200–400 mg q6–8h	T: 400, 500; ER 400, 500, 600	Fewer GI adverse events (L)
(Lodine XL)	400–1000 mg/d	C: 200, 300	
Fenoprofen▲ (Nalfon)	200–600 mg q6–8h	C: 200, 300; T: 600	Higher risk of GI adverse events (L)
Flurbiprofen▲ (Ansaid)	200–300 mg/d in 2, 3, or 4 doses	T: 50, 100	(L)
✔Ibuprofen▲	1200–3200 mg/d in 3 or 4 doses	T: 100, 200, 300, 400, 600, 800; ChT: 50, 100; S: 100 mg/5 mL	Fewer GI adverse events (L)
with famotidine (Duexis)	1 tab q8h	T: 800 with 26.6 mg famotidine	
Injectable (Caldolor)	400–800 mg IV q6h (max 3200 mg/d)	Inj	
✔Ketoprofen▲ (Orudis)	50–75 mg q8h	T: 12.5; C: 50, 75	(L)
Sustained release (Oruvail [Canadian brand])	200 mg/d	C: 200	(L)
Ketorolac▲ (Toradol)	10 mg q4–6h, 15 mg IM or IV q6h	T: 10 Inj	Duration of use should be limited to 5 d (K)
Meclofenamate sodium▲	200–400 mg/d in 3 or 4 doses	C: 50, 100	High incidence of diarrhea (L)
Mefenamic acid▲ (Ponstel)	250 mg q6h	C: 250	(L)
✔Meloxicam▲ (Mobic)	7.5–15 mg/d	T: 7.5, 15 S: 7.5 mg/5mL	Has some COX-2 selectivity; fewer GI adverse events (L)

(cont.)

✔ = preferred for treating older adults
* Also OTC in a lower tab strength

Table 70. **APAP and NSAIDs (cont.)**			
Class, Drug	Usual Dosage for Arthritis	Formulations	Comments (Metabolism, Excretion)
✔Nabumetone▲ (Relafen)	500–1000 mg q12h	T: 500, 750	Fewer GI adverse events (L)
✔Naproxen▲ (Naprosyn)	220–500 mg q12h	T: 220, 375, 500, 750 S: 125 mg/5 mL	(L)
Delayed release (EC-Naprosyn)	375–500 mg q12h	T: 375, 500	(L)
Extended release (Naprelan)	750–1000 mg/d	T: 250, 375, 500	(L)
Naproxen sodium▲ (Anaprox)	275 mg or 550 mg q12h	T: 275, 550	(L)
✔Oxaprozin▲ (Daypro)	1200 mg/d	C: 600	(L)
Piroxicam▲ (Feldene)	10 mg/d	C: 10, 20	Can cause delirium (L)
Sulindac▲ (Clinoril)	150–200 mg q12h	T: 150, 200	May have higher rate of renal impairment (L)
Tolmetin▲ (Tolectin)	600–1800 mg/d in 3 or 4 doses	T: 200, 600 C: 400	(L)
Selective COX-2 Inhibitor			
✔Celecoxib (Celebrex)	100–200 mg q12h	C: 50, 100, 200, 400	Increased risk of MI; less GI ulceration; do not inhibit platelets; may increase INR if taking warfarin▲; avoid if moderate or severe hepatic insufficiency; may induce renal impairment; contra-indicated if allergic to sulfonamides (L)

✔ = preferred for treating older adults
* Also OTC in a lower tab strength

RHEUMATOID ARTHRITIS

Diagnosis

Table 71. **2010 American College of Rheumatology/European League Against Rheumatism (ACR/EULAR) Criteria***	
A. Joint involvement (any swollen or tender joint excluding first carpometacarpal, metatarsophalangeal, and distal proximal interphalangeal joints)	
1 large joint (shoulders, elbows, hips, knees, ankles)	0
2 to 10 large joints	1
1 to 3 small joints (with or without involvement of large joints)	2
4 to 10 small joints (with or without involvement of large joints)	3
>10 joints (at least 1 small joint)	5

(cont.)

B. Serology (at least 1 test result is needed for classification)	
Negative rheumatoid factor (RF) and negative anticitrullinated protein antibody (ACPA)	0
Low-positive (<3 × upper limit of normal) RF or low-positive ACPA	2
High-positive (>3 × upper limit of normal) RF or high-positive ACPA	3
C. Acute-phase reactants (at least one test result is needed for classification)	
Normal C-reactive protein and normal ESR	0
Abnormal C-reactive protein or abnormal ESR	1
D. Duration of symptoms (by patient self-report)	
<6 wk	0
≥6 wk	1

Scoring: Add score of categories A–D; a score of ≥6/10 is needed for classification of a patient as having definite RA.

* Aimed at classifying newly presenting patients; patients with erosive disease or longstanding disease with a hx of presenting features consistent with these criteria should be classified as having RA.

Note: Adapted from Aletaha D, Neogi T, Silman AJ, et al. 2010 Rheumatoid arthritis classification criteria: an American College of Rheumatology/European League Against Rheumatism collaborative initiative. *Arthritis Rheum* 2010;62(9):2569–2581. This material is reproduced with permission of John Wiley & Sons, Inc.

Staging

- Duration: early <6 mo, intermediate 6–24 mo, late >24 mo
- Activity: low, moderate, high by various criteria; see www.rheumatology.org/practice/clinical/guidelines/Disease_Activity_Measure_RA_Clinical_Trials.pdf
- Poor prognostic factors: functional limitation, extra-articular disease, RF positivity ± anti-CCP antibodies, and/or bony erosions by radiography

Management
Nonpharmacologic

- Patient education
- Exercise
- Physical and occupational therapy
- Splints and orthotics
- Surgery for severe functional abnormalities due to synovitis or joint destruction

Pharmacologic

All patients with established disease should be offered disease-modifying antirheumatoid drugs (DMARDs) as soon as possible; goal is to induce remission and then lower dosages to maintain remission.

- Analgesics (see **Table 70** and Pain, p 203)
- NSAIDs (see **Table 70**)
- Glucocorticoids (eg, prednisone ≤15 mg/d or equivalent) with osteoporosis prevention measures (see Osteoporosis, p 198)
- Use biologic DMARDs only after failure of nonbiologic DMARDs (**Table 72**). Dual and triple nonbiologic DMARD combinations are also used. See www.rheumatology.org/practice/clinical/guidelines.

- Biologic DMARDs: Not used in early RA and only low or moderate disease activity; increased risk of serious infections and reactivation of latent infections; check PPD and make sure patient is up-to-date on all vaccinations before starting; check baseline CBC, LFTs, Cr when using any biologic. Hold therapy for any infection but can start shortly after bacterial infection is successfully treated; may increase risk of skin cancers. Avoid live vaccinations while on biologics.
  - Anti-TNF-α agents: Used if inadequate response to methotrexate, if moderate disease activity and poor prognostic features, or if high activity regardless of poor prognostic features. May be added to or substituted for methotrexate. Combinations of biologic DMARDs are not recommended.
    - Adalimumab *(Humira)* 400 mg SC every other week, or 40 mg SC every week if not taking methotrexate
    - Certolizumab *(Cimzia)* 400 mg SC at 0, 2, and 4 wk; then 200 mg q2wk or 400 mg q4wk
    - Etanercept *(Enbrel)* 50 mg SC once/wk or 25 mg SC twice/wk
    - Infliximab *(Remicade)* 3 mg/kg IV in conjunction with methotrexate; repeat in 2–6 wk, then q8wk
    - Golimumab *(Simponi)* 50 mg SC every month
  - Interleukin-1 receptor antagonist: anakinra *(Kineret)* 100 mg SC daily
- Medications used when response to DMARD has been inadequate:
  - T-cell activation inhibitor: abatacept *(Orencia)*—<60 kg: 500 mg; 60–100 kg: 750 mg; >100 kg: 1 g IV at 0, 2, and 4 wk, then q4wk (do not use with anti-TNF-α agents or with anakinra)
  - Anti-CD20 monoclonal antibody: rituximab *(Rituxam)* 1000 mg IV in conjunction with methotrexate; repeat in 2 wk
  - IL-6 inhibitor: tocilizumab *(Actemra)* 4 mg/kg IV over 1h q4wk; if response is not adequate, can increase to 8 mg/kg q4wk

		Table 72. Nonbiologic DMARDs		
Medication	**Starting/ Usual Dosage**	**Formulations**	**Indications**	**Comments***
Hydroxy-chloroquine▲	Begin 200–400 mg/d; dose at <6.5 mg/kg/d to reduce risk of retinal toxicity	T: 200	Monotherapy for durations <24 mo, low disease activity, and without poor prognostic features	Baseline and annual eye examination; contraindicated in G6PD deficiency
Sulfasalazine▲ *(Azulfidine, Azulfidine EN-tabs)*	Begin at 500 mg/d to avoid GI upset; increase dosage by 500 mg every 3–4 d until taking 2–3 g/d split between 2 doses	T: 500	Monotherapy for all disease durations and all degrees of disease activity, and without poor prognostic features	Check CBC, LFTs q8wk

(cont.)

Table 72. Nonbiologic DMARDs (cont.)				
Medication	Starting/ Usual Dosage	Formulations	Indications	Comments*
Methotrexate▲ *(Rheumatrex, Trexall)*	10–25 mg/wk, adjust dosage for renal impairment (hold if CrCl <30 mL/min	T: 2.5 T: 2.5, 5, 7.5, 10, 15	Monotherapy for all disease durations and all degrees of disease activity, irrespective of poor prognostic features	Check for hepatitis B and C; check CBC (hold if WBC <3000/mm³), LFTs q8wk; give folic acid 1 mg/d; may cause oral ulcers, hepatotoxicity, pulmonary toxicity, cytopenias; avoid if liver disease
Leflunomide▲ *(Arava)*	Begin 100 mg/d × 3 d, then 20 mg/d	T: 10, 20	Monotherapy for all disease durations and all degrees of disease activity, irrespective of poor prognostic features	Check for hepatitis B and C; check CBC (hold if WBC <3000/mm³), LFTs q8wk; may cause hepatotoxicity, cytopenias; avoid if liver disease

* Check baseline CBC, LFTs, Cr for all.

GOUT

Definition

Urate crystal disease that may be expressed as acute gouty arthritis, usually in a single joint of foot, ankle, knee, or olecranon bursa; or chronic arthritis.

Precipitating Factors

- Alcohol, heavy ingestion
- Allopurinol, stopping or starting
- Binge eating
- Dehydration
- Diuretics
- Fasting
- Infection
- Serum uric acid concentration, any change up or down
- Surgery

Evaluation of Acute Gouty Arthritis

Joint aspiration to remove crystals and microscopic examination to establish diagnosis; serum urate (can be normal during flare).

Management

Treatment of Acute Gouty Flare: Experts differ regarding order of choices:

- Intra-articular injections (see p 178) if only 1 or 2 joints involved
- NSAIDs (see **Table 70**); avoid ASA
- Colchicine 1.2 mg (2 tabs) for the first dose, followed 1 h later by 0.6 mg (total dose 1.8 mg)
- Prednisone▲ 20–40 mg/d po until response, then rapid taper
- If polyarticular involvement, consider methylprednisolone 20 mg po q12h with taper or ACTH 75 IU SC or cosyntropin *(Cortrosyn)* 75 mcg SC; may repeat daily for 3 d

Treatment of Hyperuricemia After Acute Flare: Colchicine 0.5–0.6 mg/d for 2–4 wk before beginning any treatment in **Table 73** and continued for up to 6 mo after serum urate has returned to normal.

Table 73. Medications Useful in Managing Chronic Gout

Medication	Usual Dosage	Formulations	Comments (Metabolism, Excretion)
✔Allopurinol▲ *(Zyloprim, Lopurin)*	100–800 mg/d in divided doses if >300 mg/d	T: 100, 300	Consider if nephrolithiasis, tophi, Cr ≥2 mg/dL, 24-h urinary uric acid >800 mg. Do not initiate during flare; reduce dosage in renal or hepatic impairment; increase dose by 100 mg every 2–4 wk to normalize serum urate level; monitor CBC; rash is common (K)
Colchicine▲*	0.5–0.6 mg/d	T: 0.5, 0.6; Inj	May also be effective in prevention of recurrent pseudogout; monitor CBC (L)
Febuxostat *(Uloric)*	40–80 mg/d	T: 40, 80	Begin 40 mg/d; increase to 80 mg/d if uric acid >6 mg/dL at 2 wk; not recommended if CrCl <30 mL/min (K)
Losartan *(Cozaar)*	12.5–100 mg q12–24h	T: 25, 50, 100	Modest uricosuric effect that plateaus at 50 mg/d; may be useful in patients with HTN or HF
Pegloticase *(Krystexxa)*	8 mg IV q2wk	8 mg/1-mL vial	Effective in reducing flares in allopurinol intolerant or refractory patients with high uric acid levels; may cause anaphylaxis, gout flares, and infusion reactions; contraindicated if G6PD deficiency (K)
Probenecid▲* *(Benemid)*	500–1500 mg in 2–3 divided doses	T: 500	Adjust dose to normalize serum urate level or increase urine urate excretion; inhibits platelet function; may not be effective if renal impairment (K, L)

✔ = preferred for treating older adults

* Probenecid (500 mg) and colchicine (0.5 mg) combinations *(ColBenemid, Col-Probenecid, Proben-C)* are available.

PSEUDOGOUT

Definition
Crystal-induced arthritis (especially affecting wrists and knees) associated with calcium pyrophosphate

Risk Factors
- Advanced osteoarthritis
- Diabetes mellitus
- Gout
- Hemochromatosis
- Hypercalcemia
- Hyperparathyroidism
- Hypomagnesemia
- Hypophosphatemia
- Hypothyroidism
- Neuropathic joints
- Older age

Precipitating Factors
- Acute illness
- Dehydration
- Minor trauma
- Surgery

Evaluation of Acute Arthritis
Joint aspiration and microscopic examination to establish diagnosis; radiograph indicating chondrocalcinosis (best seen in wrists, knees, shoulder, symphysis pubis)

Management of Acute Flare
If single joint, aspiration and intra-articular glucocorticoid may be effective. If multiple joints, see Gout, management (p 185). Colchicine is less effective in pseudogout.

Prevention of Recurrence

If >3 attacks/yr, consider colchicine 0.6 mg q12h.

POLYMYALGIA RHEUMATICA, GIANT CELL (TEMPORAL) ARTERITIS

Definitions and Evaluation

Polymyalgia Rheumatica: Proximal limb and girdle stiffness usually lasting ≥30 min without tenderness but with constitutional symptoms (eg, fatigue, malaise, weight loss) for ≥1 mo and sedimentation rate elevated to >50 mm/hr (7%–22% will have normal sedimentation rate), and C-reactive protein; consider ultrasound to demonstrate effusions within shoulder bursae or MRI to demonstrate tenosynovitis or subacromial and subdeltoid bursitis if diagnosis is uncertain.

Giant Cell (Temporal) Arteritis: Medium to large vessel vasculitis that presents with symptoms of polymyalgia rheumatica, headache, unexplained fever or anemia, scalp tenderness, jaw or tongue claudication, visual disturbances, TIA or stroke, and elevated sedimentation rate and C-reactive protein. The presence of synovitis suggests an alternative diagnosis. Giant cell arteritis is confirmed by temporal artery biopsy. The value of other diagnostic tests (Doppler ultrasound, MRI, positron-emission tomography) is still unproved.

Management

Polymyalgia Rheumatica:

- Low-dosage (eg, 5–20 mg/d) prednisone or its equivalent; increase dosage if symptoms are not controlled within 1 wk.
- Methylprednisolone▲ 120 mg IM q3–4 wk is also effective. After 2–4 wk, begin gradual taper to lowest dose that will control symptoms and C-reactive protein or sedimentation rate. Once-daily dose is 10 mg, taper in 1-mg decrements.
- Some patients with milder symptoms may respond to NSAIDs alone.
- Monitor symptoms and C-reactive protein or sedimentation rate.
- Maintain therapy for ≥1 yr to prevent relapse. Relapse occurs in 25%–50%, and resuming or increasing steroid dosage is necessary.
- Consider osteoporosis prevention medication (see p 199).

Giant Cell (Temporal) Arteritis:

- Treatment should not be delayed while waiting for pathologic diagnosis from temporal artery biopsy. Begin prednisone (40–60 mg/d) or its equivalent while biopsy and pathology are pending.
- Adding methotrexate▲ po 7.5–15 mg/wk and folate 5–7.5 mg/d may reduce the amount of steroid needed and the risk of relapse, but the effect is moderate at best.
- After 2–4 wk, begin taper with moderate dosage (eg, 20 mg prednisone/d) at 2 mo and gradual taper over 9–12 mo. Once-daily dose is 10 mg, taper in 1-mg decrements.
- High-dose parenteral steroids (eg, 1000 mg methylprednisolone IV daily for 3 d) for visual loss is controversial.
- Use low-dosage ASA (81–100 mg/d) to reduce risk of visual loss, TIA, or stroke. Combine with PPI or misoprostol.
- Monitor symptoms and C-reactive protein or sedimentation rate.
- Maintain therapy for ≥1 yr to prevent relapse.
- Consider osteoporosis prevention medication (see p 199).
- Monitor for development of thoracic aortic aneurysm with CXR yearly for up to 10 yr.

TREMORS

Table 74. Classification of Tremors

Tremor Type	Hz (cycles/sec)	Associated Conditions	Features	Treatment
Cerebellar	3–5	Cerebellar disease	Present only during movement; ↑ with intention; ↑ amplitude as target is approached	Symptomatic management
Essential	4–12	Familial in 50% of cases	Varying amplitude; common in upper extremities, head, neck; ↑ with antigravity movements, intention, stress, medications	Long-acting propranolol▲ or atenolol▲ (see **Table 24**); or primidone *(Mysoline)* 100 mg qhs start, titrate to 0.5–1 g/d in 3–4 divided doses [T: 50, 250; S: 250 mg/5 mL]; or gabapentin▲ (see **Table 79**)
Parkinson	3–7	Parkinson disease, parkinsonism	"Pill rolling;" present at rest; ↑ with emotional stress or when examiner calls attention to it; commonly asymmetric	See Parkinson disease (p 192)
Physiologic	8–12	Normal	Low amplitude; ↑ with stress, anxiety, emotional upset, lack of sleep, fatigue, toxins, medications	Treatment of exacerbating factor

DIZZINESS

Table 75. Classification of Dizziness

Primary Symptom	Features	Duration	Diagnosis	Management
Dizziness	Lightheadedness 1–30 min after standing	Seconds to minutes (E)	Orthostatic hypotension	See **Table 46**
	Impairment in >1 of the following: vision, vestibular function, spinal proprioception, cerebellum, lower-extremity peripheral nerves	Occurs with ambulation (C)	Multiple sensory impairments	Correct or maximize sensory deficits; PT for balance and strength training
	Unsteady gait with short steps; ↑ reflexes and/or tone	Occurs with ambulation (C)	Ischemic cerebral disease	ASA▲; modification of vascular risk factors; PT
	Provoked by head or neck movement; reduced neck range of motion	Seconds to minutes (E)	Cervical spondylosis	Behavior modification; reduce cervical spasm and inflammation

(cont.)

Table 75. Classification of Dizziness (cont.)

Primary Symptom	Features	Duration	Diagnosis	Management
Drop attacks	Provoked by head or neck movement, reduced vertebral artery flow seen on Doppler or angiography	Seconds to minutes (E)	Postural impingement of vertebral artery	Behavior modification
Vertigo	Brought on by position change, positive Dix-Hallpike test	Seconds to minutes (E)	Benign paroxysmal positional vertigo	Epley maneuver to reposition crystalline debris (see www.merck.com/mmpe/sec08/ch086/ch086c.html); exercises provoking symptoms may be of help
	Acute onset, nonpositional	Days	Labyrinthitis (vestibular neuronitis)	Methylprednisolone▲, 100 mg/d po × 3 d with subsequent gradual taper over 3 wk to improve vestibular function recovery; meclizine▲ (see **Table 50**) for acute symptom relief
	Low-frequency sensorineural hearing loss and tinnitus	Minutes to hours (E)	Ménière disease	Meclizine▲ (see **Table 50**) for acute symptom relief; diuretics and/or salt restriction for prophylaxis
	Vascular disease risk factors, cranial nerve abnormalities	10 min to several hours (E)	TIAs	ASA▲; modification of vascular risk factors

Note: C = chronic; E = episodic

MANAGEMENT OF ACUTE STROKE

Examination

- Cardiac (murmurs, arrhythmias, enlargement)
- Neurologic (serial examinations)
- Optic fundi
- Vascular (carotids and other peripheral pulses)

Tests

- Bloodwork: ABG, BUN, CBC with platelet count, creatinine, electrolytes, glucose, cardiac troponins, INR, PT, PTT, oxygen saturation
- Brain MRI or noncontrast CT
- ECG
- The National Institutes of Health Stroke Scale (NIHSS; see www.ninds.nih.gov/doctors/NIH_Stroke_Scale.pdf) can quantify stroke severity and prognosis. NIHSS score >15 signifies major or severe stroke with high risk of death or significant permanent neurologic disability; NIHSS score <8 has a good prognosis for neurologic recovery.

- Other tests as indicated by clinical presentation:
  ○ Transesophageal echocardiography is preferred over transthoracic echocardiography for detection of cardiogenic emboli.
  ○ Carotid duplex and transcranial Doppler studies can detect carotid and vertebrobasilar embolic sources, respectively.

Provide Supportive Care
- O₂ if hypoxic.
- Correct metabolic and hydration imbalances.
- Detect and treat coronary ischemia, HF, arrhythmias.
- In patients with ischemic stroke and restricted mobility, implement DVT/PE prophylaxis with unfractionated heparin▲ or LMWH (see **Table 15**).
- Monitor and treat for hypoxia and hyperthermia.
- Monitor for depression.
- Refer to rehabilitation when medically stable.
- Discharge on statin drug (**Table 23**) if not contraindicated with goal of LDL <70 mg/dL.

Antithrombotic Therapy for Ischemic Stroke
- Consider IV thrombolysis if patient presents within 180 min of symptom onset.
  ○ Data on overall risk/benefit ratio of IV thrombolysis in adults >75 yr old are limited.
  ○ Contraindications:
    - onset of symptoms >180 min before IV therapy
    - BP ≥185/110 mmHg
    - intracranial hemorrhage or hx of intracranial hemorrhage
    - head trauma, stroke, or MI in past 3 mo
    - GI bleed or urinary hemorrhage in past 21 d
    - major surgery in past 14 d
    - active bleeding or acute trauma
    - INR >1.7
    - heparin use in past 48 h
    - platelet count <100,000 mm³
    - blood glucose <50 mg/dL
    - seizure with postictal neurologic impairment
  ○ Use recombinant tissue plasminogen activator (tPA), 0.9 mg/kg IV, max dose 90 mg.
  ○ Risk of intracranial hemorrhage 3%–7%; age >75 yr old and NIHSS >20 are among risk factors for intracranial hemorrhage.
- Antiplatelet therapy: use ASA▲ 162–325 mg/d, begun within 24–48 h of onset in patients not receiving thrombolytic therapy.
- Anticoagulants are not recommended except in DVT/PE prophylactic dosages for medical patients with restricted mobility (see **Table 15**).

Management of Acute Hypertension in Ischemic Stroke

- If patient is otherwise eligible for IV thrombolysis (see contraindications, p 190), attempt to lower BP to <185/110 mmHg so that patient may undergo reperfusion therapy. Options for lowering BP are:
  - Labetolol▲ *(Normodyne, Trandate)*: 10–20 mg IV over 1–2 min, may repeat once; *or*
  - Nitroglycerin 2% ointment▲ *(Nitro-Bid, Nitrol)*: 1–2 inches; *or*
  - Nicardipine▲ *(Cardene)*: 5 mg/h IV, increasing by 2.5 mg/h q5–15 min to max of 15 mg/h
- If patient is ineligible or not being considered for thrombolytic therapy, do not lower BP if SBP ≤220 mmHg or if DBP ≤120 mmHg; higher BP may be lowered gently, with goal of 15% reduction over first 24 h. Choice of BP-lowering agent should reflect patient's comorbidities (see **Table 25**).

STROKE PREVENTION

Risk Factor Modification

- Stop smoking.
- Reduce BP to at least 140/90 mmHg; <120/80 mmHg is desirable.
- In patients ≥80 yr old with few cardiovascular comorbidities, 150/80 mmHg is a reasonable BP treatment goal.
- Treat dyslipidemia (see **Table 22** and **Table 23**).
- Start anticoagulation (see p 24) or antiplatelet therapy for AF (see p 52).
- Low-sodium (≤2–3 g/d), high-potassium (≥4.7 g/d) diet
- Exercise (≥30 min of moderate intensity activity daily)
- Weight reduction (BMI <25 kg/m^2)

Antiplatelet Therapy for Patients With Prior TIA or Stroke

- First-line therapy is ASA▲ 81–325 mg/d.
- Addition of a combination form of ASA and long-acting dipyridamole *(Aggrenox)* 1 tab q12h [T: 25/200] may provide additional benefit. Watch for adverse event of headache.
- Clopidogrel *(Plavix)* 75 mg/d [T: 75] if intolerant to ASA or ASA ineffective.
- In the absence of AF, warfarin therapy is no more effective and is associated with more bleeding than ASA in preventing strokes.

Table 76. Treatment Options for Carotid Stenosis

Presentation	% Stenosis	Preferred Treatment	Comments
Prior TIA or stroke	≥70	CA or CE	CE superior to medical therapy only if patient is reasonable surgical risk and facility has track record of low complication rate for CE (<6%)
Prior TIA or stroke	50–69	CE or MM	Serial carotid Doppler testing may identify rapidly developing plaques
Prior TIA or stroke	<50	MM	CE of no proven benefit in this situation
Asymptomatic	≥80	CA/CE or MM	CA/CE should be considered over MM only for the most healthy
Asymptomatic	<80	MM	CE of no proven benefit in this situation

Note: CA = carotid angioplasty with stent placement in patients with multiple comorbidities and/or at high surgical risk; CE = carotid endarterectomy; MM = medical management

PARKINSON DISEASE

Diagnosis Requires:

- Bradykinesia, eg:
  - ○ Slowness of initiation of voluntary movements (eg, glue-footedness when starting to walk)
  - ○ Reduced speed and amplitude of repetitive movements (eg, tapping index finger and thumb together)
  - ○ Difficulty switching from one motor program to another (eg, multiple steps to turn during gait testing)
- *and* one or more of the following:
  - ○ Muscular rigidity (eg, cogwheeling)
  - ○ 4–6 Hz resting tremor
  - ○ Impaired righting reflex (eg, retropulsed during sternal nudge)
- Other clinical features of Parkinson disease:
  - ○ Postural instability and falls
  - ○ Hyposmia
  - ○ Hypophonia
  - ○ Micrographia
  - ○ Sleep disorder
  - ○ Constipation
  - ○ Masked facies
  - ○ Infrequent blinking
  - ○ Drooling
  - ○ Seborrhea of face and scalp
  - ○ Festinating gait
- Neuropsychiatric conditions are also common usually later in the clinical course: anxiety, depression, dementia, visual hallucinations, dysthymia, psychosis, delirium

Table 77. Distinguishing Early Parkinson Disease From Other Parkinsonian Syndromes

Condition	Tremor	Asymmetric Involvement	Early Falls	Early Dementia	Postural Hypotension
Parkinson disease	+	+	−	−	−
Drug-induced parkinsonism	+/−	−	−	−	−
Vascular parkinsonism	−	+/−	+/−	+/−	−
Dementia with Lewy bodies	+/−	+/−	+/−	+	+/−
Progressive supranuclear palsy	−	−	+	+/−	−
Corticobasilar ganglionic degeneration	−	+	+	−	+
Multiple system atrophy	−	+/−	+/−	−	+

Note: + = usually or always present, +/− = sometimes present, − = absent
Source: Adapted from Christine CW, Aminoff MJ. *Am J Med* 2004;117:412–419.

Nonpharmacologic Management

- Patient education is essential, and support groups are often helpful; see p 295 for telephone numbers, Web sites.
- Monitor for orthostatic hypotension (see p 57).
- Exercise program

Surgical Treatment—Deep Brain Stimulation (DBS)

- DBS of the globus pallidus or subthalamic nucleus is used for treatment of motor complications of Parkinson disease or its therapy.
- DBS is best suited for patients who have fluctuating motor problems (tremor and other dyskinesias) despite medical therapy and who have few comorbidities.
- Compared with medical therapy in selected patients, DBS can significantly increase motor function (several more hours per day of "on" time) and decrease troubling dyskinesias.
- Early (0–3 mo) complications include surgical site infection (~10%), intracranial hemorrhage (~2%), death (~1%), cognitive and speech problems (10%–15%), and an increased risk of falls.

Pharmacologic Treatment (see Table 78)

- Begin treatment when symptoms interfere with function.
- Start at low dose and titrate upward gradually.
- Monitor orthostatic BP during titration of medications.

Table 78. Medications for Parkinson Disease

Class, Medication	Initial Dosage	Formulations	Comments (Metabolism, Excretion)
Dopamine			
✔ Carbidopa-levodopa▲* *(Sinemet, Parcopa)*	1/2 tab of 25/100 q8–12h	T: 10/100, 25/100, 25/250	Mainstay of Parkinson disease therapy; increase dose by 1/2-1 tab q1-2wk to achieve minimal target dose of 1 tab q8h, then titrate upward gradually as needed; watch for GI adverse events, orthostatic hypotension, confusion; long-term therapy associated with motor fluctuations and dyskinesias (addition of dopamine agonist may attenuate these effects) (L)
✔ Sustained-release carbidopa-levodopa▲* *(Sinemet CR)*	1 tab/d	T: 25/100, 50/200	Useful at daily dopamine requirement ≥300 mg; slower absorption than carbidopa-levodopa; can improve motor fluctuations (L)
Dopamine Agonists			More CNS adverse events than dopamine
Apomorphine *(Apokyn)*	2 mg SC	Inj: 10 mg/mL	Use with extreme caution; can cause severe orthostasis; indicated only for "off" episodes associated with levodopa therapy
Bromocriptine▲ *(Parlodel)*	1.25 mg q12–24h	T: 2.5 C: 5	Increase by 1.25-mg increments q2–5d, titrating to effective dosage (10–30 mg/d) (L)

✔ = preferred for treating older adults
* = first-line therapy

(cont.)

Table 78. Medications for Parkinson Disease (cont.)

Class, Medication	Initial Dosage	Formulations	Comments (Metabolism, Excretion)
✔ Pramipexole▲* *(Mirapex)*	0.125 mg/d	T: 0.125, 0.25, 0.5, 1, 1.5	Increase gradually to effective dosage (0.5–1.5 mg q8h) (K)
✔ Ropinirole* *(Requip)*	0.25 mg/d	T▲: 0.25, 0.5, 1, 2, 3, 4, 5 CR: 4, 8	Increase gradually to effective dosage (up to 1–8 mg q8h) (L)
Catechol *O*-Methyl-transferase (COMT) Inhibitors			Adjunctive therapy with L-dopa
✔ Tolcapone *(Tasmar)*	100 mg q8h	T: 100, 200	Monitor LFTs q6mo (L, K)
✔ Entacapone *(Comtan)*	200 mg with each L-dopa dose	T: 200	Watch for nausea, orthostatic hypotension (K)
Anticholinergics			
Benztropine▲ *(Cogentin)*	0.5 mg/d	T: 0.5, 1, 2	Can cause confusion and delirium; helpful for drooling (L, K)
Trihexyphenidyl▲ *(Artane, Trihexy)*	1 mg/d	T: 2, 5 S: 2 mg/5 mL	Same as above (L, K)
Dopamine Reuptake Inhibitor			
Amantadine▲ *(Symmetrel)*	100 mg q12–24h	T: 100 C: 100 S: 50 mg/5 mL	Useful in early and late Parkinson disease; watch closely for CNS adverse events; do not D/C abruptly (K)
MAO B Inhibitors			
Rasagiline *(Azilect)*	0.5 mg/d	T: 0.5, 1	Interactions with numerous drugs and tyramine-rich foods; expensive (L, K)
Selegiline▲ *(Carbex, Eldepryl, Zelapar)*	5 mg qam; 1.25 mg/d for ODT	T: 5 ODT: 1.25	Use as adjunctive therapy with dopamine; do not exceed a total dosage of 10 mg/d; metabolized to amphetamine derivatives (L, K)
Combination Medication			
Carbidopa-levodopa + entacapone *(Stalevo)*	1 tab/d	T: 12.5/50/200, 25/100/200, 37.5/150/200	Should be used only after individual dosages of carbidopa, levodopa, and entacapone have been established (L, K)

✔ = preferred for treating older adults

* = first-line therapy

SEIZURES

Classification

- Generalized: All areas of brain affected with alteration in consciousness.
- Partial: Focal brain area affected, not necessarily with alteration in consciousness; can progress to generalized type.

Initial Evaluation, Assessment

- History: neurologic disorders, trauma, drug and alcohol use
- Physical examination: general, with careful neurologic
- Routine tests: BUN, calcium, CBC, creatinine, ECG, EEG, electrolytes, glucose, head CT, LFTs, magnesium

- Tests as indicated: head MRI, lumbar puncture, oxygen saturation, urine toxic or drug screen

Common Causes

- Advanced dementia
- CNS infection
- Drug or alcohol withdrawal
- Idiopathic causes
- Metabolic disorders
- Prior stroke (most common)
- Toxins
- Trauma
- Tumor

Management

- Treat underlying causes.
- Institute anticonvulsant therapy (see **Table 79**). Virtually all anticonvulsant medications can cause sedation and ataxia.

Table 79. Anticonvulsant Therapy in Older Adults

Medication	Dosage (mg)	Target Blood Concentration (mcg/mL)	Formulations	Comments (Metabolism, Excretion)
◆Carbamazepine▲ (Tegretol, Epitol) (Tegretol XR, Carbatrol, Equetro)	200–600 q12h	4–12	T: 200▲ ChT: 100 S: 100/5 mL▲ T: 100, 200, 400▲ C: ER 100, 200, 300	Many drug interactions; mood stabilizer; may cause SIADH, thrombocytopenia, leukopenia (L, K)
◆Gabapentin▲ (Neurontin)	300–600 q8h	NA	C: 100, 300, 400 T: 600, 800 S: 250/5 mL	Used as adjunct to other agents; adjust dosage on basis of CrCl (K)
Lamotrigine▲ (Lamictal)	100–300 q12h	2–4	T: 25, 100, 150, 200 ChT: 2, 5, 25▲	Prolongs PR interval; risk of severe rash; when used with valproic acid, begin at 25 mg q48h, titrate to 25–100 mg q12h (L, K)
Levetiracetam▲ (Keppra)	500–1500 q12h	NA	T▲: 250, 500, 750 S▲: 100/mL CR: 500, 750	Reduce dosage in renal impairment: CrCl 30–50: 250–750 q12h CrCl 10–29: 250–500 q12h CrCl <10: 500–1000 q24h
Oxcarbazepine (Trileptal)	300–1200 q12h	NA	T▲: 150, 300, 600 ChT: 2, 5, 25 S: 300/5 mL	Can cause hyponatremia, leukopenia (L)
Phenobarbital▲ (Luminal)	30–60 q8–12h	20–40	T: 15, 16, 30, 32, 60, 100 S: 20/5 mL	Many drug interactions; not recommended for use in older adults (L)
Phenytoin▲ (Dilantin)	200–300/d	5–20	C: 30, 100▲ ChT: 50 S: 125/5 mL▲	Many drug interactions; exhibits nonlinear pharmacokinetics (L)
◆Pregabalin▲ (Lyrica)	50–200 q8–12h		C: 25, 50, 75, 100, 150, 200, 225, 300	Indicated as adjunct therapy for partial-onset seizures only; not well studied in older adults (K)

(cont.)

Table 79. **Anticonvulsant Therapy in Older Adults (cont.)**

Medication	Dosage (mg)	Target Blood Concentration (mcg/mL)	Formulations	Comments (Metabolism, Excretion)
Tiagabine *(Gabitril Filmtabs)*	2–12 q8–12h	NA	T: 2, 4, 12, 16, 20	Adverse-event profile in older adults less well described (L)
Topiramate▲ *(Topamax)*	25–100 q12–24h	NA	T: 25, 100, 200 C, sprinkle: 15, 25	May affect cognitive functioning at high dosages (L, K)
Valproic acid▲ *(Depacon, Depakene, Depakote)*	250–750 q8–12h	50–100	T: 125, 250, 500 C: 125, 250 S: 250/5 mL	Can cause weight gain, tremor, hair loss; several drug interactions; mood stabilizer; monitor LFTs and platelets (L)
(Depakote ER)			T: 500	
Zonisamide▲ *(Zonegran)*	100–400/d	NA	C: 25, 100	Anorexia; contraindicated in patients with sulfonamide allergy (K)

Note: NA = not available   ◆ = also has primary indication for neuropathic pain.

APHASIA

Table 80. **Aphasias in Which Repetition Is Impaired**

Type	Fluency	Auditory Comprehension	Associated Neurologic Deficits	Comments
Broca's	−	+	Right hemiparesis	Patient aware of deficit; high rate of associated depression; message board helpful for communication
Wernicke's	+	−	Often none	Patient frequently unaware of deficit; speech content usually unintelligible; therapy often focuses on visually based communication
Conduction	+	+	Occasional right facial weakness	Patient usually aware of deficit; speech content usually intelligible
Global	−	−	Right hemiplegia with right field cut	Most commonly due to left middle cerebral artery thrombosis, which has a poor prognosis for meaningful speech recovery

Note: + = present; − = absent

PERIPHERAL NEUROPATHY

Diagnosis

• Establish pattern of involvement:
  ○ Focal (entrapment syndromes, compression neuropathies, vasculitis)
  ○ Multifocal (vasculitis, diabetes)
  ○ Symmetric
• If symmetric, determine location:
  ○ Proximal—many causes, including Guillain-Barré syndrome, porphyria, chronic inflammatory demyelinating polyneuropathy, Lyme disease

- Distal—nerve conduction studies can help distinguish the more common axonal pathologies (diabetes, medication effects, alcohol abuse, kidney failure, malignancy) from demyelinating ones (including Guillain-Barré syndrome and chronic inflammatory demyelinating polyneuropathy)

Treatment

Prevention of Complications:

- Protect distal extremities from trauma—appropriate shoe size, daily foot inspections, good skin care, avoidance of barefoot walking.
- Prevent falls (see pp 104–105)
- Maintain tight glycemic control in diabetic neuropathy.

Treatment of Painful Neuropathy: Start at low dosage, increase as needed and tolerated:

- Nortriptyline▲ *(Aventyl, Pamelor)* 10–100 mg qhs [T: 10, 25, 50, 75]; desipramine▲ *(Norpramin)* 10–75 mg qam [T: 10, 25, 50, 75]
- Gabapentin▲ *(Neurontin)* can begin 100–200 mg qhs but may need up to 100–600 mg q8h [C: 100, 300, 400; T: 600, 800; S: 250/5 mL]
- Pregabalin *(Lyrica)* 75–300 mg po q12h [C: 25, 50, 75, 100, 150, 200, 225, 300]: primary indication is for management of post-herpetic neuralgia, diabetic peripheral neuropathy, and fibromyalgia
- Other oral agents that may be effective include:
  - Carbamazepine▲ *(Tegretol)* 200–400 mg q8h [T: 200; ChT: 100; S: 100 mg/5 mL]; *(Tegretol XR)* 200 mg q12h [T: 100, 200, 400; C: CR 200, 300]
  - Duloxetine *(Cymbalta)* 60 mg/d [C: 20, 30, 60]
  - SSRIs have not been shown to be as effective as TCAs (**Table 35**)
  - Lamotrigine▲ (*Lamictal*, see **Table 79**) 400–600 mg/d
  - Opioids (**Table 86**); watch for adverse events of itching, mood changes, weakness, confusion
  - Tramadol▲ *(Ultram, see **Table 86**)* 200–400 mg/d
- Topical agents that may be effective include:
  - Capsaicin cream▲ (eg, *Zostrix*) 0.075% applied q6–8h [0.025%, 0.075%]
  - Capsaicin cutaneous pch *(Qutenza)* applied by health professional, using a local anesthetic, to the most painful skin areas (max of 4 pchs). Apply for 30 min to feet, 60 min for other locations. Risk of significant rise in BP following placement; monitor patient for at least 1 h [179-mg pch].
  - Transcutaneous electrical nerve stimulation
  - Lidocaine 5% pch *(Lidoderm)* 1–3 patches covering the affected area up to 24 h/d [700-mg pch]

COMMONLY USED DEFINITIONS

- Established osteoporosis: occurrence of a minimal trauma fracture of any bone (WHO).
- Osteoporosis: a skeletal disorder characterized by compromised bone strength (bone density and bone quality) predisposing to an increased risk of fracture (NIH Consensus Development Panel. Osteoporosis prevention, diagnosis, and therapy. *JAMA* 2001;285 (6):785–795.)
- Osteoporosis: BMD 2.5 SD or more below that of younger normal individuals (T score) (WHO). Scores between 1 and 2.5 SD below are termed osteopenia. Some experts prefer to use Z score, which compares an individual with a population adjusted for age, sex, and race. For each SD decrement in BMD, hip fracture risk increases about 2-fold; for each SD increment in BMD, hip fracture risk is about halved.

Estimation of 10-yr probability of major osteoporotic or hip fracture based on risk factors with or without BMD can be calculated using FRAX, the World Health Organization Fracture Risk Assessment Tool (www.shef.ac.uk/FRAX/tool.jsp?locationValue=2).

RISK FACTORS FOR OSTEOPOROTIC FRACTURE

- Previous fracture as adult
- Dementia
- Depression
- Low calcium intake
- Impaired vision
- Low physical activity

- Fracture in 1st-degree relative
- Frailty
- Alcoholism
- Female sex
- Kidney failure (GFR <45 mL/min/1.73 m^2) body surface area

- BMI <20 kg/m^2
- Cigarette smoking
- Early menopause (<45 yr)
- Recurrent falls

TOXINS AND MEDICATIONS THAT CAN CAUSE OR AGGRAVATE OSTEOPOROSIS

- Alcohol (>2 drinks/d)
- Androgen deprivation therapy
- Anticonvulsants
- Antipsychotics

- Corticosteroids
- Heparin
- Lithium
- Nicotine (ie, smoking)

- Phenytoin
- PPIs (if ≥1 yr)
- SSRIs
- Thyroxine (if overreplaced or in suppressive dosage)

EVALUATION

- BMD at least once in all women after age 65, in all men after age 70 (NOF), and in men with prior clinical fracture after age 65 (NOF) (see **Table 92**). Uncertain how often to repeat. Some suggest in 3 yr for patients with osteopenia and in 5 yr for those with normal bone density. Although some professional societies recommend monitoring BMD q2yr, the value of monitoring BMD in patients already receiving treatment is unproved.
- Serum 25-hydroxy vitamin D (treat if <30 ng/mL) expected rise is 1 ng/mL/100 IU vitamin D$_3$; if <20 ng/mL, consider 50,000 U vitamin D$_2$ (ergocalciferol) once a week.
- Some experts recommend excluding secondary causes (serum PTH, TSH, calcium, phosphorus, albumin, alkaline phosphatase, bioavailable testosterone in men, kidney and liver function tests, CBC, UA, electrolytes, protein electrophoresis). Less consensus on 24-h urinary calcium excretion, cortisol, antibodies associated with gluten enteropathy.

MANAGEMENT

Universal Recommendations

- Calcium (elemental) 1200 mg/d. For most patients, calcium carbonate is sufficient and least expensive. For patients on PPIs (see **Table 47**) or who have achlorhydria, calcium citrate should be used. For patients who have difficulty swallowing calcium citrate tabs, smaller tabs of 125 mg *(Freeda Mini Cal-citrate)* and granules, 1 tsp = 760 mg *(Freeda Calcium Citrate Fine Granular)*, are available. Initiating calcium is associated with a modest increased risk of cardiovascular events (MI or stroke) in women, and the benefits vs risks of supplementation remains to be clarified.
- Vitamin D at least 800 IU; D_3 (cholecalciferol) is preferred form
- OTC calcium plus vitamin D preparations vary considerably in amounts of each, so ask patients to read labels to ensure they are getting adequate amounts.

- Avoid tobacco
- Exercise for muscle strengthening and balance training

- Falls prevention (see **Table 46**)
- No more than moderate alcohol use

Pharmacologic Prevention

- The National Osteoporosis Foundation (NOF) has recommended initiating pharmacologic management (**Table 81**) in women with BMD T scores below -2.5 in the absence of risk factors and in women with T scores of -1 to -2.5 if 10-yr risk of hip fracture is >3% or 10-yr risk of major osteoporotic fracture (cervical spine, forearm, hip, or shoulder) is >20%.
- Some question NOF guidelines because application would result in pharmacologic therapy for 72% of white women >65 yr old and 93% of women >75 yr old compared with bone density criteria alone, which would result in pharmacologic treatment of 50% of women in both age groups.
- The risk of fracture can be determined from the WHO/FRAX tool (www.shef.ac.uk/FRAX/tool.jsp?locationValue=2).
- Begin bisphosphonate therapy in patients receiving chronic glucocorticoids ($\geq$5 mg prednisone or equivalent for $\geq$3 mo) who have other fracture risk factors or if T score is less than -1.0.
- Bisphosphonate treatment of patients with locally advanced or high-risk prostate cancer receiving androgen deprivation therapy is cost-effective if osteoporosis on BMD, prior fracture, or age >80.
- Some experts recommend using bisphosphonates that have demonstrated efficacy in reducing hip fractures as preferred initial therapy (see **Table 82**).
- PPIs reduce the effectiveness of oral bisphosphonates, and some experts recommend holding the PPI the day before bisphosphonate administration and not administering the PPI until >60 min after the bisphosphonate has been taken.
- Bisphosphonates are more effective in preventing hip fracture when adherence is >80% (compared with adherence <50%).
- The duration of bisphosphonate treatment is uncertain. Some experts recommend 3–5 yr, but there is no clear evidence weighing benefit vs risk of harm.

Table 81. Pharmacologic Prevention and Treatment of Osteoporosis[a]			
Medication	**Dosage**	**Formulations**	**Comments**
Bisphosphonates			*Class effect:* Esophagitis; bone, joint, or muscle pain; osteonecrosis of jaw (estimated 0.01%–0.0001% with oral therapy)[b]; occipital inflammation; possibly serious atrial fibrillation (≤1.5%); association with atypical femoral fractures rare (<6/10,000 patient-years) Consider discontinuing after 5 yr
Alendronate▲ *(Fosamax)*	Prevention: 5 mg/d or 35 mg/wk Treatment: 10 mg/d or 70 mg/wk	T: 5, 10, 35, 40, 70; 70 sol	Must be taken fasting with water; patient must remain upright and npo for ≥30 min after taking; do not use if CrCl <35 mL/min; relatively contraindicated in GERD
Ibandronate *(Boniva)*	Treatment and prevention: po: 150 mg/mo or 2.5 mg/d IV: 3 mg q3mo	T: 2.5, 150 IV: 1 mg/mL (available in 3-mL prefilled syringes)	Must be taken fasting with water; patient must remain upright and npo for ≥60 min after taking; do not use if CrCl <30 mL/min
Risedronate *(Actonel)*	Treatment and prevention: 35 mg/wk, 5 mg/d, or 150 mg/mo	T: 5, 30, 35, 150	Must be taken fasting or ≥2 h after evening meal; patient must remain upright and npo for 30 min after taking; do not use if CrCl <30 mL/min
Zoledronic acid *(Reclast)*	5 mg IV given over >15 min every yr for treatment or q2yr for prevention	5 mg/100 mL	Not recommended if CrCl <35 mL/min; may cause acute renal failure in patients using diuretics
Others			
Raloxifene *(Evista)*	60 mg/d	T: 60	Used more often for prevention because of reduced risk of breast cancer; may cause hot flushes
Calcitonin *(Calcimar, Cibacalcin, Miacalcin, Osteocalcin, Salmonine)*	Treatment and prevention: 100 IU/d SC (human) or 200 IU intranasally (salmon) in alternate nostrils q48h	Inj: human *(Cibacalcin)* 0.5 mg/vial Intranasal▲: salmon 200 units/mL *(Miacalcin)*	May also be helpful for analgesic effect in patients with acute vertebral fracture (see also p 173); rhinitis in 10%–12%
Estrogen▲	See **Table 118**		For use in select patients; for risks and benefits see **Table 115**
Teriparatide *(Forteo)*	Treatment: 20 mcg/d for up to 24 mo	Inj: 3 mL, 28-dose disposable pen device	Contraindicated in patients with Paget disease or prior skeletal radiation therapy (L, K); treatment for 1 yr followed by 1 yr of bisphosphonates or raloxifene can maintain 1-yr gains in BMD

(cont.)

Table 81. Pharmacologic Prevention and Treatment of Osteoporosis[a] (cont.)			
Medication	**Dosage**	**Formulations**	**Comments**
Denosumab *(Prolia)*	60 mg SC q6mo	Inj: 60 mg/mL in pre-filled syringe	Skin infections, dermatitis, osteoneorosis of jaw, hypocalcemia especially if CrCl <30 mL/min and uncorrected calcium

[a] Unless specified, medication can be used for prevention or treatment.

[b] Risk factors include IV treatment (little data on osteoporosis doses); cancer; dental extractions, implants, and poor-fitting dentures; glucocorticoids; smoking; and preexisting dental disease. Some experts recommend that bisphosphonates be stopped for several months before and after elective complex oral procedures (or, if procedures are emergent, that bisphosphonates be held for several months after).

Pharmacologic Treatment Regimens for Those with Prior Osteoporotic Fractures

- BMD measurement is unnecessary. See **Table 81** for treatment regimens.
- Combination therapy (eg, estrogen plus bisphosphonate or calcitonin) is slightly more effective in improving BMD but has not been proved to affect fracture rates.
- For high-risk patients with multiple fractures who continue to fracture after 1 yr of bisphosphonate therapy or who are intolerant of bisphosphonates, consider teriparatide.
- Denosumab is an alternative for those who are intolerant of bisphosphonates.

Table 82. Bone Outcomes of Medications for Osteoporosis Based on Randomized Clinical Trials[a]				
Medication	**Spine BMD and Fracture**	**Hip BMD**	**Hip Fracture**	**All Nonspinal Fractures**
Estrogen▲	improved	improved	reduced	reduced
Raloxifene	improved	improved	no data	no effect
Alendronate▲	improved	improved	reduced	reduced
Ibandronate	improved	improved	no data	no effect
Risedronate	improved	improved	reduced	reduced
Calcitonin (nasal)[b]	improved	no effect	no effect	no effect
Zoledronic acid	improved	improved	reduced	reduced
Teriparatide[c]	improved	improved	no data	reduced
Denosumab	improved	improved	reduced	reduced

[a] The populations studied, sample sizes of individual studies, and duration of follow-up vary considerably; hence, this summary must be interpreted cautiously. Moreover, several randomized clinical trials are currently in progress and new findings may appear.

[b] Based on observational data, calcitonin appears to be less effective in preventing nonspinal fractures.

[c] More effective than bisphosphonates in increasing BMD and reducing spinal fractures in patients receiving systemic glucocorticoid therapy for ≥3 mo.

Table 83. Effects on Other Outcomes, Level of Evidence,[a] and Risks of Medications for Osteoporosis

Medication	CHD Risk Factors	CHD Prevention	CHD Treatment	Breast Cancer	Deep-vein Thrombosis
Estrogen[▲][b]	improved–R	↑ risk–R	no effect–R	↑ risk–R	↑ risk–R
Raloxifene	improved–R	no effect	↓ risk–R	↓ risk–R	↑ risk–R
Bisphos-phonates[c]	no data	no data	no data	↓ risk of invasive ↑ risk of ductal carcinoma in situ–O	no data
Calcitonin (nasal)	no data	no data	no data	no data	no data

Note: CHD = coronary heart disease; R = randomized clinical trial; O = observational study

[a] The populations studied, sample sizes of individual studies, and duration of follow-up vary considerably; hence, this summary must be interpreted cautiously. Moreover, several randomized clinical trials are currently in progress and new findings may appear.

[b] In the Women's Health Initiative estrogen-alone trial, only stroke and pulmonary embolism risk were increased.

[c] Alendronate[▲], ibandronate, risedronate, zoledronic acid

PAIN

DEFINITION
An unpleasant sensory and emotional experience associated with actual or potential tissue damage (International Association for Study of Pain taxonomy)

Acute Pain
Distinct onset, usually evident pathology, short duration; common causes: trauma, postsurgical pain

Persistent Pain
Pain due to ongoing nociceptive, neuropathic, or mixed pathophysiologic processes, often associated with functional and psychologic impairment; can fluctuate in character and intensity over time (see **Table 84**)

Table 84. Types of Pain, Examples, and Treatment

Type of Pain and Examples	Source of Pain	Typical Description	Effective Drug Classes and Nonpharmacologic Treatments
Nociceptive: somatic			
Arthritis, acute postoperative, fracture, bone metastases	Tissue injury, eg, bones, soft tissue, joints, muscles	Well localized, constant; aching, stabbing, gnawing, throbbing	APAP, opioids, NSAIDs; physical and cognitive-behavioral therapies
Nociceptive: visceral			
Renal colic, constipation	Viscera	Diffuse, poorly localized, referred to other sites, intermittent, paroxysmal; dull, colicky, squeezing, deep, cramping; often accompanied by nausea, vomiting, diaphoresis	Treatment of underlying cause, APAP, opioids; physical and cognitive-behavioral therapies
Neuropathic			
Cervical or lumbar radiculopathy, post-herpetic neuralgia, trigeminal neuralgia, diabetic neuropathy, post-stroke syndrome, herniated intervertebral disc	Peripheral or central nervous system	Prolonged, usually constant, but can have paroxysms; sharp, burning, pricking, tingling, squeezing; associated with other sensory disturbances, eg, paresthesias and dysesthesias; allodynia, hyperalgesia, impaired motor function, atrophy, or abnormal deep tendon reflexes	TCAs, SNRIs, anticonvulsants, opioids, topical anesthetics; physical and cognitive-behavioral therapies
Undetermined			
Myofascial pain syndrome, somatoform pain disorders	Poorly understood	No identifiable pathologic processes or symptoms out of proportion to identifiable organic pathology; widespread musculoskeletal pain, stiffness, and weakness	Antidepressants, antianxiety agents; physical, cognitive-behavioral, and psychological therapies

EVALUATION

Key Points, Approach

- Perform comprehensive evaluation for cause of pain, pain characteristics, and impact of physical and psychosocial function.
- Refer to PT for evaluation of function.
- Consider patient's report as the most reliable evidence of pain intensity.
- Assess for pain on each presentation (older adults may be reluctant to report pain).
- Use synonyms for pain (eg, burning, aching, soreness, discomfort).
- Use a standard pain scale (eg, Numeric Rating Scale, Verbal Descriptor Scale, or Faces Pain Scale; see www.geriatricsatyourfingertips.org); adapt for sensory impairments (eg, large print, written vs spoken).
- Treat those with behavioral disturbances/agitation suspected of an underlying pain etiology for which other causes have been ruled out using a stepwise approach such as:
  - Use simple tools or questions with yes/no answers.
  - Systematically assess pain (see **Figure 11**) and treat in a stepwise approach:
    Step 1: Oral APAP, max increase to 3 g/d
    Step 2: Oral morphine sulfate (5 mg q12h to max 10 mg q12h) or topical NSAIDs (second or as add-on therapy)
    Step 3: Buprenorphine transdermal patch 5 mcg/h to max 10 mcg/hr
    Step 4: Pregabalin 25 mg/d, max 300 mg/d for suspected neuropathic pain
  - The first step of an analgesic trial of APAP is often effective in improving behaviors and/or function.
  - Carefully monitor response to analgesics at each step of an analgesic trial as agent and dose are titrated to effect or undesirable adverse events.
  - Ask caregiver about recent changes in function, gait, behavior patterns, mood.
- Reassess regularly for improvement, deterioration, and complications/adverse events, and document.

History and Physical Examination

- Focus on a complete examination of pain source and on musculoskeletal and neurologic systems.
- Distinguish new illness from chronic condition.
- Analgesic history: effectiveness and adverse events, current and previous prescription drugs, OTC drugs, "natural" remedies.
- Assess effectiveness of prior nondrug treatments.
- Laboratory and diagnostic tests to establish etiologic diagnosis.

Characteristics of Pain Complaint

Provocative (aggravating) and **P**alliative (relieving) factors
Quality (eg, burning, stabbing, dull, throbbing)
Region (eg, pain map)
Severity (eg, scale of 0 for no pain to 10 for worst pain possible)
Timing (eg, when pain occurs, frequency and duration)

Psychosocial Assessment

Depression (see pp 288–290 for screen), anxiety, mental status (see p 285 for screen). Impact on family or significant other. Enabling behaviors by others (eg, oversolicitousness, codependency, reinforcing debility).

Prevention of Opioid Misuse and Withdrawal

- Assess for risk of addition (see Substance Abuse, p 273).
- Physical dependence is expected with long-term opioid use (can occur with several weeks of around-the-clock use); it is not the same as substance abuse or addiction.
- Be aware of early symptoms of opioid withdrawal, including agitation, anxiety, muscle aches, increased tearing, insomnia, runny nose, sweating, and yawning.
- Approach to weaning off long-term opioid use can range from a slow 10% dose reduction per week to a more rapid 25%–50% reduction every 2–3 d. Adapt based on comorbidities and withdrawal symptoms when process is begun.

Figure 11. Pain Assessment in Older Adults with Severe Cognitive Impairment

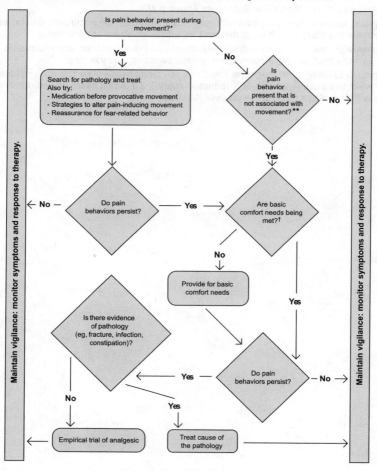

* Examples: grimacing, guarding, combativeness, groaning with movement; resisting care

** Examples: agitation, fidgeting, sleep disturbance, diminished appetite, irritability, reclusiveness, disruptive behavior, rigidity, rapid blinking

† Examples: toileting, thirst, hunger, visual or hearing impairment

Sources: American Geriatrics Society. The management of persistent pain in older persons. *J Amer Geriatr Soc* 2002; 50(6, Suppl): S205–S240; and Weiner D, Herr K, Rudy T, eds. Persistent Pain in Older Adults: An Interdisciplinary Guide for Treatment, 2002, Copyright Springer Publishing Company, Inc., New York 10036.

Functional Assessment
ADLs, impact on activities (see pp 286–287 for screens), and quality of life

Brief Pain Inventory
Use for comprehensive assessment of pain and its impact (see www.geriatricsatyourfingertips.org).

MANAGEMENT
Goal: To find optimal balance in pain relief, functional improvement, and adverse events.

Acute Pain and Short-term Management
- Identify cause of pain and treat if possible.
- Use fixed schedule of APAP, NSAIDs (consider nonselective vs COX-2 inhibitors depending on risk factors and comorbidities, see **Figure 10**), or opioids.
- Refer to PT for nonpharmacologic strategies (eg, relaxation, heat or cold, TENS, joint mobilization, stabilizing exercises, assistive devices).
- Patient-controlled analgesia (PCA): Requires patient comprehension of PCA instructions
  - Indications
    - Acute pain (eg, postoperative pain, trauma)
    - Persistent pain in patients who are npo
  - Dosing strategies (see **Table 85**)
    - Titrate up PCA dose 25%–50% if pain still not well controlled after 12 h.
    - Unless patient is awakened by pain during sleep, continuous opioid infusion not recommended because of increased risk of opioid accumulation and toxicity.
    - If basal rate used, hourly monitoring of sedation and respiratory status is warranted. If low respiratory rate (≤8) and moderate sedation (difficulty arousing patient from sleep) after expected peak of opioid, withhold further opioid until respiratory rate rises or pain returns. If needed, a small dose of dilute naloxone can be given and repeated.
    - D/C PCA when patient able to take oral analgesics or unable to self medicate due to altered mental status or physical limitations.

Table 85. Typical Initial Dosing of PCA for Older Adults with Severe Pain

Medication (usual concentration)	Usual Dose Range*	Usual Lockout (min)
Morphine▲ (1 mg/mL)	0.5–2.5 mg	5–10
Hydromorphone▲ (0.2 mg/mL)	0.05–0.3 mg	5–10

* For opioid-naive patients, consider lower end of dosage range.

Persistent Pain
- Identify cause of pain and treat if possible.
- Use multidisciplinary assessment and treatment (eg, pharmacists, physical therapists, psychologists) when possible.
- Educate patient for self-management and coping.
- Combine pharmacologic and nonpharmacologic strategies.
- Anticipate and attend to depression and anxiety.

Nonpharmacologic Treatment
- Educate patient and caregiver.
  - www.healthinaging.org/public_education/pef/persistent_pain.php
  - Explain difference between addiction, physical dependence, and tolerance.
  - www.ampainsoc.org/resources/people.htm

- Emphasize self-administered therapies (eg, heat, cold, massage, liniments and topical agents, distraction, relaxation, music).
- Prescribe exercise, especially for persistent pain (see p 232).
- Add therapy taught and/or conducted by professionals (eg, coping skills, biofeedback, imagery, hypnosis) as needed.
- When appropriate, obtain:
  - Consult PT and OT for mechanical devices to minimize pain and facilitate activity (eg, splints), transcutaneous electrical nerve stimulation, range-of-motion and ADL programs.
  - Psychiatric pain management consult for somatization or severe mood or personality disorder.
  - Anesthesia pain management consult for possible interventional therapy (eg, neuroaxial analgesia, injection therapy, neuromodulation) when more conservative approaches are ineffective.
  - Pain or chemical dependency specialist referral for management of at-risk patients and ongoing chemical dependency, "chemical coping," aberrant drug-related behaviors, and drug withdrawal.

Pharmacologic Treatment
Selection of Agent(s)
- Base initial choice of analgesic on the severity and type of pain; consider cost, availability, patient preference, comorbidity, and impairments (see **Figure 10**):
  - Consider nonopioids for mild pain (rating 1–3) (see **Table 70**).
  - Consider low-dose combination agents (see **Table 86**) for mild to moderate pain (rating 4–6).
  - Consider potent and titratable opioid agonists (see **Table 86**) for more severe pain (rating 7–10).
  - Consider adjuvant drugs (see **Table 88**) alone or in conjunction with opioids or nonopioids for neuropathic pain and other selected chronic conditions.
  - Select agents with lowest adverse-event profiles.
- APAP should be considered initial and ongoing pharmacotherapy in treating persistent musculoskeletal pain with maximal dose of 4 g in healthy patients. Advise against alcohol use.
- Avoid long-term use of nonselective NSAIDs and COX-2 selective inhibitors for chronic conditions (see **Figure 10**).
  - Nonselective NSAIDS and COX-2 selective inhibitors may be considered rarely and with extreme caution in highly selected individuals.
  - If using nonselective NSAID or COX-2 selective inhibitor with ASA, use a PPI or misoprostol for GI protection.
  - Do not use ibuprofen when also using ASA for cardioprophylaxis.
  - Consider COX-2 inhibitor for patients who would benefit from anti-inflammatory medication on a continuous, long-term basis based on risk/benefit assessment (see **Figure 10** and **Table 70**).
  - Routinely assess for GI and renal toxicity, hypertension, HF, and drug-drug and drug-disease interactions in patients taking NSAIDs.
- All patients with moderate to severe pain, pain-related functional impairment, or diminished quality of life due to pain should be considered for opioid therapy.
  - Consider fixed-dose combinations (eg, APAP▲ and hydrocodone or tramadol) for mild to moderate pain; do not exceed max dose for APAP.
  - Fall prevention when initiating opioid therapy.

- Avoid using multiple opioids or nonopioids.
- Select least invasive route (usually oral) and fast-onset, short-acting analgesics for episodic or breakthrough pain.
- Use long-acting or sustained-release analgesics for continuous pain after stabilizing dose with short-acting opioid.
  - Medications with long half-life or depot effects (eg, methadone, levorphanol, transdermal fentanyl) should be used and titrated cautiously, with close supervision of effects; duration of effect may exceed usual dose intervals because of reduced metabolism and clearance.
  - Methadone is an option if other long-acting agents are not affordable but should be used with extreme caution and only with expertise and monitoring ability because of highly variable half-life and risk of dose accumulation (see www.geriatricsatyour fingertips.org for details on methadone prescribing and monitoring).
  - Assess for ongoing attainment of therapeutic goals, adverse effects and safe and responsible medication use.
- Consider adjuvant analgesics, including antidepressants and anticonvulsants, for patients with neuropathic pain, fibromyalgia, or refractory persistent pain.
  - Effects may be enhanced when used in combination with other pain analgesics and/or nondrug strategies.
  - Begin low and titrate slowly; allow adequate therapeutic trial (may require 2–3 wk for onset of efficacy).
  - Consider topical lidocaine for patients with localized neuropathic and non-neuropathic pain.
  - Consider topical NSAIDs for localized non-neuropathic persistent pain.

Adjustment of Dosage
- Begin with lowest dose possible, usually 25%–50% adult dose, increasing slowly.
- Titrate dose on basis of persistent need for and use of medications for breakthrough pain. If using ≥3 doses/d of breakthrough pain medication, consider increased dosage of sustained-release medication.
- Dose to therapeutic ceiling of nonopioid or NSAID as limited by drug adverse events or risk factors.
- Increase opioid dosage until pain relief achieved or adverse events unmanageable before changing medications (there is no max dose or analgesic ceiling with opioids).
- Use morphine equivalents as a common denominator for all dose conversions to avoid errors, and titrate to effectiveness. See www.hopweb.org.
- When changing opioids, decrease equivalent analgesic dose by 25%–50% because of incomplete cross-tolerance.
- Administer around-the-clock for continuous pain.
- Reassess, reexamine, and readjust therapy until pain is relieved.
- Opioid analgesics should not be discontinued abruptly. Gradual tapering is necessary to avoid withdrawal symptoms (eg, nausea, abdominal cramps, irritability, anxiety, diaphoresis, tachycardia, hypertension). Decreasing the daily dosage by 10%–20% each day for 10 d can wean most patients without adverse responses. Tapering may require conversion to short-acting opioids. For patients at cardiovascular risk, a slower taper with close monitoring for sympathetic hyperactivity is recommended, and low-dose clonidine may be useful in preventing some of the physiologic (and symptomatic) stress related to opioid withdrawal.

Management of Adverse Events

- Anticipate, prevent, and vigorously treat adverse events; expect older adults to be more sensitive to adverse events.
- Warn patient about risk of sedation with opioids and that gradual resolution occurs within a week.
- Warn about risk of APAP toxicity and importance of including all OTC products with APAP in daily total (not to exceed 4 g/d in healthy older adults).
- Begin prophylactic, osmotic, or stimulant laxative when initiating opioid therapy (see **Table 49**); if patient has sufficient fluid intake, cautiously increase fiber or psyllium▲; titrate laxative dose up with opioid dose. Instances of severe opioid-induced constipation may respond to oral naloxone 0.8–2 mg q12h, titrated to a max of 12 mg/d given in water or juice, along with routine bowel regimen; or methylnaltrexone bromide *(Relistor)* SC 8 mg (38–62 kg) to 12 mg (62–114 kg) and 0.15 mg/kg for other weights with one dose q48h. Careful titration and observation are necessary because some patients may experience partial analgesia reversal. (See also p 111.)
- Monitor for dry mouth, constipation, sedation, nausea, delirium, urinary retention, and respiratory depression; tolerance develops to mild sedation, nausea, and impaired cognitive function. Reduce dosage and/or consider adding medication to counter adverse medication events if troublesome until tolerance develops.
- Avoid the following medications: carisoprodol, chlorzoxazone, cyclobenzaprine, indomethacin, meperidine, metaxalone, methocarbamol, nalbuphine, pentazocine (see also www.cms.gov/transmittals/downloads/R22SOMA.pdf).

Table 86. Short-acting Opioid Analgesic Drugs

Class, Medication	MS Equiv[a] (Route)	Starting Dosage in Opioid-naive Patients	Formulations
Mild to Moderate Pain			
Codeine▲	200 mg (po)	15 mg q4–6h	T: 15, 30, 60; S: 15/5 mL; Inj
Codeine + APAP▲b	200 mg (po)	1–2 15/325 tabs q4–6h; if 1 tab used, add 325 mg APAP	T: 15/325, 30/325, 60/325, 30/500, 30/650, 7.5/300, 15/300, 30/300, 60/300; S: 12/120/5 mL
Hydrocodone + APAP▲b (eg, *Lorcet, Lortab, Norco, Vicodin*)	30 mg (po)	2.5–5 mg q4–6h	T: 10/325, 5/400, 7.5/400, 10/400, 2.5/500, 5/500, 7.5/500, 10/500, 7.5/650, 7.5/750, 10/650, 10/660; C: 5/500; S: 2.5/167/5 mL (contains 7% alcohol)
Hydrocodone + ibuprofen▲ (eg, *Vicoprofen*)	30 mg	7.5/200	T: 7.5/200
Oxycodone▲ *(Oxy IR, Roxicodone)*	20 mg (po)	2.5–5 mg q3–4h	T: 5, 15, 30; C: 5; S: 5 mg/mL, 20 mg/mL
Oxycodone + APAP▲b *(Percocet, Tylox)*	20 mg (po)	2.5–5 mg oxycodone q6h	T▲: 2.5/325, 5/325, 5/500, 7.5/325, 7.5/500, 10/325, 10/650; C: 5/500; S: 5/325/5 mL
(Magnacet)			T: 2.5/400, 5/400, 7.5/400, 10/400
Oxycodone + ASA▲ *(Percodan)*	20 mg (po)	2.25–4.5 mg oxycodone q6h	T: 2.25/325, 4.5/325

(cont.)

Table 86. Short-acting Opioid Analgesic Drugs (cont.)

Class, Medication	MS Equiv[a] (Route)	Starting Dosage in Opioid-naive Patients	Formulations
Moderate to Severe Pain			
Oxycodone + ibuprofen▲ (Combunox)[c]	20 mg (po)	1 tab po q6h; do not exceed 4 tabs in 24h	T: 5/400
Morphine▲ (MSIR, Astramorph PF, Duramorph, Infumorph, Roxanol, OMS Concentrate, MS/L, RMS, MS/S)	30 mg (po), 10 mg (IV, IM, SC)	5 mg po q4h; 1–2 mg IV q3–4h; 2.5–5 mg IM, SC q4h; 5–10 mg Sp q3–4h	C: 15, 30; soluble T: 15, 30; S: 10 mg/5 mL, 20 mg/5 mL, 100 mg/5 mL, 4 mg/mL, 20 mg/mL; Sp: 5, 10, 20, 30; Inj
Hydromorphone▲ (Dilaudid, Hydrostat)	7.5 mg (po), 1.5 mg (IV, IM, SC), 6 mg (rectal)	1–2 mg po q3–6h; 0.1–0.3 mg IV q2–3h; 0.4–0.5 mg IM, SC q4–6h; 3 mg Sp q4–8h	T: 2, 4, 8; S: 5 mg/5 mL; Sp: 3; Inj
Oxymorphone (Opana, Opana injectable)	10 mg (po), 1 mg (IV, IM, SC)	5 mg po q4–6h; 0.5 mg IM, IV, SC q4–6h	T: 5, 10; Sp: 5; Inj
Tramadol▲ (Ultram)[d]	150–300 mg (po)	25 mg q4–6h; not >300 mg for those >75 yr old	T: 50
Tramadol + APAP▲ (Ultracet)[b,d]	37.5/325 mg (po)	2 tabs q4–6h; max 8 tabs/d	T: 37.5/325
Tapentadol (Nucynta)[e]	20 mg (po)	50 mg q4–6h	T: 50, 75, 100
Fentanyl (Actiq, Fentora)[f]	NA	Suck on 200 mcg loz over 15 min, effect begins within 10 min	Loz on a stick: 200, 400, 600, 800, 1200, 1600 mcg
Fentanyl (Onsolis)[f]	NA	One 200-mcg film, titrate using multiples of the 200-mcg film until patient reaches a dose that provides adequate analgesia with tolerable adverse events; do not use >4 of the 200-mcg films simultaneously	Buccal film: 200, 400, 600, 800, 1200 mcg
Fentanyl HCl iontophoric transdermal system (ITS)[f]	NA	40-mcg dose with 10-min lockout through electrical stimulus	System pch with battery contains 80 doses of 40 mcg each

[a] MS Equiv = morphine sulfate (MS) equivalent dose: morphine equivalency = dose of opioid equivalent to 10 mg of parenteral morphine or 30 mg of oral morphine with chronic dosing.

[b] Caution: total APAP dosage should not exceed 4 g/d.

[c] Treatment not to exceed 7 d.

[d] Risk of suicide for patients who are addiction prone, taking tranquilizers or antidepressant drugs, and at risk of overdosage. Additive effects with alcohol and other opioids.

[e] Lowest available dose may be high in opioid-naive patients in unmonitored settings; additional caution is warranted to observe for signs of excessive sedation.

[f] Do not use in opioid-naive; use is for breakthrough pain in those on opioid therapy.

Table 87. Long-acting Opioids for Opioid-tolerant[a] Patients with Moderate to Severe Pain

Class, Medication	MS Equiv[b] (Route)	Starting Dose	Formulations
ER Hydromorphone hydrochloride *(Exalgo)*	7.5 mg	*Exalgo:* 8 mg q24h[c]	T: 8, 12, 16
ER Morphine▲ *(MS Contin, Kadian, Oramorph SR, Avinza)*	*MS Contin:* 30 mg (po)	*MS Contin:* 20–30 mg q24h, 15 mg q12h	T: CR 15, 30, 60, 100, 200
	Kadian: 30 mg (po)	*Kadian:* 20 mg q24h	C: ER 10, 20, 30, 50, 60, 80, 100, 200
	Oramorph SR: 30 mg (po)	*Oramorph SR:* 15 mg q24h	T: SR 15, 30, 60, 100
	Avinza: 60 mg (po)	*Avinza:* 30 mg q24h	C: ER 30, 45, 60, 75, 90, 120
ER Morphine/naltrexone hydrochloride *(Embeda)*[d]	30 mg (po)	20 mg/0.8 mg q12–24h	C: ER 20/0.8, 30/1.2, 50/2, 60/2.4, 80/3.2, 100/4
ER Oxycodone▲ *(OxyContin)*	20–30 mg (po)	20 mg q24h, 10 mg q12h	T: CR 10, 20, 40, 80, 160
Oxymorphone ER *(Opana ER)*	10 mg	5 mg q12h; titrate dosage by 5-mg increments q12h	T: 5, 10, 20, 40
Tapentadol ER *(Nucynta ER)*	20 mg (po)	50 mg q12h	T: 50, 100, 150, 200, 250
Tramadol ER *(Ultram ER, Ryzolt)*	150–300 mg (po)	100 mg q24h or calculate 24-h total dose for immediate-release tramadol	T: 100, 200, 300
Transdermal buprenorphine[e] *(Butrans Transdermal System CIII)*	NA (see package insert)	5 mcg/h if <30 MS equiv for opioid-naive or if taking <30 mg oral morphine equiv; 10 mcg/h if 30–80 oral MS equiv with 1 pch × 7 d.[f]	5, 10, 20 mcg/h
Transdermal fentanyl▲[g] *(Duragesic)*	NA (see package insert)	12 mcg/h or higher q72h (if able to tolerate 60 mg oral morphine equiv/24 h)	12 mcg/h, 25 mcg/h, 50 mcg/h, 75 mcg/h, 100 mcg/h

Note: Conversion from any oral immediate-release opioid should be based on conversion ratios; start by administering 50% of calculated total daily dose of ER opioid, and titrate until adequate pain relief is achieved with tolerable adverse effects.

[a] Opioid-tolerant are those taking at least 60 mg/d of oral morphine, 25 mcg/h of transdermal fentanyl, 30 mg/d of oral oxycodone, 8 mg/d of oral hydromorphone, 25 mg/d of oral oxymorphone, or an equianalgesic dosage of another opioid for ≥1 wk.

[b] MS Equiv = morphine sulfate (MS) equivalent dose: morphine equivalency = dose of opioid equivalent to 10 mg of parenteral morphine or 30 mg of oral morphine with chronic dosing.

[c] Starting dose for ER formulation equivalent to total daily dose of oral hydromorphone, taken q24h; titrate every 3–4 d to adequate pain relief. Tablets should be swallowed whole or can lead to rapid release and absorption of potentially fatal dose of hydromorphone.

[d] These products contain an opioid antagonist intended to decrease misuse/abuse. If the product is used as intended and taken whole, analgesia is effected. If the product is altered (eg, chewed, crushed, dissolved), the opioid antagonist is released and can reverse analgesia effects.

e Do not exceed one 20 mcg/h Butrans system due to the rise of QT_c prolongation. Avoid exposing Butrans application site and surrounding area to direct external heat sources (eg, heating pads). Temperature-dependent increases in buprenorphine release from the system may result in overdose and death. Caution if switching from pure mu-opioid agonist. Careful patient selection because of abuse potential—monitor for signs of misuse, abuse, and addiction. Indicated for severe, chronic pain requiring around-the-clock analgesia for extended time.

f Initiate dosing regimen on individual basis and consult conversion instructions; do not titrate dose until exposed continuously for 72 h at previous dose.

g *Caution:* Active ingredient accumulates in subcutaneous fat; thus, duration of action may be >17 h. Remove patch before MRI. Do not use in opioid-naive patients. Not recommended for treatment of acute pain.

NA = not applicable

Table 88. Adjuvant Medications for Pain Relief in Older Adults

Class, Medication	Formulations and Dosage	Comments
Anticonvulsants (see also **Table 79** and p 197)		If one does not work, try another.
Carbamazepine▲ *(Tegretol)*	T: 200▲ ChT: 100 S: 100/5 mL▲ 200–400 mg q8h	Many drug interactions; mood stabilizer; used for trigeminal or glossopharyngeal neuralgia; may cause SIADH, thrombocytopenia, leukopenia
(Tegretol XR)	T: 100, 200, 400▲ C: CR 200, 300 200 mg q12h	
Gabapentin▲ *(Neurontin)*	C: 100, 300, 400 T: 600, 800 S: 250 mg/5 mL Begin 100–200 mg qhs but may need up to 200–700 mg q12h	If CrCl >15–29 mL/min: dose at 200–700 mg/d; if CrCL >30–59 mL/min, dose at 200–700 mg q12h; if CrCL ≤15 mL/min, dose at 100–300 mg/d; used for post-herpetic neuralgia and postoperative and chronic pain
Pregabalin *(Lyrica)*	C: 25, 50, 75, 100, 150, 200, 225, 300 75–300 mg q12h	Primary indication is for management of post-herpetic neuralgia, diabetic peripheral neuropathy, and fibromyalgia
Lamotrigine▲ *(Lamictal)*	T: 25, 100, 150, 200 ChT: 2, 5, 25▲ 400–600 mg q24h	Prolongs PR interval; risk of severe rash
Antidepressants (see **Table 35**)		Use low-dose desipramine▲ or nortryptyline▲; data on SSRIs lacking.
Duloxetine *(Cymbalta)*	C: 20, 30, 60 30 mg/d	For management of pain associated with diabetic peripheral neuropathy and treatment of chronic musculoskeletal pain, including osteoarthritis and chronic low back pain; most common adverse events: nausea, dry mouth, constipation, diarrhea, urinary hesitancy; significant drug-drug interactions.
Venlafaxine▲ *(Effexor)*	T: 25, 37.5, 50, 75, 100 Begin 25–50 mg q12h; 75–225 mg q24h in divided doses	Low anticholinergic activity; minimal sedation and hypotension; may increase BP and QT_c; may be useful when somatic pain present; EPS, withdrawal symptoms, hyponatremia
(Effexor XR)	C: 37.5, 75, 150 Begin 75 mg qam; 75–225 mg q24h	

(cont.)

Table 88. Adjuvant Medications for Pain Relief in Older Adults (cont.)		
Class, Medication	**Formulations and Dosage**	**Comments**
Milnacipran *(Savella)*	T: 12.5, 25, 50, 100 Begin 12.5 mg q24h; up to 100 mg q24h in divided doses	Dual reuptake inhibitor; used to treat pain of fibromyalgia; contraindicated with MAOI or within 2 wk of MAOI discontinuation
Corticosteroids (see **Table 42**)		Low-dose medical management may be helpful in inflammatory conditions.
Counterirritants		
✔Camphor-menthol-phenol▲ *(Sarna)**	lot: camphor 5%, menthol 5%, phenol 5% prn; max q6h	May be effective for arthritic pain, but effect limited when pain affects multiple joints; can cause skin injury, especially if used with heat or occlusive dressing.
✔Camphor and phenol▲ *(Campho-Phenique)**	S: camphor 5%, phenol 4.7% prn; max q8h	
✔Methylsalicylate and menthol▲		
(Ben-Gay oint*, *Icy Hot* crm*)	methylsalicylate 18.3%, menthol 16% q6–8h	Apply to affected area.
(Ben-Gay extra strength crm*)	methylsalicylate 30%, menthol 10% q6–8h	Apply to affected area.
✔Trolamine salicylate▲ *(Aspercreme* rub*)	trolamine salicylate 10% q6h or more frequently	Apply to affected area.
Other		
Baclofen▲ *(Lioresal)*	T: 10, 20; Inj 5 mg up to q8h	Probably increased sensitivity and decreased clearance; monitor for weakness, urinary dysfunction; avoid abrupt discontinuation because of CNS irritability.
Tizanidine▲ *(Zanaflex)*	T: 2, 4 2 mg up to q8h	Monitor for muscle weakness, urinary function, cognitive effects, sedation, orthostasis; potential for many drug-drug interactions.
Clonazepam *(Klonopin)*	T: 0.5, 1, 2 ODT: 0.125, 0.25, 0.5, 1, 2 0.25–0.5 mg hs	Monitor sedation, memory, CBC.
✔Capsaicin▲ (eg, *Capsin, Capzasin, No Pain-HP, R-Gel, Zostrix, Qutenza)*	crm, lot, gel, roll-on: 0.025%, 0.075%; 179-mg cutaneous pch q6–8h	Renders skin and joints insensitive by depleting and preventing reaccumulation of substance P in peripheral sensory neurons; may cause burning sensation up to 2 wk; instruct patient to wash hands after application to prevent eye contact; do not apply to open or broken skin. Pch should be applied by health professional, using a local anesthetic, to the most painful skin areas (max of 4 pchs). Apply for 30 min to feet, 60 min to other locations. Risk of significant rise in BP after placement; monitor patient for at least 1 h.

(cont.)

Table 88. Adjuvant Medications for Pain Relief in Older Adults (cont.)		
Class, Medication	**Formulations and Dosage**	**Comments**
✔Lidocaine *(Lidoderm)*	transdermal pch 5% 12 h on, 12 h off; up to 24 h on	Apply over affected area up to 4 patches for 24 h; used for neuropathic pain, may be helpful for low back pain, osteoarthritis.
Onabotulinumtoxin A *(Botox)*	Individualized based on muscle affected, severity of muscle activity, prior experience; not to exceed 360 U q12–16wk	Injected into muscles to treat myofascial pain syndrome resulting from skeletal muscle spasm and migraines when source is neck or facial muscles.

✔ = preferred for treating older adults
* Available OTC
Note: Various adjuvant classes are useful for treatment of neuropathic pain. TCAs are often helpful for migraine or tension headaches and arthritic conditions. Baclofen is particularly useful for muscle-related problems, such as spasms.

PALLIATIVE CARE

DEFINITION

"Palliative care means patient and family-centered care that optimizes quality of life by anticipating, preventing and treating suffering. Palliative care throughout the continuum of illness involves addressing physical, intellectual, emotional, social and spiritual needs to facilitate patient autonomy, access to information and choice." (From National Quality Forum's *National Framework and Preferred Practices for Palliative and Hospice Care*, 2006.)

PRINCIPLES

- Support, educate, and treat both patient and family.
- Address physical, psychologic, social, and spiritual needs.
- Use multidisciplinary team (physicians, nurses, social workers, chaplain, pharmacist, physical and occupational therapists, dietitian, family and caregivers, volunteers).
- Focus on symptom management, comfort, meeting goals, completion of "life business," healing relationships, and bereavement.
- Make care available 24 h/d, 7 d/wk.
- Educate, plan, and document advance directives; health care proxy; family awareness of decisions.
- Coordinate care among various providers. Help integrate potentially curative, disease-modifying, and palliative therapies.
- Offer bereavement support.
- Provide therapeutic environment (palliation can be given in any location).
- Advocate comprehensive palliative care for all dying patients.

QUALITY OF LIFE

Ways to help patient and family enhance quality of life at the end of life:

- Communicate, listen
- Teach stress management, coping
- Use all available resources
- Support decision making
- Encourage conflict resolution
- Help complete unfinished business
- Urge focus on nonillness-related affairs
- Urge a focus on one day at a time
- Help anticipate grief, losses
- Help focus on attainable goals
- Encourage spiritual practices
- Promote physical, psychologic comfort
- Refer to PT

DECISIONS ABOUT PALLIATIVE CARE

Follow principles involved in informed decision making (see **Figure 2**).

Communicating Bad News (SPIKES)

S=Setting: Prepare for discussion by ensuring all information/facts/data are available. Deliver in person in private area without interruptions or physical barriers. Determine individuals who patient may want involved.

P=Establish patients' perception of their illness (knowledge and understanding) by asking open-ended questions. Use vocabulary patient uses when breaking bad news.

I=Secure invitation to impart medical information. Determine what/how much patient wants to know.

K=Deliver information in sensitive, straightforward manner; avoid technical language and euphemisms. Check for understanding after small chunks of information and clarify concepts and terms.

E=Use empathetic and exploratory responses; use active listening, encourage expression of emotions, acknowledge patient's feelings.

S=Strategize and summarize and organize an immediate therapeutic plan addressing patient's concerns and agenda. Provide opportunity to raise important issues. Reassess understanding of condition and treatment plan and determine need for further education and follow-up with patient and family.

Hospice Referral

- Patients, families, or other health care providers can refer, but a physician's certification of limited life expectancy (prognosis of ≤6 mo for most hospice programs [see **Table 89**]).
- Encourage nursing home staff to interview residents to determine goals, preferences, and palliative care needs suggestive of appropriateness for hospice. Fax request for hospice referral to primary health care provider.
- Referral is appropriate when curative treatment is no longer indicated (ie, ineffective, adverse events too burdensome) and life is limited to months.
- Course of disability in last year of life does not follow predictable pattern based on the condition leading to death. For advanced dementia, high levels of disability are common. However, for cancer, organ failure, frailty, sudden death, and other conditions, very low levels of disability are seen until only a few months before death. Need for services to assist with ADLs is as great for persons dying from organ failure and frailty as for those with cancer and greater for those with advanced dementia.
- Hospice must be accepted by the patient or family, or both, and can be rescinded at any time.
- Hospice provides palliative medications, durable medical supplies and equipment, team member visits as needed and desired by patient and family (physician, nurses, home health aide, social worker, chaplain), and volunteer services.
- Optimal hospice care requires adequate time in the program; referral when death is imminent does not take full advantage of hospice care.
- Hospice care is usually delivered in patient's home, but it can be delivered in a nursing home or residential care facility (long-term care, assisted living) or in an inpatient setting (hospice-specific or contracted facility) if acuity or social circumstances warrant.
- Coverage of hospice services variable (eg, inpatient availability, amount of home care, sites for care), so determine and discuss with patient/family.

Table 89. Typical Trajectory and Hospice Eligibility for Selected Diseases	
Disease	**Typical Determinants for Hospice Eligibility***
Cancer	Clinical findings of malignancy with widespread, aggressive, or progressive disease evidenced by increasing symptoms, worsening laboratory values, and/or evidence of metastatic disease Impaired performance status with a Palliative Performance Scale (PPS; see p 291) value of ≤70% Refuses further curative therapy or continues to decline in spite of definitive therapy

(cont.)

Table 89. Typical Trajectory and Hospice Eligibility for Selected Diseases (cont.)	
Disease	**Typical Determinants for Hospice Eligibility***
Dementia	FAST Scale Stage 7 (see p 292) **and** Comorbid or secondary conditions that contribute to structural or functional impairments suggesting a prognosis of ≤6 mo
Failure to thrive	BMI <22 kg/m^2 Karnofsky score < 40 or PPS value < 40% (see p 290)
End-stage heart disease	Optimally treated with diuretics and vasodilators, which may include ACEIs or combination of hydralazine and nitrates **or** has angina pectoris at rest, resistant to standard nitrate treatment and is either not candidate for or declines invasive procedures **and** Significant symptoms of recurrent HF at rest and classified as NYHA Class IV (ie, unable to carry on any physical activity without symptoms, symptoms present at rest, symptoms increase if any physical activity is undertaken) Additional support needed for treatment-resistant symptomatic supraventricular or ventricular arrhythmia, history of cardiac arrest or resuscitation or unexplained syncope, brain embolism of cardiac origin, concomitant HIV disease, documented ejection fraction of ≤20%
End-stage liver disease	Prothrombin time ≥5 sec longer than control, or INR >1.5 **and** serum albumin <2.5 g/dL **and** At least one of the following: ascites, refractory to treatment or patient noncompliant; spontaneous bacterial peritonitis; hepatorenal syndrome (elevated Cr and BUN with oliguria [<400 mL/d]) and urine sodium concentration <10 mEq/L; hepatic encephalopathy, refractory to treatment, or patient noncompliant; recurrent variceal bleeding despite intensive therapy Additional support with progressive malnutrition; muscle wasting with reduced strength and endurance; continued active alcoholism (ethanol intake >80 g/d); hepatocellular carcinoma; hepatitis B positivity (HBsAg); hepatitis C refractory to interferon treatment Awaiting liver transplant may be certified for Medicare hospice benefit, but if donor organ is procured, patient should be discharged from hospice
End-stage pulmonary disease	Disabling dyspnea at rest, poorly or unresponsive to bronchodilators, resulting in decreased functional capacity, eg, bed to chair existence, fatigue, and cough (documentation of FEV$_1$, after bronchodilator, <30% of predicted is objective evidence for disabling dyspnea, but is not necessary to obtain) Progression of end-stage pulmonary disease, as evidenced by *prior* increased visits to emergency department or *prior* hospitalization for pulmonary infections and/or respiratory failure (documentation of serial decrease of FEV$_1$ >40 mL/yr is objective evidence for disease progression, but is not necessary to obtain) **and** Hypoxemia at rest on room air, as evidenced by pO$_2$ ≤55 mmHg or O$_2$ sat ≤88% or hypercapnia, as evidenced by pCO$_2$ ≥50 mmHg Additional support needed for cor pulmonale and right heart failure secondary to pulmonary disease, unintentional progressive weight loss of >10% of body weight over preceding 6 mo, resting tachycardia >100 bpm
Acute renal failure	Not seeking dialysis or renal transplant CrCl <10 mL/min (<15 mL/min for diabetes) Serum creatinine >8 mg/dL (>6 mg/dL for diabetes) Additional support needed for comorbid conditions such as malignancy, chronic lung disease (eg, mechanical ventilation), advanced cardiac disease, advanced liver disease

(cont.)

	Table 89. Typical Trajectory and Hospice Eligibility for Selected Diseases (cont.)
Disease	Typical Determinants for Hospice Eligibility*
Chronic renal failure	Not seeking dialysis or renal transplant CrCl <10 mL/min (<15 mL/min for diabetes) Serum creatinine >8 mg/dL (>6 mg/dL for diabetes) Additional support needed for following signs and symptoms of renal failure: uremia, oliguria (<400 mL/day), intractable hyperkalemia (>7) not responsive to treatment, uremic pericarditis, hepatorenal syndrome

* May vary depending on fiscal intermediary; additional supportive indications available for most diagnoses. Source: Adapted from Palmetto GBA (www.palmettogba.com).

Advance Directives
Designed to respect patient's autonomy and determine his/her wishes about future life-sustaining medical treatment if unable to indicate wishes. (See Assessment regarding Informed Decision-making and Patient Preferences for Life-sustaining Care, p 9.)

Oral Statements
- Conversations with relatives, friends, clinicians are most common form; should be thoroughly documented in medical record for later reference.
- Properly verified oral statements carry same ethical and legal weight as those recorded in writing.

Instructional Advance Directives (DNR Orders, Living Wills, POLST)
- Written instructions regarding the initiation, continuation, withholding, or withdrawal of particular forms of life-sustaining medical treatment.
- May be revoked or altered at any time by the patient.
- Clinicians who comply with such directives are provided legal immunity for such actions.
- POLST form can be very useful in formalizing patient preferences (www.polst.org).

Durable Power of Attorney for Health Care or Health Care Proxy
A written document that enables a capable person to appoint someone else to make future medical treatment choices for him or her in the event of decisional incapacity (see **Figure 2**).

Key Interventions, Treatment Decisions to Include in Advance Directives
- Resuscitation procedures
- Mechanical respiration
- Chemotherapy, radiation therapy
- Dialysis
- Simple diagnostic tests
- Pain control
- Blood products, transfusions
- Intentional deep sedation
- ICD and pacemakers

Withholding or Withdrawing Therapy
- There is no ethical or legal difference between withholding an intervention (not starting it) and withdrawing life-sustaining medical treatment (stopping it after it has been started).
- Beginning a treatment does not preclude stopping it later; a time-limited trial may be appropriate.
- Palliative care should not be limited, even if life-sustaining treatments are withdrawn or withheld.
- Decisions on artificial feeding should be based on the same criteria applied to use of ventilators and other medical treatment.
- Initiate discussion about pacemaker deactivation only if there is a potential patient benefit; consider the potential negative effects of deactivation before disabling the pacemaker.

Note pacemaker is not a resuscitative device and usually does not keep palliative-care patients alive.

- Reanalyze risk-to-benefit ratio of ICD therapy in patients with terminal illness. Life-prolonging treatment may no longer be desired.

Euthanasia

- Active euthanasia: direct intervention, such as lethal injection, intended to hasten a patient's death; a criminal act of homicide.
- Passive euthanasia: withdrawal or withholding of unwanted or unduly burdensome life-sustaining treatment; appropriate in certain circumstances.
- Assisted suicide: the patient's intentional, willful ending of his or her own life with the assistance of another; a criminal offense in most states.

MANAGEMENT OF COMMON END-OF-LIFE SYMPTOMS

Pain

- Primary goal: to alleviate suffering at end of life. See Pain (p 203) for assessment and interventions.
- The most distressing symptom for patients and caregivers.
- If intent is to relieve suffering, the risk that sufficient medication appropriately titrated will produce an unintended effect (hastening death) is morally acceptable (double effect).
- Alternate routes may be needed, eg, transdermal, transmucosal, rectal, vaginal, topical, epidural, and intrathecal.
- Recommend expert pain management consult if pain not adequately relieved with standard analgesic guidelines and interventions.
- Additional treatment may include:
  - radionuclides and bisphosphonates (for metastatic bone pain)
  - treatments (eg, radiotherapy, chemotherapy) directed at source of pain
- Pain crisis: Palliative sedation for intractable pain and suffering is an important option to discuss with patients. Ketamine▲ *(Ketalar)* 0.1 mg/kg IV bolus. Repeat as needed q5min. Follow with infusion of 0.015 mg/kg/min IV (if IV access not available, SC at 0.3–0.5 mg/kg). Decrease opioid dosage by 50%. A benzodiazepine may be useful. Observe for problems with increased secretions and treat (see p 222).

Weakness, Fatigue
Nonpharmacologic

- Modify environment to decrease energy expenditure (eg, placement of phone, bedside commode, drinks).
- Adjust room temperature to patient's comfort.
- Teach reordering tasks to conserve energy (eg, eating first, resting, then bathing).
- Modify daily procedures (eg, sitting while showering rather than standing).

Pharmacologic

- Treat remediable causes such as pain, medication toxicity, insomnia, anemia, and depression.
- Consider psychostimulants (eg, dextroamphetamine▲ *[Dexedrine]* 2.5 mg po qam or q12h, methylphenidate▲ *[Ritalin]* 5–10 mg po qam or q12h, or modafinil *[Provigil]* 200 mg qam); monitor for signs of psychosis, agitation, or sleep disturbance.

Dysphagia (see also p 106)
Nonpharmacologic
- Feed small, frequent amounts of pureed or soft foods.
- Avoid spicy, salty, acidic, sticky, and extremely hot or cold foods.
- Keep head of bed elevated for 30 min after eating.
- Instruct patient to wear dentures and to chew thoroughly.
- Use suction machine when necessary.

Pharmacologic
- For painful mucositis: local preparation of "magic mouthwash" (eg, 1:2:8 mixture of diphenhydramine elixir: lidocaine [2%–4%]: magnesium-aluminum hydroxide▲ [eg, *Maalox*] as a swish-and-swallow suspension before meals).
- For candidiasis: clotrimazole 10-mg troches▲, 5 doses/d, *or* fluconazole▲ 150 mg po followed by 100 mg/d po × 5 d.
- For severe halitosis: antimicrobial mouthwash; fastidious oral and dental care; treat putative respiratory tract infection with broad-spectrum antibiotics.

Dyspnea (see p 242)
Nonpharmacologic
- Teach positions to facilitate breathing, elevate head of bed.
- Teach relaxation techniques.
- Eliminate smoke and allergens.
- Assure brisk air circulation (facial breeze) with a room fan; oxygen is indicated only for symptomatic hypoxemia (ie, SaO_2 <90% by pulse oximetry).

Pharmacologic
- Opioids: oral morphine▲ concentration (20 mg/mL: 1/4 to 1/2 mL sl, po; repeat in 10–15 min prn) *or* morphine tabs 5–10 mg po q2h; if oral route not tolerated, nebulized morphine 2.5 mg in 2–4 mL NS *or* fentanyl 25–50 mcg in 2–4 mL NS; *or* IV morphine 1 mg or equivalent opioid q5–10min.
- Bronchodilators (see **Table 107**).
- Diuretics, if evidence of volume overload (see **Table 24**).
- Anxiolytics (eg, lorazepam▲ po, sl, SC 0.5–2 mg q2–4h or prn); titrate slowly to effect.

Constipation (see p 111)
- Most common cause: adverse effects of opioids, medications with anticholinergic adverse effects. Use stimulant or osmotic laxative (see **Table 49**). Consider enema if no bowel movement for 4 d. Evaluate for bowel obstruction or fecal impaction.
- Opioid-induced constipation not responsive to laxative treatment: methylnaltrexone bromide *(Relistor)* SC 8 mg (38–62 kg) to 12 mg (62–114 kg) and 0.15 mg/kg for other weights with one dose q48h.

Bowel Obstruction
Indications for Radiographic Evaluation
- To differentiate between constipation and mechanical obstruction
- To confirm the obstruction, determine site and nature if surgery is being considered

Nonpharmacologic Management
- Nasogastric intubation: only if surgery is being considered, for high-level obstructions, and poor response to pharmacotherapy
- Percutaneous venting gastrostomy: for high-level obstructions and profuse vomiting not responsive to antiemetics
- Palliative surgery
- Hydration: IV or hypodermoclysis

Pharmacologic Management (aimed at specific symptoms)
- Nausea and vomiting: haloperidol▲ *(Haldol)* po, IM 0.5–5 mg (≤10 mg) q4–8h prn; ondansetron▲ *(Zofran)* IV (over 2–5 min) 4 mg q12h, po 8 mg q12h [inj; T: 4, 8, 24; S: 4 mg/5 mL]; see also **Table 50**.
- Spasm, pain, and vomiting: scopolamine▲ IM, IV, SC 0.3–0.65 mg q4–6h prn; po 0.4–0.8 mg q4–8h prn; transdermal 2.5 cm² pch applied behind the ear q3d [inj; T: 0.4; pch 1.5 mg] *or* hyoscyamine▲ *(Levsin/SL)* sl [T: 0.125; S: 0.125 mg/mL] 0.125–0.25 q6–8h.
- Diarrhea and excessive secretions: loperamide▲ *(Imodium A-D)*, see **Table 51**; octreotide▲ *(Sandostatin)* SC 0.15–0.3 mg q12h [inj], very expensive.
- Pain: see **Table 86**.
- Inflammation due to malignant obstruction: dexamethasone▲ *(Decadron)* po 4 mg q6h × 5–7 d.

Excessive Secretions
Nonpharmacologic: Positioning and suctioning, as needed
Pharmacologic: Glycopyrrolate▲ 0.1–0.4 mg IV, SC q4h prn *or* scopolamine▲ 0.3–0.6 mg SC prn *or* transdermal scopolamine pch q72h *or* atropine▲ 0.3–0.5 mg SC, sl, nebulized q4h prn

Cough (see p 241)

Nausea, Vomiting (see p 113)
Determine cause to select appropriate antiemetic based on pathway-mediating symptoms and neurotransmitter involved (see **Table 50**). For refractory nausea and vomiting (ie, not amenable to other therapies), a trial of dexamethasone (2 mg q8h) can be tried; risks are dyspepsia, altered mental status

Anorexia, Cachexia, Dehydration
See also Malnutrition (p 166) and volume depletion (p 161). Universal symptom of patients with serious and life-threatening illness.

Nonpharmacologic
- Educate patient and family on effects of disease progression resulting in lack of appetite and weight loss.
- Promote interest, enjoyment in meals (eg, alcoholic beverage if desired, involve patient in meal planning, small frequent feedings, cold or semi-frozen nutritional drinks).
- Good oral care is important.
- Alleviate dry mouth with ice chips, popsicles, moist compresses, or artificial saliva.

Pharmacologic
- Corticosteroids: dexamethasone▲ 1–2 mg po q8h; methylprednisolone▲ 1–2 mg po q12h; prednisone▲ 5 mg po q8h
- Hormone therapy: megestrol acetate▲ 200–800 mg/d

Altered Mental Status, Delirium (see Delirium, p 59)

Anxiety, Depression
- Provide opportunity to discuss feelings, fears, existential concerns
- Referral to appropriate team members (spiritual, nursing)
- Medicate (see Anxiety, p 30, and Depression, p 68)

Source: Fine P. *Hospice Companion: Best Practices for Interdisciplinary Assessment and Care of Common Problems During the Last Phase of Life.* Oxford University Press; 2008.

PREOPERATIVE CARE

Cardiac Risk Assessment

Figure 12. Assessing Cardiac Risk in Noncardiac Surgery

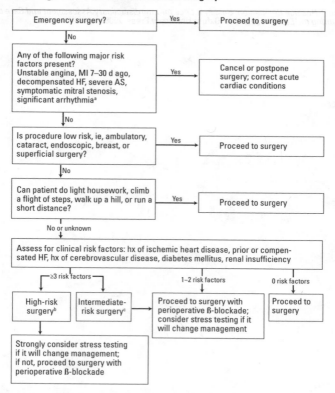

[a] High-grade AV block, Mobitz II AV block, third-degree AV block, symptomatic ventricular arrhythmias, or supraventricular arrhythmias with resting HR >100, newly recognized VT

[b] Open aortic or other major vascular surgery, peripheral vascular surgery

[c] Intraperitoneal or intrathoracic surgery, carotid endarterectomy, endovascular AAA repair, head and neck surgery, orthopedic surgery, prostate surgery

Source: Adapted from Fleisher LA, Beckman JA, Brown KA et al: ACC/AHA 2007 guidelines on perioperative cardiovascular evaluation and care for noncardiac surgery. A report of the American College of Cardiology/American Heart Association Task Force on Practice Guidelines (Writing Committee to Revise the 2002 Guidelines on Perioperative Cardiovascular Evaluation for Noncardiac Surgery). *Circulation* 2007;116:e418-e499.

Pulmonary Risk Assessment

Major risk factors for postoperative pulmonary complications:

- COPD
- ASA Class II – V (I – healthy; II – mild systemic disease; III – moderate/severe systemic disease; IV – life-threatening systemic disease; V – moribund)
- ADL dependence
- HF
- Prolonged (>3 h) surgery; abdominal, thoracic, neurologic, head and neck, or vascular surgery; AAA repair; emergency surgery
- General anesthesia
- Serum albumin <3.5 mg/dL

Minor risk factors:

- Confusion/delirium
- Weight loss
- Elevated BUN
- Alcohol use

Reducing risk of postoperative pulmonary complications:

- Smoking cessation 6–8 wk before surgery
- Preoperative training in incentive spirometry, active-cycle breathing techniques, and forced-expiration techniques
- Postoperative incentive spirometry, chest physical therapy, coughing, postural drainage, percussion and vibration, suctioning and ambulation, intermittent positive-pressure breathing, and/or continuous positive-airway pressure
- Nasogastric tube use for patients with postoperative nausea or vomiting, inability to tolerate oral intake, or symptomatic abdominal distention

Other Assessments

Cognitive Status: Unrecognized dementia is a risk factor for postoperative delirium. Measure preoperative cognitive status with Mini-Cog (see p 285) or MMSE.

Nutritional Status: Poor nutritional status can impair wound healing. Measure height, weight, serum albumin.

Routine Laboratory Tests: Recommended—Hb, hematocrit, electrolytes, creatinine, BUN, albumin. ECG and/or CXR should be obtained as necessary to assess cardiac or pulmonary risk. Optional—CBC, platelets, ABG, PT, PTT.

Cataract Surgery: Routine laboratory testing or cardiopulmonary risk assessment is unneccessary for cataract surgery performed under local anesthesia. Use of α_1-blockers for BPH (see p 233) within 14 d of cataract surgery is associated with increased risk of complications (intraoperative floppy iris syndrome), but it is unknown if cessation of α_1-blockers before surgery lowers risk.

Antiplatelet Therapy: If surgery poses high bleeding risk (eg, CABG, intracranial surgery, prostate surgery), D/C antiplatelet therapy 5–7 d before procedure.

Patients With Drug-Eluting Stents (DES) on Dual Antiplatelet Therapy:

- If possible, postpone surgery until 12 mo after DES was placed.
- If surgery cannot be delayed until 12 mo after DES placement:
  - For most surgeries, which are at low risk of bleeding, continue dual antiplatelet therapy.

- For surgeries at intermediate risk of bleeding (visceral, cardiovascular, major orthopedic, ENT, and urologic reconstruction surgery), continue dual antiplatelet therapy if DES placement was <12 mo previous.
- For surgeries at intermediate risk of bleeding in patients with DES placement >12 mo previous, D/C thienopyradine and maintain ASA therapy. D/C clopidogrel or prasugrel 5–7 d before procedure. Because the platelet inhibition of ticagrelor is irreversible, it should be stopped 1 d before procedure.
- For surgeries at high risk of catastrophic bleeding (intracranial, spinal canal, or posterior chamber eye surgery), D/C thienopyradine (clopidogrel or prasugrel 5 d before procedure and ticagrelor 1 d before procedure) and consider D/C of ASA 5 d before procedure. Stopping ASA is an individual decision based on patient's risk factors for stent thrombosis and on assessed bleeding risk.
- If both antiplatelet agents need to be stopped, consider bridging therapy (requires admitting patient 2–4 d before surgery) with tirofiban or eptifibatide (see **Table 18**) in patients felt to be at very high risk of stent thrombosis (consult with cardiology).
- If antiplatelet therapy is discontinued, resume it the day of the surgical procedure.

Anticoagulation: See **Table 90.**

Table 90. Cessation of Warfarin Before Surgery [a]

Thromboembolic Risk	Patient Conditions Determining Risk	Recommendations for Cessation of Anticoagulation
Low	• No VTE in past 12 mo • AF without prior TIA/stroke and 0–2 SRF • Bileaflet mechanical aortic valve without AF, prior TIA/stroke, or SRF	If INR therapeutic, stop warfarin 5 d before surgery, earlier if INR is supertherapeutic or >3; bridging therapy with LMWH at prophylactic dose is optional
Intermediate	• VTE in past 3–12 mo • Recurrent VTE • Active malignancy • AF without prior TIA/stroke and with 3–4 SRF • Bileaflet mechanical aortic valve with AF, prior TIA/stroke, or any SRF	Stop warfarin 5 d before surgery and begin LMWH at therapeutic (preferred) or prophylactic (optional) dose 3 d before surgery; give last preoperative LMWH dose at one-half total daily dose 24 hr before surgery
High	• VTE within past 3 mo • TIA/stroke within 3 mo • Rheumatic heart disease • AF with prior TIA/stroke and 3–4 SRF • Mechanical mitral valve or ball/cage mechanical aortic valve	Stop warfarin 5 d before surgery and begin LMWH at therapeutic dose 3 d before surgery; give last preoperative LMWH dose at one-half total daily dose 24 hr before surgery

Note: SRF = stroke risk factors: age ≥75 yr, HTN, diabetes mellitus, HF

[a] If patient is on dabigatran without prior TIA/stroke and 0–2 SRF, dabigatran can be discontinued 1–2 d before surgery (3–5 d if CrCl <50 mL/min); consider stopping it earlier for patients undergoing major surgery, spinal puncture, or placement of spinal or epidural catheter/port. For AF patients with higher thromboembolic risk (>2 SRF), risk of discontinuing dabigatran must be weighed against risk of bleeding with surgery. Bleeding risk can be assessed by ecarin clotting time or, if not available, activated PTT.

Source: Adapted from Douketis JD, Berger PB, Dunn AS, et al. The perioperative management of antithrombotic therapy. American College of Chest Physicians Evidence-Based Clinical Practice Guidelines (8th ed.). *Chest* 2008;133:299-339S.

Diuretics and Hypoglycemic Agents: Withhold on day of surgery.
SSRIs: SSRIs increase risk of bleeding with surgery, but discontinuing them before surgery is not recommended unless routine medication review indicates no therapeutic need.
Advance Directives: Establish or update.

PERIOPERATIVE MANAGEMENT

Table 91. Perioperative Medical Therapy to Reduce Cardiovascular Complications of Surgery

Agent	Target Conditions to be Prevented	Dosage	Clinical Situation
β-Blocker	MI, cardiac ischemia, death	Long-acting agent begun days to weeks before surgery to achieve resting HR of 60 bpm, and continued throughout postoperative period	Recommended in patients with >1 clinical risk factors and/or demonstrated coronary artery disease undergoing vascular (ie, high-risk) or intermediate-risk surgery[a]
			Consider in patients with 1 clinical risk factor undergoing intermediate-risk surgery or in patients with no clinical risk factors undergoing vascular surgery[a]
			Continue at usual dosage for patients already on a β-blocker.
Statin	MI, cardiac ischemia, death	Uncertain timing, specific drug, and dosage; one randomized trial used atorvastatin 20 mg po q24h begun an average of 30 d before surgery (see **Table 23**)	Consider in all patients undergoing vascular surgery.
			Consider in patients with >1 clinical risk factor undergoing intermediate-risk surgery[a].
			Continue at usual dosage for patients already on a statin.
Antiplatelet	Coronary events, TIA, stroke	ASA[▲] 81–325 mg po q24h; clopidogrel 75 mg po q24h	Begin ASA <24 h after CABG. For patients already on ASA, consider not withdrawing it before surgery unless patient is undergoing prostate or intracranial surgery.
			For patients already on clopidogrel, D/C it 5–7 d before CABG and other procedures judged to be high risk for bleeding (see p 226).
Anticoagulant	DVT, PE	See pp 24–29.	For patients >60 yr old, begin after most types of surgery.
			For patients already on an anticoagulant, see **Table 90** for management guidelines.

(cont.)

Table 91. Perioperative Medical Therapy to Reduce Cardiovascular Complications of Surgery (cont.)

Agent	Target Conditions to be Prevented	Dosage	Clinical Situation
Amoxicillin▲	Infective endocarditis	2 g po 30–60 min before procedure[b]	Use in patients with selected cardiac conditions undergoing selected dental, respiratory tract, infected skin, or infected musculoskeletal tissue procedures[b].
Amiodarone▲	AF	5 mg/kg po q12h from 6 d before surgery to 6 d after	Consider in patients undergoing CABG or cardiac valvular surgery.
Hydrocortisone▲	AF	100 mg IV the evening of the operative day, followed by 100 mg IV q8h × 3 d	Consider in patients undergoing CABG or cardiac valvular surgery; concomitant treatment with oral metoprolol is advised: 25 mg q12h if HR is 60–70 bpm, 50 mg q12h if HR is 71–80, or 50 mg q8h if HR is >80. Concomitant treatment with amiodarone (above) has not been studied.
Insulin	ICU morbidity and mortality	Titrate to maintain blood glucose 140–180 mg/dL (see **Table 41**)	CABG or carotid endarterectomy patients; surgical ICU patients

[a] See **Figure 12** for definitions of clinical risk factors, high-risk surgery, and intermediate-risk surgery.
[b] See Prevention, p 229, for alternative dosing regimens and specific indications.

PREVENTIVE TESTS AND PROCEDURES

Table 92. Recommended Primary and Secondary Disease Prevention for People Aged 65 and Older

Preventive Strategy	Frequency
USPSTF or CDC[a] Recommendations for Primary Prevention	
Bone mineral density (women)	at least once after age 65
BP screening	yearly
Diabetes mellitus screening	every 3 yr in people with BP >135/80 mmHg
Herpes zoster immunization	once after age 50 in immunocompetent people[b]
Influenza immunization	yearly
Lipid disorder screening	every 5 yr, more often in CAD, diabetes mellitus, PAD, prior stroke
Obesity (height and weight)	yearly
Pneumonia immunization	once at age 65[c]
Smoking cessation	at every office visit
Tetanus immunization	every 10 yr
USPSTF[a] Recommendations for Secondary Prevention	
Abdominal aortic aneurysm ultrasonography	once between age 65–75 in men who have ever smoked
Alcohol abuse screening	unspecified but should be done periodically
Depression screening	yearly
FOBT/sigmoidoscopy/colonoscopy	yearly/every 5 yr/every 10 yr from age 50 to age 75
Mammography[d]	every 2 yr in women age 50–74
Pap smear[e]	at least every 3 yr
Other[f] Recommendations for Primary Prevention	
ASA to prevent MI	daily
Bone mineral density (men)	at least once after age 70
Calcium (1200 mg) and vitamin D (≥800 IU) to prevent osteoporosis	daily
Measurement of serum C-reactive protein	at least once in people with one CAD risk factor
Omega-3 fatty acids to prevent MI, stroke	at least 2 ×/wk (see MI care, p 37)
Multivitamin	1–2/d

(cont.)

Table 92. Recommended Primary and Secondary Disease Prevention for People Aged 65 and Older (cont.)

Preventive Strategy	Frequency
Other[f] Recommendations for Secondary Prevention	
Skin examination	yearly
Cognitive impairment screening	yearly
Electron-beam CT	at least once in people with multiple CAD risk factors
Glaucoma screening	yearly
Hearing impairment screening	yearly
Inquiry about falls	yearly
TSH in women	yearly
Visual impairment screening	yearly

[a] US Preventive Services Task Force (see www.ahrq.gov/clinic/uspstfix.htm); Centers for Disease Control and Prevention (see www.cdc.gov/vaccines/recs/schedules/adult-schedule.htm)

[b] May vaccinate patients 1 yr after zoster infection; patients on chronic acyclovir, famcyclovir, or valacyclovir treatment should D/C the medication 24 h before zoster vaccination and resume the medication 14 d after vaccination.

[c] Consider repeating pneumococcal vaccine every 6–7 yr.

[d] Mammograms to age 70 are almost universally recommended; many organizations recommend that mammography should be continued in women over 70 who have a reasonable life expectancy.

[e] Pap smear testing can be stopped in most women after age 65. Women without a cervix should not have pap smears.

[f] Not endorsed by USPSTF/CDC for all older adults, but recommended in selected patients or by other professional organizations.

For individualized age- and sex-specific USPSTF prevention recommendations, see http://epss.ahrq.gov/ePSS/search.jsp.

The USPSTF recommends **against** screening for:

- Asymptomatic bacteriuria with urinalysis
- Bladder cancer with hematuria detection, bladder tumor antigen measurement, NMP22 urinary enzyme immunoassay, or urine cytology
- CAD with ECG, exercise treadmill test, or electron-beam CT in people with few or no CAD risk factors
- Carotid artery stenosis with duplex ultrasonography
- Colon cancer with FOBT/sigmoidoscopy/colonoscopy in people ≥85 yr old. Screening may be modestly beneficial in people 76–85 yr old with long life expectancy and no or few comorbidities.
- COPD with spirometry
- Ovarian cancer with transvaginal ultrasonography or CA-125 measurement
- PAD with measurement of ABI
- Pancreatic cancer with ultrasonography or serologic markers
- Prostate cancer with PSA and/or digital rectal examination

CANCER SCREENING AND MEDICAL DECISION MAKING

- Many decisions about whether or not to perform preventive activities are based on the estimated life expectancy of the patient. Refer to **Table 7** for life expectancy data by age and sex.

- Most cancer screening tests do not realize a survival benefit for the patient until after 5 yr from the time of the test. Cancer screening should be discouraged or very carefully considered in patients with ≤5 yr of estimated life expectancy.

ENDOCARDITIS PROPHYLAXIS (AHA GUIDELINES)

Antibiotic Regimens Recommended (see Table 93)

Cardiac Conditions Requiring Prophylaxis

- Prosthetic cardiac valve
- Previous infective endocarditis
- Cardiac transplant recipients who develop cardiac valvulopathy
- Unrepaired cyanotic congenital heart disease
- Repaired congenital heart disease with residual defects at the site or adjacent to the site of a prosthetic patch or device
- Congenital heart disease completely repaired with prosthetic material or device (prophylaxis needed for only the first 6 mo after repair procedure)

Cardiac Conditions Not Requiring Prophylaxis

All cardiac conditions or procedures not listed above.

Procedures Warranting Prophylaxis (only in patients with cardiac conditions listed above)

- Dental procedures requiring manipulation of gingival tissue, manipulation of the periapical region of teeth, or perforation of the oral mucosa (includes extractions, implants, reimplants, root canals, teeth cleaning during which bleeding is expected)
- Invasive procedures of the respiratory tract involving incision or biopsy of respiratory tract mucosa
- Surgical procedures involving infected skin, skin structures, or musculoskeletal tissue

Procedures Not Warranting Prophylaxis

- All dental procedures not listed above
- All noninvasive respiratory procedures
- All GI and GU procedures

Table 93. Endocarditis Prophylaxis Regimens

Situation	Regimen (Single Dose 30-60 Min Before Procedure)*
Oral	Amoxicillin▲ 2 g po
Unable to take oral medication	Ampicillin▲ 2 g, cefazolin▲ 1 g, or ceftriaxone▲ 1 g IM or IV
Allergic to penicillins or ampicillin	Cephalexin▲ 2 g, clindamycin▲ 600 mg, azithromycin▲ 500 mg, or clarithromycin▲ 500 mg po
Allergic to penicillins or ampicillin and unable to take oral medication	Cefazolin▲ 1 g, ceftriaxone▲ 1 g, or clindamycin▲ 600 mg IM or IV

* For patients undergoing invasive respiratory tract procedures to treat an infection known to be caused by *Staph aureus*, or for patients undergoing surgery for infected skin, skin structures, or musculoskeletal tissue, regimen should include an antistaphylococcal penicillin or cephalosporin.

Source: Wilson W, Taubert KA, Gewitz M et al. Prevention of infective endocarditis. Guidelines from the American Heart Association. A guideline from the American Heart Association Rheumatic Fever, Endocarditis, and Kawasaki Disease Committee, Council on Cardiovascular Disease in the Young, and the Council on Clinical Cardiology, Council on Cardiovascular Surgery and Anesthesia, and the Quality of Care and Outcomes Research Interdisciplinary Working Group. *Circulation* (online) 2007: http://circ.ahajournals.org/content/116/15/1736.full.pdf.

ANTIBIOTIC PROPHYLAXIS FOR PATIENTS WITH TOTAL JOINT REPLACEMENTS (TJR)

Risk Factors Prompting Consideration of Prophylaxis

- All patients with prior TJR, regardless of when joint was replaced, who are undergoing dental, ophthalmic, orthopedic, vascular, GI, head and neck, gynecologic, or genitorurinary procedures
- Additional risk factors: immunocompromised state; disease-, radiation-, or drug-induced immunosuppression; inflammatory arthropathies; previous prosthetic joint replacement; malnourishment; hemophilia; HIV infection; type 1 diabetes mellitus; malignancy; megaprostheses; comorbidities (eg, diabetes mellitus, obesity, smoking)

Conditions Not Requiring: patients with pins, plates, or screws

Suggested Prophylactic Regimens:

- Dental procedures (see those listed on p 231 for endocarditis): amoxicillin▲, cephalexin▲, or cephradine▲ 2 g po 1 h before procedure
- Prophylactic antibiotic recommendations for other types of procedures vary by procedure (see: Antimicrobial Prophylaxis for Surgery. *The Medical Letter, Treatment Guidelines* 2006;4(52):83–88 or www.aaos.org/about/papers/advistmt/1033.asp).

Source: Excerpted from Antibiotic Prophylaxis for Bacteremia in Patients with Joint Replacements, American Academy of Orthopaedic Surgeons Information Statement, February 2009. See entire statement at: www.aaos.org/about/papers/advistmt/1033.asp.

EXERCISE PRESCRIPTION

Before Giving an Exercise Prescription

Screen patient for:

- Musculoskeletal problems: decreased flexibility, muscular rigidity, weakness, pain, ill-fitting shoes
- Cardiac disease: consider stress test if patient is beginning a vigorous exercise program and is sedentary with ≥2 cardiac risk factors (male gender, HTN, smoking, diabetes mellitus, dyslipidemia, obesity, family hx, sedentary lifestyle).

Individualize the Prescription

Specify short- and long-term goals; include the following components (American College of Sports Medicine/AHA recommendations):

Flexibility: Static stretching, at least twice a week for ≥10 min of flexibility exercises, 10–30 sec per stretch, 3–4 repetitions of major muscle/tendon groups

Endurance: Moderate-intensity activity, ≥30 min ≥5 times per week

- Moderate-intensity activities are those that increase HR and would be rated 5–6 on a 10-point intensity scale by the patient (includes activities like brisk walking).
- Using pedometers to record the number of steps in a walking program has been demonstrated to increase physical activity, lower BMI, and lower BP.

Strength: Weight (resistance) training at least twice a week, 10 exercises on major muscle groups, 10-15 repetitions per exercise

Balance: Balance exercises are recommended for people with mobility problems or who fall frequently.

Patient information: See www.nia.nih.gov/health/publication/exercise-physical-activity-your-everyday-guide-national-institute-aging-1.

See also Assessment and Management of Falls, **Figure 5**.

BENIGN PROSTATIC HYPERPLASIA

Evaluation

Detailed medical hx focusing on physical examination of the urinary tract, including abdominal examination, digital rectal examination, and a focused neurologic examination; UA and culture if pyuria or hematuria; measurement of serum creatinine. Postvoid residual if neurologic disease or prior procedure that can affect bladder or sphincter function, urinary incontinence, or reports of incomplete emptying. Measurement of PSA is optional.

Management

Mild Symptoms: (eg, AUA/International Prostate Symptom Score [IPSS] ≤7; see p 293) watchful waiting

Moderate to Severe Symptoms: (eg, AUA score ≥8) watchful waiting, medical or surgical treatment

Nonpharmacologic Treatment: Avoid fluids before bedtime, reduce mild diuretics (eg, caffeine, alcohol), double voiding to empty bladder completely.

Pharmacologic Treatment: Combining drugs from different classes may have better long-term effectiveness than single-agent therapy. Because of immediate onset of benefit, many recommend beginning with α-adrenergic blockers.

- α_1-**Blockers** (reduce dynamic component by relaxing prostatic and bladder detrusor smooth muscle). Nonselective and selective agents are equally effective.
  - **First-generation** (can cause orthostatic hypotension and dizziness, which may be potentiated by sildenafil *[Viagra]*, vardenafil *[LEVITRA]*, and perhaps tadalafil *[Cialis]*)
    - Terazosin▲ *(Hytrin)* increase dosage as tolerated—days 1–3, 1 mg/d hs; days 4–7, 2 mg; days 8–14, 5 mg; day 15 and beyond, 10 mg [T: 1, 2, 5, 10]
    - Doxazosin▲ *(Cardura)* start 0.5 mg with max of 16 mg/d [T: 1, 2, 4, 8]
  - **Second-generation** (less likely to cause hypotension or syncope)
    - Tamsulosin▲ *(Flomax)* 0.4 mg 30 min after the same meal each day and increase to 0.8 mg if no response in 2–4 wk [T: 0.4]; decreases ejaculate volume; increases risk of retinal detachment, lost lens or lens fragment, or endophthalmitis if taken within 14 d before cataract surgery
    - Silodosin *(Rapaflo)* 8 mg/d, 4 mg/d in moderate kidney impairment; not recommended in severe kidney or liver impairment [C: 4, 8]; decreases ejaculate volume; retrograde ejaculation in ~30%
    - Alfuzosin ER▲ *(Uroxatral)* 10 mg after the same meal every day [T: 10]
- **5-α Reductase inhibitors** (reduce prostate size and are more effective with large [>30 g] glands; treatment for 6–12 mo may be needed before symptoms improve) can decrease libido, ejaculation, and erectile function. Both finasteride and dutasteride reduce the incidence of prostate cancer buy may lead to higher incidence of high-grade tumors in later years.
  - Finasteride▲ *(Proscar)* 5 mg/d [T: 5]
  - Dutasteride *(Avodart)* 0.5 mg/d [C: 0.5]
- **Antimuscarinic agents** (bladder relaxants) may have additional benefit beyond α_1-blockers on urinary frequency and urgency (see **Table 59**)
- **Phosphodiesterase-5 (PDE-5) inhibitors** may improve symptoms of BPH/lower urinary tract symptoms in men with or without erectile dysfunction but do not improve flow rates.

Surgical Management: Indicated if recurrent UTI, recurrent or persistent gross hematuria, bladder stones, or renal insufficiency are clearly secondary to BPH or as indicated by severe symptoms (AUA score >16), patient preference, or ineffectiveness of medical treatment.*
For men with moderate symptoms (AUA scores 8–15), surgical therapy is more effective than watchful waiting, but the latter is a reasonable alternative.

* Source: McConnell JD, Barry MJ, Bruskewitz RC, et al. *Benign Prostatic Hyperplasia: Diagnosis and Treatment.* Clinical Practice Guideline No. 8. Rockville, MD: Agency for Health Care Policy and Research, Public Health Service, US Dept. of Health and Human Services, February 1994. AHCPR Publication No. 94-0582.

Surgical options are:

- Transurethral resection of the prostate (TURP); standard treatment, best long-term outcome data
- Transurethral incision of the prostate (TUIP), which is limited to prostates with an estimated resected tissue weight (if done by TURP) of ≤30 g
- Open prostatectomy for large glands (>50 g)
- For laser prostatectomy, microwave therapy, and electrovaporization, data to support effectiveness and safety are limited.
- Transurethral needle ablation (TUNA) is less effective than TURP but may be an option for men with substantial comorbidity who are poor surgical candidates.
- Microwave thermotherapy delivered transurethrally or transrectally.
- Urethral stents may be an option for poor surgical candidates.
- Botulinum toxin may be effective but requires further study before it can be recommended.

PROSTATE CANCER
Screening is not recommended for older men.
Evaluation
Predicting extent of disease:
- PSA (see p 230)
- Biopsy
- Digital rectal examination
- CT abdomen and pelvis (selectively)
- Bone scan (selectively)

Histology
- Gleason score 2–6 has low 15–20 yr morbidity and mortality; watchful waiting usually appropriate.
- Gleason score ≥7, higher PSA and younger age associated with higher morbidity and mortality; best treatment strategy (surgery, radiation, androgen suppression, etc) is not known.

Treatment of Early Prostate Cancer
- Based on aggressiveness risk of cancer (National Comprehensive Cancer Network):
  - Very low: T_{1c}, Gleason score <6, <3 positive biopsy cores, <50% cancer in each core, PSA <10 ng/mL, and PSA density 0.15 ng/mL
    If <20 yr expected survival, treat with active surveillance.
  - Low: Stage T_1 or T_{2a}, Gleason score 2–6, PSA <10 ng/mL
    Treat with active surveillance (only if >65 yr old), prostatectomy, brachytherapy, or external radiation with adjuvant short-term androgen-deprivation therapy.

- Intermediate stage: T_{2b} *or* PSA 10–20 ng/mL, *or* Gleason score 7
  Treat with prostatectomy, brachytherapy, or external radiation therapy with short-term androgen deprivation therapy. If <10 yr expected survival, can treat with active surveillance.
- High: T_{3a} *or* Gleason score 8–10, PSA >20 ng/mL
  Treat with prostatectomy or external radiation therapy with adjuvant androgen suppressive therapy. At 24 mo, sexual dysfunction rates are similar with both treatments.
- Radical prostatectomy (reduced short- and long-term overall and disease-specific mortality, metastasis, and local progression compared with watchful waiting in men <65 yr old with early disease, regardless of histology and PSA, including those who are at low risk. Urinary incontinence is more common but treatable (see therapy for post-prostatectomy UI, p 134) and may gradually improve.
- Radiation therapy may cause transient PSA increase that does not reflect cancer recurrence. Irritative or obstructive urinary symptoms and bowel frequency and urgency are more common.
  - External beam
  - Brachytherapy (radioactive seed implantation) has greater effect on prostate than external beam.
- Proton-beam therapy is controversial and remains unproved.
- Hormonal therapy is reserved for locally advanced or metastatic disease.

Monitoring
After surgery or radiation therapy, PSA should be <0.1 ng/mL or undetectable. A PSA doubling time of 3–12 mo in the absence of clinical recurrence indicates a higher risk of development of systemic disease and cancer-specific death.

Therapy for Locally Advanced and Metastatic Disease
- For locally advanced (T3) disease (tumor extension beyond prostate capsule or invasion of seminal vesicles), and local disease with unfavorable prognostic factors (eg, Gleason score ≥7, PSA >10 ng/mL), external beam radiation is commonly used with androgen deprivation therapy (ADT). However, among men with moderate or severe comorbidity, there may be no benefit of ADT beyond radiation therapy alone.
- For T3, T4 (invading bladder, levator muscles, and/or pelvic wall), or metastatic disease, use ADT **(Table 94)**.
- Monotherapy can be either bilateral orchiectomy or a GnRH agonist.
- Combined androgen blockade (GnRH agonist plus antiandrogen) is used to avoid "flare" phenomenon (ie, increased symptoms early in treatment), but survival benefit is uncertain and side effects are greater than with monotherapy.
- In case of relapse, sequential hormonal manipulations are often used first:
  - Withdrawal of antiandrogen may induce remission.
  - Patients often respond when changed to a second antiandrogen.
  - When antiandrogens no longer control disease, adrenal suppression with aminoglutethimide or ketoconazole and hydrocortisone replacement may be effective.
- If castration-recurrent metastatic disease, maintain castrate levels of testosterone and:
  - If minimally symptomatic, sipuleucel-T *(Provenge)*, autologous cellular immunotherapy, may prolong survival (very expensive and available only at a limited number of cancer centers).

- If severely symptomatic or rapidly progressing, chemotherapy (docetaxel, mitoxantrone, abiraterone acetate); cabazitaxel *(Jevtana)* may prolong survival if progression during or after treatment with docetaxel.
- Treating patients with locally advanced or high-risk cancer receiving ADT with bisphosphonates (see p 199) is cost-effective if osteoporosis on BMD, prior fracture, or age ≥80 yr.

Therapy for PSA-only Recurrence (no evidence of other disease)
Consider salvage surgical, radiation, or cryotherapy treatment if less advanced disease at presentation, long lag between recurrence (>3 yr), or after radical prostatectomy with no nodal involvement. If patient is not a candidate for local treatment, than ADT.

Therapy for Metastatic Bone Disease
In men receiving long-term ADT or hormone therapy for cancer and in those with bone metastasis, zoledronic acid or denosumab reduces the proportion of patients with skeletal-related events or fracture.

Table 94. Common Medications for Prostate Cancer Therapy

Class, Medication	Dosage	Metabolism	Adverse Events/Comments
GnRH Agonists			*Class adverse events:* certain symptoms (urinary obstruction, spinal cord compression, bone pain) may be exacerbated early in treatment; risk is less when combined with antiandrogens
Goserelin acetate implant *(Zoladex)*	3.6 mg SC q28d or 10.8 mg q3mo	Rapid urinary and hepatic excretion, no dosage adjustment in renal impairment	Hot flushes (60%), breast swelling, libido change, impotence, nausea
Leuprolide acetate▲ *(Lupron Depot)*	7.5 mg IM qmo or 22.5 mg q3mo or 30 mg q4mo	Unknown; active metabolites for 4–12 wk, dose-dependent	Hot flushes (60%), edema (12%), pain (7%), nausea, vomiting, impotence, dyspnea, asthenia (all 5%), thrombosis, PE, MI (all 1%); headache as high as 32%
Triptorelin *(Trelstar Depot, Trelstar LA)*	Depot: 37.5 mg q28d IM LA: 11.25 mg q84d	Hepatic metabolism and renal excretion (42% as intact peptide)	Hot flushes, ↑ glucose, ↓ Hb, ↓ RBC, ↑ alkaline phosphatase, ↑ ALT or AST, skeletal pain, ↑ BUN
Histrelin acetate *(Vantas)*	50-mg SC implant q12mo	Hepatic metabolism	Hot flushes, fatigue, headaches, nausea, mild renal impairment
Antiandrogens (most often used in combination with GnRH agonists)			*Class adverse events:* nausea, hot flushes, breast pain, gynecomastia, hematuria, diarrhea, liver enzyme elevations, galactorrhea

(cont.)

Table 94. Common Medications for Prostate Cancer Therapy (cont.)

Class, Medication	Dosage	Metabolism	Adverse Events/Comments
Bicalutamide▲ *(Casodex)*	50 mg/d po [T: 50]	Metabolized in liver, excreted in urine; half-life 10 d at steady state	
Flutamide▲ *(Eulexin)*	250 mg po q8h [C: 125]	Renal excretion; half-life 5–6 h	Greatest GI toxicity in the class; severe liver dysfunction reported
Nilutamide *(Nilandron)*	300 mg/d po for 30 d, then 150 mg/d po [T: 50]	80% protein bound; liver metabolism, renal excretion; half-life 40–60 h	Delayed light adaptation
GnRH Antagonist			
Degarelix *(Firmagon)*	240 mg SC, then 80 mg SC q28d	Liver 70%–80%, renal 20%–30%	Prolonged QT interval, hot flushes, weight gain, fatigue, ↑AST and ALT

PROSTATITIS

Definition
Acute or chronic inflammation of the prostate secondary to bacterial and nonbacterial causes

Symptoms and Diagnosis
Acute: fever; chills; dysuria; tender, tense, or boggy on examination (examination should be minimal to avoid bacteremia); Gram stain and culture of urine
Chronic: obstructive or irritative symptoms with voiding, perineal pain, normal examination; compare first void or midstream urine with prostatic secretion or postmassage urine: bacterial if leukocytosis and bacteria in expressed sample, nonbacterial if sample sterile with leukocytosis

Treatment (see Table 65)
Antibiotic therapy should be based on Gram stain and culture.

Acute prostatitis (recommend treatment for 4–6 wk)
- Co-trimoxazole▲ DS 1 po q12h, *or*
- Ciprofloxacin▲ 500 mg po or 400 mg IV q12h, *or*
- Ofloxacin▲ 400 mg po once, then 300 mg q12h, *or*
- 3rd-generation cephalosporin▲ or aminoglycoside▲ IV
- If patient is toxic, then combine aminoglycoside with fluoroquinolone.

Chronic prostatitis (fluoroquinolones have good penetration of inflamed prostate)
- Co-trimoxazole▲ DS 1 po q12h × 2–4 mo, *or*
- Ciprofloxacin▲ 500 mg po q12h × 1 mo, *or*
- Levofloxacin 500 mg po q24h × 1 mo, *or*
- Ofloxacin▲ 200 mg q12h × 3 mo

DIFFERENTIAL DIAGNOSIS

- Bipolar affective disorder
- Delirium
- Dementia
- Medications/drugs: eg, antiparkinsonian agents, anticholinergics, benzodiazepines or alcohol (including withdrawal), stimulants, corticosteroids, cardiac medications (eg, digitalis), opioid analgesics
- Late-life delusional (paranoid) disorder
- Major depression
- Physical disorders: hypo- or hyperglycemia, hypo- or hyperthyroidism, sodium or potassium imbalance, Cushing's syndrome, Parkinson disease, B_{12} deficiency, sleep deprivation, AIDS
- Pain, untreated
- Schizophrenia
- Structural brain lesions: tumor or stroke
- Seizure disorder: eg, temporal lobe

Risk Factors for Psychotic Symptoms in Older Adults: chronic bed rest, cognitive impairment, female gender, sensory impairment, social isolation

MANAGEMENT

- Establish a trusting therapeutic relationship with the patient; focus on empathizing with the distress that symptoms cause rather than reality orientation.
- Encourage patients to maintain significant, supportive relationships.
- Alleviate underlying physical causes.
- Address identifiable psychosocial triggers.
- If psychotic symptoms are severe, frightening, or may affect safety, use antipsychotic.
- Aripiprazole, olanzapine, quetiapine, risperidone▲ are first choice because of fewer adverse events (TD extremely high in older adults taking first-generation antipsychotics). See **Table 96** and **Table 97** for adverse events of second-generation antipsychotics.
- All antipsychotics are associated with increased mortality in older adults.

Table 95. Representative Medications for Treatment of Psychosis

Class, Medication	Dosage*	Formulations	Comments (Metabolism)
Second-generation Antipsychotics			
✒Aripiprazole *(Abilify)*	2–5 (1) initially; max 30/d	T: 2, 5, 10, 15, 20, 30 ODT: 10, 15 IM: 9.75 mg/1.3 mL S: 1 mg/mL	Wait 2 wk between dosage changes (CYP2D6, -3A4) (L)
Clozapine▲ *(Clozaril)*	25–150 (1)	T: 25, 100 ODT: 12.5, 25, 100	May be useful for parkinsonism and TD; significant risk of neutropenia and agranulocytosis; weekly CBCs × 6 mo, then biweekly (L)

(cont.)

Table 95. Representative Medications for Treatment of Psychosis (cont.)

Class, Medication	Dosage*	Formulations	Comments (Metabolism)
Lurasidone (Latuda)	40 mg	T: 40–80 mg	Very limited geriatric data
✔Olanzapine (Zyprexa)	2.5–10 (1)	T: 2.5, 5, 7.5, 10, 15, 20 ODT: 5, 10, 15, 20 IM: 5 mg/mL	Weight gain (L)
Paliperidone (Invega)	3–12 (1)	T: ER 3, 6, 9	CrCl 51–80 mL/min, max 6 mg/d; CrCl ≤50 mL/min, max 3 mg/d; very limited geriatric data (K)
✔Quetiapine (Seroquel)	25–800 (1–2)	T: 25, 100, 200, 300 T: ER 50, 150, 200, 300, 400	Ophthalmic examination recommended q6mo (L, K)
✔Risperidone▲ (Risperdal)	0.25–1 (1–2)	T: 0.25, 0.5, 1, 2, 3, 4 ODT: 0.5, 1, 2, 3, 4 S: 1 mg/mL IM long-acting: 25, 37.5, and 50 mg/2 mL	Dose-related EPS; IM not for acute treatment; do not exceed 6 mg (L, K)
Ziprasidone (Geodon)	20–80 (1–2)	C: 20, 40, 60, 80 IM: 20 mg/mL	May increase QT$_c$; very limited geriatric data (L)
Low Potency First Generation			
Thioridazine▲ (eg, Mellaril)	25–200 (1–3)	T: 10, 15, 25, 50, 100, 150, 200 S: 30 mg/mL	Substantial anticholinergic effects, orthostasis, QT$_c$ prolongation, sedation, TD; for acute use only (L, K)
Intermediate Potency First Generation			
Perphenazine▲ (Trilafon)	2–32 (1–2)	T: 2, 4, 8, 16	Risk of TD with long-term use (L, K)
High Potency First Generation			
Haloperidol▲ (Haldol)	0.5–2 (1–3); depot 25–200 mg IM q4wk	T: 0.5, 1, 2, 5, 10, 20 S: conc 2 mg/mL Inj: 5 mg/mL (lactate)	EPS, TD; for acute use only (L, K) Depot form is for chronic use; monitor for TD and D/C if signs appear
Fluphenazine	1–2.5 mg/d (max 5 mg/d) (1)	T: 1, 2.5, 5, 10 S: conc 5 mg/mL IM: 2.5 mg/mL (decanoate)	EPS, TD, akathisia (L, K)

✔ = preferred for treating older adults but does not imply low risk; mortality may be increased in patients
with dementia.
* Total mg/d (frequency/d)

Table 96. Adverse Events of Preferred Second-generation Antipsychotics

	Aripiprazole	Olanzapine	Quetiapine	Risperidone
Level of Evidence	CR	RCT	RCT	RCT
Cardiovascular				
Hypotension	?	+	+++	+
QT$_c$ prolongation[a]	?	+	+	+

[a] QT$_c$ upper limit of normal = 44 millisec

(cont.)

Table 96. Adverse Events of Preferred Second-generation Antipsychotics (cont.)				
	Aripiprazole	**Olanzapine**	**Quetiapine**	**Risperidone**
Level of Evidence	CR	RCT	RCT	RCT
Endocrine/Metabolic				
Weight gain	?	+++	++	++
Diabetes	?	+++	++	++
Hypertriglyceridemia	0	+	0	?
Hyperprolactinemia	?	?	?	+++
Gastrointestinal				
Nausea, vomiting, constipation	0	0	+	?
Neurologic				
EPS	++	+	+	+++
Seizures	?	?	?	ND
Sedation	?	+	+	+
Systemic				
Anticholinergic	0	++	+	0
Neuroleptic malignant syndrome	ND	ND	ND	+

CR = case reports; RCT = randomized clinical trials; ND = no data

? = uncertain effect

0 = no effect

+ = mild effect; ++ = moderate effect; +++ = severe effect

Table 97. Management of Adverse Events of Antipsychotic Medications		
Adverse Event	**Treatment**	**Comment**
Drug-induced parkinsonism	Reduce dosage or change drug or drug class	Often dose related; avoid anticholinergic agents
Akathisia (motor restlessness)	Consider adding β-blocker (eg, propranolol▲ *[Inderal]* 20–40 mg/d) or low-dose benzodiazepine (eg, lorazepam▲ 0.5 mg q12h)	Also seen with second-generation antipsychotics; more likely with traditional agents
Hypotension	Slow titration; reduce dosage; change drug class	More common with low-potency agents
Sedation	Reduce dosage; give at bedtime; change drug class	More common with low-potency agents
TD	Stop drug (if possible); consider second-generation antipsychotic (eg, aripiprazole, quetiapine) with lower potential for EPS	Increased risk in older adults; may be irreversible

Note: Periodic (q4mo) reevaluation of antipsychotic dosage and ongoing need is important (see CMS guidance on unnecessary drugs in the nursing home: www.cms.gov/transmittals/downloads/R22SOMA.pdf). Older adults are particularly sensitive to adverse events of antipsychotic drugs. They are also at higher risk of developing TD. Periodic use of an adverse-event scale such as the AIMS is highly recommended. (see: www.geriatricsatyourfingertips.org)

COUGH
Among the most common symptoms in office practice; consider likely diagnosis based on duration of symptoms and treat the specific disorder **(Table 98)**. **Table 99** lists agents sometimes used in symptomatic management of cough.

Table 98. Diagnosis and Treatment of Cough by Duration of Symptoms

Cause	Preferred Treatment
Acute cough: duration up to 3 wk	
Common cold	Sinus irrigation or nasal ipratropium *(Atrovent NS,* see **Table 102)**. Not recommended: sedating antihistamines (dry mouth, urinary retention, confusion); oral pseudoephedrine (hypertension, tachycardia, urinary retention)
Allergic rhinitis	See p 243.
Bacterial sinusitis	Oxymetazaline▲ nasal spr (eg, *Afrin)* × 5 d; antibiotic against *Haemophilus influenzae* and streptococcal pneumonia × 2 wk
Pertussis	Macrolide or trimethoprim-sulfa antibiotic × 2 wk
Other: pneumonia, HF, asthma, COPD exacerbation	See pneumonia, p 141; HF, p 37; asthma, p 248; COPD, p 246.
Subacute cough: duration 3–8 wk*	
Postinfectious	Inhaled ipratropium *(Atrovent)*; systemic steroids tapered over 2–3 wk; if protracted, dextromethorphan with codeine; use bronchodilators if there is bronchospasm (see **Table 107)**
Subacute bacterial sinusitis	As for acute bacterial sinusitis, but treat for 3 wk
Asthma	See treatment, p 249.
Pertussis	Macrolide or trimethoprim-sulfa antibiotic × 2 wk; may need to treat as above for postinfectious cough
Chronic cough: duration >8 wk*	
Perennial rhinitis *or* vasomotor rhinitis	See p 243.
Chronic bacterial sinusitis	Oxymetazaline▲ nasal spr (eg, *Afrin)* × 5 d; antibiotic against *Haemophilus influenzae,* streptococcal pneumonia, and mouth anaerobes × 3 wk; may need follow-up course of nasal steroids
Asthma	See treatment, p 249.
Other: ACEIs, reflux esophagitis	Stop ACEI; treat reflux for ≥3 mo using a PPI
Aspiration	See Dysphagia, p 106.

*Obtain chest radiograph, sputums to exclude malignancy, TB, etc.

Management
- Do not suppress cough in stable COPD.
- For symptomatic relief, see **Table 99**.

Table 99. Antitussives and Expectorants		
Medication	Dosage and Formulations	Adverse Events (Metabolism)
Benzonatate[▲a] (Tessalon Perles)	100 mg po q8h (max: 600 mg/d) C: 100, 200	CNS stimulation or depression, headache, dizziness, hallucination, constipation (L)
Dextromethorphan[▲a] (eg, Robitussin DM)	10–30 mL po q4–8h C: 30 S: 10 mg/5 mL	Mild drowsiness, fatigue; interacts with SSRIs and SNRIs; combination may cause serotonin syndrome (L)
Guaifenesin[▲b] (eg, Robitussin)	5–20 mL po q4h S: 100 mg/5 mL	None at low dosages; high dosages cause nausea, vomiting, diarrhea, drowsiness, abdominal pain (L)
Codeine phosphate/Guaifenesin[▲c]	S: 10 mg/5 mL/100 mg/5 mL; 10 mg/5 mL/300 mg/5 mL T: 10 mg/300 mg	Sedation, constipation (L)
Hydrocodone/Homatropine[▲a] (Hycodan)	5 mL po q4–6h S: 5 mg/5 mL/1.5 mg/mL T: 5 mg/1.5 mg	Sedation, constipation, confusion (L)

[a] Antitussive

[b] Expectorant

[c] Antitussive and expectorant

DYSPNEA

Definition

A subjective experience of breathing discomfort that consists of qualitatively distinct sensations that vary in intensity (ATS)

Characteristics

- >65 yr: occurs in 17% at rest at least occasionally; in 38% when hurrying on level ground or on slight hill
- Hx: consider if level of dyspnea is appropriate to level of exertion (vs suggests pathology)
  - Consider age, peers, usual activities, level of fitness
  - Ask, "What activities have you stopped doing?"
- Associated symptoms: cough, sputum, wheezing, chest pain, orthopnea, paroxysmal nocturnal dyspnea

Evaluation

Hx and physical examination should suggest organ system; then evaluate for cause (**Table 100**).

Table 100. Diagnosis of Dyspnea		
Suspected System	Diagnostic Strategy	Diagnosis
Cardiac	Chest radiograph, ECG, echocardiogram, radionuclide imaging, BNP (p 37)	Ischemic or other form of heart disease
Lung	Spirometry	Asthma or COPD
	Diffusing capacity	Emphysema or interstitial lung disease
	Echocardiogram	Pulmonary hypertension

(cont.)

Table 100. Diagnosis of Dyspnea (cont.)		
Suspected System	**Diagnostic Strategy**	**Diagnosis**
Respiratory muscle dysfunction	Inspiratory and expiratory mouth pressures	Neuromuscular disease
Deconditioning/obesity vs psychological disorders	Cardiopulmonary exercise test	Deconditioning shows decreased maximal oxygen consumption but normal cardiorespiratory exercise responses.

Therapy
Nonpharmacologic
- Exercise reduces dyspnea and improves fitness in almost all older adults regardless of cause; physical conditioning reduces dyspnea during ADLs and exercise, and is primary treatment for deconditioning.
  - Use low-impact, indoor activity
  - Base intensity on heart rate or symptom of dyspnea
  - Recommend 20–30 min on most days
- Indications for pulmonary rehabilitation include the following:
  - Dyspnea during rest or exertion
  - Hypoxemia, hypercapnia
  - Reduced exercise tolerance or a decline in ADLs
  - Worsening dyspnea and a reduced but stable exercise tolerance level
  - Pre- or postoperative lung resection, transplantation, or volume reduction
  - Chronic respiratory failure and the need to initiate mechanical ventilation
  - Ventilator dependence
  - Increasing need for emergency department visits, hospitalization, and unscheduled office visits

Pharmacologic: See specific diseases elsewhere in this chapter.

ALLERGIC RHINITIS
Description
- The most common atopic disorder.
- Symptoms include rhinorrhea; sneezing; and irritated eyes (see Allergic Conjunctivitis, p 98), nose, and mucous membranes.
- May be seasonal, but in older adults is more often perennial.
- Postnasal drip, mainly from chronic rhinitis, is the most common cause of chronic cough.

Therapy
Nonpharmacologic: Avoid allergens, eliminate pets and their dander, dehumidify to reduce molds; saline and sodium bicarbonate nasal irrigation (eg, Sinu*Cleanse*) are helpful as primary or adjunctive therapy; reduce outdoor exposures during pollen season; reduce house dust mites by encasing pillows and mattresses. Arachnocides reduce mites.

Pharmacologic: Target therapy to symptoms and on whether symptoms are seasonal or perennial; see **Table 101** and **Table 102**.

Stepped therapy: For mild or intermittent symptoms, begin with an oral second-generation antihistamine; for moderate or severe symptoms, begin a nasal steroid; if symptoms uncontrolled, add the other agent; if still uncontrolled, add or substitute a leukotriene modifier for one of the other agents.

Ocular symptoms: Oral H₁ antihistamine or topical ophthalmic H₁ antihistamine are drugs of choice (see allergic conjunctivitis, p 98 and **Table 101**).

Table 101. Choosing Medication for Allergic Rhinitis or Conjunctivitis

Medication or Class	Rhinitis	Sneezing	Pruritus	Congestion	Eye Symptoms
Nasal steroids[a]	+++	+++	++	++	++
Ipratropium, nasal[a]	++	0	0	0	0
Antihistamines[b,c]	++	++	++	+	+++
Pseudoephedrine, nasal[d]	0	0	0	++++	0
Cromolyn, nasal[c]	+	+	+	+	0
Leukotriene modifiers	+	+	+	+	++

Note: 0 = drug is not effective; the number of "+'s" grades the drug's effectiveness.

[a] Effective in seasonal, perennial, and vasomotor rhinitis.

[b] Better in seasonal than in perennial rhinitis; nasal, ocular, and oral forms; ocular form effective only for eye symptoms, but nasal form may help ocular symptoms.

[c] Start before allergy season.

[d] Topical therapy rapid in onset but results in rebound if used for more than a few days; enhances effectiveness of nasal steroids and improves sleep during severe attacks.

Table 102. Medications for Allergic Rhinitis

Type, Medication	Geriatric Dosage	Formulations	Adverse Events/Comments
H₁-Receptor Antagonists or Antihistamines			*Class adverse events:* bitter taste, nasal burning, sneezing (nasal preparations); eye burning, stinging, injection (ocular preparations)
Oral			
✔Cetirizine▲ (*Zyrtec**)	5 mg/d (max)	T: 5, 10▲; syr 5 mg/5 mL	
✔Desloratadine (*Clarinex*)	5 mg/d	T: 5	
Fexofenadine▲ (✔*Allegra, Allegra-D*[a])	60 mg po q12h; q24h if CrCl <40 mL/min	T▲: 30, 60, 180; C: 60 ODT: 30 S▲: 30/5 mL	Least sedating in the class; fruit juice reduces absorption, so take 4 h before or 1–2 h after ingestion of juice
Levocetirizine (*Xyzal*)	2.5 mg/d po if CrCl 50–80 mL/min; q48h if CrCl 30–50; 2 ×/wk if CrCl 10–30. Not recommended if CrCl <10 mL/min.	T: 5 mg S: 0.5 mg/mL	Somnolence, pharyngitis, fatigue
Loratadine▲* (✔*Claritin, Claritin-D*[a])	5–10 mg/d	T: 10; rapid disintegrating tab 10 mg; syr 1 mg/mL	

*OTC

(cont.)

Table 102. Medications for Allergic Rhinitis (cont.)			
Type, Medication	**Geriatric Dosage**	**Formulations**	**Adverse Events/Comments**
Chlorpheniramine▲ (eg, *ChlorTrimeton**)	8–12 mg q12h	T: 4, 8, 12; ChT: 2; CR: 8, 12; S: 2 mg/5 mL	Sedation, dry mouth, confusion, urinary retention; dries lung secretions
Diphenhydramine▲ (eg, *Benadryl/**)	25–50 mg q12h	T: 25, 50; S: elixir 12.5 mg/mL	Same as chlorpheniramine
Hydroxyzine▲ (eg, *Atarax*)	25–30 mg q12h	T: 10, 25, 50	Same as chlorpheniramine
Nasal			
✔Azelastine (*Astelin*) (*Astepro*)	2 spr q12h[b]	topical spr 0.1% 0.1%, 0.15%	
✔Olopatadine (*Patanase*)	2 spr q12h	0.6%	Epistaxis
Decongestant			
Pseudoephedrine▲ (eg, *Sudafed*, combinations*)	60 mg po q4–6h	T: 30, 60; SR: 120; S: elixir 30 mg/5 mL	Arrhythmia, insomnia, anxiety, restlessness, elevated BP, urinary retention in men
Nasal Steroids			
✔Beclomethasone (eg, *Beconase, Vancenase*)	1–2 spr q12h[b]	80 spr	*Class adverse events:* nasal burning, sneezing, bleeding; septal perforation (rare); fungal overgrowth (rare); no significant systemic effects
✔Budesonide (eg, *Rhinocort*)	1–4 spr/d[b]	200 spr	
✔Ciclesonide (*Omnaris*)	1–2 spr/d[b]	250 spr	
✔Flunisolide▲ (eg, *Nasalide, Nasarel*)	2 spr/d[b] or 1 spr q8–12h	200 spr	
✔Fluticasone▲ furoate (*Veramyst*)	2 spr/d[b]	120 spr	
✔Fluticasone propionate▲ (eg, *Flonase*)	2 spr/d[b]	120 spr	
✔Mometasone (*Nasonex*)	2 spr/d[b]	120 spr	
✔Triamcinolone (eg, *Nasacort*)	2–4 spr/d[b]	100 spr	
Mast Cell Stabilizer			
Cromolyn▲ (*NasalCrom*)	1 spr q6–8h[b]; begin 1–2 wk before exposure to allergen	2%, 4%	Nasal irritation, headache, itching of throat
Leukotriene Modifier (see also p 252)			
Montelukast (*Singulair*)	10 mg/d po	T: 10 mg; gran 4 mg/packet	Less effective than nasal steroids

(cont.)

* OTC

Table 102. Medications for Allergic Rhinitis (cont.)			
Type, Medication	**Geriatric Dosage**	**Formulations**	**Adverse Events/Comments**
Other			
Ipratropium▲ *(Atrovent NS)*	2 spr q6–12h[b]	0.03, 0.06%[c] sol	Epistaxis, nasal irritation, upper respiratory infection; sore throat, nausea Caution: Do not spray in eyes.

✔ = preferred for treating older adults

[a] *Allegra-D* and *Claritin-D*, also available as *Allegra-D 24 Hour* and *Claritin-D 24 Hour,* are not recommended; all contain pseudoephedrine. Contraindicated in narrow angle glaucoma, urinary retention, MAOI use within 14 d, severe HTN, or CAD. May cause headache, nausea, insomnia.

[b] Spr per nares

[c] Use 0.06% for treatment of viral upper respiratory infection.

CHRONIC OBSTRUCTIVE PULMONARY DISEASE

Definition

A spectrum of chronic respiratory diseases characterized by:

- Not completely reversible airflow limitation
- Cough
- Dyspnea on exertion
- Frequent pulmonary infection
- Impaired gas exchange
- Sputum production

Therapy

Smoking Cessation: Essential at any age. See p 275.

Anxiety or Major Depression: Seen in up to 40% of patients and should be treated.

Mucolytic Therapy: Not recommended in stable COPD. Consider for patients with chronic productive cough; continue if reduced cough and sputum during a trial. Example therapy: guiafenesin▲ long-acting 600 mg po q12h

Rehabilitation: Patients at all stages benefit from exercise training, ie, increased exercise tolerance results in decreased dyspnea and fatigue (p 243).

Long-term Oxygen Therapy: For indications, see **Table 104**. Assess patients with FEV_1 <30%, cyanosis, edema, HF, resting O_2 sats ≤92%.

Stepped Approach: Add steps when symptoms inadequately controlled; D/C medication if no improvement. Assess improvement in symptoms, ADLs, exercise capacity, rapidity of symptom relief. See **Table 103** and **Table 107**. Long-term therapy with long-acting anticholinergics (eg, tiotropium), long-acting β-agonists, and inhaled steroids slows the loss of FEV_1 and reduces the number of exacerbations and/or hospitalization.

Table 103. COPD Therapy

Stage	Treatment
At all stages	Reduce risk factors Short-acting β_2-agonist when needed for symptom control Influenza vaccination
Mild COPD $FEV_1 \geq 80\%$ FEV_1/FVC or $FEV_1/FEV_6{}^a < 0.7$	See above
Moderate COPD $50\% \leq FEV_1 < 80\%$ FEV_1/FVC or $FEV_1/FEV_6{}^a < 0.7$	Regular treatment with one or more long-acting bronchodilators[b] Rehabilitation Add short-acting bronchodilator if needed
Severe COPD $30\% \leq FEV_1 < 50\%$ FEV_1/FVC or $FEV_1/FEV_6{}^a < 0.7$	Regular treatment with one or more bronchodilators[b] Rehabilitation Add inhaled steroids[c] if ≥ 3 exacerbations in last 3 yr Consider roflumilast
Very Severe COPD $FEV_1 < 30\%$ or $FEV_1 < 50\%$ plus chronic respiratory failure FEV_1/FVC or $FEV_1/FEV_6{}^a < 0.7$	Regular treatment with one or more bronchodilators[b] Inhaled steroids[c] if repeated exacerbations Treatment of complications Long-term O_2 therapy if respiratory failure Consider lung reduction or endobronchial valve placement in select patients Consider roflumilast
COPD Exacerbation (assess cardinal symptoms: increased dyspnea, sputum volume, and sputum purulence)	
Mild exacerbation (1 cardinal symptom)	Increase dosage and/or frequency of β_2-agonist; no antibiotics; monitor for worsening
Moderate or severe exacerbation (2 or 3 cardinal symptoms)	Add steroid (eg, methylprednisolone 30–40 mg po q24h × 7–10 d)
	Add respiratory fluoroquinolone (moxifloxacin, levofloxacin, or gemifloxacin) or amoxicillin-clavulanate; if at risk of *Pseudomonas*, consider ciprofloxacin and obtain sputum culture; if antibiotics in last 3 mo, use alternative class CBC, CXR, ECG, ABG; titrate O_2 to 90% sat and recheck ABG
	If 2 or more of severe dyspnea, respiratory rate ≥ 25, or PCO_2 45–60, then noninvasive positive-pressure ventilation reduces risk of ventilator use and mortality and length of hospital stay.

[a] FEV_1/FEV_6 is an alternative measurement and easier to obtain in older adults and in those with severe lung disease.

[b] β_2-agonists, anticholinergics, or slow-release theophylline (caution in older adults with other conditions and taking other medications). It is uncertain whether anticholinergics or long-acting β-agonists should be used as initial therapy.

[c] Consider osteoporosis prophylaxis.

Source: www.goldcopd.org (2010)

| Table 104. Indications for Long-term Oxygen Therapy[a] |

PaO$_2$ Level	SaO$_2$ Level	Other
≤55 mmHg	≤88%	>15 h/d for benefit[a], greater if 20 h/d[b]
55–59 mmHg	≥89%	Signs of tissue hypoxia (eg, cor pulmonale by ECG, HF, hematocrit >55%); or nocturnal desaturation, sats <90% for >30% of the time
≥60 mmHg	≥90%	Desaturation with exercise Desaturation with sleep apnea not corrected by CPAP

[a] Titrate O$_2$ saturation to ~90%.
[b] Improves survival, hemodynamics, polycythemia, exercise capacity, lung mechanics, and cognition.
Source: www.goldcopd.org (2010)

ASTHMA

Definition

- A chronic inflammatory disorder of airways causing airway hyperresponsiveness and episodic wheezing, breathlessness, chest tightening, and coughing, particularly at night or in the early morning.
- Episodes are usually associated with reversible airflow obstruction.

Diagnosis in Older Adults

- Half of older people with asthma have not been diagnosed.
- Diagnosis is based on symptoms, and after age 65 requires spirometry.
  - Aging reduces FEV$_1$/FVC and may result in overdiagnosis of COPD. For this reason, some older adults with asthma are misdiagnosed with COPD.
  - If FEV$_1$/FVC is low and the diffusing capacity of carbon dioxide is reduced, then COPD is likely. The diffusing capacity of carbon dioxide is normal in asthma.
  - If a short-acting β_2-agonist does not reverse airflow obstruction during pulmonary function tests (asthma is not excluded), do one of the following:
    - Perform bronchial provocative testing (induce obstruction), *or*
    - Repeat testing after 2 wk of oral steroids to determine if obstruction seen in the initial test is reversible.
  - Over half of people >65 yr old with airflow obstruction have both COPD and asthma ("overlap" syndrome).

Additional Considerations

- Some adults >65 yr old may have had asthma from a young age, while others develop asthma for the first time in late life. Second peak in incidence after 65 yr; 5–10% after 65 yr are affected and account for two-thirds of asthma deaths.
- Those with long-standing asthma develop fixed obstruction (reduced FEV$_1$/FVC that is not reversed by bronchodilators) as an effect of both the disease and aging.
- Cough is a common presentation for asthma in those >65 yr old.
- Symptoms may be confused with those of HF, COPD, GERD, chronic aspiration.
- Typical triggers: aeroallergens, irritants (eg, smoke, paint, household aerosols), viral URI, GERD, allergic rhinitis, metabisulfate ingestion (eg, wine, beer, food preservatives), medications (eg, ASA, NSAIDs, β-blockers).

Therapy
Nonpharmacologic
Avoid triggers; educate patients on disease management. Peak flow meters are less helpful in monitoring older adults; aging decreases peak flow and increases variability.

Pharmacologic
Good evidence on best treatment for older adults with asthma is lacking because most clinical trials exclude people >65 yr old and those with comorbidities or a hx of smoking >10 pack-years.

Stepped approach:
- Based on level of symptom control (see **Table 105**).
- Long-acting β-agonists should not be used unless given in combination with an inhaled steroid. Long-acting β-agonists as monotherapy are associated with increased mortality and are contraindicated as monotherapy.
- When symptoms controlled for 3 mo, try stepwise reduction, eg, step down from twice-daily steroid and long-acting β-agonist combination to once daily.
- If control not achieved, step up, but first review medication technique, adherence, and avoidance of triggers (see **Table 105** and **Table 106**).

Use separate AeroChamber for steroids; wash AeroChamber monthly.

Table 105. **Levels of Asthma Control**

Characteristic	Controlled (all of the following)	Partly Controlled (any measure present in any week)	Uncontrolled
Daytime symptoms	0–2 times/wk	>2 times/wk	Three or more features of partly controlled asthma present in any week
Limitations of activities	None	Any	
Nighttime symptoms/awakening	None	Any	
Need for reliever/rescue treatment	0–2 times/wk	>2 times/wk	
Lung function (PEF or FEV_1)	Normal	<80% predicted or personal best (if known)	
Exacerbations	None	$\geq$1/yr[a]	One in any week[b]

[a] Any exacerbation should prompt review of maintenance treatment to ensure that it is adequate.
[b] By definition, an exacerbation in any week makes that an uncontrolled asthma week.
Source: www.ginasthma.com

Table 106. **Asthma Therapy for Older Adults**

Step*	Treatment Options	Comments
Step 1	Inhaled β-agonist prn	Anticholinergics are an alternative rescue agent.
Step 2	Low-dose inhaled glucocorticoid (IGC) *or* leukotriene modifier	
Step 3	Low-dose IGC + long-acting β-agonist *or* medium- to high-dose IGC *or* low-dose IGC + leukotriene modifier *or* low-dose IGC + tiotropium or SR-theophylline	The anticholinergic tiotropium is superior to doubling the dose of inhaled steroid and equivalent to adding a long-acting β-agonist in uncontrolled asthma in adults. Leukotriene modifiers are equivalent to long-acting β-agonists in uncontrolled asthma in adults. Many drug interactions with theophylline.

(cont.)

Table 106. Asthma Therapy for Older Adults (cont.)		
Step*	Treatment Options	Comments
Step 4	**Add**: medium- to high-dose IGC + long-acting β-agonist **and/or** leukotriene modifier **and/or** SR-theophylline	Inhaled steroids are associated with bone loss. Never use long-acting β-agonists without an inhaled steroid.
Step 5	**Add**: oral glucocorticoid (lowest dose) and/or anti-IgE treatment	Oral steroids are associated with bone loss.

* Go to next step if symptoms not controlled.

Source: Adapted from: www.ginasthma.com (2010); and Gibson PG, McDonald VM, Marks GB. Asthma in older adults. *Lancet.* 2010;376:803–813.

DELIVERY DEVICES FOR ASTHMA AND COPD

Metered-dose inhalers (MDIs): prescribed as number of puffs. Spacers (require a separate prescription) improve drug delivery and should be used for essentially all older patients. Use separate spacers for steroids. Wash spacer monthly.

Dry powder inhalers (DPIs): prescribed as caps or inhalations; require moderate to high inspiratory flow. DPIs are not used correctly by 40% of people >60 yr old and 60% of those >80 yr old. Instructions should be repeated and reinforced for proper use and effective treatment.

Nebulizers: prescribed as milligrams or milliliters of solution. Consider for patients with disabling or distressing breathlessness on maximal therapy with inhalers. Often the best choice for patients with cognitive impairment. Caution when patients with glaucoma use nebulized anticholinergics; the mask should fit well, or a T-type delivery device should be used. Ultrasonic and jet nebulizers are available; the latter can be used with supplemental oxygen.

Table 107. Asthma and COPD Medications		
Packaging Color (Body/Cap)[a]	Dosage	Adverse Events (Metabolism, Excretion)
Anticholinergics		
✔ Ipratropium *(Atrovent)* (silver/green)	2–6 puffs q6h or 0.5 mg by nebulizer▲ q6h	Dry mouth, urinary retention, possible increase in cardiovascular mortality (lung, poorly absorbed; F)
Tiotropium *(Spiriva)* (gray/green)	1 inhalation cap (18 mcg) daily	Same as ipratropium except good data on cardiovascular safety (14% K, 86% F)
Short-acting β₂-Agonists[b]		*Class adverse events:* tremor, nervousness, headache, palpitations, tachycardia, cough, hypokalemia. Caution: use half-doses in patients with known or suspected coronary disease (L)
✔ Albuterol▲ *(Proventil, Ventolin)* (yellow/orange)	2–6 puffs q4–6h or 2.5 mg by nebulizer q6h; T: ER 4–8 mg po q12h	Adverse events more common with oral formulation
(Ventolin Rotacaps) (light blue/dark blue)	1–2 caps q4–6h; 200 mcg/cap	

(cont.)

Table 107. Asthma and COPD Medications (cont.)

Packaging Color (Body/Cap)[a]	Dosage	Adverse Events (Metabolism, Excretion)
✔ Bitolterol *(Tornalate)*	1–3 puffs q4–6h	
Levalbuterol *(Xopenex)*	0.31, 0.63, 1.25 mg q6–8h by nebulizer; inhaler 2 puffs q4–6h	Expensive; no advantage over racemic albuterol (intestine, L)
Pirbuterol *(Maxair)* (blue/white)	2–3 puffs q4–6h	Mechanism may be difficult for older adults to trigger (L, K)
Long-acting β-Agonists		*Class adverse events:* tremor, nervousness, headache, palpitations, tachycardia, cough, hypokalemia. Caution: use half-doses in patients with known or suspected coronary disease; not for acute exacerbation. These agents should not be used in asthma without an inhaled steroid. (L)
Arformoterol *(Brovana)*	2 mL q12h by nebulizer	
✔ Salmeterol *(Serevent Diskus)* (teal/light teal)	1 cap q12h; 50 mcg/cap	
✔ Formoterol *(Foradil)* (white/light blue)	1 puff q12h; 20 mcg/2 mL q12h per nebulizer	Onset of action 1–3 min (L, K)
Corticosteroids: Inhaled ✔ Beclomethasone *(Beclovent)* (white/brown) *(Vanceril)* (pink/dark pink)	2–4 puffs q6–12h [42, 84 mcg/puff, max 840 mcg/d]	*Class adverse events:* nausea, vomiting, diarrhea, abdominal pain; oropharyngeal thrush; dysphonia; dosages >1 mg/d may cause adrenal suppression, reduce calcium absorption and bone density, and cause bruising (L)
✔ Budesonide▲ (eg, *Pulmicort*) (white/brown)	1–2 puffs q6–12h [100, 200, 400 mcg/puff]	
Budesonide inhalation solution (eg, *Pulmicort Respules*)	0.5 mg/2 mL q12h	
Ciclesonide *(Alvesco)* (dark orange)	1–2 puffs q12h [80, 160 mcg/puff]	
✔ Flunisolide▲ (eg, *AeroBid*) (gray/purple or green)	2–4 puffs q12h [250 mcg/puff]	
✔ Fluticasone▲ (eg, *Flovent*) (orange/light orange)	1 puff q12h [44, 110, 220 mcg/puff]	
Mometasone *(Asmanex)*	1 inhalation/d [220 mcg]	
✔ Triamcinolone▲ (eg, *Azmacort*) (white/white)	2 puffs q6–8h or 4 puffs q12h [100 mcg/puff]	
Corticosteroids: Oral Prednisone▲ (eg, *Deltasone, Orasone*)	20 mg po q12h [T: 1, 2.5, 5, 10, 20, 50; elixir 5 mg/5 mL]	Leukocytosis, thrombocytosis, sodium retention, euphoria, depression, hallucination, cognitive dysfunction; other effects with long-term use (L)

(cont.)

Table 107. Asthma and COPD Medications (cont.)

Packaging Color (Body/Cap)[a]	Dosage	Adverse Events (Metabolism, Excretion)
Methylxanthines		
Long-acting theophyllines▲ (eg, *Quibron-T/SR*)	300–400 mg/d po [T: 300 bisect, trisect tabs]	*Class adverse events:* atrial arrhythmias, seizures, increased gastric acid secretion, ulcer, reflux, diuresis; clearance ↓ by 30% after 65 yr; initial dosage ≤400 mg/d, titrate using blood levels; 16-fold greater risk of life-threatening events or death after age 75 at comparable blood levels (L)
(eg, *Theo-Dur, Slo-Bid*)	100–200 mg po q12h [T: 100, 200, 300, 450]	
(eg, *Uniphyl, Theo-24*)	400 mg/d po [T: 100, 200, 300, 400]	
Leukotriene Modifiers		
Montelukast *(Singulair)*	10 mg po in AM [T: 10; ChT: 4, 5]	Headache, drowsiness, fatigue, dyspepsia; minimal data in older adults; leukotriene-receptor antagonist (L)
Zafirlukast *(Accolate)*	20 mg po q12h 1 h before or 2 h after meals [T: 10, 20]	Headache, somnolence, dizziness, nausea, diarrhea, abdominal pain, fever; monitor LFTs; monitor coumarin anticoagulants; leukotriene-receptor antagonist (L, reduced by 50% if >65 yr)
Zileuton *(Zyflo)*	600 mg po q6h [T: 600]	Dizziness, insomnia, nausea, abdominal pain, abnormal LFTs, myalgia; monitor coumarin anticoagulants; other drug interactions; inhibits synthesis of leukotrienes (L)
Other Medications		
✔ Albuterol-Ipratropium *(Combivent)* (silver/orange) *(Duoneb)*	0.09/0.018 mg/puff, 2-3 puffs q6h; 3 mg/0.5 mg by nebulizer▲ q6h	Same as individual agents (L, K)
✔ Budesonide-Formoterol *(Symbicort)* (red/gray)	2 puffs q12h (80 mcg/4.5 mcg or 160 mcg/4.5 mcg)	Same as individual agents (L, K)
Cromolyn sodium (eg, *Intal*) (white/blue)	2–4 puffs or 20-mg caps q6h	Because of propellant, use MDI with caution in coronary disease or arrhythmia (L, K)
✔ Formoterol-Mometasone *(Dulera)*	1 puff (5 mcg/100, 200 mcg per inhalation)	Nasopharyngitis, sinusitis, headache
Nedocromil *(Tilade)* (white/white)	2 puffs q6h	Bitter taste, headache, dizziness, sore throat, cough, chest tightness (K, F)

(cont.)

Table 107. Asthma and COPD Medications (cont.)		
Packaging Color (Body/Cap)[a]	Dosage	Adverse Events (Metabolism, Excretion)
Omalizumab *(Xolair)*	150–375 mg SC q2–4wk based on body weight and pretreatment IgE level	Malignancy, anaphylaxis; half-life 26 d (L, bile); expensive ($6,000–$25,000/yr)
Roflumilast *(Daliresp)*	500 mcg/d po, for use in severe COPD (FEV$_1$ <50%) associated with chronic bronchitis but not emphysema [T: 500 mcg]	Weight loss, nausea, headache, back pain, influenza, insomnia; do not use if acute bronchospasm or moderate or greater liver impairment; caution in patients with depression (suicidality); inhibits CYP3A4 and -1A2 (eg, erythromycin) (L)
✔Salmeterol-Fluticasone combination *(Advair Diskus)* (purple/light purple)	1 puff q12h (50 mcg/100, 250, or 500 mcg/cap	

✔ = preferred for treating older adults
[a] Generics may have different color on body and cap.
[b] Older nonselective β_2-agonists such as isoproterenol, metoproterenol, or epinephrine are not recommended and are more toxic.

IMPOTENCE (ERECTILE DYSFUNCTION)

Definition

Inability to achieve sufficient erection for intercourse. Prevalence nearly 70% by age 70.

Causes

Often multifactorial; >50% of cases arterial, venous, or mixed vascular cause. Also:

- Chronic high-dose opioids
- Diabetes mellitus
- Drug adverse events
- Hyperprolactinemia
- Hypogonadism
- Neurologic: eg, disorders of the CNS, spinal cord, or PNS; autonomic neuropathy; temporal lobe epilepsy
- Psychologic: eg, depression, anxiety, bereavement
- Thyroid or adrenal disorders

Low testosterone is associated more with decreased libido than with erectile dysfunction.

Evaluation

History: Type and duration of problem; relation to surgery, trauma, medication. Problems with orgasm, libido, or penile detumescence are not erectile dysfunction.

Physical Findings:

- Neuropathy: orthostatic hypotension, impaired response to Valsalva's maneuver, absent bulbocavernosus or cremasteric reflexes
- Peyronie's disease: penile bands, plaques
- Hypogonadism: diminished male pattern hair, gynecomastia, small (<20–25 mm long) testes

Assessment:

- Reduced penile-to-brachial pressure index suggests vascular disease.
- Cavernosometry used for diagnosing venous leak syndrome; reserved for surgical candidates.
- Test dose of prostaglandin E or papaverine can exclude vascular disease or confirm venous leak syndrome.
- For libido problems check total testosterone, luteinizing hormone, TSH, and prolactin. Most late-life hypogonadism is hypothalamic failure.

Diagnosis of Hypogonadism in Middle-aged and Older Men

- Diagnose testosterone deficiency only in men with consistent symptoms and unequivocally low testosterone levels.
- Morning total testosterone level <320 ng/dL (11 nmol/L) that remains <320 ng/dL on repeat testing and a free testosterone level of <640 pg/dL (<220 pmol/L) using a reliable assay suggests deficiency.
- Ask the following questions from the European Male Aging Study Sexual Function Questionnaire. If the answer to **all 3 questions** is the response in **bold**, hypogonadism is likely present.
  - How often did you think about sex? This includes times of just being interested in sex, daydreaming, or fantasizing about sex, as well as times when you wanted to have sex.
    - **2 or 3 times or less in the last month**
    - Once a week or more often

○ It is common for men to experience erectile problems. This may mean that one is not always able to get or keep an erection that is rigid enough for satisfactory activity (including sexual intercourse and masturbation). In the *last month*, are you:
- Always able to keep an erection that would be good enough for sexual intercourse, or usually able to get and keep an erection that would be good enough for sexual intercourse
- **Sometimes or never able to get and keep an erection that would be good enough for sexual intercourse**
○ How frequently do you awaken with full erection?
- **Once in the last month or less often**
- 2 or 3 times or more often in the last month

Therapy

Table 108. Management of Male Sexual Dysfunction

Cause	Therapy	Comments
Hypogonadism	Testosterone (preparation, formulation, usual dosage) ***Injectable*** Testosterone enanthate▲ 200 mg/mL, 50–400 mg IM q2–4wk Testosterone cypionate▲ 100, 200 mg/mL, 50–400 mg IM q2–4wk ***Transdermal*** *Androderm* 2.5 mg/24-h pch *AndroGel* 1% 2.5-g packet (25 mg), 5 mg qhs; 5-g packet (50 mg), 5-g packet qd *Fortesta* 60-g canister (10 mg/spr), 4 spr/d *Testim* 5-g tube (50 mg), 1 tube/d ***Buccal*** *Striant* T: 30 mg, 1 tab q12h	Not recommended with breast or prostate cancer, prostate nodule or induration or PSA >3 ng/dL, hematocrit >50%, untreated sleep apnea, HF, significant prostate obstructive symptoms. Probably effective in the treatment of opioid-induced androgen deficiency. Check serum testosterone concentration and adjust dose to achieve concentration in midrange of normal. Monitor adverse events and response q3mo. *Adverse events:* polycythemia, fluid retention, liver dysfunction. Possible increase in cardiovascular events in men with cardiovascular risk factors and poor mobility. Review cautions for individual preparations.
Neuropathic, vascular, or mixed	Vacuum tumescence devices (*Osbon-Erec Aid, Catalyst Vacuum Device, Pos-T-Vac, Rejoyn*)	*Rare:* ecchymosis, reduced ejaculation, coolness of penile tip. Good acceptance in older population; intercourse successful in 70%–90% of cases.
	Intracavernosal [5, 10, 20, 40 mcg] *or* intraurethral [125, 250, 500, 1000 mcg] prostaglandin E (*Alprostadil*)	*Risks:* hypotension, bruising, bleeding, priapism; erection >4 h requires emergency treatment; intraurethral safer and more acceptable.
	Penile prosthesis	*Complications:* infection, mechanical failure, penile fibrosis

(cont.)

Table 108. Management of Male Sexual Dysfunction (cont.)		
Cause	**Therapy**	**Comments**
Organic, psychogenic, or mixed	PDE5 inhibitors	*All agents:* contraindicated with use of nitrates; caution in vascular disease, least effective in vascular impotence. Caution with use of α-blockers; hypotension may occur with higher dosages of PDE5 inhibitors. Metabolism reduced in liver, kidney disease. Adverse events: headache, flushing, dyspepsia, dizziness, rhinitis. Nonarteritic ischemic optic neuropathy has been reported, but cause and effect have not been proved. Caution with CYP3A4 inhibitors.
	Sildenafil *(Viagra)* [25, 50, 100]: start 25 mg 1 h before sexual activity	*Other adverse events:* color tinge in vision, increased sensitivity to light, blurred vision
	Vardenafil *(LEVITRA)* [2.5, 5, 10, 20]: start 2.5 mg 1 h before sexual activity	*Other adverse events:* Avoid using in congenital or acquired QT prolongation and in patients taking class IA or III antiarrhythmics.
	Tadalafil *(Cialis)* [2.5, 5, 10, 20]: start 5 mg 30–60 min before sexual activity; lasts 24 h; 2.5 mg/d may be as effective as taking higher doses prn.	*Other adverse events:* back pain, myalgia, pain in limbs

FEMALE SEXUAL DYSFUNCTION

Definition
May involve reduced sex drive, dislike of sexual activity, difficulty with arousal, inability to achieve orgasm, or dyspareunia (pain with intercourse)

Factors Aggravating Dyspareunia
- Anticholinergic medications (produce vaginal dryness)
- Gynecologic tumors
- Interstitial cystitis
- Myalgia from overexertion during Kegel exercises
- Osteoarthritis
- Pelvic fractures
- Retroverted uterus
- Sacral nerve root compression
- Vaginal atrophy from estrogen deprivation
- Vulvar or vaginal infection

Evaluation
- Ask about sexual problems (eg, changes in libido, partner's function, and health issues).
- Screen for depression.
- Perform pelvic examination for vulvovaginitis, vaginal atrophy, conization (decreased distensibility and narrowing of the vaginal canal), scarring, pelvic inflammatory disease, cystocele, and rectocele.

Management
- Identify and treat clinical pathology.
- Educate and counsel patients and/or refer to a certified sex therapist (www.nlm.nih.gov/medlineplus/femalesexualdysfunction.html).
- Water-soluble lubricants (eg, *Replens*) are highly effective as monotherapy for dyspareunia in those who cannot or will not use hormones, or as a supplement to estrogen.

- For vaginismus (vaginal muscle spasm), trial cessation of intercourse and gradual vaginal dilation may help.
- For diminished libido, short-term use of androgens, eg, 300 mcg testosterone pch, provides modest but meaningful improvement (not yet available in the United States).
- Topical estrogens (**Table 119**) treat symptoms and complications of estrogen deficiency such as dyspareunia and recurrent urinary tract infections with minimal systemic absorption.
- The OTC botanical massage oil *Zestra* appears to improve desire and arousal in women with mixed desire/interest/arousal/orgasm disorders but can cause vaginal burning.
- Studies of sildenafil have not consistently shown effectiveness.

DRUG-INDUCED SEXUAL DYSFUNCTION

Agents Associated with Sexual Dysfunction

The following drugs and drug classes are believed to sometimes cause sexual dysfunction. In cases of suspected drug-induced sexual dysfunction, improvement after drug withdrawal provides the best evidence for the adverse effect. Therapy with a drug from an alternative class to treat an underlying condition may be necessary.

- Antidepressants: SSRIs (see below), lithium (erectile dysfunction), MAOIs
- Antipsychotics: olanzapine produces less loss of libido/impotence than risperidone, clozapine, and oral and depot first-generation agents.
- Antihypertensives: any agent related to reduced genital blood flow
  - Spironolactone has antiandrogen effect.
  - Centrally acting sympatholytics, eg, clonidine, produce relatively high rates of sexual dysfunction.
  - Peripherally acting sympatholytics, eg, reserpine
- Digoxin: possibly related to reduced testosterone levels
- Lipid-lowering agents: fibrates (gynecomastia and erectile dysfunction) and many statins (eg, lovastatin, pravastatin, simvastatin, atorvastatin) are the subject of case reports of both erectile dysfunction and gynecomastia. Statins affect the substrate for sex hormones and have been shown to reduce total and sometimes also bioavailable testosterone.
- Acid-suppressing drugs: The histamine$_2$-blockers cimetidine and more rarely ranitidine cause gynecomastia. Famotidine has caused hyperprolactinemia and galactorrhea. The PPI omeprazole has caused gynecomastia.
- Metaclopramide: induces hyperprolactinemia
- Anticonvulsants: phenobarbital, phenytoin, carbamazepine, primidone; all increase metabolism of androgen.
- Alcohol: high dosages reduce libido.
- Opioids: reduce libido and produce anorgasmia in men and women; mechanism related to reduced testosterone.

Management of SSRI-Induced Sexual Dysfunction

- Wait for tolerance to develop (12 wk of treatment may be needed).
- Pharmacologic management:
  - For escitalopram and sertraline (not other SSRIs), reducing dosage or "drug holidays" (skip or reduce weekend dose) may help.
  - In both men and women, sildenafil 50–100 mg po improved sexual function in prospective, parallel-group, randomized, double-blind, placebo-controlled clinical trials.

CHRONIC WOUND ASSESSMENT AND TREATMENT

Wound Assessment

Evaluation of chronic wounds should include the following (see **Table 110** for wound characteristics specific to ulcer type):

• Location
• Wound size and shape: length, width, depth, stage (pressure ulcer), grade (diabetic foot ulcer)
• Wound bed: color, presence of slough, necrotic tissue, granulation tissue, epithelial tissue, undermining or tunneling
• Exudate: purulent vs nonpurulent (serous, serosanguineous)
• Wound edges: distinct, diffuse, rolled under
• Periwound skin and soft tissue: erythema, edema, induration, temperature
• Presence of pain at rest and with wound care procedures
• Signs of wound infection
  ◦ Increased necrotic tissue
  ◦ Foul odor
  ◦ Purulent exudate
  ◦ Halo of erythema at wound edges
  ◦ Wound breakdown
  ◦ Increasing pain
  ◦ Marked edema
  ◦ Friable granulation tissue
  ◦ Serous exudate with nonspecific inflammation
  ◦ Nonhealing or enlarging wound
  ◦ Heat
• Swab culture of wound surface exudates is of no value in diagnosing infection due to wound contamination.
  ◦ Levine's technique (cleanse with normal saline followed by rotating a swab over a 1-cm square area with sufficient pressure to express fluid from the wound tissue beneath the wound surface) produces culture findings most comparable to those of tissue specimens.

Principles of Wound Treatment

• Remove debris from wound surface.
  ◦ Cleanse using normal saline or lactated Ringer's with each dressing change. Avoid antiseptics because of cytotoxicity.
  ◦ Irrigate using 4–15 psi to cleanse adherent debris. Use 8 mmHg pressure (19-gauge catheter and 35-mL syringe) when wound is deep, tunneled, or undermined.
• Remove necrotic tissue. Consider combining autolytic or topical enzyme debridement methods with sharp debridement to facilitate more rapid removal of necrotic tissue.
  ◦ Sharp debridement
  ◦ Autolytic methods (eg, moisture-retaining dressings or hydrogels)
  ◦ Mechanical (eg, wet-to-dry dressings)
  ◦ Chemical (eg, topical enzymes such as *Accuzyme, Santyl*)
• Pack dead space (tunnels, undermining) with moistened gauze dressings or strips of calcium alginate.
• Control pain associated with wound care procedures.
  ◦ For moderate to severe pain not managed by oral medications or with dose-limiting adverse events, topical opioids may be used, eg, mixture of 10 mg morphine sulfate injectable

combined with 8 g of neutral water-based gel applied 2 ×/d. Can titrate up to 10 mg morphine sulfate injectable with 5 g neutral water-based gel applied 2–3 ×/d.

- Control bacterial burden/infection.
  ○ Monitor for signs of infection.
  ○ Debride all necrotic tissue (*except* in lower extremity with arterial insufficiency).
  ○ If infection is suspected, assess type and quantity of bacteria by validated quantitative swab or tissue biopsy. Suspect infection if epithelialization from margin is not progressing within 2 wk of debridement and initiation of offloading (use of cast, splint, or special shoe to shift pressure from wound to surrounding support structure).
  ○ For ulcers with ≥1 million CFU/g of tissue or any tissue level of β-hemolytic streptococci, use a topical antimicrobial (eg, *Silvadene* or dressings with bioavailable silver, cadexomer iodine at concentrations up to 0.45%; see **Table 112**). Limit duration of use of topical antimicrobials to avoid cytotoxicity or bacterial resistance.
  ○ Consider 2-wk trial of topical antibiotic for clean ulcers that are not healing after 2–4 wk optimal care; antibiotic spectrum should include gram-negative, gram-positive, and anaerobic organisms.
  ○ Use systemic antibiotics if obvious signs of localized infection, cellulitis, osteomyelitis, or systemic inflammatory response (see **Table 109**).
  ○ Treat cellulitis surrounding ulcer with a systemic gram-positive bactericidal antibiotic (see cellulitis, p 75) unless gram-negative organisms are suspected and require aggressive IV treatment.
  ○ If osteomyelitis is suspected, evaluate with radiographs, MRI, CT, or radionuclide scan.
  ○ Referral for surgical evaluation is warranted.

Table 109. Empiric Antibiotic Therapy to Treat Infections in Chronic Wounds

Severity of Infection	Clinical Features	Medication Options	Duration of Treatment
Mild	Superficial, localized signs of inflammation/infection, without signs of a systemic response or osteomyelitis, and ambulatory management planned	Cephalexin Clindamycin Amoxicillin/clavulanate Clindamycin plus ciprofloxacin, moxifloxacin, or linezolid (for MRSA)	2 wk
Moderate	Superficial to deep tissue involvement, a systemic response, no osteomyelitis, and either planned ambulatory or inpatient management	Clindamycin plus ciprofloxacin Clindamycin po plus ceftriaxone IV Vancomycin IV (for MRSA) Linezolid IV (for MRSA)	2–4 wk
Severe	Requires inpatient care and involves deep tissue with a systemic response, presence of osteomyelitis, or is life/limb threatening	Clindamycin po plus ceftriaxone IV Piperacillin/tazobactam IV Clindamycin po plus gentamicin IV Imipenem IV Meropenem IV Vancomycin IV (for MRSA) Linezolid IV (for MRSA)	2–12 wk (Bone and joint involvement requires prolonged oral therapy after IV therapy completed.)

Source: Adapted from Landis, SJ. Chronic wound infection and antimicrobial use. *Advances in Skin and Wound Care* 2008;21:531–540.

- Provide moist wound environment and control exudates.
  ○ Dressings (see **Table 111** and **Table 112**)

- Adjunctive therapies to support wound healing process
  - Negative-pressure wound therapy (ie, vacuum-assisted closure [VAC])
    - Indications: Stage III and IV pressure ulcers, neuropathic ulcers, venous ulcers, dehisced incisions with trapping of third-space fluid around wound
    - Contraindications: Presence of *any* nonviable, necrotic tissue in wound; untreated osteomyelitis; malignancy in or surrounding wound
    - Precautions: unstable hemostasis, anticoagulant therapy
    - Guidelines for use:
      - Negative pressure = 75–125 mmHg depending on wound characteristics
      - Dressing change regimen: 48 h after placement, then every other day
      - Cycle: continuous for initial 48 h, then intermittent (5 min negative pressure followed by 2 min of no pressure) for remainder of treatment
      - Specialized training in application and monitoring of therapy essential for successful outcome
  - Electrical stimulation
    - Indications: Stage III and IV pressure ulcers, arterial ulcers, diabetic foot ulcers, and venous ulcers if no evidence of measurable improvement after ≥30 d of standard wound care
    - Contraindications: presence of cardiac pacemaker, malignancy, osteomyelitis
    - Precautions: avoid placement of electrodes over topical substances containing metal ions, tangential to the heart, or over the carotid sinus
    - Guidelines for use:
      - Refer to PT for stimulation parameters
      - Predominant type of current used is pulsed current (either low- or high-voltage)
      - Electrode placement—two options:
        - One electrode placed directly in contact with saline-moistened gauze on wound surface and second electrode 15–30 cm from wound edge
        - Electrodes placed on skin at wound edges on opposite sides of wound
      - Pulse frequency: 100 pulses/sec with current sufficient to produce tingling sensation
      - Treatment administered for 1 h, 5–7 days/wk, continued as long as wound is progressing toward closure
  - Growth factor therapy
    - *Regranex*, a recombinant platelet-derived growth factor, applied topically in thin layer to a clean wound bed for 12 h followed by 12 h of saline-moistened gauze dressing
    - Indications: Currently for diabetic foot ulcers but may have benefit in other nonhealing wounds.
    - Contraindications: Not recommended for use in patients with known malignancies.
    - Guidelines for use:
      - Must be used in conjunction with offloading of pressure on foot, regular sharp debridement, and maintenance of uninfected status.
      - If wound closure is not ≥30% in 10 wk or complete in 20 wk, reevaluate treatment plan and consider surgical intervention (especially if osteomyelitis is present).
- Prevent further injury
  - Use pressure-reducing mattresses, chair cushions, and heel protectors
  - Reposition q2h and avoid any pressure on the wound

- Support repair process
  - Protein (1.25–1.5 g/kg/d) and calories (30–35/kg/d) unless contraindicated because of impaired renal function
  - Correct deficiencies of vitamin C and zinc if suspected
  - Avoid exposure to cold; vasoconstriction reduces blood flow to wound
  - Assure adequate hydration with oral or parenteral fluids
- If ulcer does not show signs of healing over 2-wk period of optimal therapy, reevaluate wound management strategies and factors affecting healing.

Table 110. Typical Wound Characteristics by Ulcer Type

	Arterial	Diabetic	Pressure	Venous
Location	Tips of toes or between toes, on pressure points of foot (eg, heel or lateral foot), or in areas of trauma	Plantar surface of foot, especially over metatarsal heads, toes, and heel	Over bony prominences (eg, trochanter, coccyx, ankle)	Gaiter area, particularly medial malleolus
Size and shape	Shallow, well-defined borders	Wound margins with callus	Variable length, width, depth depending on stage (see staging system, p 263)	Edges may be irregular with depth limited to dermis or shallow subcutaneous tissue
Wound bed	Pale or necrotic	Granular tissue unless PAD present	Varies from bright red, shallow crater to deeper crater with slough and necrotic tissue; tunneling and undermining	Ruddy red; yellow slough may be present; undermining or tunneling uncommon
Exudate	Minimal amount due to poor blood flow	Variable amount; serous unless infection present	May be purulent, becoming serous as healing progresses; foul odor with infection	Copious; serous unless infection present
Surrounding skin	Halo of erythema or slight fluctuance indicates infection	Normal; may be calloused	May be distinct, diffuse, rolled under; erythema, edema, induration if infected	May appear macerated, crusted, or scaly; presence of stasis dermatitis, hyperpigmentation
Pain	Cramping or constant deep aching	Variable intensity; none with advanced neuropathy	Painful, unless sensory function impaired or with deep, extensive tissue necrosis	Variable; may be severe, dull, aching, or bursting in character

ARTERIAL ULCERS

Definition
Any lesion caused by severe tissue ischemia secondary to atherosclerosis and progressive arterial occlusion.

Wound Assessment
- See Chronic Wound Assessment (p 258).

- Assess ankle-brachial index (ABI): If ABI <0.5, wound healing unlikely without revascularization.

Management (see also PAD, p 54, and Diabetes, p 82)
Protect from Injury
- Avoid friction and pressure by using lamb's wool or foam between toes
- Use positioning devices to avoid pressure on feet (eg, heel protectors)
Local Wound Care
Treatment dictated by adequacy of perfusion and status of wound bed:
- Avoid debridement of necrotic tissue until perfusion status is determined.
- Assess vascular perfusion and refer for surgical intervention if consistent with overall goals of care.
- If wound is infected, revascularization procedures, surgical removal of necrotic tissue, and systemic antibiotics are treatments of choice.
- Topical antibiotics should not be used solely to treat infected ischemic wounds and may cause sensitivity reactions.
- If wound is uninfected and dry eschar is present, maintain dry intact eschar as a barrier to bacteria. Application of an antiseptic may decrease bacterial burden on wound surface although evidence is lacking.
- If wound is uninfected and soft slough and necrotic tissue are present, apply moisture-retaining dressings that allow frequent inspection of wound for signs of infection.

DIABETIC (NEUROPATHIC FOOT) ULCERS
Definition
Any lesion on the plantar surface of the foot caused by neuropathy and repetitive pressure on foot.

Wound Assessment
- See Chronic Wound Assessment (p 258).
- Assess for specific diabetes-related signs of infection:
  ○ Sudden increase in blood glucose
  ○ Wound can be probed to the bone—highly sensitive indicator of osteomyelitis
  ○ Exclude gross arterial disease by assessment for palpable pedal pulses, toe:brachial index >0.7 (or ankle:brachial index >0.9), a transcutaneous oxygen pressure of >30 mmHg, or normal Doppler-derived wave form.
- Determine grade of ulcer (Wagner Classification)
  Grade 0: Preulcerative lesions; healed ulcers present; bony deformity present
  Grade 1: Superficial ulcer without subcutaneous tissue involvement
  Grade 2: Penetration through subcutaneous tissue
  Grade 3: Osteitis, abscess, or osteomyelitis
  Grade 4: Gangrene of digit
  Grade 5: Gangrene of foot requiring disarticulation

Management (see also Diabetes, p 82)
Local Wound Care
In addition to recommendations under Chronic Wound Treatment (see p 258):
- Debride devitalized tissue and callus: surgical debridement is method of choice for effective, rapid removal of nonviable tissue
- Avoid occlusive dressings to reduce risk of wound infection
- Offload pressure and stress from foot
  - Avoidance of pressure on foot essential to management of diabetic foot ulcer
  - Use orthotic that redistributes weight on plantar surface of foot when ambulating (eg, total contact cast, *DH Pressure Relief Walker*)
- If ulcer does not reduce in size by ≥50% after 4 wk of therapy, reassess treatment and consider alternative options (eg, negative-pressure wound therapy, growth factor therapy, hyperbaric oxygen therapy).
  - Hyperbaric oxygen therapy effective in promoting healing of complicated chronic diabetic foot ulcers is covered by Medicare and some insurance companies. Caution in patients with HF, advanced COPD, and those treated wtih anticancer drugs. Treatments applied in chamber for 1.5–2 h/d for 20–40 d.

PRESSURE ULCERS
Definition
Any lesion caused by unrelieved pressure resulting in damage of underlying tissue; usually develops over bony prominence.

Wound Assessment
- See Chronic Wound Assessment (p 258).
- Determine level of tissue injury by using Pressure Ulcer Staging System:
  - **Stage I:** An observable pressure-related alteration of intact skin that, as compared with an adjacent or opposite area on the body, may include changes in one or more of the following: skin temperature (warmth or coolness), tissue consistency (firm or boggy feel), and/or sensation (pain, itching). The ulcer appears as a defined area of persistent redness in lightly pigmented skin, whereas in darker skin tones, it may appear with persistent red, blue, or purple hues.
  - **Stage II:** Partial-thickness skin loss involving epidermis and/or dermis; presents as abrasion, blister, or shallow crater.
  - **Stage III:** Full-thickness skin loss involving damage or necrosis of subcutaneous tissue that may extend down to, but not through, underlying fascia; presents as deep crater with or without undermining of adjacent tissue.
  - **Stage IV:** Full-thickness skin loss with extensive destruction; tissue necrosis; or damage to muscle, bone, or supporting structures. May have associated undermining of sinus tracts. *Note:* eschar-covered ulcers cannot be staged until eschar is removed.
  - **Suspected Deep Tissue Injury:** Localized area of purple or maroon discoloration of intact skin or blood-filled blister indicating underlying soft-tissue injury due to pressure and/or shear. May be preceded by pain, tissue firmness, mushiness, or bogginess; and cooler or warmer temperature than adjacent tissue.

Table 111. Wound and Pressure Ulcer Products, by Drainage and Stage							
	Drainage			Wound Stage			
Product	Light	Moderate	Heavy	I	II	III	IV
Transparent film	•			•	•		
Foam island	•	•			•	•	
Hydrocolloids	•	•			•	•	
Petroleum-based nonadherent	•				•	•	
Alginate		•	•				•
Hydrogel	•				•	•	
Gauze packing (moistened with saline)		•	•			•	•

Table 112. Common Dressings for Pressure Ulcer Treatment		
Dressing	Indications/Use	Contraindications
Transparent film (eg, *Bioclusive, Tegaderm, Op-site, Invacore, Mepore Film, Polyskin II, Reliamed, Uniflex*)	Stage I, II Protection from friction Superficial scrape Autolytic debridement of slough Apply skin prep to intact skin to protect from adhesive	Draining ulcers Suspicion of skin infection or fungus
Foam island (eg, *Allevyn, Lyofoam, COPA, Invacore*)	Stage II, III Low to moderate exudate Can apply as window to secure transparent film	Excessive exudate Dry, crusted wound
Hydrocolloids (eg, *DuoDERM, Extra thin film DuoDERM, Tegasorb, RepliCare, Comfeel, Nu-derm, Cutinova Hydro, Hydrocol II, MediHoney, Restore, Ultec*)	Stage II, III Low to moderate drainage Good periwound skin integrity Autolytic debridement of slough Leave in place 3–5 d Can apply as window to secure transparent film Can apply over alginate to control drainage Must control maceration Apply skin prep to intact skin to protect from adhesive	Poor skin integrity Infected ulcers Wound needs packing
Alginate (eg, *Sorbsan, Kaltostat, Algosteril, AlgiDERM*, Maxorb, *Nu-derm, Tegaderm*)	Stage III, IV Excessive drainage Apply dressing within wound borders Requires secondary dressing Must use skin prep Must control maceration	Dry or minimally draining wound Superficial wounds with maceration

(cont.)

Table 112. Common Dressings for Pressure Ulcer Treatment (cont.)

Dressing	Indications/Use	Contraindications
Hydrogel (amorphous gels) (eg, *IntraSite gel, SoloSite gel, Restore gel, AmeriGel, Biafine, Carrasmart, Carrysyn, Curafil Gel, Curasol Gel, Elta Dermal Gel, Gentell, Hypergel and Normigel, Purilon Gel, Saf-Gel, Tegaderm Wound Filler*)	Stage II, III, IV Needs to be combined with gauze dressing Stays moist longer than saline gauze Changed 1–2 times/d Used as alternative to saline gauze for packing deep wounds with tunnels, undermining Reduces adherence of gauze to wound Must control maceration	Macerated areas Wounds with excess exudate
(gel sheet) (eg, *Vigilon, Restore Impregnated Gauze, Tegagel, ClearSite, AQUASORB, FLEXDERM, NU-GEL, CURAGEL, Derma-Gel, FlexiGel*)	Stage II Needs to be held in place with topper dressing	Macerated areas Wounds with moderate to heavy exudate
Gauze packing▲ (moistened with saline) (eg, square 2 × 2s/ 4 × 4s, *Fluffed Kerlix, CURITY*)	Stage III, IV Wounds with depth, especially those with tunnels, undermining Must be remoistened often to maintain moist wound environment	
Silver dressings▲ (silver with alginates, gels, charcoal) (eg, *Silvercel, Silvadene, Aquacel Ag, Acticoat, Alleveyn Ag, Arglaes, Biostep, Colactive Ag, Contreet, InterDry Ag, Kendall AMD, Maxorb, Melgisorb, Meplix, Optifoam, Restore, Seasorb, Select Silver, SilvaSorb, SilverMed, Tegaderm*)	Malodorous wounds High level of exudates Wound highly suspicious for critical bacterial load Periwound with signs of inflammation Slow-healing wound	Systemic infection Cellulitis Signs of systemic side effects, especially erythema multiforme Fungal proliferation Sensitivity of skin to sun Interstitial nephritis Leukopenia Skin necrosis Concurrent use with proteolytic enzymes

Source: Copyright © 2012 by Rita Frantz. Used with permission.

Surgical Repair
Surgical referral is warranted for Stage IV pressure ulcers and for severely undermined or tunneled wounds.

VENOUS ULCERS

Definition
Any lesion caused by venous insufficiency precipitated by venous hypertension

Wound Assessment
- See Chronic Wound Assessment (p 258).
- Assess lower-extremity edema.
- Assess pedal pulses to exclude ischemic ulcers.

Management
Compression Therapy
- Essential component of venous ulcer treatment
- Provides externally applied pressure to lower extremity to facilitate normal venous return
- Therapeutic level of compression is 30–40 mmHg at ankle, decreasing toward knee
- Avoid compression therapy when ABI ≤0.8
- Types of compression therapy:
  - Static compression device
    - Layered compression wraps *(Profore, ProGuide, Dynapress)*
    - Short-stretch wraps *(Comprilan)*
    - Paste-containing bandages *(Unna's boot, Duke boot)*
      - Preferable for actively ambulating patient; support compression of calf muscle "pump"
  - Dynamic compression devices (indicated when static compression not feasible)
    - Pneumatic compression device (intermittent pneumatic pumps)
    - Powered devices that propel venous blood upward when applied to lower leg
  - Compression therapy for long-term maintenance
    - Therapeutic compression stockings *(Jobst, Juzo, Sig-Varis, Medi-Strumpf, Therapress Duo)*

Local Wound Care
In addition to recommendations under Chronic Wound Treatment (see p 258):
- Use exudate-absorbing dressings (eg, calcium alginate dressings, foam dressings)
- Use skin sealant to protect skin around wound from exudates
- Infected venous ulcers should be treated with systemic antibiotics because of development of resistant organisms with topical antibiotics.

Surgical Intervention
If manifestations of chronic venous insufficiency and ulceration are resistant to more conservative therapies or if venous obstruction is present, surgical repair (eg, skin graft) is treatment of choice.

CLASSIFICATION

- Circadian rhythm disorders (eg, jet lag)
- **Insomnia** (difficulty initiating or maintaining sleep, or poor quality sleep)
- Parasomnias (disorders of arousal, partial arousal, and sleep stage transition)
- Hypersomnea of central origin (eg, narcolepsy)
- **Sleep-related breathing disorders** (central and obstructive sleep apnea and sleep-related hypoventilation-hypoxia syndromes)
- **Sleep-related movement disorders** (eg, restless legs syndrome, periodic limb movement disorder)

Bolded disorders are covered here. Others are covered in *JAGS* 2009;57:761–789.

INSOMNIA

Risk Factors and Aggravating Factors

Treatable Associated Medical and Psychiatric Conditions: adjustment disorders, anxiety, bereavement, cough, depression, dyspnea (cardiac or pulmonary), GERD, nocturia, pain, paresthesias, Parkinson disease, stress, stroke

Medications That Cause or Aggravate Sleep Problems: alcohol, antidepressants, β-blockers, bronchodilators, caffeine, clonidine, corticosteroids, diuretics, levodopa, methyldopa, nicotine, phenytoin, progesterone, quinidine, reserpine, sedatives, sympathomimetics including decongestants

Management

- For most patients, behavioral therapy should be initial treatment.
- Combined behavioral and pharmacologic therapy is more effective than either alone.
- Sleep improvements are better sustained over time with behavioral treatment, including discontinuing pharmacologic therapy after acute therapy.

Nonpharmacologic

- Stimulus control
  Measures recommended to improve sleep hygiene:
  - During the daytime:
    - Get out of bed at the same time each morning regardless of how much you slept the night before.
    - Exercise daily but not within 2 h of bedtime.
    - Get adequate exposure to bright light during the day.
    - Decrease or eliminate naps, unless necessary part of sleeping schedule.
    - Limit or eliminate alcohol, caffeine, and nicotine, especially before bedtime.
  - At bedtime:
    - If hungry, have a light snack before bed (unless there are symptoms of GERD or it is otherwise medically contraindicated), but avoid heavy meals at bedtime.
    - Don't use bedtime as worry time. Write down worries for next day and then don't think about them.
    - Sleep only in your bedroom.

- Control nighttime environment, ie, comfortable temperature, quiet, dark.
  - Wear comfortable bedclothes.
  - If it helps, use soothing noise (eg, a fan or other appliance or a "white noise" machine).
  - Remove or cover the clock.
  - No television watching in the bedroom.
- Maintain a regular sleeping time, but don't go to bed unless sleepy.
- Develop a sleep ritual (eg, hot bath 90 min before bedtime followed by preparing for bed for 20–30 min, followed by 30–40 min of relaxation, meditation, or reading).
- If unable to fall asleep within 15–20 min, get out of bed and perform soothing activity, such as listening to soft music or reading (but avoid exposure to bright light or computer screens).
- Cognitive-behavioral therapy combines multiple behavioral approaches (eg, sleep restriction, stimulus control, cognitive therapy).
- Sleep restriction: reduce time in bed to estimated total sleep time (min 5 h) and increase by 15 min/wk when ratio of time asleep to time in bed is ≥90%.
- Relaxation techniques—physical (progressive muscle relaxation, biofeedback); mental (imagery training, meditation, hypnosis)
- Bright light: 2,500 lux for 2 h/d to 10,000 lux for 30 min/d

Pharmacologic—Principles of Prescribing Medications for Sleep Disorders:
- Use lowest effective dose.
- All increase risk of falls.
- Do not use OTC antihistamines to treat insomnia in older adults.
- For sleep-onset insomnia, use a shorter-acting agent (eg, zolpidem, zaleplon). For sleep-maintenance insomnia, use a longer-acting agent (eg, eszopiclone, zolpidem ER, doxepin).
- Use intermittent dosing (2–4 times/wk).
- Prescribe medications for short-term use (no more than 3–4 wk).
- D/C medication gradually.
- Be alert for rebound insomnia after discontinuation.

Table 113. Useful Medications for Sleep Disorders in Older Adults

Class, Medication	Usual Dose	Formulations	Half-life	Comments (Metabolism, Excretion)
Antidepressant, sedating				
Trazodone▲ (Desyrel)	25–100 mg	T: 50, 100, 150, 300	12 h	Moderate orthostatic effects; effective for insomnia with or without depression (L)
Benzodiazepines, intermediate-acting[a]				
Estazolam▲ (ProSom)	0.5–1 mg	T: 1, 2	12–18 h	Rapidly absorbed, effective in initiating sleep; slightly active metabolites that may accumulate (K)
Lorazepam▲ (Ativan)	0.25–2 mg	T: 0.5, 1, 2	8–12 h	Effective in initiating and maintaining sleep; associated with falls, memory loss, rebound insomnia (K)

(cont.)

Table 113. Useful Medications for Sleep Disorders in Older Adults (cont.)

Class, Medication	Usual Dose	Formulations	Half-life	Comments (Metabolism, Excretion)
Temazepam▲ (Restoril)	7.5–15 mg	C: 7.5, 15, 30	8–10 h[b]	Daytime drowsiness may occur with repeated use; effective for sleep maintenance; delayed onset of effect (K)
Nonbenzodiazepines, short-acting[a]				
Eszopiclone (Lunesta)	1–2 mg	T: 1, 2, 3	5–6 h	CYP3A4 interactions; avoid administration with high-fat meal; not for treatment of anxiety (L)
Zaleplon▲ (Sonata)	5 mg	C: 5, 10	1 h	Avoid taking with alcohol or food (L)
Zolpidem▲ (Ambien)	5 mg	T: 5, 10	1.5–4.5 h[c]	Confusion and agitation may occur but are rare (L)
(Ambien CR)	6.25 mg	T: 6.25, 12.5	1.6–5.5 h	Do not divide, crush, or chew
(Edluar)	5 mg	T: 5, 10 (sl)	2.8 h	
Hormone and Hormone Receptor Agonist				
Melatonin▲	0.3–5 mg	various	1 h	Not regulated by FDA
Ramelteon (Rozerem)	8 mg within 30 min of bedtime	T: 8	Ramelteon: 1–2.6 h; active metabolite: 2–5 h	Do not administer with or immediately after high-fat meal (L, K)
Antihistamine				
Doxepin (Silenor)	3–6 mg	T: 3, 6	15.3 h	May cause next-day sedation; many potential drug interactions

[a] May cause severe allergic reactions and complex sleep-related behavioral disturbances
[b] Can be as long as 30 h in older adults
[c] 3 h in older adults; 10 h in those with hepatic cirrhosis

SLEEP APNEA

Definition

Repeated episodes of apnea (cessation of airflow for ≥10 sec) or hypopnea (transient reduction [≥30% decrease in thoracoabdominal movement or airflow and with ≥4% oxygen desaturation, or an arousal] of airflow for ≥10 sec) during sleep with excessive daytime sleepiness or altered cardiopulmonary function.

Classification

Obstructive (OSA) (90% of cases): Airflow cessation as a result of upper airway closure in spite of adequate respiratory muscle effort

Central (CSA): Cessation of respiratory effort

Mixed: Features of both obstructive and central

Associated Risk Factors

Family hx, increased neck circumference, male gender, Asian ethnicity, hx of hypothyroidism (in women), obesity, smoking, upper airway structural abnormalities (eg, soft palate, tonsils), HTN, HF, atrial fibrillation, stroke

Clinical Features

Excessive daytime sleepiness, snoring, choking or gasping on awakening, morning headache, nocturia

Evaluation

- Epworth Sleepiness Scale (www.umm.edu/sleep/epworth_sleep.htm) is useful for documenting and monitoring daytime sleepiness.
- Full night's sleep study (polysomnography) in sleep laboratory is indicated for those who habitually snore and either report daytime sleepiness or have observed apnea.
- Results are reported as the apnea-hypopnea index (AHI), which is the number of episodes of apneas and hypopneas per hour of sleep.
- Medicare reimbursement threshold for CPAP based on a minimum of 2 h sleep by polysomnography is AHI (1) ≥15 or (2) ≥5 and ≤14 with documented symptoms of excessive daytime sleepiness, impaired cognition, mood disorders, or insomnia, or documented HTN, ischemic heart disease, or hx of stroke.

Management
Nonpharmacologic

- Weight loss (eg, using very low-calorie diet) with active lifestyle counseling is effective in mild OSA.
- Bariatric surgery improves but does not cure moderate or severe OSA.
- CPAP by nasal mask, nasal prongs, or mask that covers the nose and mouth is considered initial treatment for clinically important sleep apnea. A short course (14 d) of eszopiclone may facilitate adherence when initiating CPAP.
- Oral appliances that keep the tongue in an anterior position during sleep or keep the mandible forward; less effective than CPAP in reducing AHI but may be better tolerated. Generally used in mild to moderate OSA (AHI <30) for patients who do not want CPAP.
- For moderate sleep apnea (>15 and <30 AHI), oropharyngeal exercises, including tongue, soft palate, and lateral pharyngeal wall, performed daily improves symptoms and reduces AHI.
- Avoidance of alcohol or sedatives.
- Lying in lateral rather than supine position; may be facilitated by soft foam ball in a backpack.
- Weight loss (obese patients) via dieting or bariatric surgery.

Pharmacologic

- Modafinil (Provigil) 200 mg qam for excessive daytime sleepiness (CYP3A4 inducer and CYP2C19 inhibitor) [T: 100, 200]; use in addition to (not instead of) CPAP

Surgical

- Palatal implants (for mild to moderate OSA)
- Tracheostomy (indicated for patients with severe apnea who cannot tolerate positive pressure or when other interventions are ineffective)
- Uvulopalatopharyngoplasty (curative in fewer than 50% of cases)
- Maxillofacial surgery (rare cases)

SLEEP-RELATED MOVEMENT DISORDERS
Nocturnal Leg Cramps

Stretching exercises or use of heating pad 10 min before bedtime may be helpful. Despite evidence of effectiveness, quinine is not recommended for nocturnal leg cramps because of the potential for serious though uncommon adverse events. Small studies have supported the use of vitamin B complex and diltiazem. Gabapentin has been used but with little evidence to support its effectiveness.

Restless Legs Syndrome (RLS; the majority will also have periodic limb movement disorder)
Diagnostic Criteria
• A compelling urge to move the limbs, usually associated with paresthesias or dysesthesias
• Motor restlessness (eg, floor pacing, tossing and turning in bed, rubbing legs)
• Vague discomfort, usually bilateral, most commonly in calves
• Symptoms occur while awake and are exacerbated by rest, especially at night
• Symptoms relieved by movement—jerking, stretching, or shaking of limbs; pacing
Secondary Causes: Iron deficiency, spinal cord and peripheral nerve lesions, uremia, diabetes, Parkinson disease, venous insufficiency, medications/drugs (eg, TCAs, SSRIs, lithium, dopamine antagonists, caffeine)
Nonpharmacologic Treatment
• Sleep hygiene measures (see p 267).
• Avoid alcohol, caffeine, nicotine.
• Rub limbs.
• Use hot or cold baths, whirlpools.
Pharmacologic Treatment
• Exclude or treat iron deficiency, peripheral neuropathy. Some recommend a trial of iron therapy in all patients with RLS.
• If possible, avoid SSRIs, TCAs, lithium, and dopamine antagonists.
Start at low dosage, increase as needed:
• First line: dopamine agonists (preferred for daily symptoms) (see **Table 78**) or carbidopa-levodopa (preferred for intermittent symptoms) *(Sinemet)* 25/100 mg, 1–2 h before bedtime. Symptom augmentation may develop earlier in the day (eg, afternoon instead of evening) and may be more severe with carbidopa-levodopa; treatment may require reducing dosage or switching to dopamine agonist.
• Gabapentin may be beneficial if daily symptoms (see **Table 79**).
• Extended-release formulation, gabapentin enacarbil *(Horizant)* 600 mg [T: 600] daily at 5 PM, has been FDA approved for RLS.
• For refractory cases, gabapentin benzodiazepines (eg, clonazepam), benzodiazepine agonists, or low-potency opioids can be tried.

Periodic Limb Movement Disorder (a minority will also have RLS)
Diagnostic Criteria
• Insomnia or excessive sleepiness
• Repetitive, highly stereotyped limb muscle movements (eg, extension of big toes with partial flexion of ankle, knee, and sometimes hip) that occur during nonREM sleep
• Polysomnographic monitoring showing >15 episodes of muscle contractions per hour and associated arousals or awakenings
• No evidence of a medical, mental, or other sleep disorder that can account for symptoms
Treatment: Indicated for clinically significant sleep disruption or frequent arousals documented on a sleep study.
• Nonpharmacologic: See sleep hygiene measures, p 267.
• Pharmacologic: See RLS, pharmacologic treatment, above.

Rapid-Eye Movement (REM) Sleep Behavior Disorder

- Loss of atonia during REM sleep (ranging from simple limb twitches to acting out dreams), exaggeration of features of REM sleep (eg, nightmares), and intrusion of aspects of REM sleep into wakefulness (eg, sleep paralysis)
- High risk of developing neurodegenerative disorder (eg, Parkinson disease, multisystem atrophy, Lewy body dementia)

Pharmacologic Treatment: clonazepam 0.25–1 mg hs, high-dose melatonin 3–6 mg; if associated with Parkinson disease, levodopa or pramipexole

SLEEP DISORDERS IN LONG-TERM–CARE FACILITIES
Risk Factors

- Medical and medication factors (see insomnia, p 267)
- Environmental factors (eg, little physical activity, infrequent daytime bright light exposure, extended periods in bed, nighttime noise and light interruptions)

Nonpharmacologic Treatment

- Morning bright light therapy
- Exercise (eg, stationary bicycle, Tai Chi) and physical activity
- Reduction of nighttime noise and light interruptions
- Multicomponent interventions combining the above and a bedtime routine

SUBSTANCE USE DISORDERS

SCOPE OF THE PROBLEM
- Alcohol abuse is the primary substance abuse problem of those ≥50 yr old.
- Baby boomers are likely to maintain higher alcohol consumption than the current cohort of older people.
- 10% of people >65 yr old (12% of men, 8% of women) are current smokers.
- Marijuana use is higher than use of any other illicit drug among baby boomers.
- Although supporting data are sparse, prescription drug misuse is an important problem in the older population.

ALCOHOL USE DISORDERS
Hazardous or At-Risk Drinking
- Will probably eventually cause harm
- No current alcohol problems; whether or not the definitions applied to the general adult population apply to older adults is not clear.
- The World Health Organization defines at-risk drinking as drinking more than the recommended limit (14 units/wk in men, 7 units/wk in women) or binge drinking (8 units/d in men, 6 units/d in women); 1 unit = 14 g of alcohol = 1 glass of wine or 1 beer or 1 oz of spirits
- The National Institute on Alcohol Abuse and Alcoholism (NIAAA) defines at-risk drinking for both men and women >65 yr old as >3 units on any one occasion or >7 units/wk.

Harmful Drinking
- Already causing damage to physical or mental health
- Damage may be acute (eg, acute pancreatitis) or chronic (eg, alcohol-related brain damage).
- Do not usually seek treatment.

Dependent Drinking (≥3 of the following in the previous year)
- A strong desire or compulsion to drink
- Difficulty controlling drinking
- Physiologic withdrawal syndrome (tremors, sweating, anxiety, nausea and vomiting, agitation, insomnia)
- Evidence of tolerance
- Neglect of other pursuits because of drinking
- Persistent drinking despite clear evidence of harm

Evaluation
Alcohol use disorders are often missed in older adults because of reduced social and occupational functioning; signs more often are poor self-care, malnutrition, and medical illness.

Alcohol Misuse Screening: CAGE questionnaire has been validated in the older population.

C Have you ever felt you should **C**ut down?

A Does others' criticism of your drinking **A**nnoy you?

G Have you ever felt **G**uilty about drinking?

E Have you ever had an "**E**ye opener" to steady your nerves or get rid of a hangover? *(Positive response to any suggests problem drinking.)*

Detecting Harmful or Hazardous Drinking:

May be missed by CAGE; ask:

- How many days per week?
- How many drinks on those days?
- Maximal intake on any one day?
- What type (ie, beer, wine, or liquor)?
- What is in "a drink"?

Aggravating Factors

Alcohol and Aging: Higher blood concentrations per amount consumed due to decreased lean body mass and total body water; concomitant medications may interact with alcohol. Abstain if cognitively impaired, on medications that interact, or comorbidities or disability are present.

Age-related Diseases: Cognitive impairment, HTN.

Medications: Many drug interactions, eg, APAP, anesthetics, antihypertensives, antihistamines, antipsychotics, narcotic analgesics, NSAIDs, sedatives, antidepressants, anticonvulsant medications, nitrates, β-blockers, oral hypoglycemic agents, anticoagulants.

Management of Alcohol Misuse/Abuse
Psychosocial Interventions:

- Hazardous or harmful drinking: Brief intervention; educate patient on effects of current drinking, point out current adverse events, specify safe drinking limits. Patients who cannot moderate should abstain.
- Dependent drinking: Self-help groups (eg, Alcoholics Anonymous); professional help (eg, psychodynamic, cognitive-behavioral, counseling, social support, family therapy, age-specific inpatient or outpatient).
- The NIAAA provides an online resource: Helping Patients Who Drink Too Much: A Clinician's Guide (www.niaaa.nih.gov/Publications/EducationTrainingMaterials/guide.htm).

Drug Therapy: Is useful only when used as an adjunct to psychosocial therapy.

- Naltrexone▲ *(Depade, REVIA, Trexan)* 25 mg × 2 d po, then 50 mg/d [T: 50]; *(Vivitrol)* 380 mg IM monthly; monitor LFTs, avoid in kidney failure, hepatitis, cirrhosis, and with opioid use; ~10% get nausea, headache (L, K).
- Acamprosate *(Campral)* 666 mg q8h po, reduce dosage to 333 mg q8h if CrCl 30–50 mL/min or weight <132 lb (60 kg) [T: 333]; contraindicated if CrCl <30 mL/min; diarrhea is most common adverse drug event (K). Large US trials have not shown efficacy.
- Topiramate 300 mg/d po is effective at reducing relapse. The magnitude of the effect may be greater than with either acamprosate or naltrexone.
- The duration of drug therapy should be at least 3 mo, or up to 12 mo, which is the period when relapse is highest.
- Combining these agents does not improve effectiveness.
- If significant depression persists after 1 wk of abstinence, treatment for depression improves outcomes.

Acute Alcohol Withdrawal: See p 61.

SMOKING CESSATION

Nonpharmacologic Therapy

What Health Providers Should Do:

• **Ask** about tobacco use at every visit. **Advise** all users to quit. **Assess** willingness to quit. **Assist** the patient with a quit plan, education, pharmacotherapy.

Making the Decision to Quit:

Patients are more likely to stop smoking if they believe they could get a smoking-related disease and can make an honest attempt at quitting, that the benefits of quitting outweigh the benefits of continued smoking, or if they know someone who has had health problems as a result of smoking.

Setting a Quit Date and Deciding on a Plan:

Pick a specific day within the next month (gives time to develop a plan). Will nicotine replacement therapy be used? Will the patient attend a smoking cessation class? On quit day, get rid of all cigarettes and related items.

Managing Symptoms of Withdrawal:

• **Physical:** Pharmacotherapy (**Table 114**) helps physical symptoms.

  ○ Nicotine replacement, bupropion, and varenicline are all effective in improving quit rates.

  ▪ Nicotine replacement is contraindicated with recent MI, uncontrolled high BP, arrhythmias, severe angina, gastric ulcer

  ▪ May not be needed if patient smokes fewer than 10 cigarettes/d.

  ▪ The long-term benefits of combining pharmacotherapies remain uncertain.

• **Psychological:**

  ○ Avoid people and places where tempted to smoke.

  ○ Alter habits: 1) switch to juices or water instead of alcohol or coffee, 2) take a walk instead of a coffee break, 3) use oral substitutions, eg, sugarless gum or hard candy.

  ○ Effective interventions include advice from health care provider to quit, self-help materials, proactive telephone counseling, group counseling, individual counseling, intra-treatment social support (from a clinician), extra-treatment social support (family, friends, coworkers, and smoke-free home).

Maintaining Smoking Cessation: Use the same methods that helped during withdrawal.
Source: Adapted from www.goldcopd.org (2010).

Table 114. Pharmacotherapy for Tobacco Abuse

Drug	Dosage	Formulations	Comments (Metabolism, Excretion)
Tobacco Abuse			
Bupropion▲ *(Wellbutrin SR, Zyban)*	150 mg q12h × 7–12 wk	SR: 100, 150	Contraindicated with seizure disorders (L)
Varenicline *(Chantix)* [a]	0.5 mg × 3 d, 0.5 mg q12h × 4 d, then 1 mg q12h × 12–24 wk or longer	0.5, 1	Adverse events: nausea, vivid dreams, constipation, depression, suicide (L, K); reduce dosage if CrCl <30 mL/min

(cont.)

Table 114. Pharmacotherapy for Tobacco Abuse (cont.)

Drug	Dosage	Formulations	Comments (Metabolism, Excretion)
Nicotine Replacement			
Transdermal patches▲ (eg, *Habitrol, NicoDerm*)	21 mg/d × 4–8 wk[b] 14 mg/d × 2–4 wk 7 mg/d × 2–4 wk	7, 14, 21	Apply to clean, nonhairy skin on upper torso, rotate sites; start 14 mg/d with cardiovascular disease or body wt <100 lb or if smoking <10 cigarettes/d (L)
(Nicotrol)	15 mg/d × 8 wk[b] 10 mg/d × 4–6 wk 5 mg/d × 4–6 wk	5, 10, 15	Gradually released over 16 h (L)
(ProStep)	22 mg/d × 4–8 wk[b] 11 mg/d × 4–8 wk	11, 22	People <100 lb start at lower dosage; reduce or D/C after 4–8 wk (L)
Polacrilex gum▲ *(Nicorette)*	9–12 pieces/d	2, 4	Chew 1 piece when urge to smoke; usual 10–12/d, max 30/d; 4 mg if smoking >21 cigarettes/d (L)
Nasal spray *(Nicotrol NS)*[c]	1 spr each nostril q30–60min	0.5 mg/spr	Do not exceed 5 applications/h or 40 in 24 h (L)
Inhaler *(Nicotrol Inhaler)*[c]	6–16 cartridges/d	4 mg delivered/ cartridge	Max 16 cartridges/d with gradual reduction after 6–12 wk if needed (L)
Lozenge	1 po prn	2, 4	Do not exceed 20/d; do not bite or chew; wean over 12 wk
Lollipop[c]	1 po prn	1, 2, 3, 4	Place in mouth when urge to smoke; remove when craving passes; gradually reduce dose over 4–8 wk; do not exceed 7/d

[a] Partial nicotine agonist that eases withdrawal and blocks effects of nicotine if patients resume smoking.

[b] The next lower dosage is less toxic and probably equally effective.

[c] Available by prescription only.

PRESCRIPTION DRUG MISUSE

Definition

Use of a drug that was not prescribed, or using a drug for an experience or feelings it causes rather than for treatment of a medical condition

Commonly Abused Prescription Medications

Although many prescription medications can be abused, according to the National Institute of Drug Abuse, the following 3 classes are abused most commonly:

- Opioids—usually prescribed to treat pain
- CNS depressants—used to treat anxiety and sleep disorders
- Stimulants—prescribed to treat attention deficit hyperactivity disorder and narcolepsy

Adverse Events

- Benzodiazepines: falls, mobility and ADL disability, cognitive impairment, motor vehicle accidents, pressure ulcers, UI
- Nonbenzodiazepine sedatives: anxiety, depression, nervousness, hallucinations, dizziness, headache, sleep-related behavioral disturbances
- Opioids: falls and fractures

Assessing for Risk of Medication Misuse/Abuse

- General risk factors include use of a psychoactive drug with abuse potential, use of other substances (alcohol, tobacco, etc), female gender, possibly social isolation, and hx of mental health disorder.
- Addiction to opioids is rare in those without prior hx of substance abuse.
- Screen for risk of opioid misuse/abuse with the Opioid Risk Tool (see p 294); this instrument differentiates low-risk from high-risk patients.

Detection of Medication Misuse/Abuse

- Detection relies on clinical judgment; monitor at-risk patients when prescribing benzodiazepines, stimulants, and opioid analgesics.
- Observe for behavior that may suggest nonadherence to prescribed medication schedule (eg, early fill request, frequent lost prescriptions).
- Record any suspicious drug-seeking or other aberrant behaviors observed or reported by others, along with actions taken.
- Document evaluation process, rationale for long-term therapy, and periodic review of patient status.

Treatment for Prescription Drug Abuse/Misuse

- Opioids
  - May need to undergo medically supervised detoxification
  - Gradual tapering of opioids is necessary (see Adjustment of Dosage, p 209).
  - Behavioral treatments, usually combined with medications (methadone, buprenorphine), *are* effective.
  - Opioid abuse-deterrent products (eg, *Embeda*) may reduce diversion. These agents do not have street value because they release naltrexone if not used as intended.
- CNS depressants or stimulants
  - Primary provider encouragement to reduce use
  - Short-term substitution of other medications (eg, trazodone) for sleep
  - Gradual slow tapering of the drug
  - Cognitive-behavioral therapies (CBT) that teach patients skills to cope more effectively with problems; if drug is used for sleep, specific CBT techniques are available (see Sleep Disorders, p 267).

COMMON DISORDERS

Breast Cancer

• Mammography (see **Table 92**)

Also assess breast cancer risk using http://cancer.gov/bcrisktool; then consider prophylaxis for women at moderate to high risk with the agents in **Table 115**.

Table 115. Agents that Reduce Breast Cancer Risk and Alter Other Outcomes

Outcomes	Agents			
	Tamoxifen	**Raloxifene**	**Exemestane**	**Bisphosphonates**
Invasive breast cancer	↓	↓	↓	↓[a]
Noninvasive breast cancer	↓	—	↓	↑[a]
Endometrial cancer	↑	↓	—	—
DVT risk	↑↑	↑	—	—
BMD	↑[b]	↑	↓	↑

[a] Data from the Women's Health Initiative
[b] Increases BMD in postmenopausal women and decreases BMD in premenopausal women

Monitoring:

• History, physical examination q6mo for 5 yr, then annually

• Increase surveillance for second primary in breasts, ovaries, colon, and rectum

• Annual mammography and monthly breast self-examination

• Annual pelvic examination for patients on tamoxifen (risk of uterine cancer)

Oral Hormone Adjuvant Therapy: Postmenopausal women with estrogen-receptor- or progesterone-receptor-positive tumors at high risk of recurrence (tumors >1 cm, or positive nodes) should be treated with oral adjuvant therapy. Therapy should include an aromatase inhibitor, which may be the initial treatment. Options include an aromatase inhibitor for 5 yr, or sequential treatment with tamoxifen for 2–3 yr followed by an aromatase inhibitor to complete 5 yr, or tamoxifen for 4.5–6 yr followed by an aromatase inhibitor for 5 yr. See **Table 116**.

Adjuvant Chemotherapy: Is used after resection. Reduces risk of recurrence and improves survival, especially when risk of recurrence is >10% at 10 yr. Recurrence is reduced by 30%–50% with greater benefit in estrogen-receptor-poor or absent breast cancer.

Therapy for Metastatic Bone Disease: Pamidronate or zoledronic acid reduces morbidity and delays time to onset of bone symptoms. Consult oncology.

Table 116. Oral Agents for Breast Cancer Treatment

Class, Medication	Dosage and Formulations	Monitoring	Adverse Events, Interactions (Metabolism)
Antiestrogen Drugs			
Fulvestrant (Faslodex)	250 mg/mo IM in 1 or 2 injections Inj: 250 mg/5 mL; 125 mg/2.5 mL	Blood chemistry, lipids	Metabolized through CYP3A4; GI reactions, anesthesia, pain (back, pelvic, headache), hot flushes (L)
Tamoxifen▲ᵃ (Nolvadex)	20 mg/d po T: 10, 20	Annual eye examination; endometrial cancer screening	Activated through CYP2D6; avoid fluoxetine, paroxetine, buproprion, duloxetine, and other potent CYPD26 inhibitors that reduce tamoxifen activity; ↑ risk of thrombosis (L)
Toremifene (Fareston)	60 mg/d po T: 60	CBC, Ca, LFTs, BUN, Cr	Drug interactions: CYP3A4–6 inhibitors and inducers (see **Table 10**); ↑ warfarin effect (L)
Aromatase Inhibitors			
Anastrozole (Arimidex)	1 mg/d po T: 1	Periodic CBC, lipids, serum chemistry profile	Common: arthritis, arthralgia, bone pain, asthenia, cough, dyspnea, pharyngitis, depression, headache, nausea, rash, edema. Less common: anemia, leukopenia, thromboembolism, thrombophlebitis, hypercholesterolemia, fractures, vaginal hemorrhage (L)
Exemestane (Aromasin)	25 mg/d po T: 25	Periodic WBC count with differential, lipids, serum chemistry profile	Common: anxiety, depression, fatigue, insomnia, dyspnea, hot flushes, weight gain, nausea, pain at tumor site. Rare: myocardial infarction (L)
Letrozole (Femara)	2.5 mg/d po T: 2.5	Periodic CBC, LFTs, TSH	Common: arthralgia, back pain, bone pain, dyspnea, hot flushes, nausea. Less common: fracture, myocardial infarction or ischemia, pancytopenia, thromboembolism, pleural effusion, pulmonary embolism. Metabolized by CYP3A4, CYP2A6; strongly inhibits CYP2A6 and moderately inhibits CYP2C19 (L)

ᵃ Reduce dosage if CrCl <10 mL/min

Vulvar Diseases
Non-neoplastic:

• Lichen sclerosus—Common on vulva of middle-aged and older women; causes 1/3 of benign vulvar lesions, extends to perirectal areas (classic hourglass appearance); lesions are white to pink macules or papules, may coalesce; asymptomatic or itching, soreness, or dyspareunia. Must biopsy for diagnosis. Lichen sclerosus is a precursor to vulvar interepithelial neoplasia (VIN). Associated with squamous cell cancer in 4%–5%. Treatment: clobetasol propionate 0.05% q12–24h for 8–12 wk; then taper gradually to zero. Long-term follow-up advised.

• Squamous hyperplasia—Raised white keratinized lesions difficult to distinguish from VIN; must biopsy to exclude malignancy. Treatment: betamethasone dipropionate 0.05% for 6–8 wk, then 1% hydrocortisone if symptoms persist. Long-term follow-up advised.

Neoplastic:
- VIN—Most often seen in postmenopausal women; asymptomatic or may cause pruritus; hypo- or hyperpigmented keratinized lesions; often multifocal; inspection ± colposcopy of the entire vulva with biopsy of most worrisome lesions; lesions graded on degree of atypia. Treatment: surgical or other ablative therapy. Imiquimod 5% topical crm often effective in human papillomavirus-positive patient.
- Vulvar malignancy—Half of cases are in women >70 yr old; 80% are squamous cell, with melanoma, sarcoma, basal cell, and adenocarcinoma <20%; biopsy any suspicious lesion. Treatment: radical surgery is preferred treatment.

Postmenopausal Bleeding
Bleeding after 1 yr of amenorrhea:
- Exclude malignancy, identify source, treat symptoms.
- Examine genitalia, perineum, rectum.
- If endometrial source, use endometrial biopsy or vaginal probe ultrasound to assess endometrial thickness (<5 mm virtually excludes malignancy).
- D&C when endometrium not otherwise adequately assessed.
- Evaluation is needed for:
  - Women on combination continual estrogen and progesterone who bleed after 12 mo.
  - Women on cyclic replacement with bleeding at unexpected times (ie, bleeding other than during the second week of progesterone therapy).
  - Women on unopposed estrogen who bleed at any time.

Vaginal Prolapse
- Child-bearing and other causes of increased intra-abdominal pressure weaken connective tissue and muscles supporting the genital organs, leading to prolapse.
- Symptoms include pelvic pressure, back pain, fecal or urinary incontinence, difficulty evacuating the rectum. Symptoms may be present even with mild prolapse.
- The degree of prolapse and organs involved dictate therapy; no therapy if asymptomatic.
- Estrogen and Kegel exercises (p 140) may help in mild cases.
- Pessary or surgery indicated with increase in symptoms. Surgery needed for fourth-degree symptomatic prolapse.
- Precise anatomic defect(s) dictates the surgical approach. Surgical closure of the vagina is a simple option for frail patients who are not sexually active.
- A common classification (ACOG) for degrees of prolapse:
  - First degree—extension to mid-vagina
  - Second degree—approaching hymenal ring
  - Third degree—at hymenal ring
  - Fourth degree—beyond hymenal ring

HORMONE THERAPY

Symptoms Associated with the Postmenopausal State

- Hot flushes and night sweats
- Sleep disturbances
- Vaginal dryness and dyspareunia
- Depression
- Insufficient evidence exists to link the following commonly reported symptoms to the postmenopausal state: cognitive disturbances, fatigue, sexual dysfunction.

Therapy for Menopausal Symptoms

- Vasomotor and vaginal symptoms respond to estrogen (see **Table 118**) in dose-response fashion; start at low dosage, titrate to effect. Dyspareunia and vaginal dryness respond to topical estrogen (see **Table 119**).
- "Bioidentical hormone therapy" refers to the use of naturally occurring (rather than synthetic or animal-derived) forms of progesterone, estradiol, and estriol. These preparations are compounded by pharmacies and readily available over the Internet but are not FDA approved. The FDA and the Endocrine Society believe there is insufficient evidence to evaluate the safety and efficacy of these agents relative to FDA-approved hormone therapies.

Risk of Hormone Therapy

- Risks associated with HT use may vary based on the length of time between menopause and initiation of HT. For information on the risks and benefits of HT initiated within the first 5 yr after menopause, see the position statement of the North American Menopause Society (www.menopause.org/PSht10.pdf).
- For current understanding of risks for women who start HT ≥10 yr after menopause (generally >63 yr old), see **Table 117**.
- If the woman has a uterus, estrogen combined with progesterone reduces risk of endometrial cancer but increases breast cancer risk and mortality.
- Some women prefer unopposed estrogen and annual endometrial biopsy.
- For common regimens, see **Table 118**.
- Older women can get hot flushes if estrogen is discontinued suddenly. Tapering (eg, q48h for 1–2 mo and then q72h for a few months) is better tolerated.
- The fracture-protective effect from HT is lost rapidly after discontinuation; women at risk of fracture should be evaluated and treated with alternative therapy (see Osteoporosis, p 198).

Table 117. Risks and Benefits of Systemic Hormone Therapy Initiated After Age 63		
Systemic Outcome	**Estrogen**	**Estrogen/Progesterone**
MI	none	↑
Thromboembolic disease	↑ DVT	↑ DVT, PE
Stroke	↑	↑
Breast cancer	↓	↑[a]
Hip fracture	↓	↓
Colon cancer	none	uncertain
Kidney stones	↑	↑
Endometrial cancer	↑	no change or ↓

(cont.)

Systemic Outcome	Estrogen	Estrogen/Progesterone
Gallbladder disease	↑	↑
Urogenital disease[b]	↓	↓
Dementia	possibly ↑	↑
Ovarian cancer	↑	↑

Note: ↑ = increased risk; ↓ = decreased risk

[a] Both incidence and breast cancer mortality are increased.

[b] Dyspareunia, UTI, and vaginal dryness; oral HT worsens urinary incontinence

Contraindications to Hormone Therapy

- Undiagnosed vaginal bleeding
- Thromboembolic disease
- Breast cancer
- Prior stroke or TIA
- Endometrial cancer more advanced than Stage 1
- Possibly gallbladder disease
- CHD

Intolerable Vasomotor Symptoms

- 10% of women continue with vasomotor symptoms 12 yr after menopause.
- Note contraindications above.
- Assess risk of venous thromboembolism (VTE) and cardiovascular disease:
  - VTE risk increased by history of VTE, malignancy/myeloproliferative disorder, leg immobilization, or both smoking and obesity.
  - Cardiovascular disease risk increased by known CAD, PAD, abdominal aortic aneurysm, carotid artery disease, diabetes mellitus, or risk factors that confer a 10-yr risk of coronary disease >20% (http://hp2010.nhlbihin.net/atpiii/calculator.asp?usertype=prof)
- If increased cardiovascular or VTE risk, then oral standard dosage estrogen-progestin should not be used.
- If increased cardiovascular risk (but not VTE risk), attempt to control symptoms with transdermal estrogen.
- If risk of VTE is increased and risk of cardiovascular disease is usual and patient has no uterus, transdermal estrogen may be appropriate; if patient has uterus, adding a progestin raises additional concerns.
- If neither VTE nor cardiovascular disease risk is increased, estrogen or estrogen-progestin may be appropriate given orally or transdermally at lowest dosage to control symptoms.
- Continue to advocate tapering (see p 281) at 2-yr intervals.
- If estrogen cannot be taken or if risks exceed benefits, try one of the less effective alternatives for vasomotor symptoms; the following dosages have been studied:
  - SSRIs: citalopram 10–30 mg/d; escitalopram 10–20 mg/d; fluoxetine 10–30 mg/d; sertraline 25–250 mg/d; paroxetine 12.5–25 mg/d. Avoid these agents if patients are receiving tamoxifen; tamoxifen levels will be subtherapeutic.
  - SNRIs: venlafaxine 75 mg/d; desvenlafaxine 50–200 mg/d
  - Anticonvulsants: gabapentin 900–2700 mg/d
  - α_2-Adrenergic agonists: clonidine 0.5–1.5 mg/d; watch for orthostatic hypotension and rebound increase in BP if used intermittently.

Table 118. Common Regimens for Systemic Hormone Therapy

Preparation	Starting Dosage (mg/d)	Cyclic Dosing	Continual Dosing	Formulations
Oral				
Conjugated equine estrogen (Premarin)*	0.3–0.625	—	Daily	T: 0.3, 0.625, 0.9, 1.25, 2.5
Conjugated synthetic estrogen (Cenestin)	0.625	—	Daily	T: 0.625, 0.9, 1.25
Esterified estrogen (eg, Estratab, Menest)*	0.3–0.625	—	Daily	T: 0.3, 0.625, 1.25, 2.5
Estradiol acetate▲ (Femtrace)	0.45	—	Daily	T: 0.45, 0.9, 1.8
Estropipate (Ogen, Ortho-Est)*	0.625	—	Daily	T: 0.625, 1.25, 2.5
Micronized 17-β estradiol (Estrace)*	0.5–1	—	Daily	T: 0.5, 1, 2
Synthetic conjugated estrogens, B (Enjuvia)	0.625	—	Daily	T: 0.625, 1.25
Oral Combinations				
Conjugated estrogen and medroxyprogesterone (Prempro)	0.625, 0.45 1.5, 2.5, 5	—	Daily	Fixed dose 0.625/2.5 or 0.625/5 or 0.45/1.5
Conjugated estrogen and medroxyprogesterone (Premphase)	0.625 5	Days 1–28 Days 15–28	—	Fixed dose 0.625 days 1–14, 0.625/5 days 15–28
Estradiol and norethindrone▲ (FEMHRT 1/5)	1/5	—	Daily	Fixed dose 1/5
Transdermal				
Estradiol▲				
(Alora)	0.05	—	Biweekly	Pch: 0.05, 0.075, 0.1
(Climara)	0.025–0.05	—	Weekly	Pch: 0.025, 0.05, 0.06, 0.075, 0.1
(Divigel)	0.25	—	Daily	Gel: 0.25, 0.5, 1
(Elestrin)	0.52	—	Daily	Gel: 0.06%
(Estraderm)	0.05	—	Biweekly	Pch: 0.05, 0.1
(Estrogel)	0.75	—	Daily	Gel: 0.06%
(Evamist)	1–3 sprays	—	Daily (applied to inside of forearm)	1.7% sol (1.53 mg estradiol per spray)
(Fempatch)	0.025	—	Weekly	Pch: 0.025
(Vivelle)	0.025	—	Biweekly	Pch: 0.025, 0.0375, 0.05, 0.075, 0.1
Estradiol and norethindrone (CombiPatch)	0.05/0.14	—	Biweekly	Pch: 0.05/0.14, 0.05/0.25

(cont.)

Table 118. Common Regimens for Systemic Hormone Therapy (cont.)

Preparation	Starting Dosage (mg/d)	Cyclic Dosing	Continual Dosing	Formulations
Other				
Femring	0.05	—	Vaginal ring, change q90d	0.05, 0.10
Medroxyprogesterone▲ (Cycrin, Provera)	2.5–10	5–10 mg, days 1–14	2.5–5 mg/d	T: 2.5, 5, 10

*FDA approved for long-term use to prevent osteoporosis.

Table 119. Topical Estrogens Without Systemic Effects

Estrogen	Dosage
Estrogen cream (Premarin, Ogen, Estrace)	Use min dose (0.5 g for Premarin, 2 g for Ogen and Estrace) daily × 2 wk, then 1–3 times/wk thereafter
Estradiol vaginal ring (Estring)	Insert intravaginally and change q90d
Estradiol vaginal tablets (Vagifem)	Insert 25 mcg intravaginally daily × 2 wk, then twice/wk

Some assessment instuments commonly used in geriatrics practice are included on the following pages. These instruments, as well as some additional ones, are available on the *Geriatrics At Your Fingertips* Web site (see www.geriatricsatyourfingertips.org).

MINI-COG™ SCREEN FOR DEMENTIA

The Mini-Cog™ combines an uncued 3-item recall test with a clock-drawing test (CDT) that serves as the recall distractor. The Mini-Cog™ can be administered in about 3 min, requires no special equipment, and is less influenced by level of education or language differences than many other screens.

Administration

1. Get the patient's attention. Then instruct him or her to listen carefully to, repeat back to you, and remember (now and later) 3 unrelated words. You may present the same words up to 3 times if necessary.

2. Using a blank piece of paper or one with a circle already drawn on it, ask the patient to draw the face of a clock and fill in all the numbers. After he or she adds the numbers, ask him or her to draw the hands to read a specific time (11:10 or 8:20 are most commonly used; other times that use both halves of the clock face may be effective). You can repeat these instructions, but give no additional instructions or hints. If the patient cannot complete the CDT in 3 min or less, move on to the next step.

3. Ask the patient to repeat the 3 previously presented words. Score this step even if the patient was not able to repeat the words in step 1.

Scoring

Give 1 point for each recalled word after the CDT distractor. Score 0–3 for recall.

Give 2 points for a normal CDT, and 0 points for an abnormal CDT. The CDT is considered normal if all numbers are depicted, once each, in the correct sequence and position around the circle, and the hands readably display the requested time. Do not count equal hand length as an error. Add the recall and CDT scores together to get the Mini-Cog score:

- 0–2   positive screen for dementia.
- 3–5   negative screen for dementia.

Sources: Adapted from Borson S, Scanlan J, Brush M, Vitaliano P, Dokmak A. The Mini-Cog: a cognitive "vital signs" measure for dementia screening in multi-lingual elderly. *Int J Geriatr Psychiatry*, 2000; 15(11):1021–1027; Borson S, Scanlan JM, Watanabe J, Tu SP, Lessig M. Improving identification of cognitive impairment in primary care. *Int J Geriatr Psychiatry*, 2006;21(4):349–355; and Lessig M, Scanlan JM, Nazemi H, Borson S. Time that tells: Critical clock drawing errors for dementia screening. *Int Psychogeriatr*, 2008; 20(3):459–470.

Mini-Cog™ Copyright S Borson. All rights reserved. Reprinted with permission of the author solely for use as a clinical aid. Any other use is strictly prohibited. To obtain information on the Mini-Cog™ contact Dr. Borson at soob@u.washington.edu.

PHYSICAL SELF-MAINTENANCE SCALE (ACTIVITIES OF DAILY LIVING, OR ADLS)

In each category, circle the item that most closely describes the person's highest level of functioning and record the score assigned to that level (either 1 or 0) in the blank at the beginning of the category.

A. Toilet
1. Care for self at toilet completely; no incontinence . . . . .1 ___
2. Needs to be reminded, or needs help in cleaning self, or has rare (weekly at most) accidents. 0
3. Soiling or wetting while asleep more than once a week 0
4. Soiling or wetting while awake more than once a week 0
5. No control of bowels or bladder 0

B. Feeding
1. Eats without assistance. . . . . .1 ___
2. Eats with minor assistance at meal times and/or with special preparation of food, or help in cleaning up after meals 0
3. Feeds self with moderate assistance and is untidy 0
4. Requires extensive assistance for all meals 0
5. Does not feed self at all and resists efforts of others to feed him or her 0

C. Dressing
1. Dresses, undresses, and selects clothes from own wardrobe . . . . .1 ___
2. Dresses and undresses self with minor assistance 0
3. Needs moderate assistance in dressing and selection of clothes. 0
4. Needs major assistance in dressing but cooperates with efforts of others to help. 0
5. Completely unable to dress self and resists efforts of others to help 0

D. Grooming (neatness, hair, nails, hands, face, clothing)
1. Always neatly dressed and well-groomed without assistance . . . . .1 ___
2. Grooms self adequately with occasional minor assistance, eg, with shaving. 0
3. Needs moderate and regular assistance or supervision with grooming .0
4. Needs total grooming care but can remain well-groomed after help from others. 0
5. Actively negates all efforts of others to maintain grooming 0

E. Physical Ambulation
1. Goes about grounds or city . . . . .1 ___
2. Ambulates within residence on or about one block distant. 0
3. Ambulates with assistance of (check one)
   a ( ) another person, b ( ) railing, c ( ) cane, d ( ) walker, e ( ) wheelchair 0
   1.___ Gets in and out without help. 2.___Needs help getting in and out
4. Sits unsupported in chair or wheelchair but cannot propel self without help 0
5. Bedridden more than half the time 0

F. Bathing
1. Bathes self (tub, shower, sponge bath) without help. . . . . .1 ___
2. Bathes self with help getting in and out of tub. 0
3. Washes face and hands only but cannot bathe rest of body. 0
4. Does not wash self but is cooperative with those who bathe him or her. 0
5. Does not try to wash self and resists efforts to keep him or her clean. 0

For scoring interpretation and source, see note after the next instrument.

INSTRUMENTAL ACTIVITIES OF DAILY LIVING SCALE (IADLS)

In each category, circle the item that most closely describes the person's highest level of functioning and record the score assigned to that level (either 1 or 0) in the blank at the beginning of the category.

A. Ability to Use Telephone _____
1. Operates telephone on own initiative; looks up and dials numbers. 1
2. Dials a few well-known numbers. 1
3. Answers telephone but does not dial. 1
4. Does not use telephone at all. 0

B. Shopping _____
1. Takes care of all shopping needs independently. 1
2. Shops independently for small purchases. 0
3. Needs to be accompanied on any shopping trip. 0
4. Completely unable to shop. 0

C. Food Preparation _____
1. Plans, prepares, and serves adequate meals independently. 1
2. Prepares adequate meals if supplied with ingredients. 0
3. Heats and serves prepared meals or prepares meals but does not maintain adequate diet. 0
4. Needs to have meals prepared and served. 0

D. Housekeeping _____
1. Maintains house alone or with occasional assistance (eg, domestic help for heavy work). 1
2. Performs light daily tasks such as dishwashing, bedmaking. 1
3. Performs light daily tasks but cannot maintain acceptable level of cleanliness.. 1
4. Needs help with all home maintenance tasks. 1
5. Does not participate in any housekeeping tasks. 0

E. Laundry _____
1. Does personal laundry completely. 1
2. Launders small items; rinses socks, stockings, etc. 1
3. All laundry must be done by others. 0

F. Mode of Transportation _____
1. Travels independently on public transportation or drives own car. 1
2. Arranges own travel via taxi but does not otherwise use public transportation.. 1
3. Travels on public transportation when assisted or accompanied by another.. 1
4. Travel limited to taxi or automobile with assistance of another. 0
5. Does not travel at all.. 0

G. Responsibility for Own Medications _____
1. Is responsible for taking medication in correct dosages at correct time. 1
2. Takes responsibility if medication is prepared in advance in separate dosages. 0
3. Is not capable of dispensing own medication. 0

H. Ability to Handle Finances _____
1. Manages financial matters independently (budgets, writes checks, pays rent and bills, goes to bank); collects and keeps track of income.. 1
2. Manages day-to-day purchases but needs help with banking, major purchases, etc. 1
3. Incapable of handling money. 0

Scoring Interpretation: For ADLs, the total score ranges from 0 to 6, and for IADLs, from 0 to 8. In some categories, only the highest level of function receives a 1; in others, two or more levels have scores of 1 because each describes competence at some minimal level of function. These screens are useful for indicating specifically how a person is performing at the present time. When they are also used over time, they serve as documentation of a person's functional improvement or deterioration.

Sources: Lawton MP, Brody EM. Assessment of older people: self-maintaining and instrumental activities of daily living. _Gerontologist_ 1969, 9:179–186. Katz S, Downs TD, Cash HR, Grotz RC. Progress in development of the index of ADL. _Gerontologist_ 1970;10:20–30. Copyright by the Gerontological Society of America. Reproduced by permission of the Gerontological Society of America.

PHQ-9 QUICK DEPRESSION ASSESSMENT

Instructions For Use: *for doctor or healthcare professional use only*
For initial diagnosis:

1. Patient completes PHQ-9 Quick Depression Assessment.
2. If there are at least 4 ✔s in the two right columns (including Questions #1 and #2), consider a depressive disorder. Add score to determine severity.

3. *Consider Major Depressive Disorder*
- if there are at least 5 ✔s in the two right columns (one of which corresponds to Question #1 or #2).

   Consider Other Depressive Disorder
- if there are 2 to 4 ✔s in the two right columns (one of which corresponds to Question #1 or #2).

Note: Since the questionnaire relies on patient self-report, all responses should be verified by the clinician, and a definitive diagnosis is made on clinical grounds, taking into account how well the patient understood the questionnaire, as well as other relevant information from the patient. Diagnoses of Major Depressive Disorder or Other Depressive Disorder also require impairment of social, occupational, or other important areas of functioning and ruling out normal bereavement, a history of a Manic Episode (Bipolar Disorder), and a physical disorder, medication, or other drug as the biological cause of the depressive symptoms.

To monitor severity over time for newly diagnosed patients or patients in current treatment for depression:

1. Patients may complete questionnaires at baseline and at regular intervals (eg, q2wk) at home and bring them in at their next appointment for scoring, or they may complete the questionnaire during each scheduled appointment.
2. Add up ✔s by column. For every ✔:
   "Several days" = 1   "More than half the days" = 2   "Nearly every day" = 3
3. Add together column scores to get a TOTAL score.
4. Refer to PHQ-9 Scoring to interpret the TOTAL score.
5. Results may be included in patients' files to assist you in setting up a treatment goal, determining degree of response, as well as guiding treatment intervention.

PHQ-9 Scoring For Severity Determination
for healthcare professional use only

Scoring—add up all checked boxes on PHQ-9
For every ✔: Not at all = 0; Several days = 1; More than half the days = 2;
Nearly every day = 3

Interpretation of Total Score

Total Score	Depression Severity
0–4	None
5–9	Mild
10–14	Moderate
15–19	Moderately severe
20–27	Severe

PATIENT HEALTH QUESTIONNAIRE-9

THIS SECTION FOR USE BY STUDY PERSONNEL ONLY.

Were data collected? **No** ☐ (provide reason in comments)
If **Yes**, data collected on visit date ☐ or specify date:_____

Comments

Only the patient (subject) should enter information onto this questionnaire.

Over the *last 2 weeks*, how often have you been bothered by any of the following problems?	Not at all	Several days	More than half the days	Nearly every day
1. Little interest or pleasure in doing things	0	1	2	3
2. Feeling down, depressed, or hopeless	0	1	2	3
3. Trouble falling or staying asleep, or sleeping too much	0	1	2	3
4. Feeling tired or having little energy	0	1	2	3
5. Poor appetite or overeating	0	1	2	3
6. Feeling bad about yourself — or that you are a failure or have let yourself or your family down	0	1	2	3
7. Trouble concentrating on things, such as reading the newspaper or watching television	0	1	2	3
8. Moving or speaking so slowly that other people could have noticed? Or the opposite — being so fidgety or restless that you have been moving around a lot more than usual	0	1	2	3
9. Thoughts that you would be better off dead or of hurting yourself in some way	0	1	2	3

SCORING FOR USE BY STUDY PERSONNEL ONLY

___0___ + _____ + _____ + _____

=Total Score: _____

If you checked off *any* problems, how *difficult* have these problems made it for you to do your work, take care of things at home, or get along with other people?

Not difficult at all	Somewhat difficult	Very difficult	Extremely difficult
☐	☐	☐	☐

Developed by Drs. Robert L. Spitzer, Janet B.W. Williams, Kurt Kroenke and colleagues, with an educational grant from Pfizer Inc.

I confirm this information is accurate.	Patient's/Subject's initials:	Date:

GERIATRIC DEPRESSION SCALE (GDS, SHORT FORM)

Choose the best answer for how you felt over the past week.

1. Are you basically satisfied with your life? — yes/**no**
2. Have you dropped many of your activities and interests? — **yes**/no
3. Do you feel that your life is empty? — **yes**/no
4. Do you often get bored? — **yes**/no
5. Are you in good spirits most of the time? — yes/**no**
6. Are you afraid that something bad is going to happen to you? — **yes**/no
7. Do you feel happy most of the time? — yes/**no**
8. Do you often feel helpless? — **yes**/no
9. Do you prefer to stay at home, rather than going out and doing new things? — **yes**/no
10. Do you feel you have more problems with memory than most? — **yes**/no
11. Do you think it is wonderful to be alive now? — yes/**no**
12. Do you feel pretty worthless the way you are now? — **yes**/no
13. Do you feel full of energy? — yes/**no**
14. Do you feel that your situation is hopeless? — **yes**/no
15. Do you think that most people are better off than you are? — **yes**/no

Score 1 point for each bolded answer. Cut-off: normal 0–5; above 5 suggests depression.

Source: Courtesy of Jerome A. Yesavage, MD. For 30 translations of the GDS, see www.stanford.edu/~yesavage/GDS.html

For additional information on administration and scoring, refer to the following references:

Sheikh JI, Yesavage JA. Geriatric Depression Scale: recent evidence and development of a shorter version. *Clin Gerontol* 1986;5:165–172.

Feher EP, Larrabee GJ, Crook TH 3rd. Factors attenuating the validity of the Geriatric Depression Scale in a dementia population. *J Am Geriatr Soc* 1992;40:906–909.

Yesavage JA, Brink TL, Rose TL et al. Development and validation of a geriatric depression rating scale: a preliminary report. *J Psychiatr Res* 1983;17:27.

KARNOFSKY SCALE

This 10-point scale is a quick and easy way to indicate how a person is feeling on a given day, without going through several multiple-choice questions or symptom surveys.

Score	Description
100	Able to work; normal, no complaints, no evidence of disease
90	Able to work; able to carry on normal activity, minor symptoms
80	Able to work; normal activity with effort, some symptoms
70	Unable to work or carry on normal activity, cares for self independently
60	Mildly disabled, dependent; requires occasional assistance, cares for most needs
50	Moderately disabled, dependent; requires considerable assistance and frequent care
40	Severely disabled, dependent; requires special care and assistance
30	Severely disabled; hospitalized, death not imminent
20	Very sick; active supportive treatment needed
10	Moribund; fatal processes rapidly progressing

Source: Karnofsky DA, Burchenal JH. The clinical evaluation of chemotherapeutic agents in cancer. In: MacLeon CM, ed. *Evaluation of Chemotherapeutic Agents*. Columbia University Press; 1949:196.

PALLIATIVE PERFORMANCE SCALE, VERSION 2 (PPSv2)

PPS Level (%)	Ambulation	Activity and Evidence of Disease	Self-care	Intake	Conscious Level
100	Full	Normal activity and work, no evidence of disease	Full	Normal	Full
90	Full	Normal activity and work, some evidence of disease	Full	Normal	Full
80	Full	Normal activity with effort, some evidence of disease	Full	Normal or reduced	Full
70	Reduced	Unable to do normal job or work, significant disease	Full	Normal or reduced	Full
60	Reduced	Unable to do hobby or housework, significant disease	Occasional assistance required	Normal or reduced	Full or confusion
50	Mainly sit/lie	Unable to do any work, extensive disease	Considerable assistance required	Normal or reduced	Full or confusion
40	Mainly in bed	Unable to do most activity, extensive disease	Mainly assistance	Normal or reduced	Full or drowsy, ± confusion
30	Totally bed bound	Unable to do any activity, extensive disease	Total care	Normal or reduced	Full or drowsy, ± confusion
20	Totally bed bound	Unable to do any activity, extensive disease	Total care	Minimal to sips	Full or drowsy, ± confusion
10	Totally bed bound	Unable to do any activity, extensive disease	Total care	Mouth care only	Drowsy or coma, ± confusion
0	Death	—	—	—	—

Instructions: PPS level is determined by reading left to right to find a 'best horizontal fit.' Begin at left column reading downwards until current ambulation is determined, then read across to next and downwards until each column is determined. Thus, 'leftward' columns take precedence over 'rightward' columns. Also, see 'definitions of terms' for interpretation of PPSv2 and complete instructions at www.victoriahospice.org. Victoria Hospice Society©

Palliative Performance Scale, Version 2 (PPSv2). *Medical Care of the Dying, 4th ed.* Victoria, BC, Canada: Victoria Hospice Society; 2006:120-121. Reprinted with permission.

REISBERG FUNCTIONAL ASSESSMENT STAGING (FAST) SCALE

This 16-item scale is designed to parallel the progressive activity limitations associated with AD. Stage 7 identifies the threshold of activity limitation that would support a prognosis of ≤6 mo remaining life expectancy.

FAST Scale Item	Activity Limitation Associated with AD
Stage 1	No difficulty, either subjectively or objectively
Stage 2	Complains of forgetting location of objects; subjective work difficulties
Stage 3	Decreased job functioning evident to coworkers; difficulty in traveling to new locations
Stage 4	Decreased ability to perform complex tasks (eg, planning dinner for guests, handling finances)
Stage 5	Requires assistance in choosing proper clothing
Stage 6	Decreased ability to dress, bathe, and toilet independently
Substage 6a	Difficulty putting clothing on properly
Substage 6b	Unable to bathe properly, may develop fear of bathing
Substage 6c	Inability to handle mechanics of toileting (ie, forgets to flush, does not wipe properly)
Substage 6d	Urinary incontinence
Substage 6e	Fecal incontinence
Stage 7	Loss of speech, locomotion, and consciousness
Substage 7a	Ability to speak limited (1–5 words a day)
Substage 7b	All intelligible vocabulary lost
Substage 7c	Nonambulatory
Substage 7d	Unable to smile
Substage 7e	Unable to hold head up

Source: Reisberg, B. Functional assessment staging (FAST), *Psychopharmacol Bull* 1988;24(4):653–659. Copyright MedWorks Media Global, LLC. Reprinted with permission.

AUA SYMPTOM INDEX FOR BPH

Questions to be answered (circle one number on each line)	Not at all	Less than 1 time in 5	Less than half the time	About half the time	More than half the time	Almost always
1. Over the past month or so, how often have you had a sensation of not emptying your bladder completely after you finished urinating?	0	1	2	3	4	5
2. Over the past month or so, how often have you had to urinate again less than 2 hours after you finished urinating?	0	1	2	3	4	5
3. Over the past month or so, how often have you found you stopped and started again several times when you urinated?	0	1	2	3	4	5
4. Over the past month or so, how often have you found it difficult to postpone urination?	0	1	2	3	4	5
5. Over the past month or so, how often have you had a weak urinary stream?	0	1	2	3	4	5
6. Over the past month or so, how often have you had to push or strain to begin urination?	0	1	2	3	4	5
7. Over the last month, how many times did you most typically get up to urinate from the time you went to bed at night until the time you got up in the morning?	none	1 time	2 times	3 times	4 times	>5 times

AUA Symptom Score = sum of responses to questions 1–7 =____. For interpretation, see p 233.

Source: Barry MJ, Fowler FJ Jr, O'Leary MP et al. The American Urological Association symptom index for benign prostatic hyperplasia. *J Urol* 1992;148(5):1549–1557. Reprinted with permission.

OPIOID RISK TOOL*

Factor	Score**	
	Women	**Men**
Family hx of substance abuse		
Alcohol	1	3
Illegal drugs	2	3
Prescription drugs	4	4
Personal hx of substance abuse		
Alcohol	3	3
Illegal drugs	4	4
Prescription drugs	5	5
Age (if between 16 and 45)	1	1
Hx of preadolescent sexual abuse	3	0
Psychological disease		
Attention-deficit disorder, obsessive-compulsive disorder, bipolar, schizophrenia	2	2
Depression	1	1
TOTAL		

* Main drawback is susceptibility to deception.

** Scoring: 0–3 = low risk, 4–7 = moderate risk, ≥8 = high risk

Note: Adapted from Webster LR, Webster RM. Predicting aberrant behaviors in opioid-treated patients: preliminary validation of the Opioid Risk Tool. *Pain Med* 2005;6:432–442.

IMPORTANT TELEPHONE NUMBERS AND WEB SITES

General Information on Aging

AGS Foundation for Health in Aging	www.healthinaging.org	800-563-4916
Administration on Aging	www.aoa.gov	202-619-0724
American Association of Retired Persons	www.aarp.org	888-OUR-AARP (888-687-2277)
American Geriatrics Society	www.americangeriatrics.org	800-247-4779
American Medical Directors Association	www.amda.com	800-876-2632
American Society of Consultant Pharmacists	www.ascp.com	800-355-2727
Assisted Living Federation of America	www.alfa.org	703-894-1805
CDC National Prevention Information Network	www.cdcnpin.org	800-458-5231
Children of Aging Parents	www.caps4caregivers.org	800-227-7294
Family Caregiver Alliance	www.caregiver.org	800-445-8106
Medicare Hotline	www.medicare.gov	800-MEDICARE (800-633-4227) TTY: 877-486-2048
National Adult Day Services Association	www.nadsa.org	877-745-1440
National Council on the Aging	www.ncoa.org	202-479-1200
National Institute on Aging	www.nia.nih.gov	301-496-1752 TTY: 800-222-4225

End-of-Life

National Hospice and Palliative Care Organization	www.nhpco.org	800-658-8898 877-658-8896 (multilingual helpline)

Mistreatment of Older Adults

National Center on Elder Abuse	www.ncea.aoa.gov	855-500-3537 800-677-1116 (help hotline)

Smoking Cessation

CDC National Center for Chronic Disease Prevention and Health Promotion	www.cdc.gov/tobacco/how2quit.htm	800-CDC-INFO (800-232-4636) TTY: 888-232-6348
National Cancer Institute	www.smokefree.gov	800-QUITNOW (800-784-8669) TTY: 800-332-8615

Specific Health Problems

Alzheimer's Association	www.alz.org	800-272-3900 TDD: 866-403-3073
Alzheimer's Disease Education and Referral Center	www.nia.nih.gov/alzheimers	800-438-4380
American Academy of Ophthalmology	www.aao.org	877-887-6327
American Association for Geriatric Psychiatry	www.aagponline.org	301-654-7850
American Cancer Society	www.cancer.org	800-ACS-2345 (800-227-2345) TTY: 866-228-4327
American College of Obstetricians and Gynecologists	www.acog.org	800-673-8444

American Diabetes Association	www.diabetes.org	800-DIABETES (800-342-2383)
American Foundation for the Blind	www.afb.org	800-AFB-LINE (800-232-5463)
American Heart Association	www.americanheart.org	800-AHA-USA1 (800-242-8721)
American Lung Association	www.lungusa.org	800-LUNG-USA (800-586-4872)
American Pain Society	www.ampainsoc.org	847-375-4715
American Parkinson Disease Association	www.apdaparkinson.org	800-223-2732
American Stroke Association	www.strokeassociation.org	888-4-STROKE (888-478-7653)
American Urological Association	www.auanet.org	866-746-4282
Arthritis Foundation	www.arthritis.org	800-283-7800
Better Hearing Institute	www.betterhearing.org	800-EAR-WELL (800-327-9355)
Endocrine Society and Hormone Foundation (obesity)	www.obesityinamerica.org	301-941-0200
Geriatric Mental Health Foundation	www.gmhfonline.org	301-654-7850
Hearing Loss Association of America	www.hearingloss.org	301-657-2248 (V-TTY)
Lighthouse International	www.lighthouse.org	800-829-0500 TTY: 212-821-9713
Meals On Wheels Association of America	www.mowaa.org	703-548-5558
National Association for Continence	www.nafc.org	800-BLADDER (800-252-3337)
National Diabetes Information Clearinghouse	www.diabetes.niddk.nih.gov	800-860-8747 TTY: 866-569-1162
National Digestive Diseases Information Clearinghouse	www.digestive.niddk.nih.gov	800-891-5389 TTY: 866-569-1162
National Eye Institute	www.nei.nih.gov	301-496-5248
National Heart, Lung, and Blood Institute	www.nhlbi.nih.gov	301-592-8573 TTY: 240-629-3255
National Institute of Arthritis and Musculoskeletal and Skin Diseases	www.niams.nih.gov	877-22-NIAMS (877-226-4267) TTY: 301-565-2966
National Institute of Mental Health	www.nimh.nih.gov	866-615-NIMH (866-615-6464) TTY: 866-415-8051
National Institute of Neurological Disorders and Stroke	www.ninds.nih.gov	800-352-9424 TTY: 301-468-5981
National Institute on Deafness and Other Communication Disorders	www.nidcd.nih.gov	800-241-1044 TTY: 800-241-1055
National Kidney and Urologic Diseases Information Clearinghouse	www.kidney.niddk.nih.gov	800-891-5390 TTY: 866-569-1162
National Osteoporosis Foundation	www.nof.org	800-231-4222
National Parkinson Foundation	www.parkinson.org	800-473-4636 (helpline)
Sexuality Information and Education Council of the US	www.siecus.org	212-819-9770
The Simon Foundation for Continence	www.simonfoundation.org	800-23-SIMON (800-237-4666)

INDEX

Page references followed by *t* and *f* indicate tables and figures, respectively.

Trade names are in *italics*.

About the American Geriatrics Society

WHAT IS THE AMERICAN GERIATRICS SOCIETY DOING TO IMPROVE THE HEALTH OF OLDER ADULTS?

We are expanding the geriatrics knowledge base through activities that promote basic, clinical, and translational research regarding the health of older adults, such as:
- The AGS Annual Scientific Meeting
- *The Journal of the American Geriatrics Society*
- The Geriatrics-for-Specialists Initiative
- Scholarship programs

We are increasing the number of healthcare professionals who employ the principles of geriatrics when caring for older people through AGS products, including:
- *Geriatrics At Your Fingertips*
- The *Doorway Thoughts* Series on Cross-Cultural Health Care for Older Adults
- The *Geriatrics Review Syllabus (GRS)*, *GRS* Teaching Slides, *Case-Based Geriatrics Review,* and *Geriatric Nursing Review Syllabus*

We are recruiting physicians and other healthcare professionals into careers in geriatrics through strategies such as:
- The Student Researcher Fund
- Free AGS membership for students and residents
- Innovative recruiting methods
- Mentoring

We are guiding public policy to advocate for improved health and healthcare of seniors. Five years ago, through a strategic planning process, the AGS invested in expanding its public policy efforts. Our investments are now paying off. We are making an impact in Washington, through activities such as:
- Crafting new legislation
- Working with federal agencies
- Staying active on the Hill and with the White House
- Responding to requests for comments on legislation and regulations
- Forging partnerships with other aging advocacy groups

We are raising public awareness of the need for high quality, culturally sensitive geriatric healthcare, through the following activites:
- Producing useful and accessible information for older adults and caregivers
- Making the news

Visit www.americangeriatrics.org Today and Find Out More About the AGS and the Exciting Benefits It Offers to Members!

From the American Geriatrics Society
GERIATRICS *At Your* FINGERTIPS®
2012, 14th Edition
(ISSN 1553-152X) (ISBN 978-1-886775-57-2)

A guide to the evaluation and management of the diseases and disorders that most commonly affect older adults.

Portable, Practical, Fully Indexed, and Up-to-Date!

Send completed order form with payment to:

Fry Communications, Inc.
American Geriatrics Society
800 West Church Road
Mechanicsburg, PA 17055

For fast service
Call: 1-800-334-1429 ext. 2529
Order online at: www.geriatricsatyourfingertips.org

Please send me _____ copies of *Geriatrics At Your Fingertips*, 2012, 14th Edition
@ $14.95 each ($12.95 for AGS Members)

Subtotal ⎯⎯⎯⎯

Shipping and Handling
North America: $3.00 + $1.00 ea additional ⎯⎯⎯⎯
Overseas: please call 1-717-766-0211 ext. 2529 for rates

TOTAL ⎯⎯⎯⎯

Method of Payment: _____ Check or money order payable to Fry Communications
_____ MasterCard   _____ VISA
Card Number _____ Exp. Date _____
Signature _____

Shipping Instructions (must be complete)

Name: _____
Address: _____
City: _____ State: _____ Zip: _____
Phone: _____
E-mail Address: _____

GAYF 2012

Your request places you on the AGS e-alert electronic mailing list. You will be among the first in your discipline to find out about new releases, special offers, and program announcements from AGS. After you receive your first e-alert, you have the option of canceling the service at any time. Prices subject to change without notice.